PLAYFAIR
CRICKET ANNUAL 1975
28th EDITION

EDITED BY GORDON ROSS

Statistics by Michael Fordham and Barry McCaully

Front cover: Dennis Amis...
batting average of 53.92 in...

GILLETTE 'PICK–A–TEAM' COMPETITION
£500 TO BE WON

Prizes 1st; £200   2nd; £100   3rd; £50   4th; £25
Twenty-five runners-up; £5 each

Plus A selection of Gillette products, from the range shown opposite, for each winner

How to Enter: **Pick the Greatest Gillette Cup Team of all time!**
From the list below of famous cricketers who have appeared in the Gillette Cup since 1963, choose the greatest Gillette team of all time, placing them in batting order, and assuming them all to be at the top of their form. Then write in 20 words the reasons for the success of the Gillette Cup.
Write the names on the entry form on the opposite page with your name and address and post to the address shown.

Your Choice
Dennis Amiss, Geoff Arnold, Asif Iqbal, Trevor Bailey, Bob Barber, Ken Barrington, Geoff Boycott, Brian Close, Colin Cowdrey, Greg Chappell, Mike Denness, Ted Dexter, Basil D'Oliveira, John Edrich, Bill Edrich, Keith Fletcher, Tom Graveney, Tony Greig, Ray Illingworth, Rohan Kanhai, Alan Knott, Brian Luckhurst, Peter Lever, Tony Lock, Clive Lloyd, David Lloyd, Majid Jahangir, Roy Marshall, Colin Milburn, Chris Old, Jim Parks, Mike Procter, Barry Richards, Mike (M.J.K.) Smith, John Snow, Gary Sobers, Brian Statham, Fred Trueman, Derek Underwood, Bob Willis.

Rules: Judging; Each entry will be considered by a panel of cricket experts, and the entry which, in the opinion of the judges, constitutes the greatest Gillette Cup team of all time will be adjudged the winner. The decision of the judges is final and binding; no correspondence will be entered into.
Employees of Gillette and Queen Anne Press and their families are not eligible to compete.
Proof of entry: All entries must be on the entry form provided.
Proof of posting is not proof of entry.

ENTRY FORM

Your team in batting order:

1	7
2	8
3	9
4	10
5	11
6	

Why is the Gillette Cup such a big success (20 words) ?

Closing Date: 12.00 noon Wednesday, 10 September, 1975

Your name and address:

....

....

Post to   Gillette Industries Limited,
             Cricket Competition (P.R. Department)
             Great West Road,
             Isleworth, Middlesex.

OH, ENGLAND
by Gordon Ross

Very few tours of Australia by an England side have aroused so much disappointment at home as this one. Although it must have been a great tonic to our players to win the last Test after multifarious problems and setbacks, there is not much gilt on the gingerbread for the rest of us when the final score is 4–1. It would be extremely ungenerous to our players to suggest that the last match was a hollow victory – it had to be won – but the absence of Thomson and Lillee from the Australian attack merely emphasised our inability to cope with this considerable amount of extra pace. There was unquestionably a large number of short-pitched balls sent down throughout the series which could give rise to future discussions on the subject, but one can only presume that the umpires were satisfied, and they can only operate within the framework of the law. The crux of the matter was that we had no bowler anything like as fast, as a retaliatory weapon, leaving it as a rather one-sided affair.

But let us not detract from the merits of Australia as a team. They were stronger in every department of the game, not least of which was the fielding; some of their catches were superlative – and there was not much wrong with their batting, either! They will surely be a great attraction in England this summer when they undertake a dual purpose tour: to compete in the one-day World Cup competition, and then to the more serious business of four Test matches.

INDIA V WEST INDIES

Because of the all too familiar pressure on space, it was not possible to include in this year's annual the fine series between India and West Indies, which West Indies won 3–2 after being level at 2–2. In order to maintain Playfair's continuity of the complete coverage of world Test matches, this series will be included next year, together with England's Test matches in New Zealand which were too late for inclusion this year.

The World Cup, to give it its popular title, though it is actually called The Prudential Cup, is an ambitious scheme that deserves success, and most of all, good weather; in cricket these go hand in hand. The matches will be fought out on similar terms to Gillette Cup matches – one day, and 60 overs. There are eight competitors, divided into two groups: England, East Africa, India, and New Zealand are in Group A, with Australia, Pakistan, Sri Lanka, and West Indies in Group B. Each team in each group will play each other once; then the first two teams in each group will go forward to the semi-finals. The tournament begins on 7 June and the final will be played at Lord's on 21 June. In the group matches, the winning team will gain four points. In the event of a no-result match, each team will gain two points. The organisers of this ambitious scheme know full well how important it is to have the host nation in the final, and despite England's shortcomings displayed in Australia, they seem likely to emerge victorious from their league. Group B, however, is substantially harder for Australia, who will find West Indies and Pakistan two worthy competitors. England must be favourites by virtue of the draw and their extra know-how on the one-day cricket scene, but Australia will start as favourites when the Test series begins.

What new measures will England adopt in preparation for the series? Will Alec Bedser remain in the high office which he has graced with dedication for so long, or is it time for a change? Will Mike Denness hang on precariously to the captaincy? We shall see, although presumably something positive must be seen to be done. Our Test record over the last year or two has suggested that a wind of change might be necessary. It is merely confusing to lose a series, and then win the final Test, as if to suggest that all is well; we have done this a time or two. The three hidings that we handed out to India in England last summer, completely mesmerising their hitherto magic triumvirate of spinners, was short-lived triumph when we came up against Pakistan. They gave no ground at all in a three-match drawn series, although the weather and Derek Underwood could have been their undoing. Underwood's 13 wickets in the Lord's Test match on a rain-affected pitch showed just what a devastating effect he can have in such conditions. For a period he was virtually unplayable.

On the purely domestic scene in England in 1974, honours were spread in the major competitions. Worcestershire won the County Championship, Kent the Gillette Cup, Surrey the Benson and Hedges Cup, and Leicestershire the John Player League, but supporters of Hampshire and Somerset will never stop telling their descendants how near they were to success. Hampshire will say, with ample justification, that weather, and weather alone, robbed them of another County Championship, and Somerset will imply that they might have won at Leicester, but for the rain; this may or may not have been. Kent won the first Gillette Cup final in 12 years to be washed out on the scheduled Saturday, on a pitch which was never to be completely trusted. This is borne out by the fact that Kent won the Cup and yet not one of their players reached an individual score of 20; a comparison with the truly brilliant innings which have characterised this final in the past proves the point. With the amount of rain that had bucketed down for days it was remarkable to get a pitch at all.

The Benson and Hedges final, too, had been a low-scoring affair which Leicester looked to have in their pocket at one time; but Surrey, at last, won a one-day title which they had promised to do for so long, but always before had failed somewhere along the line.

EWAN CHATFIELD

Just before this annual went to press, news came of the distressing serious accident to Ewan Chatfield, the New Zealand no. 11 batsman, who deflected a bouncer from Peter Lever into his face. The stricken batsman needed heart massage and mouth-to-mouth resuscitation before he could be moved to an ambulance. This sort of accident can always happen and Lever can have a clear conscience, but it does bring into sharp focus again the whole question of short-pitched balls in cricket. It is surely a matter which must be looked into very seriously.

AUSTRALIA v ENGLAND, 1974–75

FIRST TEST MATCH

PLAYED AT BRISBANE, 29, 30 NOV, 1, 3, 4 DECEMBER
AUSTRALIA WON BY 166 RUNS

AUSTRALIA

I. R. Redpath b Willis	5	b Willis	25
W. J. Edwards c Amiss b Hendrick	4	c Knott b Willis	5
†I. M. Chappell c Greig b Willis	90	c Fletcher b Underwood	11
G.S. Chappell c Fletcher b Underwood	58	b Underwood	71
R. Edwards c Knott b Underwood	32	c Knott b Willis	53
K. D. Walters c Lever b Willis	3	not out	62
‡R. W. Marsh c Denness b Hendrick	14	not out	46
T. J. Jenner c Lever b Willis	12		
D. K. Lillee c Knott b Greig	15		
M. H. N. Walker not out	41		
J. R. Thomson run out	23		
Extras (LB4, NB8)	12	(B1, LB7, W1, NB6)	15
	---		---
Total	309	(5 wkts dec)	288

ENGLAND

D. L. Amiss c Jenner b Thomson	7	c Walters b Thomson	25
B. W. Luckhurst c Marsh b Thomson	1	c I. Chappell b Lillee	3
J. H. Edrich c I. Chappell b Thomson	48	b Thomson	6
†M. H. Denness lbw b Walker	6	c Walters b Thomson	27
K. W. R. Fletcher b Lillee	17	c G. Chappell b Jenner	19
A. W. Greig c Marsh b Lillee	110	b Thomson	2
‡A. P. E. Knott c Jenner b Walker	12	b Thomson	19
P. Lever c I. Chappell b Walker	4	c Redpath b Lillee	14
D. L. Underwood c Redpath b Walters	25	c Walker b Jenner	30
R. G. D. Willis not out	13	not out	3
M. Hendrick c Redpath b Walker	4	b Thomson	0
Extras (B5, LB2, W3, NB8)	18	(B8, LB3, W2, NB5)	18
	---		---
Total	265		166

BOWLING

ENGLAND	O	M	R	W	O	M	R	W
Willis	21.5	3	56	4	15	3	45	3
Lever	16	1	53	0	18	4	58	0
Hendrick	19	3	64	2	13	2	47	0
Greig	16	2	70	1	13	2	60	0
Underwood	20	6	54	2	26	6	63	2
AUSTRALIA								
Lillee	23	6	73	2	12	2	25	2
Thomson	21	5	59	3	17.5	3	46	6
Walker	24.5	2	73	4	9	4	32	0
Walters	6	1	18	1	2	0	0	0
Jenner	6	1	24	0	16	5	45	2

Fall of Wickets

	A	E	A	E
	1st	1st	2nd	2nd
1st	7	9	15	18
2nd	10	10	39	40
3rd	110	33	59	44
4th	197	57	173	92
5th	202	130	190	94
6th	205	162	—	94
7th	228	168	—	115
8th	229	226	—	162
9th	257	248	—	163
10th	309	265	—	166

SECOND TEST MATCH

PLAYED AT PERTH, 13, 14, 15, 17 DECEMBER
AUSTRALIA WON BY 9 WICKETS

ENGLAND

D. Lloyd c G. Chappell b Thomson	49	c G. Chappell b Walker	35
B. W. Luckhurst c Mallett b Walker	27	c Mallett b Lillee	23
M. C. Cowdrey b Thomson	22	lbw b Thomson	41
A. W. Greig c Mallett b Walker	23	c G. Chappell b Thomson	32
K. W. R. Fletcher c Redpath b Lillee	4	c Marsh b Thomson	0
†M. H. Denness c G. Chappell b Lillee	2	c Redpath b Thomson	20
‡A. P. E. Knott c Redpath b Walters	51	c G. Chappell b Lillee	18
F. J. Titmus c Redpath b Walters	10	c G. Chappell b Mallett	61
C. M. Old c G. Chappell b I. Chappell	7	c Thomson b Mallett	43
G. G. Arnold run out	1	c Mallett b Thomson	4
R. G. D. Willis not out	4	not out	0
Extras (W3, NB5)	8	(LB4, W1, NB11)	16
Total	**208**		**293**

AUSTRALIA

I. R. Redpath st Knott b Titmus	41	not out	12
W. J. Edwards c Lloyd b Greig	30	lbw b Arnold	0
†I. M. Chappell c Knott b Arnold	25	not out	11
G. S. Chappell c Greig b Willis	62		
R. Edwards b Arnold	115		
K. D. Walters c Fletcher b Willis	103		
‡R. W. Marsh c Lloyd b Titmus	41		
M. H. N. Walker c Knott b Old	19		
D. K. Lillee b Old	11		
A. A. Mallett c Knott b Old	0		
J. R. Thomson not out	11		
Extras (B7, LB14, NB2)	23		
Total	**481**	**(1 wkt)**	**23**

BOWLING

AUSTRALIA	O	M	R	W		O	M	R	W		Fall of Wickets			
											E	A	E	A
Lillee	16	4	48	2	...	22	5	59	2		1st	1st	2nd	2nd
Thomson	15	6	45	2	...	25	4	93	5	1st	44	64	62	4
Walker	20	5	49	2	...	24	7	76	1	2nd	99	101	106	—
Mallett	10	3	35	0	...	11.1	4	32	2	3rd	119	113	124	—
Walters	2.3	1	13	2	...	9	4	17	0	4th	128	119	124	—
I. Chappell	2	0	10	1	...					5th	132	362	154	—
ENGLAND										6th	132	416	156	—
Willis	22	0	91	2	...	2	0	8	0	7th	194	449	219	—
Arnold	27	1	129	2	...	1.7	0	15	1	8th	201	462	285	—
Old	22.6	3	85	3	...					9th	202	462	293	—
Greig	9	0	69	1	...					10th	208	481	293	—
Titmus	28	3	84	2	...									

NB In England's second innings, Lloyd retired hurt at 52, and resumed his innings when the second wicket fell at 1·06.

THIRD TEST MATCH

PLAYED AT MELBOURNE, 26, 27, 28, 30, 31 DECEMBER
MATCH DRAWN

ENGLAND

D. L. Amiss c Walters b Lillee	4	c I. Chappell b Mallett	90
D. Lloyd c Mallett b Thomson	14	c & b Mallett	44
M. C. Cowdrey lbw b Thomson	35	c G. Chappell b Lillee	8
J. H. Edrich c Marsh b Mallett	49	c Marsh b Thomson	4
†M. H. Denness c Marsh b Mallett	8	c I. Chappell b Thomson	2
A. W. Greig run out	28	c G. Chappell b Lillee	60
‡A. P. E. Knott b Thomson	52	c Marsh b Thomson	4
F. J. Titmus c Mallett b Lillee	10	b Mallett	0
D. L. Underwood c Marsh b Walker	9	c I. Chappell b Mallett	4
R.G.D. Willis c Walters b Thomson	13	b Thomson	15
M. Hendrick not out	8	not out	0
Extras (LB2, W1, NB9)	12	(B2, LB9, W2)	13
Total	242		244

AUSTRALIA

I. R. Redpath c Knott b Greig	55	run out	39
W. J. Edwards c Denness b Willis	29	lbw b Greig	0
G. S. Chappell c Greig b Willis	2	lbw b Titmus	61
R. Edwards c Cowdrey b Titmus	1	c Lloyd b Titmus	10
K. D. Walters c Lloyd b Greig	36	c Denness b Greig	32
†I. M. Chappell lbw b Willis	36	lbw b Willis	0
‡R. W. Marsh c Knott b Titmus	44	c Knott b Greig	40
M. H. N. Walker c Knott b Willis	30	not out	23
D. K. Lillee not out	2	c Denness b Greig	14
A. A. Mallett run out	0	not out	0
J. R. Thomson b Willis	2		
Extras (B2, LB2)	4	(B6, LB9, NB4)	19
Total	241	(8 wkts)	238

BOWLING

AUSTRALIA	O	M	R	W	O	M	R	W
Lillee	20	2	70	2	17	3	55	2
Thomson	22.4	4	72	4	17	1	71	4
Walker	24	10	36	1	11	0	45	0
Walters	7	2	15	0				
Mallett	15	3	37	2	24	6	60	4
ENGLAND								
Willis	21.7	4	61	5	14	2	56	1
Hendrick	2.6	1	8	0				
Underwood	22	6	62	0	19	7	43	0
Greig	24	2	63	2	18	2	56	4
Titmus	22	11	43	2	29	10	64	2

Fall of Wickets

	E	A	E	A
	1st	1st	2nd	2nd
1st	4	65	115	4
2nd	34	67	134	5
3rd	110	68	152	106
4th	110	121	156	120
5th	141	126	158	121
6th	157	173	165	171
7th	176	237	178	208
8th	213	237	182	235
9th	232	238	238	—
10th	242	241	244	—

NB Owing to injury, Hendrick could not complete his third over.

FOURTH TEST MATCH

PLAYED AT SYDNEY, 4, 5, 6, 8, 9 JANUARY
AUSTRALIA WON BY 171 RUNS

AUSTRALIA

I. R. Redpath hit wkt b Titmus	33	c sub (Old) b Underwood	105
R. B. McCosker c Knott b Greig	80		
†I. M. Chappell c Knott b Arnold	53	c Lloyd b Willis	5
G. S. Chappell c Greig b Arnold	84	c Lloyd b Arnold	144
R. Edwards b Arnold	15	not out	17
K. D. Walters lbw b Arnold	1	b Underwood	5
‡R. W. Marsh b Greig	30	not out	7
M. H. Walker c Greig b Arnold	30		
D. K. Lillee b Arnold	8		
A. A. Mallett lbw b Greig	31		
J. R. Thomson not out	24		
Extras (B1, LB4, NB11)	16	(LB2, W1, NB3)	6
Total	**405**	**(4 wkts dec)**	**289**

ENGLAND

D. L. Amiss c Mallett b Walker	12	c Marsh b Lillee	37
D. Lloyd c Thomson b Lillee	19	c G. Chappell b Thomson	26
M. C. Cowdrey c McCosker b Thomson	22	c I. Chappell b Walker	1
†J. H. Edrich c Marsh b Walters	50	not out	33
K.W.R. Fletcher c Redpath b Walker	24	c Redpath b Thomson	11
A. W. Greig c G. Chappell b Thomson	9	st Marsh b Mallett	54
‡A. P. E. Knott b Thomson	82	c Redpath b Mallett	10
F. J. Titmus c Marsh b Walters	22	c Thomson b Mallett	4
D. L. Underwood c Walker b Lillee	27	c & b Walker	5
R. G. D. Willis b Thomson	2	b Lillee	12
G. G. Arnold not out	3	c G. Chappell b Mallett	14
Extras (B15, LB7, W1)	23	(B13, LB3, NB5)	21
Total	**295**		**228**

BOWLING

ENGLAND	O	M	R	W		O	M	R	W
Willis	18	2	80	4	...	11	1	52	1
Arnold	29	6	86	5	...	22	3	78	1
Greig	23	2	104	4	...	12	1	64	0
Underwood	13	3	54	0	...	12	1	65	2
Titmus	16	2	65	1	...	7.3	1	69	2

AUSTRALIA	O	M	R	W		O	M	R	W
Lillee	19.1	2	66	2	...	21	5	65	2
Thomson	9	3	74	4	...	23	7	74	2
Walker	23	4	77	2	...	16	5	46	2
Mallett	1	0	8	0	...	16.5	9	21	4
Walters	2	2	26	2	...				
I. Chappell	4	0	21	0	...	2	1	0	1

Fall of Wickets

	A	E	A	E
	1st	1st	2nd	2nd
1st	96	36	15	68
2nd	142	46	235	70
3rd	199	69	242	74
4th	251	108	280	103
5th	255	123	—	136
6th	305	180	—	156
7th	310	240	—	158
8th	332	273	—	175
9th	368	285	—	201
10th	405	295	—	228

NB In England's second innings Edrich retired hurt at 70 and resumed his innings at the fall of the 6th wicket.

FIFTH TEST MATCH

PLAYED AT ADELAIDE, 25, 26, 27, 29, 30 JANUARY
AUSTRALIA WON BY 163 RUNS

AUSTRALIA

I. R. Redpath c Greig b Underwood	21	b Underwood	52
R. B. McCosker c Cowdrey b Underwood	35	c Knott b Arnold	11
†I. M. Chappell c Knott b Underwood	0	c Knott b Underwood	41
G. S. Chappell lbw b Underwood	5	c Greig b Underwood	18
K. D. Walters c Willis b Underwood	55	not out	71
‡R. W. Marsh c Greig b Underwood	6	c Greig b Underwood	55
T. J. Jenner b Underwood	74	not out	14
M. H. N. Walker run out	41		
D. K. Lillee b Willis	26		
A. A. Mallett not out	23		
J. R. Thomson b Arnold	5		
Extras (B4, LB4, NB5)	13	(LB4, NB6)	10
Total	**304**	**(5 wkts dec)**	**272**

ENGLAND

D. L. Amiss c I. Chappell b Lillee	0	c Marsh b Lillee	0
D. Lloyd c Marsh b Lillee	4	c Walters b Walker	5
M. C. Cowdrey c Walker b Thomson	26	c Mallett b Lillee	3
†M. H. Denness c Marsh b Thomson	51	c Jenner b Lillee	14
K. W. R. Fletcher c I. Chappell b Thomson	40	lbw b Lillee	63
A. W. Greig c Marsh b Lillee	19	lbw b Walker	20
‡A. P. E. Knott c Lillee b Mallett	5	not out	106
F. J. Titmus c G. Chappell b Mallett	11	lbw b Jenner	20
D. L. Underwood c Lillee b Mallett	0	c I. Chappell b Mallett	0
G. G. Arnold b Lillee	0	b Mallett	0
R. G. D. Willis not out	11	b Walker	3
Extras (LB2, NB3)	5	(B3, LB3, NB1)	7
Total	**172**		**241**

BOWLING

ENGLAND	O	M	R	W		O	M	R	W
Willis	10	0	46	1	...	5	0	27	0
Arnold	12.2	3	42	1	...	20	1	71	1
Underwood	29	3	113	7	...	26	5	102	4
Greig	10	0	63	0	...	2	0	9	0
Titmus	7	1	27	0	...	13	1	53	0
AUSTRALIA									
Lillee	12.5	2	49	4	...	14	3	69	4
Thomson	15	1	58	3	...				
Walker	5	1	18	0	...	20	3	89	3
Jenner	5	0	28	0	...	15	4	39	1
Mallett	9	4	14	3	...	25	10	36	2
I. Chappell					...	1	0	1	0

Fall of Wickets	A	E	A	E
	1st	1st	2nd	2nd
1st	52	2	16	0
2nd	52	19	92	8
3rd	58	66	128	10
4th	77	90	133	33
5th	84	130	245	76
6th	164	147	—	144
7th	241	155	—	212
8th	259	156	—	213
9th	295	161	—	217
10th	304	172	—	241

SIXTH TEST MATCH

PLAYED AT MELBOURNE, 8, 9, 10, 12, 13 FEBRUARY
ENGLAND WON BY AN INNINGS AND 4 RUNS

AUSTRALIA

I. R. Redpath	c Greig b Lever	1	c Amiss b Greig		83
R. B. McCosker	c Greig b Lever	0	c Cowdrey b Arnold		76
†I. M. Chappell	c Knott b Old	65	c Knott b Greig		50
G. S. Chappell	c Denness b Lever	1	b Lever		102
R. Edwards	c Amiss b Lever	0	c Knott b Arnold		18
K. D. Walters	c Edrich b Old	12	b Arnold		3
‡A. W. Marsh	b Old	29	c Denness b Lever		1
M. H. N. Walker	not out	20	c & b Greig		17
D. K. Lillee	c Knott b Lever	12	not out		0
A. A. Mallett	b Lever	7	c Edrich b Greig		0
G. Dymock	c Knott b Greig	0	c Knott b Lever		0
Extras	(B2, LB1, NB2)	5	(B9, LB5, W4, NB5)		23
Total		**152**			**373**

ENGLAND

D. L. Amiss	lbw b Lillee	0
M. C. Cowdrey	c Marsh b Walker	7
J. H. Edrich	c I. Chappell b Walker	70
†M. H. Denness	c & b Walker	188
K.W.R. Fletcher	c Redpath b Walker	146
A. W. Greig	c sub b Walker	89
‡A. P. E. Knott	c Marsh b Walker	5
C. M. Old	b Dymock	0
D. L. Underwood	b Walker	11
G. G. Arnold	c Marsh b Walker	0
P. Lever	not out	6
Extras	(B4, LB2, NB1)	7
Total		**529**

BOWLING

ENGLAND	O	M	R	W		O	M	R	W
Arnold	6	2	24	0	...	23	6	83	3
Lever	11	2	38	6	...	16	1	65	3
Old	11	0	50	3	...	18	1	75	0
Greig	8.7	1	35	1	...	37.7	7	88	4
Underwood					...	18	5	39	0

AUSTRALIA	O	M	R	W	
Lillee	6	2	17	1	...
Walker	42.2	7	143	8	...
Dymock	39	6	130	1	...
Walters	23	3	86	0	...
Mallett	29	8	96	0	...
I. Chappell	12	1	50	0	...

Fall of Wickets

	A	E	A
	1st	1st	2nd
1st	0	4	111
2nd	5	18	215
3rd	19	167	248
4th	23	359	289
5th	50	507	297
6th	104	507	306
7th	115	508	367
8th	141	514	373
9th	149	514	373
10th	152	529	373

ENGLAND v AUSTRALIA

1876-77 to 1974-75

SERIES BY SERIES

Season		Visiting Captain	P	E W	A W	D
1876–77	In Australia	J. Lillywhite (E)	2	1	1	0
1878–79	In Australia	Lord Harris (E)	1	0	1	0
1880	In England	W. L. Murdoch (A)	1	1	0	0
1881–82	In Australia	A. Shaw (E)	4	0	2	2
1882	In England	W. L. Murdoch (A)	1	0	1	0
1882–83	In Australia	Hon. Ivo Bligh (E)	4	2	2	0
1884	In England	W. L. Murdoch (A)	3	1	0	2
1884–85	In Australia	A. Shrewsbury (E)	5	3	2	0
1886	In England	H. J. H. Scott (A)	3	3	0	0
1886–87	In Australia	A. Shrewsbury (E)	2	2	0	0
1887–88	In Australia	W. W. Read (E)	1	1	0	0
1888	In England	P. S. McDonnell (A)	3	2	1	0
1890	In England	W. L. Murdoch (A)	2*	2	0	0
1891–92	In Australia	W. G. Grace (E)	3	1	2	0
1893	In England	J. McC. Blackham (A)	3	1	0	2
1894–95	In Australia	A. E. Stoddart (E)	5	3	2	0
1896	In England	G. H. S. Trott (A)	3	2	1	0
1897–98	In Australia	A. E. Stoddart (E)	5	1	4	0
1899	In England	J. Darling (A)	5	0	1	4
1901–02	In Australia	A. C. MacLaren (E)	5	1	4	0
1902	In England	J. Darling (A)	5	1	2	2
1903–04	In Australia	P. F. Warner (E)	5	3	2	0
1905	In England	J. Darling (A)	5	2	0	3
1907–08	In Australia	A. O. Jones (E)	5	1	4	0
1909	In England	M. A. Noble (A)	5	1	2	2
1911–12	In Australia	J.W.H.T. Douglas (E)	5	4	1	0
1912	In England	S. E. Gregory (A)	3	1	0	2
1920–21	In Australia	J.W.H.T. Douglas (E)	5	0	5	0
1921	In England	W. W. Armstrong (A)	5	0	3	2
1924–25	In Australia	A. E. R. Gilligan (E)	5	1	4	0
1926	In England	H. L. Collins (A)	5	1	0	4
1928–29	In Australia	A. P. F. Chapman (E)	5	4	1	0
1930	In England	W. M. Woodfull (A)	5	1	2	2
1932–33	In Australia	D. R. Jardine (E)	5	4	1	0
1934	In England	W. M. Woodfull (A)	5	1	2	2
1936–37	In Australia	G. O. Allen (E)	5	2	3	0
1938	In England	D. G. Bradman (A)	4*	1	1	2
1946–47	In Australia	W. R. Hammond (E)	5	0	3	2
1948	In England	D. G. Bradman (A)	5	0	4	1
1950–51	In Australia	F. R. Brown (E)	5	1	4	0
1953	In England	A. L. Hassett (A)	5	1	0	4

Season	Visiting Captain	P	E W	A W	D
1954–55 In Australia	L. Hutton (E)	5	3	1	1
1956 In England	I. W. Johnson (A)	5	2	1	2
1958–59 In Australia	P. B. H. May (E)	5	0	4	1
1961 In England	R. Benaud (A)	5	1	2	2
1962–63 In Australia	E. R. Dexter (E)	5	1	1	3
1964 In England	R. B. Simpson (A)	5	0	1	4
1965–66 In Australia	M. J. K. Smith (E)	5	1	1	3
1968 In England	W. M. Lawry (A)	5	1	1	3
1970–71 In Australia	R. Illingworth (E)	6*	2	0	4
1972 In England	I. M. Chappell (A)	5	2	2	1
1974–75 In Australia	M. H. Denness (E)	6	1	4	1
	At Lord's	23	5	9	9
	At The Oval	25	12	5	8
	At Manchester	21	5	4	12
	At Leeds	15	3	5	7
	At Nottingham	12	2	3	7
	At Birmingham	4	1	0	3
	At Sheffield	1	0	1	0
	At Melbourne	43	16	20	7
	At Sydney	42	18	21	3
	At Adelaide	21	6	12	3
	At Brisbane	11	3	5	3
	At Perth	2	0	1	1
	In England	101	28	27	46
	In Australia	119	43	59	17
	Total	220	71	86	63

* The Test matches at Manchester in 1890 and 1938 and the third Test match at Melbourne in 1970–71 were abandoned without a ball being bowled and are excluded from this schedule.

HIGHEST INNINGS TOTALS

England

903–7d	The Oval	1938
658–8d	Nottingham	1938
636	Sydney	1928–29
627–9d	Manchester	1934
611	Manchester	1964

Australia

729–6d	Lord's	1930
701	The Oval	1934
695	The Oval	1930
659–8d	Sydney	1946–47
656–8d	Manchester	1964
645	Brisbane	1946–47
604	Melbourne	1936–37
601–8d	Brisbane	1954–55
600	Melbourne	1924–25

LOWEST INNINGS TOTALS

England

45	Sydney	1886–87
52	The Oval	1948
53	Lord's	1888
61	Melbourne	1901–02
61	Melbourne	1903–04

Australia

36	Birmingham	1902
42	Sydney	1887–88
44	The Oval	1896
53	Lord's	1896
58	Brisbane	1936–37
60	Lord's	1888
63	The Oval	1882
65	The Oval	1912
66	Brisbane	1928–29

HIGHEST INDIVIDUAL INNINGS FOR ENGLAND

364	L. Hutton	at The Oval	1938
287	R. E. Foster	at Sydney	1903–04
256	K. F. Barrington	at Manchester	1964
251	W. R. Hammond	at Sydney	1928–29
240	W. R. Hammond	at Lord's	1938
231*	W. R. Hammond	at Sydney	1936–37
216*	E. Paynter	at Nottingham	1938
200	W. R. Hammond	at Melbourne	1928–29

A total of 154 centuries have been scored for England.

HIGHEST INDIVIDUAL INNINGS FOR AUSTRALIA

334	D. G. Bradman	at Leeds	1930
311	R. B. Simpson	at Manchester	1964
307	R. M. Cowper	at Melbourne	1965–66
304	D. G. Bradman	at Leeds	1934
270	D. G. Bradman	at Melbourne	1936–37
266	W. H. Ponsford	at The Oval	1934
254	D. G. Bradman	at Lord's	1930
244	D. G. Bradman	at The Oval	1934
234	S. G. Barnes	at Sydney	1946–47
234	D. G. Bradman	at Sydney	1946–47
232	D. G. Bradman	at The Oval	1930
232	S. J. McCabe	at Nottingham	1938
225	R. B. Simpson	at Adelaide	1965–66
212	D. G. Bradman	at Adelaide	1936–37
211	W. L. Murdoch	at The Oval	1884
207	K. R. Stackpole	at Brisbane	1970–71
206*	W. A. Brown	at Lord's	1938
206	A. R. Morris	at Adelaide	1950–51
201*	J. Ryder	at Sydney	1924–25
201	S. E. Gregory	at Sydney	1894–95

A total of 171 centuries have been scored for Australia

A CENTURY IN EACH INNINGS OF A MATCH
FOR ENGLAND

176	& 127	H. Sutcliffe	at Melbourne	1924–25
119*	& 177	W. R. Hammond	at Adelaide	1928–29
147	& 103*	D. C. S. Compton	at Adelaide	1946–47

FOR AUSTRALIA

136	& 130	W. Bardsley	at The Oval	1909
122	& 124*	A. R. Morris	at Adelaide	1946–47

A CENTURY ON DEBUT IN SERIES
FOR ENGLAND

152	W. G. Grace (on Test debut)	at The Oval	1880
154*	K. S. Rinjitsinhji (on Test debut)	at Manchester	1896
287	R. E. Foster (on Test debut)	at Sydney	1903–04
119	G. Gunn (on Test debut)	at Sydney	1907–08
115	H. Sutcliffe	at Sydney	1924–25

137	M. Leyland	at Melbourne	1928–29
173	K. S. Duleepsinhji	at Lord's	1930
102	Nawab of Pataudi (on Test debut)	at Sydney	1932–33
100	L. Hutton	at Nottingham	1938
102	D. C. S. Compton	at Nottingham	1938
109	W. Watson	at Lord's	1953
112	R. Subba Row	at Birmingham	1961
120	J. H. Edrich	at Lord's	1964

FOR AUSTRALIA

165*	C. Bannerman (on Test debut)	at Melbourne	1876–77
107	H. Graham (on Test debut)	at Lord's	1893
104	R. A. Duff (on Test debut)	at Melbourne	1903–04
116	R. J. Hartigan (on Test debut)	at Adelaide	1907–08
104	H. L. Collins (on Test debut)	at Sydney	1920–21
110	W. H. Ponsford (on Test debut)	at Sydney	1924–25
164	A. A. Jackson (on Test debut)	at Adelaide	1928–29
112	R. N. Harvey	at Leeds	1948
101*	J. W. Burke (on Test debut)	at Adelaide	1950–51
155	K. D. Walters (on Test debut)	at Brisbane	1965–66
108	G. S. Chappell (on Test debut)	at Perth	1970–71

RECORD WICKET PARTNERSHIPS FOR ENGLAND

1st	323	J. B. Hobbs & W. Rhodes at Melbourne	1911–12
2nd	382	L. Hutton & M. Leyland at The Oval	1938
3rd	262	W. R. Hammond & D. R. Jardine at Adelaide	1928–29
4th	222	W. R. Hammond & E. Paynter at Lord's	1938
5th	206	E. Paynter & D. C. S. Compton at Nottingham	1938
6th	215	L. Hutton & J. Hardstaff at The Oval	1938
7th	143	F. E. Woolley & J. Vine at Sydney	1911–12
8th	124	E. Hendren & H. Larwood at Brisbane	1928–29
9th	151	W. H. Scotton & W. W. Read at The Oval	1884
10th	130	R. E. Foster & W. Rhodes at Sydney	1903–04

RECORD WICKET PARTNERSHIPS FOR AUSTRALIA

1st	244	R. B. Simpson & W. M. Lawry at Adelaide	1965–66
2nd	451	W. H. Ponsford & D. G. Bradman at The Oval	1934
3rd	276	D. G. Bradman & A. L. Hassett at Brisbane	1946–47
4th	388	W. H. Ponsford & D. G. Bradman at Leeds	1934
5th	405	S. G. Barnes & D. G. Bradman at Sydney	1946–47
6th	346	J. H. Fingleton & D. G. Bradman at Melbourne	1936–37
7th	165	C. Hill & H. Trumble at Melbourne	1897–98
8th	243	C. Hill & R. J. Hartigan at Adelaide	1907–08
9th	154	S. E. Gregory & J. McC. Blackham at Sydney	1894–95
10th	127	J. M. Taylor & A. A. Mailey at Sydney	1924–25

HIGHEST RUN AGGREGATE IN A TEST RUBBER FOR:

England in England	562 (Av. 62.44)	D. C. S. Compton	1948
England in Australia	905 (Av. 113.12)	W. R. Hammond	1928–29
Australia in England	974 (Av. 139.14)	D. G. Bradman	1930
Australia in Australia	810 (Av. 90.00)	D. G. Bradman	1936–37

17

BEST INNINGS BOWLING FIGURES FOR:

England in England	10–53	J. C. Laker at Manchester	1956
England in Australia	8–35	G. A. Lohmann at Sydney	1886–87
Australia in England	8–31	F. Laver at Manchester	1909
Australia in Australia	9–121	A. A. Mailey at Melbourne	1920–21

TEN WICKETS OR MORE IN A MATCH

The feat has been achieved on 34 occasions for England, the last time being by D. L. Underwood at Adelaide in 1975. For Australia, it has been achieved on 29 occasions, the last instance being by D. K. Lillee at The Oval in 1972.

HIGHEST WICKET AGGREGATE IN A TEST RUBBER FOR:

England in England	46 (Av. 9.60)	J. C. Laker	1956
England in Australia	38 (Av. 23.18)	M. W. Tate	1924–25
Australia in England	31 (Av. 17.67)	D. K. Lillee	1972
Australia in Australia	36 (Av. 26.27)	A. A. Mailey	1920–21

HIGHEST MATCH AGGREGATE   1753–40 wkts Adelaide 1920–21

LOWEST MATCH AGGREGATE   291–40 wkts Lord's   1888

ENGLAND MASSACRE INDIA

There can rarely have been a Test series which was thought beforehand to be very open, yet which resulted in a complete whitewash by huge margins. The first Test was a comparatively modest victory – 113 runs – but the second was by an innings and 285 runs, and the third by an innings and 78 runs. England's score in the second match was 629; India capitulated with a paltry 42, of which one player, Solkar, scored 18. In the third match England scored 459 for 2 to complete the absolute rout of India's hitherto highly-prized spin bowlers. Bedi, Chandra, and Prasanna had caused England's batsmen immense problems in the past, but the bubble was well and truly burst in this series.

The first match was played in weather most befitting to the wastes of Siberia; small wonder that Indian cricketers could not find their best form in these conditions, but even they would hardly blame the weather entirely. England batted better, and bowled better; Fletcher, and Edrich, recalled to the Test scene, hit hundreds, and Old, Willis, Hendrick, and Greig shared the pickings among the wickets. At Lord's, however, India were humiliated, utterly and completely. Their spinners were savagely mauled, and although they had batted with a great deal of spirit in the first innings when facing a daunting score of 629, they appeared to throw in the towel in the second; no Test side in the world on any wicket should be out for 42. They allowed Arnold and Old to toy with them.

Thus with their tails very much down they travelled to Edgbaston, and as seemed possible, they were never in the match from start to finish. Their only hope had been a good start, but at 17–2 the writing appeared to be on the wall, and so it was. In only his second Test, David Lloyd hit an unbeaten 214 as the Indian bowlers were savaged yet again. The turbaned Bedi took most wickets in the series for India, but at an appalling cost – 2 for 87, 1 for 58, 6 for 226, and 1 for 152, an aggregate of 10 for 523. How the tables had been turned.

England v India, 1974

FIRST TEST MATCH

PLAYED AT OLD TRAFFORD, 6, 7, 8, 10, 11 JUNE
ENGLAND WON BY 113 RUNS

ENGLAND

G. Boycott lbw b Abid Ali	10	c Engineer b Solkar	
D. L. Amiss c Madan Lal Sharma b Chandrasekhar	56	c Gavaskar b Bedi	47
J. H. Edrich b Abid Ali	7	not out	100
†M. H. Denness b Bedi	26	not out	45
K. W. R. Fletcher not out	123		
D. L. Underwood c Solkar b Bedi	7	c Engineer b Abid Ali	9
A. W. Greig c Engineer b Madan Lal Sharma	53		
‡A.P.E. Knott lbw b Madan Lal Sharma	0		
C.M. Old c Engineer b Chandrasekhar	12		
R. G. D. Willis lbw b Abid Ali	24		
M. Hendrick did not bat			
Extras (B1, LB7, W1, NB1)	10	(B4, LB2)	9
Total (9 wkts dec)	328	(3 wkts dec)	213

INDIA

S. M. Gavaskar run out	101	c Hendrick b Old	58
E. D. Solkar c Willis b Hendrick	7	c Hendrick b Underwood	19
S. Venkataraghavan b Willis	3	not out	5
†A. L. Wadekar c Hendrick b Old	6	c Knott b Greig	14
G. R. Viswanath b Underwood	40	c Knott b Old	50
B. P. Patel c Knott b Willis	5	c Knott b Old	3
‡F. M. Engineer b Willis	0	c Knott b Hendrick	12
Madan Lal Sharma lbw b Hendrick	2	hit wkt b Willis	7
S. Abid Ali c Knott b Hendrick	71	c Boycott b Greig	4
B. S. Bedi b Willis	0	b Old	0
B. S. Chandrasekhar not out	0	st Knott b Greig	0
Extras (B3, LB3, NB5)	11	(B1, LB2, NB7)	10
Total	246		182

BOWLING

INDIA	O	M	R	W		O	M	R	W
Abid Ali	30.3	6	79	3	...	11	2	31	1
Solkar	13	4	33	0	...	7	0	24	1
Madan Lal	31	11	56	2	...	12	2	39	0
Venkataraga'n	5	1	8	0	...	9	1	17	0
Bedi	43	14	87	2	...	20	2	58	1
Ch'drasek'r	21	4	55	2	...	11	2	38	0
ENGLAND									
Willis	24	3	64	4	...	12	5	33	1
Old	16	0	46	1	...	16	7	20	4
Hendrick	20	4	57	3	...	17	1	39	1
Underwood	19	7	50	1	...	4		45	1
Greig	5	1	18	0	...	25.1	8	35	3

Fall of Wickets

	E	I	E	I
	1st	1st	2nd	2nd
1st	18	22	13	32
2nd	28	25	30	68
3rd	90	32	104	103
4th	104	105	—	111
5th	127	129	—	139
6th	231	135	—	157
7th	231	143	—	165
8th	265	228	—	180
9th	328	228	—	180
10th	—	246	—	182

SECOND TEST MATCH

PLAYED AT LORD'S, 20, 21, 22, 24 JUNE
ENGLAND WON BY AN INNINGS AND 285 RUNS

ENGLAND

D. L. Amiss lbw b Prasanna	188
D. Lloyd c Solkar b Prasanna	46
J. H. Edrich lbw b Bedi	96
†M. H. Denness c sub (Venkatarag'n) b Bedi	118
K. W. R. Fletcher c Solkar b Bedi	15
A. W. Greig c & b Abid Ali	106
‡A. P. E. Knott c & b Bedi	26
C. M. Old b Abid Ali	3
G. G. Arnold b Bedi	5
D. L. Underwood c Solkar b Bedi	9
M. Hendrick not out	1
Extras (B8, LB4, W2, NB2)	16
Total	**629**

INDIA

S. M. Gavaskar c Knott b Old	49	lbw b Arnold	5
‡F. M. Engineer c Denness b Old	86	lbw b Arnold	0
†A. L. Wadekar c Underwood b Hendrick	18	b Old	3
G. R. Viswanath b Underwood	52	c Knott b Arnold	5
B. P. Patel c Fletcher b Greig	1	c Knott b Arnold	1
E. D. Solkar c Underwood b Hendrick	43	not out	18
S. Abid Ali c Arnold b Old	14	c Knott b Old	3
Madan Lal Sharma c Knott b Old	0	c Hendrick b Old	2
E.A.S. Prasanna c Denness b Hendrick	0	b Old	5
B. S. Bedi b Arnold	14	b Old	0
B. S. Chandrasekhar not out	2	absent hurt	
Extras (B4, LB7, NB12)	23		
Total	**302**		**42**

BOWLING

INDIA	O	M	R	W		O	M	R	W
Abid Ali	22	2	79	2	...				
Solkar	6	2	16	0	...				
Madan Lal	30	6	93	0	...				
Bedi	64.2	8	226	6	...				
Ch'drasek'r	9.3	1	33	0	...				
Prasanna	51	6	166	2	...				
ENGLAND									
Arnold	24.5	6	81	1	...	8	1	19	4
Old	21	6	67	4	...	8	3	21	5
Hendrick	18	4	46	3	...	1	0	2	0
Greig	21	4	63	1	...				
Underwood	15	10	18	1	...				
Lloyd	2	0	4	0	...				

Fall of Wickets

	E	I	I
	1st	1st	2nd
1st	116	131	2
2nd	337	149	5
3rd	339	183	12
4th	369	188	14
5th	571	250	25
6th	591	280	28
7th	604	281	30
8th	611	286	42
9th	624	286	42
10th	629	302	

NB An injured thumb prevented Chandrasekhar from completing his 10th over.

THIRD TEST MATCH

PLAYED AT EDGBASTON, 4, 5, 6, 8 JULY
ENGLAND WON BY AN INNINGS AND 78 RUNS

INDIA

S. M. Gavaskar c Knott b Arnold	0	c Knott b Old		4
S. S. Naik b Arnold	4	lbw b Greig		77
†A. L. Wadekar c Knott b Hendrick	36	lbw b Old		5
G. R. Viswanath b Hendrick	28	c Greig b Hendrick		25
A. V. Mankad c Knott b Arnold	14	hit wkt b Old		43
‡F. M. Engineer not out	64	lbw b Hendrick		33
E. D. Solkar lbw b Old	3	c Edrich b Arnold		8
S. Abid Ali run out	6	b Arnold		3
S. Venkataraghavan b Underwood	0	c Lloyd b Greig		5
E. A. S. Prasanna c Greig b Hendrick	0	b Hendrick		4
B. S. Bedi c Old b Hendrick	0	not out		1
Extras (B1, LB1, NB8)	10	(LB3, NB5)		8
Total	**165**			**216**

ENGLAND

D. L. Amiss c Mankad b Prasanna	79
D. Lloyd not out	214
†M. H. Denness c & b Bedi	100
K. W. R. Fletcher not out	51
J. H. Edrich	
A. W. Greig	
‡A. P. E. Knott	
C. M. Old	did not bat
G. G. Arnold	
D. L. Underwood	
M. Hendrick	
Extras (B4, LB5, W1, NB5)	15
Total (2 wkts dec)	**459**

BOWLING

ENGLAND	O	M	R	W		O	M	R	W		Fall of Wickets		
											I	E	I
Arnold	14	3	43	3	...	19	3	61	2		1st	1st	2nd
Old	13	0	43	1	...	15	3	52	3	1st	0	157	6
Hendrick	14.2	1	28	4	...	14.4	4	43	3	2nd	17	368	12
Greig	3	0	11	0	...	16	3	49	2	3rd	62	—	21
Underwood	15	3	30	1	...	3	1	3	0	4th	81	—	59
INDIA										5th	115	—	146
Abid Ali	18	2	63	0	...					6th	129	—	172
Solkar	18	5	52	0	...					7th	153	—	183
Bedi	45	4	152	1	...					8th	156	—	196
Venkatarag'n	23	1	71	0	...					9th	165	—	211
Prasanna	35	4	101	1	...					10th	165	—	216
Gavaskar	1	0	5	0	...								

Test Match Averages

ENGLAND—BATTING AND FIELDING

	M	I	NO	HS	Runs	Avge	100	50	Ct	St
D. Lloyd	2	2	1	214*	260	260.00	1	—	1	—
K. W. R. Fletcher	3	3	2	123*	189	189.00	1	1	1	—
J. H. Edrich	3	3	1	100*	203	101.50	1	1	1	—
M. H. Denness	3	4	1	118	289	96.33	2	—	2	—
D. L. Amiss	3	4	—	188	370	92.50	1	2	—	—
A. W. Greig	3	2	0	106	159	79.50	1	1	2	—
A. P. E. Knott	3	2	0	26	26	13.00	—	—	15	1
D. L. Underwood	3	3	0	9	25	8.33	—	—	1	—
C. M. Old	3	2	0	12	15	7.50	—	—	1	—
G. G. Arnold	2	1	0	5	5	5.00	—	—	1	—
M. Hendrick	3	1	1	1*	1	—	—	—	4	—

Played in one Test: G. Boycott 10 and 6 (1 ct); R. G. D. Willis 24 (1 ct).

BOWLING

	Overs	Mdns	Runs	Wkts	Avge	Best	5 wI	10 wM
C. M. Old	89	19	249	18	13.83	5–21	—	—
M. Hendrick	85	14	215	14	15.35	4–28	—	—
R. G. D. Willis	36	8	97	5	19.40	4–64	—	—
G. G. Arnold	65.5	13	204	10	20.40	4–19	—	—
A. W. Greig	70.1	16	176	6	29.33	3–35	—	—

Also bowled: D. Lloyd 2–0–4–0; D. L. Underwood 67–25–146–4.

INDIA—BATTING AND FIELDING

	M	I	NO	HS	Runs	Avge	100	50	Ct	St
F. M. Engineer	3	6	1	86	195	39.00	—	2	4	—
S. M. Gavaskar	3	6	0	101	217	36.16	1	1	1	—
G. R. Viswanath	3	6	0	52	200	33.33	—	2	—	—
E. D. Solkar	3	6	1	43	98	19.60	—	—	4	—
S. Abid Ali	3	6	0	71	101	16.83	—	1	—	—
A. L. Wadekar	3	6	0	36	82	13.83	—	—	1	—
S. Venkataraghavan	2	4	1	5*	13	4.33	—	—	—	—
B. S. Bedi	3	6	1	14	15	3.00	—	—	2	—
Madan Lal Sharma	2	4	0	7	11	2.75	—	—	1	—
B. P. Patel	2	4	0	5	10	2.50	—	—	—	—
E. A. S. Prasanna	2	4	0	5	9	2.25	—	—	—	—
B. S. Chandrasekhar	2	3	2	2*	2	2.00	—	—	—	—

Played in one Test: A. V. Mankad 14 and 43 (1 ct); S. S. Naik 4 and 77.

BOWLING

	Overs	Mdns	Runs	Wkts	Avge	Best	5 wI	10 wM
S. Abid Ali	81.3	12	252	6	42.00	3–79	—	—
B. S. Bedi	172.2	28	523	10	52.30	6–226	1	—

Also bowled: B. S. Chandrasekhar 41.3–7–126–2; S. M. Gavaskar 1–0–5–0; Madan Lal Sharma 73–19–188–2; E. A. S. Prasanna 86–10–267–3; E. R. Solkar 44–11–125–1; S. Venkataraghavan 37–3–96–0.

Tour Averages
BATTING AND FIELDING

	M	I	NO	HS	Runs	Avge	100	50	Ct	St
S. M. H. Kirmani	9	10	7	46*	144	48.00	—	—	12	7
S. M. Gavaskar	14	26	2	136	993	41.37	3	4	6	—
S. S. Naik	11	21	3	135	730	40.55	2	4	3	—
F. M. Engineer	9	17	4	108	500	38.46	1	3	17	1
A. V. Mankad	13	22	6	66*	611	38.18	—	4	5	—
A. L. Wadekar	14	24	2	138	783	35.59	1	5	7	—
Madan Lal Sharma	12	18	6	79*	399	33.25	—	2	11	—
G. R. Viswanath	15	26	3	106	705	30.65	2	2	7	—
E. D. Solkar	15	27	2	109	709	28.36	1	3	9	—
B. P. Patel	14	22	3	107	511	26.89	2	1	6	—
S. Abid Ali	14	22	4	71	470	26.11	—	4	5	—
G. Bose	9	18	0	66	328	18.22	—	2	4	—
S. Venkataraghavan	13	17	4	28	168	12.92	—	—	8	—
B. S. Bedi	13	11	3	19	73	9.12	—	—	6	—
E. A. S. Prasanna	13	13	3	13	52	5.20	—	—	4	—
B. S. Chandrasekhar	10	5	3	2*	2	1.00	—	—	7	—

BOWLING

	Overs	Mdns	Runs	Wkts	Avge	Best	5 wI	10 wM
S. Abid Ali	324.4	64	965	32	30.15	6–23	2	—
B. S. Chandrasekhar	258.5	33	789	26	30.34	5–80	1	—
B. S. Bedi	604	150	1651	53	31.15	6–110	5	—
Madan Lal Sharma	412.4	89	1263	31	40.74	7–95	1	—
E. A. S. Prasanna	425.4	88	1261	28	45.03	4–59	—	—
E. D. Solkar	250.2	62	680	14	48.57	3–73	—	—
S. Venkataraghavan	356	75	970	18	53.88	4–35	—	—

Also bowled: G. Bose 15.4–1–42–4; S. M. Gavaskar 19–3–60–2; A. V. Mankad 15–1–58–1; G. R. Viswanath 3–0–26–0.

PAKISTAN, A DIFFERENT STORY

If England were riding on the crest of a wave after the battering they had given India, they found Pakistan a very different proposition. On paper, every match was drawn, but this by no means tells the full story. Especially notable was the hiatus at Lord's, when the Pakistan manager accused the amiable Lord's groundsman, Jim Fairbrother, of carelessness in his attempts to cover the wicket during heavy rains. When rain prevented play on the last day at Headingley there was nothing in it, and both captains could say that they would have won if play had been possible. England, needing 282 to win, were 238 for 6, with Fletcher 67 not out, and Old as his accomplice. If Fletcher was out early, then things were very much in favour of Pakistan. If Fletcher stayed, then it was England's match. We shall never know, but at Lord's, Pakistan were ravaged twice by Underwood, in the second innings when heavy rain had seeped underneath the covers (with that amount of rain and the added hazard of the Lord's slope nothing in the world could have prevented it). Pakistan from 192–3 were all out 226, Underwood being as near unplayable as makes no difference. England's task on the last day was an easy one, but as the tourists' manager fumed, the rain appeared again; with play impossible, Pakistan were spared the defeat that had seemed inevitable.

So the two sides came to the Oval all square, and on the most placid wicket in the world Pakistan simply decided to put themselves beyond defeat. (Had they been looking for victory they would scarcely have batted on to a total of 600, since they could have had precious little hope of bowling any Test side out twice on that wicket.) The only course left open to England was a similar one – they went wearily and wearily on, just as Pakistan had done. It was a match condemned to death from the start; a Bank Holiday crowd of very useful dimensions sat it out peacefully, for they could do little else. Fletcher batted 518 minutes for a piece of cricket that was little better than drudgery. So despite all sorts of ramifications the teams finished level.

England v Pakistan, 1974

FIRST TEST MATCH

PLAYED AT HEADINGLEY, 25, 26, 27, 29 JULY
MATCH DRAWN

PAKISTAN

Sadiq Mohammad c Lloyd b Hendrick	28	c Greig b Old	12
Shafiq Ahmed b Old	7	c Greig b Arnold	18
Majid Khan c & b Greig	75	c Knott b Arnold	4
Mushtaq Mohammad c Fletcher b Underwood	6	c Greig b Hendrick	43
Zaheer Abbas c Knott b Hendrick	48	c Knott b Greig	19
Asif Iqbal c Knott b Arnold	14	b Old	8
†Intikhab Alam c Knott b Arnold	3	lbw b Old	10
Imran Khan c Greig b Old	23	c Greig b Hendrick	31
‡Wasim Bari c Denness b Old	2	b Hendrick	3
Sarfraz Nawaz b Arnold	53	c Fletcher b Arnold	2
Asif Masood not out	4	not out	2
Extras (LB5, W2, NB15)	22	(B14, W1, NB12)	27
Total	**285**		**179**

ENGLAND

D. L. Amiss c Sadiq b Sarfraz	13	lbw b Sarfraz	8
D. Lloyd c Sadiq b Masood	48	c Wasim b Sarfraz	9
J. H. Edrich c Iqbal b Masood	9	c Sadiq b Imran	70
†M. H. Denness b Masood	9	c Sarfraz b Intikhab	44
K. W. R. Fletcher lbw b Sarfraz	11	not out	67
A. W. Greig c Wasim b Imran	37	c Majid b Sarfraz	12
‡A. P. E. Knott c Wasim b Iqbal	35	c Majid b Sarfraz	5
C. M. Old c Masood b Imran	0	not out	10
G. G. Arnold c Intikhab b Sarfraz	1		
D. L. Underwood run out	9		
M. Hendrick not out	1		
Extras (B1, LB3, W4, NB2)	10	(B4, LB2, W1, NB5)	13
Total	**183**	**(6 wkts)**	**238**

BOWLING

ENGLAND	O	M	R	W		O	M	R	W		Fall of Wickets			
											P	E	P	E
Arnold	31.5	8	67	3	...	23.1	11	36	3		1st	1st	2nd	2nd
Old	21	4	65	3	...	17	0	54	3	1st	12	25	24	17
Hendrick	26	4	91	2	...	18	6	39	3	2nd	60	69	35	22
Underwood	12	6	26	1	...	1	0	0	0	3rd	70	79	38	94
Greig	11	4	14	1	...	9	3	23	1	4th	170	84	83	174
PAKISTAN										5th	182	100	97	198
Asif Masood	16	3	50	3	...	19	2	63	0	6th	189	172	115	213
Sarfraz	22	4	51	3	...	36	14	56	4	7th	198	172	154	—
Imran	21	1	55	2	...	29	7	55	1	8th	209	172	168	—
Mushtaq	1	1	0	0	...	4	1	8	0	9th	223	182	177	—
Intikhab	6	2	14	0	...	14	4	25	1	10th	285	183	179	—
Asif Iqbal	6	3	3	1	...	5	1	18	0					

SECOND TEST MATCH

PLAYED AT LORD'S, 8, 9, 10, 12, 13 AUGUST
MATCH DRAWN

PAKISTAN

Sadiq Mohammad lbw b Hendrick	40	lbw b Arnold	43
Majid Khan c Old b Greig	48	lbw b Underwood	19
Zaheer Abbas c Hendrick b Underwood	1	c Greig b Underwood	1
Mushtaq Mohammad c Greig b Underwood	0	c Denness b Greig	76
Wasim Raja c Greig b Underwood	24	c Lloyd b Underwood	53
Asif Iqbal c Amiss b Underwood	2	c Greig b Underwood	0
†Intikhab Alam b Underwood	5	b Underwood	0
Imran Khan c Hendrick b Greig	4	c Lloyd b Underwood	0
‡Wasim Bari lbw b Greig	4	lbw b Underwood	1
Sarfraz Nawaz not out	0	c Lloyd b Underwood	1
Asif Masood did not bat		not out	17
Extras (NB2)	2	(LB8, NB7)	15
Total (9 wkts dec)	130		226

ENGLAND

D. L. Amiss c Sadiq b Asif Masood	2	not out	14
D. Lloyd c Zaheer b Sarfraz	23	not out	12
J. H. Edrich c Sadiq b Intikhab	40		
†M. H. Denness b Imran	20		
K. W. R. Fletcher lbw b Imran	8		
A. W. Greig run out	9		
‡A. P. E. Knott c Wasim Bari b Asif Masood	83		
C. M. Old c Wasim Bari b Mushtaq	41		
G. G. Arnold c Wasim Bari b Masood	10		
D. L. Underwood not out	12		
M. Hendrick c Imran b Intikhab	6		
Extras (LB14, W1, NB1)	16	(NB1)	1
Total	270	(No wkt)	27

BOWLING

ENGLAND	O	M	R	W	O	M	R	W
Arnold	8	1	32	0	15	3	37	1
Old	5	0	17	0	14	1	39	0
Hendrick	9	2	36	1	15	4	29	0
Underwood	14	8	20	5	34.5	17	51	8
Greig	8.5	4	23	3	19	6	55	1
PAKISTAN								
Asif Masood	25	10	47	3	4	0	9	0
Sarfraz	22	8	42	1	3	0	7	0
Imran	18	2	48	2				
Intikhab	26	4	80	2	1	1	0	0
Wasim Raja	2	0	8	0				
Mushtaq	7	3	16	1				
Asif Iqbal	5	0	13	0				
Majid Khan					2	0	10	0

Fall of Wickets

	P	E	P	E
	1st	1st	2nd	2nd
1st	71	2	55	—
2nd	91	52	61	—
3rd	91	90	77	—
4th	91	94	192	—
5th	103	100	192	—
6th	111	118	220	—
7th	130	187	200	—
8th	130	231	206	—
9th	130	254	208	—
10th	—	270	226	—

THIRD TEST MATCH

PAKISTAN

Sadiq Mohammad c Old b Willis	21	c & b Arnold	4
Majid Khan b Underwood	98	c Denness b Old	18
Zaheer Abbas b Underwood	240	c Knott b Arnold	15
Mushtaq Mohammad b Arnold	76	b Underwood	8
Asif Iqbal c & b Greig	29		
Wasim Raja c Denness b Greig	28	not out	30
Imran Khan c Knott b Willis	24	not out	10
†Intikhab Alam not out	32		
Sarfraz Nawaz not out	14		
‡Wasim Bari ⎱ did not bat			
Asif Masood ⎰			
Extras (B6, LB18, NB14)	38	(B5, NB4)	9
Total (7 wkts dec)	600	(4 wkts	94

ENGLAND

D. L. Amiss c Majid b Intikhab	183
D. Lloyd c Sadiq b Sarfraz	4
D. L. Underwood lbw b Wasim Raja	43
J. H. Edrich c Wasim Bari b Intikhab	25
†M. H. Denness c Imran b Asif Masood	18
K. W. R. Fletcher run out	122
A. W. Greig b Intikhab	32
‡A. P. E. Knott b Intikhab	9
C. M. Old lbw b Intikhab	65
G. G. Arnold c Wasim Bari b Mushtaq	2
R. G. D. Willis not out	1
Extras (B8, LB13, NB20)	41
Total	545

BOWLING

ENGLAND	O	M	R	W		O	M	R	W
Arnold	37	5	106	1	...	6	0	22	2
Willis	28	3	102	2	...	7	2	27	0
Old	29.3	3	143	2	...	6	0	61	0
Underwood	44	14	106	2	...	8	2	15	1
Greig	25	5	92	2	...	7	1	15	0
Lloyd	2	0	13	0					
PAKISTAN									
Asif Masood	40	13	66	1					
Sarfraz	38	8	103	1					
Intikhab	51.3	14	116	5					
Imran	44	16	100	0					
Mushtaq	29	12	51	1					
Wasim Raja	23	6	68	1					

Fall of Wickets

	P	E	P
	1st	1st	2nd
1st	66	14	8
2nd	166	143	33
3rd	338	209	41
4th	431	244	68
5th	503	383	—
6th	550	401	—
7th	550	531	—
8th	—	539	—
9th	—	539	—
10th	—	545	—

Note: Amiss retired hurt at 305 and resumed his innings after the 8th wicket fell at 539.

Test Match Averages

ENGLAND—BATTING AND FIELDING

	M	I	NO	HS	Runs	Avge	100	50	Ct	St
K. W. R. Fletcher	3	4	1	122	208	69.33	1	1	2	—
D. L. Amiss	3	5	1	183	220	55.00	1	—	1	—
C. M. Old	3	4	1	65	116	38.66	—	1	2	—
J. H. Edrich	3	4	0	70	144	36.00	—	1	—	—
A. P. E. Knott	3	4	0	83	132	33.00	—	1	7	—
D. L. Underwood	3	3	1	43	64	32.00	—	—	1	—
D. Lloyd	3	5	1	48	96	24.00	—	—	4	—
M. H. Denness	3	4	0	44	91	22.75	—	—	4	—
A. W. Greig	3	4	0	37	90	22.50	—	—	11	—
M. Hendrick	2	2	1	6	7	7.00	—	—	2	—
G. G. Arnold	3	3	0	10	13	4.33	—	—	1	—

Played in one Test: R. G. D. Willis 1*.

BOWLING

	Overs	Mdns	Runs	Wkts	Avge	Best	5 wI	10 wM
D. L. Underwood	113.5	48	218	17	12.82	8–51	2	1
A. W. Greig	79.5	23	222	8	27.75	3–23	—	—
G. G. Arnold	121	28	300	10	30.00	3–36	—	—
M. Hendrick	68	16	195	6	32.50	3–39	—	—
C. M. Old	88.3	8	324	7	46.28	3–54	—	—

Also bowled: D. Lloyd 2–0–13–0; R. G. D. Willis 35–4–129–2.

PAKISTAN—BATTING AND FIELDING

	M	I	NO	HS	Runs	Avge	100	50	Ct	St
Zaheer Abbas	3	6	0	240	324	54.00	1	—	1	—
Wasim Raja	2	4	1	53	135	45.00	—	1	—	—
Majid Khan	3	6	0	98	262	43.66	—	2	3	—
Mushtaq Mohammad	3	6	0	76	209	34.83	—	1	—	—
Sadiq Mohammad	3	6	0	43	148	24.66	—	—	6	—
Sarfraz Nawaz	3	5	2	53	70	23.33	—	1	1	—
Imran Khan	3	6	1	31	92	18.40	—	—	2	—
Intikhab Alam	3	5	1	32*	50	12.50	—	—	1	—
Asif Iqbal	3	5	0	29	53	10.60	—	—	1	—
Wasim Bari	3	4	0	4	10	2.50	—	—	8	—
Asif Masood	3	3	3	17*	23	—	—	—	1	—

Played in one Test: Shafiq Ahmed 7 and 18.

BOWLING

	Overs	Mdns	Runs	Wkts	Avge	Best	5 wI	10 wM
Sarfraz Nawaz	121	34	259	9	28.77	4–56	—	—
Intikhab Alam	98.4	25	235	8	29.37	5–116	1	—
Asif Masood	104	28	235	7	33.57	3–47	—	—
Imran Khan	112	26	258	5	51.60	2–48	—	—

Also bowled: Asif Iqbal 16–4–34–1; Majid Khan 2–0–10–0; Mushtaq Mohammad 41–17–75–2; Wasim Raja 25–6–76–1.

Tour Averages

BATTING AND FIELDING

	M	I	NO	HS	Runs	Avge	100	50	Ct	St
Wasim Raja	11	15	6	139*	486	54.00	1	2	5	—
Zaheer Abbas	16	23	4	240	975	51.31	4	2	10	—
Shafiq Ahmed	7	12	3	100*	451	50.11	1	3	5	—
Majid Khan	14	23	4	134*	1000	50.00	3	5	13	—
Sadiq Mohammad	14	24	2	106	1007	45.77	2	8	17	—
Mushtaq Mohammad	14	21	3	101*	730	40.55	1	5	7	—
Asif Iqbal	12	16	2	77	447	31.92	—	3	6	—
Imran Khan	8	10	2	56*	249	31.12	—	1	3	—
Aftab Gul	6	10	0	112	293	29.30	1	1	1	—
Aftab Baloch	7	8	4	42*	101	25.25	—	—	4	—
Asif Masood	12	5	4	17*	25	25.00	—	—	3	—
Intikhab Alam	13	18	2	61	323	20.18	—	3	4	—
Sarfraz Nawaz	11	12	4	53	161	20.12	—	1	6	—
Naseer Malik	7	5	1	21	48	12.00	—	—	4	—
Wasim Bari	14	14	3	30*	104	9.45	—	—	35	5
Mohammad Nazir jr	6	4	3	9*	9	9.00	—	—	3	—
Mazullah Khan	4	2	1	1	1	1.00	—	—	3	—

BOWLING

	Overs	Mdns	Runs	Wkts	Avge	Best	5 wI	10 wM
Mushtaq Mohammad	227.3	57	662	37	17.89	7-59	3	—
Asif Iqbal	78	20	200	10	20.00	4-46	—	—
Sarfraz Nawaz	326.4	91	774	37	20.91	8-27	3	—
Asif Masood	260	64	603	29	21.00	5-35	1	—
Sadiq Mohammad	30.5	5	155	7	22.14	5-126	1	—
Intikhab Alam	328.3	75	994	44	22.59	5-66	3	—
Naseer Malik	127.1	14	538	20	26.90	5-61	2	—
Imran Khan	211	45	625	15	41.66	3-65	—	—
Wasim Raja	123	23	400	9	44.44	3-92	—	—

Also bowled: Aftab Baloch 21-2-106-2; Majid Khan 3-1-10-0; Mazullah Khan 68-16-183-1; Mohammad Nazir jr 118-33-366-4; Zaheer Abbas 1-0-5-0.

ENGLAND DRAW SERIES
IN WEST INDIES

When last year's annual went to press, two Test matches had been played in West Indies, at Port of Spain and Kingston. West Indies had won the first by 7 wickets, and had scored 583 for 9 declared in the second, in reply to England's 353. Amiss, alone, had saved that match, with a massive undefeated score of 262. In doing so he saved the series, for after two drawn games in the third and fourth Tests, England won an elusive, but thoroughly deserved, victory in the last encounter back at Port of Spain, where West Indies achieved their only success in the first Test.

It was a hard series for bowlers of both sides with 12 centuries, plus a 99 (which prevented Boycott from getting a century in each innings of the fifth Test), a 98, and two 93s (one of these by Boycott). The man of the series was undoubtedly Amiss from the English point of view, whilst West Indies owed much to Rowe, who even exceeded Amiss's huge score by landing 302 in the third Test. For the bowlers it was a heartbreak story and Pocock's 9 wickets at 61 apiece was obviously a preliminary to losing his place in the England side and hence a trip to Australia. Greig emerged as an all-rounder with a twin attack – spin and seam. The bitter disappointment was the form of Frank Hayes, of whom very high hopes had been held, but in seven innings his highest score was 24. He, too, lost his place in the side as a result of this tour.

Denness had a very difficult tour as captain, and received a good deal of press criticism for one reason and another. But although having only a moderate series with the bat, he must have held morale together sufficiently to come back and win the last Test, and to gain priceless experience which was obviously to stand him in great stead when being considered to lead the side in Australia. Knott's contribution to the run effort was invaluable, his 87 in the third Test coming when England were in desperate straits.

West Indies v England, 1973-74
THIRD TEST MATCH

PLAYED AT BRIDGETOWN, BARBADOS, 6, 7, 9, 10 11 MARCH
MATCH DRAWN

ENGLAND

Batsman	1st innings		2nd innings	
†M. H. Denness	c Murray b Sobers	24	lbw b Holder	0
D. L. Amiss	b Julien	12	c Julien b Roberts	4
J. A. Jameson	c Fredericks b Julien	3	lbw b Roberts	9
G. Boycott	c Murray b Julien	10	c Kanhai b Sobers	13
K. W. R. Fletcher	c Murray b Julien	37	not out	129
A. W. Greig	c Sobers b Julien	148	c Roberts b Gibbs	25
‡A. P. E. Knott	b Gibbs	87	lbw b Lloyd	67
C. M. Old	c Murray b Roberts	1	b Lloyd	0
G. G. Arnold	b Holder	12	not out	2
P. I. Pocock	c Lloyd b Gibbs	18		
R. G. D. Willis	not out	10		
Extras	(LB5, NB28)	33	(B7, LB5, NB16)	28
Total		**395**	**(7 wkts)**	**277**

WEST INDIES

R. C. Fredericks	b Greig	32
L. G. Rowe	c Arnold b Greig	302
A. I. Kallicharran	b Greig	119
C. H. Lloyd	c Fletcher b Greig	8
V. A. Holder	c & b Greig	8
†R. B. Kanhai	b Arnold	18
G. S. Sobers	c Greig b Willis	0
‡D. L. Murray	not out	53
B. D. Julien	c Willis b Greig	1
A. M. E. Roberts	not out	9
L. R. Gibbs	did not bat	
Extras	(B3, LB8, NB35)	46
Total (8 wkts dec)		**596**

BOWLING

W INDIES	O	M	R	W		O	M	R	W
Holder	27	6	68	1	...	15	6	37	1
Roberts	33	8	75	1	...	17	4	49	2
Julien	26	9	57	5	...	11	4	21	0
Sobers	18	4	57	1	...	35	21	55	1
Gibbs	33.4	10	91	2	...	28.3	15	40	1
Lloyd	4	2	9	0	...	12	4	13	2
Fredericks	3	0	5	0	...	6	2	24	0
Rowe					...	1	0	5	0
Kallicharran					...	1	0	5	0

ENGLAND	O	M	R	W	
Arnold	26	5	91	1	...
Willis	26	4	100	1	...
Greig	46	2	164	6	...
Old	28	4	102	0	...
Pocock	28	4	93	0	...

Fall of Wickets

	E 1st	WI 1st	E 2nd
1st	28	126	4
2nd	34	375	8
3rd	53	390	29
4th	68	420	40
5th	130	465	106
6th	293	466	248
7th	306	551	248
8th	344	556	—
9th	371	—	—
10th	395	—	—

FOURTH TEST MATCH

PLAYED AT GEORGETOWN, 22, 23, 24, 26, 27 MARCH
MATCH DRAWN

ENGLAND

G. Boycott b Julien	15
D. L. Amiss c Murray b Boyce	118
†M. H. Denness b Barrett	42
K. W. R. Fletcher c Murray b Julien	41
A. W. Greig b Boyce	121
F. C. Hayes c & b Gibbs	7
‡A. P. E. Knott c Julien b Gibbs	61
J. Birkenshaw c Murray b Fredericks	0
C. M. Old c Kanhai b Boyce	14
G. G. Arnold run out	1
D. L. Underwood not out	7
Extras (B1, LB13, NB8)	22

Total   **448**

WEST INDIES

R. C. Fredericks c & b Greig	98
L. G. Rowe b Greig	28
A. I. Kallicharran b Birkenshaw	6
†R. B. Kanhai b Underwood	44
C. H. Lloyd not out	7
M. L. C. Foster	
‡D. L. Murray	
B. D. Julien } did not bat	
K. D. Boyce	
A. G. Barrett	
L. R. Gibbs	
Extras (B6, LB4, NB5)	15

Total (4 wkts)   **198**

BOWLING

W INDIES	O	M	R	W
Boyce	27.4	6	70	3
Julien	36	10	96	2
Lloyd	19	5	27	0
Foster	16	5	32	0
Gibbs	37	5	102	2
Barrett	31	6	87	1
Fredericks	5	2	12	1
ENGLAND				
Arnold	10	5	17	0
Old	13	3	32	0
Underwood	17.5	4	36	1
Greig	24	8	57	2
Birkenshaw	22	7	41	1

Fall of Wickets		
	E	WI
	1st	1st
1st	41	73
2nd	128	90
3rd	228	179
4th	244	198
5th	257	—
6th	376	—
7th	377	—
8th	410	—
9th	428	—
10th	448	—

FIFTH TEST MATCH

PLAYED AT PORT OF SPAIN, 30, 31 MARCH, 2, 3, 4, 5, APRIL
ENGLAND WON BY 26 RUNS

ENGLAND

G. Boycott c Murray b Julien	99	b Gibbs	112
D. L. Amiss c Kanhai b Sobers	44	b Lloyd	16
†M.H. Denness c Fredericks b Inshan Ali	13	run out	4
K. W. R. Fletcher c Kanhai b Gibbs	6	b Julien	45
A. W. Greig lbw b Gibbs	19	c Fredericks b Julien	1
F. C. Hayes c Rowe b Inshan Ali	24	lbw b Julien	0
‡A. P. E. Knott not out	33	lbw b Sobers	44
J. Birkenshaw c Lloyd b Julien	8	c Gibbs b Inshan Ali	7
G. G. Arnold run out	6	b Sobers	13
P. I. Pocock c Lloyd b Inshan Ali	0	c Kallicharran b Boyce	5
D. L. Underwood b Gibbs	4	not out	1
Extras (B2, LB3, NB6)	11	(LB4, NB11)	15
Total	**267**		**263**

WEST INDIES

R. C. Fredericks c Fletcher b Pocock	67	run out	36
L. G. Rowe c Boycott b Greig	123	lbw b Birkenshaw	25
A. I. Kallicharran c & b Pocock	0	c Fletcher b Greig	0
C. H. Lloyd c Knott b Greig	52	c & b Greig	13
G. S. Sobers c Birkenshaw b Greig	0	b Underwood	20
†R. B. Kanhai c & b Greig	2	c Fletcher b Greig	7
‡D. L. Murray c Pocock b Greig	2	c Fletcher b Greig	33
B. D. Julien c Birkenshaw b Greig	17	c Denness b Pocock	2
K. D. Boyce c Pocock b Greig	19	not out	34
Inshan Ali lbw b Greig	5	c Underwood b Greig	15
L. R. Gibbs not out	0	b Arnold	1
Extras (B11, LB4, NB3)	18	(B9, LB2, NB2)	13
Total	**305**		**199**

BOWLING

W INDIES	O	M	R	W	O	M	R	W
Boyce	10	3	14	0	12	3	40	1
Julien	21	8	35	2	22	7	31	3
Sobers	31	16	44	1	24.2	9	36	2
Inshan Ali	35	12	86	3	34	12	51	1
Gibbs	34.3	11	70	3	50	15	85	1
Lloyd	4	2	7	0	7	4	5	1
ENGLAND								
Arnold	8	0	27	0	5.3	1	13	1
Greig	36.1	10	86	8	33	7	70	5
Pocock	31	7	86	2	25	7	60	1
Underwood	34	12	57	0	15	7	19	1
Birkenshaw	8	1	31	0	10	1	24	1

Fall of Wickets

	E 1st	WI 1st	E 2nd	WI 2nd
1st	83	110	39	63
2nd	114	122	44	64
3rd	133	224	145	65
4th	165	224	169	84
5th	204	226	174	85
6th	212	232	176	135
7th	244	270	213	138
8th	257	300	226	166
9th	260	300	258	197
10th	267	305	263	199

Test Match Averages

WEST INDIES—BATTING AND FIELDING

	M	I	NO	Runs	HS	Avge	100	50	Ct	St
L. G. Rowe	5	7	0	616	302	88.00	3	—	5	—
R. C. Fredericks	5	7	1	397	98	66.16	—	4	10	—
A. I. Kallicharran	5	7	0	397	158	56.71	2	1	1	—
B. D. Julien	5	5	1	172	86*	43.00	—	2	3	—
D. L. Murray	5	5	2	113	53*	37.66	—	1	14	1
K. D. Boyce	4	4	1	87	34*	29.00	—	—	1	—
R. B. Kanhai	5	7	1	157	44	26.16	—	—	7	—
C. H. Lloyd	5	7	1	147	52	24.50	—	1	3	—
G. S. Sobers	4	5	0	100	57	20.00	—	1	1	—
Inshan Ali	2	3	0	29	15	9.66	—	—	—	—
L. R. Gibbs	5	4	2	9	6*	4.50	—	—	4	—
A. G. Barrett	2	1	0	0	0	0.00	—	—	—	—

Played in one Test: M. L. C. Foster did not bat; V. A. Holder 8; A. M. E. Roberts 9* (1 ct).

BOWLING

	Overs	Mdns	Runs	Wkts	Avge	Best	5 wI	10 wM
B. D. Julien	174	51	378	16	23.62	5-57	1	—
K. D. Boyce	118.4	23	324	11	29.45	4-42	—	—
G. S. Sobers	223.2	92	421	14	30.07	3-54	—	—
L. R. Gibbs	328	102	661	18	36.72	6-108	1	—
A. G. Barrett	124	46	260	7	37.14	3-86	—	—
Inshan Ali	113	34	248	5	49.60	3-86	—	—

Also bowled: M. L. C. Foster 16-5-32-0; R. C. Fredericks 34-7-93-1; V. A. Holder 42-12-105-2; A. I. Kallicharran 4-0-17-0; R. B. Kanhai 3-1-8-0; C. H. Lloyd 56-21-71-3; A. M. E. Roberts 50-12-124-3; L. G. Rowe 3-1-6-0.

ENGLAND—BATTING AND FIELDING

	M	I	NO	Runs	HS	Avge	100	50	Ct	St
D. L. Amiss	5	9	1	663	262*	82.87	3	—	—	—
A. W. Greig	5	9	0	430	148	47.77	2	—	7	—
G. Boycott	5	9	0	421	112	46.77	1	3	2	—
A. P. E. Knott	5	9	1	365	87	45.62	—	3	4	—
K. W. R. Fletcher	4	7	1	262	129*	43.66	1	—	6	—
M. H. Denness	5	9	0	231	67	25.66	—	1	5	—
R. G. D. Willis	3	5	4	25	10*	25.00	—	—	3	—
J. A. Jameson	2	4	0	73	38	18.25	—	—	—	—
D. L. Underwood	4	7	3	67	24	16.75	—	—	2	—
F. C. Hayes	4	7	0	60	24	8.57	—	—	2	—
G. G. Arnold	3	5	1	34	13	8.50	—	—	1	—
P. I. Pocock	4	7	0	52	23	7.42	—	—	3	—
C. M. Old	4	7	0	50	19	7.14	—	—	—	—
J. Birkenshaw	2	3	0	15	8	5.00	—	—	2	—

BOWLING

	Overs	Mdns	Runs	Wkts	Avge	Best	5 wI	10 wM
A. W. Greig	207.1	46	543	24	22.62	8–86	3	1
R. G. D. Willis	73	15	255	5	51.00	3–97	—	—
P. I. Pocock	200	50	550	9	61.11	5–110	1	—
C. M. Old	87.4	15	313	5	62.60	3–89	—	—
D. L. Underwood	137.5	45	314	5	62.80	2–48	—	—

Also bowled: G. G. Arnold 49.3–11–148–2; J. Birkenshaw 40–9–96–2;
K. W. R. Fletcher 0.5–0–5–0; J. A. Jameson 7–2–17–1.

Tour Averages

BATTING AND FIELDING

	M	I	NO	Runs	HS	Avge	100	50	Ct	St
D. L. Amiss	9	16	1	1120	262*	74.66	5	2	3	—
G. Boycott	10	16	3	960	261*	73.84	3	4	3	—
A. W. Greig	9	14	1	665	148	51.15	3	1	12	—
K. W. R. Fletcher	10	16	3	564	129*	43.38	2	1	9	—
M. H. Denness	10	17	2	504	67	33.60	—	4	5	—
J. Birkenshaw	5	6	2	127	53*	31.75	—	1	2	—
F. C. Hayes	9	16	2	444	88	31.71	—	3	8	—
R. G. D. Willis	6	6	5	30	10*	30.00	—	—	8	—
A. P. E. Knott	10	17	1	474	87	29.62	—	3	14	—
J. A. Jameson	7	13	0	325	91	25.00	—	2	6	—
R. W. Taylor	3	3	0	69	65	23.00	—	1	5	1
M. Hendrick	5	5	3	29	16	14.50	—	—	2	—
D. L. Underwood	7	10	3	100	24	14.28	—	—	5	—
G. G. Arnold	8	10	2	101	25	12.62	—	—	2	—
C. M. Old	6	10	0	122	53	12.20	—	1	2	—
P. I. Pocock	7	11	0	77	23	7.00	—	—	3	—

BOWLING

	Overs	Mdns	Runs	Wkts	Avge	Best	5 wI	10 wM
A. W. Greig	277.1	57	766	30	25.53	8–86	3	1
M. Hendrick	108.2	21	320	12	26.66	4–38	—	—
J. Birkenshaw	165.5	35	467	16	29.18	6–101	1	—
R. G. D. Willis	140	27	526	15	35.06	4–91	—	—
P. I. Pocock	326.3	79	844	19	44.42	5–110	1	—
D. L. Underwood	263.5	88	573	12	47.75	2–48	—	—
G. G. Arnold	174.3	40	611	12	50.91	5–44	1	—
C. M. Old	135.4	28	459	9	51.00	3–56	—	—

Also bowled: G. Boycott 9–1–33–1; K. W. R. Fletcher 20.5–4–63–3;
F. C. Hayes 0.2–0–4–0; J. A. Jameson 35–10–74–4.

NB The match between MCC and Bermuda was not first class.

Australia v New Zealand, 1973-74

FIRST TEST MATCH

PLAYED AT MELBOURNE, 29, 30 DECEMBER, 1, 2 JANUARY
AUSTRALIA WON BY AN INNINGS AND 25 RUNS

AUSTRALIA

K. R. Stackpole c Parker b Shrimpton 122
A. P. Sheahan c Wadsworth b D. Hadlee 28
†I. M. Chappell c R. Hadlee b Shrimpton 54
G. S. Chappell c Wadsworth b Congdon 60
K. D. Walters c Wadsworth b D. Hadlee 79
I. C. Davis c Wadsworth b D. Hadlee 15
‡R. W. Marsh c Parker b D. Hadlee 6
K. J. O'Keeffe not out 40
G. J. Gilmour b Congdon 52
A. A. Mallett } did not bat
A. R. Dell }
Extras (LB4, W1, NB1) 6

Total (8 wkts dec) 462

NEW ZEALAND

G. M. Turner c Gilmour b Dell 6 — absent hurt
J. M. Parker c I. Chappell b O'Keeffe 27 — c I. Chappell b Walters 23
M. J. F. Shrimpton c Marsh b Gilmour 16 — b Walters 22
B. F. Hastings b O'Keeffe 1 — c Marsh b Mallett 22
†B. E. Congdon st Marsh b Mallett 31 — c Marsh b Mallett 14
J. F. M. Morrison c Marsh b Gilmour 44 — c Marsh b Walters 16
‡K. J. Wadsworth c G. Chappell b Gilmour 80 — c Stackpole b Mallett 30
R. J. Hadlee c Marsh b Gilmour 9 — c I. Chappell b O'Keeffe 6
D. R. Hadlee run out 2 — c & b O'Keeffe 37
D. R. O'Sullivan c Davis b Mallett 6 — c & b Mallett 8
B. Andrews not out 0 — not out 5
Extras (B8, LB5, NB2) 15 — (B8, LB9) 17

Total 237 — 200

BOWLING

N ZEALAND	O	M	R	W	O	M	R	W
R. Hadlee	25	4	104	0				
Andrews	19	2	100	0				
D. Hadlee	20	2	102	4				
O'Sullivan	22	3	80	0				
Shrimpton	7	0	39	2				
Congdon	8.5	1	31	2				
AUSTRALIA								
Dell	22	1	54	1	5	0	9	0
Gilmour	22	4	75	4	3	0	16	0
G. Chappell	4	2	4	0	7	3	18	0
Mallett	16.7	2	46	2	24	4	63	4
O'Keeffe	14	4	40	2	29.6	12	51	2
I. Chappell	1	0	3	0				
Walters					13	4	26	3

Fall of Wickets

	A 1st	NZ 1st	NZ 2nd
1st	75	19	37
2nd	203	47	54
3rd	212	51	83
4th	304	89	109
5th	345	100	113
6th	363	189	134
7th	381	215	150
8th	462	230	188
9th	—	237	200
10th	—	237	—

SECOND TEST MATCH

PLAYED AT SYDNEY, 5, 6, 7, 9, 10 JANUARY

MATCH DRAWN

NEW ZEALAND

J. M. Parker c Marsh b Walker	108	c Marsh b G. Chappell	11
J. F. M. Morrison c G. Chappell b Walters	28	c Davis b I. Chappell	117
M. J. F. Shrimpton b Walters	0	c & b Walters	28
†B. E. Congdon c Marsh b Walters	4	b Gilmour	17
B. F. Hastings c Marsh b Walker	16	b G. Chappell	83
J. V. Coney c Stackpole b O'Keeffe	45	c Davis b G. Chappell	11
‡K. J. Wadsworth c Marsh b Walters	54	c G. Chappell b Gilmour	2
D. R. Hadlee c & b G. Chappell	14	not out	18
R.J. Hadlee c I. Chappell b G. Chappell	17	run out	1
D. R. O'Sullivan not out	3	lbw b Gilmour	1
B. Andrews c Marsh b Gilmour	17		
Extras (LB2, NB4)	6	(B4, LB11, W1)	16
Total	**312**	**(9 wkts dec)**	**305**

AUSTRALIA

A. P. Sheahan c Coney b Andrews	7	not out	14
K.R. Stackpole c Morrison b R. Hadlee	8	lbw b R. Hadlee	2
†I.M. Chappell c Hastings b D. Hadlee	45	lbw b R. Hadlee	6
G. S. Chappell c Coney b Andrews	0	not out	8
K. D. Walters c Coney b D. Hadlee	41		
I. C. Davis c Andrews b R. Hadlee	29		
‡R.W. Marsh c Wadsworth b D. Hadlee	10		
K. J. O'Keeffe c Wadsworth b R. Hadlee	9		
G. J. Gilmour c Wadsworth b Congdon	3		
A. A. Mallett lbw b R. Hadlee	0		
M. H. N. Walker not out	2		
Extras (LB5, NB3)	8		
Total	**162**	**(2 wkts)**	**30**

BOWLING

AUSTRALIA	O	M	R	W		O	M	R	W
Gilmour	18.6	3	70	1	...	21.2	1	70	3
Walker	22	2	71	2	...				
G. Chappell	19	2	76	2	...	16	3	54	3
Walters	11	0	39	4	...	11	0	54	1
Mallett	8	0	30	0	...	14	1	65	0
O'Keeffe	8	2	20	1	...	10	0	40	0
I. Chappell					...	3	0	6	1
N ZEALAND									
R. Hadlee	9.4	2	33	4	...	4.3	0	16	2
Andrews	9	1	40	2	...	4	0	14	0
D. Hadlee	13	3	52	3	...				
Congdon	13	2	29	1	...				

Fall of Wickets

	NZ	A	NZ	A
	1st	1st	2nd	2nd
1st	78	20	23	10
2nd	78	20	94	22
3rd	90	21	120	—
4th	113	98	244	—
5th	193	115	255	—
6th	221	133	276	—
7th	268	150	282	—
8th	292	157	292	—
9th	293	160	305	—
10th	312	162	—	—

THIRD TEST MATCH

PLAYED AT ADELAIDE, 26, 27, 28, 30, 31 JANUARY
AUSTRALIA WON BY AN INNINGS AND 57 RUNS

AUSTRALIA

K. R. Stackpole c Parker b D. Hadlee	15
A. J. Woodcock c Coney b Cairns	27
†I. M. Chappell c R. Hadlee b Cairns	22
G. S. Chappell b Congdon	42
K. D. Walters b O'Sullivan	94
I. C. Davis c Congdon b O'Sullivan	15
‡R. W. Marsh st Wadsworth b O'Sullivan	132
K. J. O'Keeffe lbw b R. Hadlee	85
A.A. Mallett c Wadsworth b O'Sullivan	11
A. G. Hurst c Hastings b O'Sullivan	16
G. Dymock not out	0
Extras (B3, LB6, NB9)	18
Total	**477**

NEW ZEALAND

J. M. Parker c Marsh b Dymock	0	c I. Chappell b Dymock	22
G. M. Turner lbw b Hurst	20	c O'Keeffe b Dymock	34
J. F. M. Morrison c I. Chappell b O'Keeffe	40	c I. Chappell b O'Keeffe	4
B.F. Hastings c Woodcock b O'Keeffe	23	c Stackpole b Dymock	7
†B. E. Congdon run out	13	not out	71
J. V. Coney c Marsh b Dymock	8	b Dymock	17
‡K. J. Wadsworth lbw b I. Chappell	48	c Marsh b O'Keeffe	16
D. R. Hadlee c G. Chappell b Mallett	29	c G. Chappell b Mallett	0
R. J. Hadlee c I. Chappell b Mallett	20	c Marsh b O'Keeffe	15
D. R. O'Sullivan b O'Keeffe	2	c I. Chappell b Dymock	4
B. L. Cairns not out	4	c I. Chappell b Mallett	0
Extras (B4, LB4, NB3)	11	(B2, LB8, NB2)	12
Total	**218**		**202**

BOWLING

N ZEALAND	O	M	R	W		O	M	R	W		Fall of Wickets		
											A	NZ	NZ
R. Hadlee	28	3	102	1	...						*1st*	*1st*	*2nd*
D. Hadlee	21	2	76	1	...					1st	21	1	56
Cairns	21	4	73	2	...					2nd	67	35	65
O'Sullivan	35.5	4	148	5	...					3rd	73	84	65
Congdon	15	1	60	1	...					4th	173	89	73
AUSTRALIA										5th	221	107	105
Hurst	19	3	56	1	...	10	2	17	0	6th	232	110	130
Dymock	19	5	44	2	...	27	7	58	5	7th	400	176	143
Walters	1	0	2	0	...	3	0	17	0	8th	452	209	170
Mallett	23	6	46	2	...	21.5	9	47	2	9th	472	214	197
O'Keeffe	24.3	9	55	3	...	28	12	51	3	10th	477	218	202
I. Chappell	1	0	4	1	...								

New Zealand v Australia, 1973-74

FIRST TEST MATCH

PLAYED AT WELLINGTON, 1, 2, 3, 5, 6 MARCH
MATCH DRAWN

AUSTRALIA

K. R. Stackpole b Webb	10	b Collinge	27
I. R. Redpath c Coney b Hadlee	19	c Howarth b Congdon	93
†I. M. Chappell c Wadsworth b Webb	145	c Hadlee b Howarth	121
G. S. Chappell not out	247	c Wadsworth b Collinge	133
I. C. Davis c Wadsworth b Hadlee	16	c Wadsworth b Howarth	8
K. D. Walters c Howarth b Collinge	32	c Morrison b Hadlee	8
‡R. W. Marsh lbw b Congdon	22	c Collinge b Congdon	17
K. J. O'Keeffe		c Howarth b Congdon	2
M. H. N. Walker	did not bat	not out	22
A. A. Mallett		not out	4
G. Dymock		did not bat	
Extras (B2, LB3, NB15)	20	(B4, LB4, W1, NB16)	25
Total (6 wkts dec)	511	(8 wkts)	460

NEW ZEALAND

G. M. Turner c Redpath b O'Keeffe	79
J. M. Parker lbw b Walker	10
J. F. M. Morrison b Walker	66
†B. E. Congdon c Davis b Mallett	132
B. F. Hastings c I. Chappell b Dymock	101
J. V. Coney c G. Chappell b Walker	13
‡K. J. Wadsworth b Dymock	5
D. R. Hadlee c Davis b O'Keeffe	9
R. O. Collinge run out	2
H. J. Howarth not out	29
M. G. Webb c O'Keeffe b Dymock	12
Extras (B10, LB5, NB11)	26
Total	484

BOWLING

N ZEALAND	O	M	R	W	O	M	R	W
Webb	21	1	114	2	19	0	93	0
Collinge	24	3	103	1	19	3	60	2
Hadlee	27	7	107	2	21	2	106	1
Howarth	21	0	113	0	25	3	97	2
Congdon	12.5	0	54	1	13	1	60	3
Coney					2	0	13	0
Hastings					2	0	6	0

AUSTRALIA	O	M	R	W
Walker	41	11	107	3
Dymock	35	7	77	3
Walters	8	0	39	0
Mallett	41	8	117	1
O'Keeffe	33	9	83	2
G. Chappell	0	2	27	0
I. Chappell	4	0	8	0

Fall of Wickets

	A	NZ	A
	1st	1st	2nd
1st	13	28	67
2nd	55	136	208
3rd	319	169	294
4th	359	398	318
5th	431	409	359
6th	511	423	414
7th	—	423	433
8th	—	430	433
9th	—	437	—
10th	—	484	—

SECOND TEST MATCH

PLAYED AT CHRISTCHURCH, 8, 9, 10, 12, 13 MARCH
NEW ZEALAND WON BY 5 WICKETS

AUSTRALIA

Batsman	1st	2nd innings	2nd
K. R. Stackpole b Collinge	4	c Wadsworth b Collinge	9
I. R. Redpath c & b Collinge	71	c Howarth b R. Hadlee	58
†I. M. Chappell b R. Hadlee	20	b Collinge	1
G. S. Chappell c Howarth b Congdon	25	c Coney b R. Hadlee	6
I. C. Davis lbw b R. Hadlee	5	c Congdon b R. Hadlee	50
K. D. Walters b R. Hadlee	6	lbw b D. Hadlee	65
‡R. W. Marsh b Congdon	38	c & b D. Hadlee	4
K. J. O'Keeffe c Wadsworth b Congdon	3	not out	23
M. H. N. Walker not out	19	c Howarth b D. Hadlee	4
A. A. Mallett b Collinge	1	c Wadsworth b R. Hadlee	11
G. Dymock c Congdon b D. Hadlee	12	c Wadsworth b D. Hadlee	0
Extras (B1, LB6, NB12)	19	(B16, LB4, NB8)	28
Total	**223**		**259**

NEW ZEALAND

Batsman	1st	2nd innings	2nd
G. M. Turner c Stackpole b G. Chappell	101	not out	110
J. M. Parker lbw b Dymock	18	c Marsh b Walker	26
J. F. M. Morrison c Marsh b G. Chappell	12	lbw b Walker	0
†B. E. Congdon c I. Chappell b Walker	8	run out	2
B. F. Hastings c Marsh b Walker	19	lbw b Mallett	46
J. V. Coney c Marsh b Dymock	15	c Marsh b G. Chappell	14
‡K. J. Wadsworth c Marsh b Mallett	24	not out	9
D. R. Hadlee c Marsh b Dymock	11		
R. J. Hadlee lbw b Walker	23		
H. J. Howarth c I. Chappell b Walker	0		
R. O. Collinge not out	1		
Extras (B4, LB8, NB11)	23	(B4, LB14, NB5)	23
Total	**255**	**(5 wkts)**	**230**

BOWLING

N ZEALAND	O	M	R	W	O	M	R	W
R. Hadlee	14	2	59	3	20	2	75	4
Collinge	21	4	70	3	19	9	37	2
Congdon	11	2	33		19	3	26	0
D. Hadlee	12.2	2	42	1	8	5	71	4
Howarth					11	2	22	0
AUSTRALIA								
Walker	19.6	5	60	4	28	10	50	2
Dymock	24	6	59	3	25	5	84	0
G. Chappell	20	2	76	2	15.6	5	38	1
Walters	7	1	34	0				
Mallett	3	1	3	1	13	4	35	1

Fall of Wickets

	A 1st	NZ 1st	A 2nd	NZ 2nd
1st	8	59	12	51
2nd	45	90	26	55
3rd	101	104	33	62
4th	120	136	139	177
5th	128	171	142	206
6th	181	213	160	—
7th	190	220	232	—
8th	194	241	238	—
9th	196	242	239	—
10th	223	255	259	—

THIRD TEST MATCH

PLAYED AT AUCKLAND 22, 23, 24 MARCH

AUSTRALIA WON BY 297 RUNS

AUSTRALIA

K. R. Stackpole c Parker b R. Hadlee		0	c Congdon b Collinge	0
I. R. Redpath c Wadsworth b Collinge		13	not out	159
†I. M. Chappell c Turner b Collinge		37	lbw b Collinge	35
G. S. Chappell c Howarth b Collinge		0	c Wadsworth b Howarth	38
I. C. Davis c Hastings b Collinge		0	c Parker b Howarth	5
K. D. Walters not out		104	c Parker b Congdon	5
‡R. W. Marsh c Hastings b Collinge		45	c R. Hadlee b Howarth	47
K. J. O'Keeffe c Morrison b Congdon		0	c Burgess b Collinge	32
G. J. Gilmour c Morrison b Congdon		7	b R. Hadlee	4
M. H. N. Walker c Burgess b Congdon		7	b R. Hadlee	0
A. A. Mallett c Turner b Congdon		7	c Parker b Collinge	6
Extras (B4, LB1, NB2)		7	(B4, LB4, W1, NB6)	15
Total		**221**		**346**

NEW ZEALAND

G. M. Turner c G. Chappell b Mallett		41	c I. Chappell b Walker	72
J. M. Parker lbw b Gilmour		11	c Marsh b Gilmour	34
J. F. M. Morrison c Marsh b Walker		9	c Marsh b Gilmour	0
†B. E. Congdon lbw b Gilmour		4	c Marsh b Walker	4
B. F. Hastings b Gilmour		0	lbw b Walker	1
M. G. Burgess c Marsh b Gilmour		7	c Stackpole b Walker	6
‡K. J. Wadsworth c Marsh b Gilmour		0	c G. Chappell b Mallett	21
H. J. Howarth c Chappell b Mallett		0	not out	3
D. R. Hadlee b Mallett		4	c Walters b Mallett	4
R. J. Hadlee c I. Chappell b Mallett		13	b O'Keeffe	1
R. O. Collinge not out		8	c I. Chappell b O'Keeffe	4
Extras		15	(B3, LB3, NB2)	8
Total		**112**		**158**

BOWLING

N ZEALAND	O	M	R	W		O	M	R	W
R. Hadlee	9	1	45	1	...	9	1	50	2
Collinge	18	4	82	5	...	16.5	0	84	4
D. Hadlee	9	0	41	0	...	7	0	48	0
Congdon	10.1	1	46	4	...	19	1	66	1
Howarth					...	28	5	83	3
AUSTRALIA									
Walker	10	4	11	1	...	19	8	39	4
Gilmour	15	3	64	5	...	16	0	52	2
Mallett	5.2	0	22	4	...	13	6	51	2
O'Keeffe					...	5	1	8	2

Fall of Wickets

	A 1st	NZ 1st	A 2nd	NZ 2nd
1st	0	16	2	107
2nd	32	28	83	107
3rd	37	34	118	112
4th	37	40	132	115
5th	64	62	143	116
6th	150	62	230	127
7th	154	63	315	145
8th	162	71	330	147
9th	191	102	330	147
10th	221	112	346	158

CAREER FIGURES FOR THE LEADING PLAYERS

The following are the abbreviated figures of the leading batsmen and bowlers based on their career averages, and fielders and wicket-keepers based on the number of their catches and dismissals. The figures are complete to the end of the 1974 season and the full career records will be found in the main table on pages 175 to 190. The qualifications for inclusion for batsmen and bowlers are 100 innings and 100 wickets respectively.

Only those players likely to play in first-class county cricket in 1975 have been included.

BATSMEN	Runs	Avge	100s	BOWLERS	Wkts	Avge
B. A. Richards	20,894	57.71	60	A. M. E. Roberts	181	17.99
G. Boycott	26,686	55.36	82	M. J. Procter	802	18.15
Zaheer Abbas	10,021	50.35	32	T. W. Cartwright	1,517	19.03
R. B. Kanhai	25,964	49.64	77	D. L. Underwood	1,333	19.44
C. H. Lloyd	14,216	47.38	35	A. G. Nicholson	866	19.76
G. M. Turner	17,313	46.66	46	R. Illingworth	1,882	19.78
J. H. Edrich	34,342	45.91	90	N. Gifford	1,264	20.24
L. G. Rowe	4,977	44.43	12	R. M. H. Cottam	944	20.71
M. J. Khan	18,251	43.97	51	G. G. Arnold	748	21.24
M. C. Cowdrey	41,618	43.44	105	B. S. Bedi	910	21.39
A. I. Kallicharran	6,981	42.30	18	A. Ward	354	21.46
M. J. K. Smith	39,127	42.11	68	J. N. Graham	561	21.97
Mushtaq Mohammad	23,900	41.85	53	C. M. Old	419	22.00
D. L. Amiss	19,298	40.03	38	F. J. Titmus	2,615	22.13
B. W. Luckhurst	20,465	39.20	44	J. A. Snow	1,003	22.19

FIELDERS	Ct	WICKET-KEEPERS	Total	Ct	St
D. B. Close	751	J. T. Murray	1,482	1,230	252
M. C. Cowdrey	618	J. M. Parks	1,179	1,086	93
P. J. Sainsbury	593	R. W. Taylor	958	856	102
M. J. K. Smith	588	A. P. E. Knott	821	729	92
P. J. Sharpe	570	A. Long	802	701	101
A. S. Brown	458	F. M. Engineer	691	578	113
F. J. Titmus	451	R. W. Tolchard	566	498	68
C. T. Spencer	380	D. L. Murray	552	476	76
R. Illingworth	379	E. W. Jones	535	484	51
K. W. R. Fletcher	359	G. R. Stephenson	402	357	45
R. G. A. Headley	357	D. L. Bairstow	293	257	36
R. T. Virgin	355	D. J. S. Taylor	286	254	32
B. W. Luckhurst	352	D. Nicholls	271	261	10
T. W. Cartwright	327	K. Goodwin	256	229	27
M. H. Denness	318	G. R. Cass	211	186	25

KENT'S GILLETTE CUP

Lancashire lose a final at last

by Gordon Ross

Kent achieved their second Gillette Cup final success (having
lost in 1971, but having beaten Somerset in 1967), by gaining
revenge over Lancashire for the 1971 defeat. Kent won a
low-scoring game by 4 wickets. For the first time since the
competition began in 1963, rain prevented any play on the
appointed Saturday – a great disappointment to thousands,
many of whom had travelled down from Lancashire. Even
more galling was the sunshine on the day, but the relentless
battering from torrential and sustained rain that the grass
had taken previously, made a serious game of cricket
absolutely out of the question. So the Lord's authorities
made the only decision possible. The weather was kind again
on the Monday – but only just – some very heavy storms
skirted Lord's and enabled the match to be finished in the
day, with bouts of sunshine and much of the atmosphere that
would have prevailed on the Saturday. All that was missing
from these traditional finals was aggressive stroke-play on a
pitch which at no time was easy, and in a match which
produces its fair share of tension anyway, this may, perhaps,
have stimulated excessive caution. In the field, Kent were
brilliant, admirably backing up sustained accuracy by their
bowlers. Lancashire's batsmen, never really getting a grip
on the game, suffered a mortal blow when Clive Lloyd, their
great hope, slipped when turning, and was run out. To make
119 looked easy for Kent, and it seemed that it was, when
they were 52–1 with all the time in the world. At 53–4,
however, it was a different kettle of fish, and at this point
Alan Knott got his head down and in the end saw Kent home
comfortably. So Kent won a Gillette final without one of
their players scoring 20, Alan Knott was the Man of the
Match, given the award by Brian Close, and I gave Alan
Ealham the fielding award, which is presented by Wombwell
Cricket Lovers Society to honour the memory of Sir Learie
Constantine. So it was very much a Kent day.

For Lancashire, it was fourth time unlucky, having won

on their three previous visits to contest a Gillette final, and having had a hard road: drawn away from Old Trafford in all the four previous rounds against Gloucestershire, Middlesex, Yorkshire, and Worcestershire, but batting first on all five occasions. Lincolnshire made a name for themselves by travelling to Wales and beating Glamorgan. They now join Durham as the only minor counties to defeat a first-class county. Lincolnshire won by 4 wickets at Swansea. But perhaps the 'match of the season' was Somerset v Surrey at Taunton, and the 'player of the season' was Peter Denning, who hit 112 when Somerset were chasing a score of 255. This created enormous interest in Somerset – for they scored the runs for a memorable victory, and a huge contingent travelled to Canterbury in the next round. At one time, at 40–4 looking for 155, Kent were in desperate straits, but Knott did his bit here, and won the Man of the Match award. What of 1975? Could Lancashire be in the final for the fifth time to equal the record held by Sussex?

THE GILLETTE CUP 1975
FIRST ROUND
Matches to be played on 25 June

Cambridgeshire v Northamptonshire at March
Middlesex v Buckinghamshire at Lord's
Nottinghamshire v Sussex at Trent Bridge
Oxfordshire v Cornwall at Oxford (Morris Motors)
Staffordshire v Leicestershire at Stoke-on-Trent
Surrey v Somerset at The Oval

SECOND ROUND
Matches to be played on 16 July

Nottinghamshire or Sussex v Kent
Yorkshire v Staffordshire or Leicestershire at Headingley
Gloucestershire v Oxfordshire or Cornwall at Bristol
Surrey or Somerset v Derbyshire
Warwickshire v Middlesex or Buckinghamshire at Edgbaston
Lancashire v Cambridgeshire or Northamptonshire at Old Trafford
Hampshire v Glamorgan at Southampton
Worcestershire v Essex at Worcester

Quarter-final 6 August; semi-final 20 August;
Final at Lord's 6 September

1974 RESULTS
FIRST ROUND—29 JUNE
Shropshire v Essex at Wellington
Essex 180 in 60 overs (B. E. A. Edmeades 39, G. Othen 4–34).
Shropshire 41 in 36.1 overs (S. Johnson 18, J. K. Lever 4–15, R. N. S. Hobbs 3–2)
Result: Essex won by 139 runs.
Man of the Match: J. K. Lever.
Adjudicator: J. D. Robertson.
Derbyshire v Hampshire at Derby
Derbyshire 86 in 48.5 overs (L. G. Rowe 20, R. S. Herman 3–21, M. N. S. Taylor 3–17)
Hampshire 87–1 in 20.2 overs (B. A. Richards 41*, D. R. Turner 35*)
Result: Hampshire won by 9 wickets.
Man of the Match: M. N. S. Taylor.
Adjudicator: C. Washbrook.
Glamorgan v Lincolnshire at Swansea
Glamorgan 155 in 54.3 overs (M. A. Nash 51, M. Maslin 3–29, J. Dale 3–33)
Lincolnshire 156–6 in 53 overs (Maslin 62*, T. Blades 50*)
Result: Lincolnshire won by 4 wickets.
Man of the Match: M. Maslin.
Adjudicator: C. J. Barnett.
Hertfordshire v Durham at Hitchin
Durham 155 in 59.3 overs (T. J. Hughes 35, B. G. Collins 3–35)
Hertfordshire 81 in 41.3 overs (J. S. Stoker 3–16, S. Greensword 3–33)
Result: Durham won by 74 runs.
Man of the Match: J. S. Stoker.
Adjudicator: F. R. Brown.
Kent v Buckinghamshire at Canterbury
Buckinghamshire 223–5 in 60 overs (J. B. Turner 88, G. A. Jones 47)
Kent 224–3 in 57 overs (G. W. Johnson 120*, M. H. Denness 42)
Result: Kent won by 7 wickets.
Man of the Match: J. B. Turner.
Adjudicator: R. T. Simpson.

29 JUNE AND 1 JULY
Gloucestershire v Lancashire at Bristol
Lancashire 201–6 in 60 overs (D. Lloyd 54, C. H. Lloyd 44)
Gloucestershire 151 in 51.1 overs (R. D. V. Knight 35, P. Lever 4–29, B. Wood 3–33)
Result: Lancashire won by 50 runs.
Man of the Match: P. Lever.
Adjudicator: K. F. Barrington.

SECOND ROUND—10 JULY
Essex v Somerset at Westcliff
Essex 216 in 59.3 overs (B. E. A. Edmeades 52, K. S. McEwan 63, S. Turner 40, H. R. Moseley 3–30)
Somerset 219–6 in 58 overs (P. W. Denning 57)
Result: Somerset won by 4 wickets.
Man of the Match: P. W. Denning.
Adjudicator: W. J. Edrich.

Kent v Durham at Canterbury
Kent 287–2 in 60 overs (B. W. Luckhurst 129*, M. C. Cowdrey 115)
Durham 171 in 59.5 overs (J. N. Graham 3–18)
Result: Kent won by 116 runs.
Man of the Match: M. C. Cowdrey.
Adjudicator: J. D. Robertson.

Leicestershire v Northamptonshire at Leicester
Leicestershire 182–8 in 60 overs (J. F. Steele 85*, C. Milburn 3–44)
Northamptonshire 62 in 34 overs (K. Higgs 3–6, N. M. McVicker 4–26)
Result: Leicestershire won by 120 runs.
Man of the Match: J. F. Steele.
Adjudicator: R. T. Simpson.

Lincolnshire v Surrey at Lincoln
Surrey 266–5 in 60 overs (D. R. Owen-Thomas 66, Younis Ahmed 76)
Lincolnshire 143 in 44.1 overs (M. Maslin 58, G. G. Arnold 5–15, P. I. Pocock 3–44)
Result: Surrey won by 123 runs.
Man of the Match: G. G. Arnold.
Adjudicator: H. Gimblett.

10 AND 11 JULY
Middlesex v Lancashire at Lord's
Lancashire 193–9 in 60 overs (C. H. Lloyd 42, D. P. Hughes 42*, B. Wood 39, K. V. Jones 6–28)
Middlesex 112 in 50 overs (Jones 27, Wood 4–26, P. Lee 3–23)
Result: Lancashire won by 81 runs.
Man of the Match: B. Wood.
Adjudicator: F. R. Brown.

Sussex v Worcestershire at Hove
Worcestershire 259–9 in 60 overs (B. L. d'Oliveira 102, G. R. Cass 43 A. W. Greig 4–52)
Sussex 110 in 45.5 overs (P. J. Graves 44, J. Cumbes 4–23)
Result: Worcestershire won by 149 runs.
Man of the Match: B. L. d'Oliveira.
Adjudicator: A. V. Bedser.

Warwickshire v Nottinghamshire at Edgbaston
Warwickshire 225–7 in 60 overs (D. L. Murray 72*, G. S. Sobers 3–38)
Nottinghamshire 228–6 in 59.1 overs (M. J. Harris 52, M. J. Smedley 63*, R. G. D. Willis 3–32)
Result: Nottinghamshire won by 4 wickets.
Man of the Match: M. J. Smedley.
Adjudicator: C. J. Barnett.

Yorkshire v Hampshire at Bradford
Yorkshire 233–6 in 60 overs (J. H. Hampshire 87*)
Hampshire 192 in 54.5 overs (D. R. Turner 68, B. Leadbeater 3–47)
Result: Yorkshire won by 41 runs.
Man of the Match: J. H. Hampshire.
Adjudicator: C. Washbrook.

QUARTER-FINALS—31 JULY
Kent v Leicestershire at Canterbury
Kent 295–8 in 60 overs (B. W. Luckhurst 125, M. H. Denness 72, A. G. E. Ealham 46, N. M. McVicker 3–61)
Leicestershire 229 in 54.1 overs (B. F. Davidson 82, J. Birkenshaw 45, D. L. Underwood 4–57, R. A. Woolmer 3–48)

Result: Kent won by 66 runs.
Man of the Match: B. W. Luckhurst.
Adjudicator: F. R. Brown.

Somerset v Surrey at Taunton

Surrey 254–7 in 60 overs (J. H. Edrich 59, Younis Ahmed 53, H, R. Moseley 4–31)
Somerset 257–5 in 58.2 overs (P. W. Denning 112, J. M. Parks 42*)
Result: Somerset won by 5 wickets.
Man of the Match: P. W. Denning.
Adjudicator: C. J. Barnett.

31 JULY AND 1 AUGUST

Worcestershire v Nottinghamshire at Worcester

Worcestershire 251–9 in 60 overs (K. W. Wilkinson 95, J. M. Parker 41, B. Stead 5–44)
Nottinghamshire 233–9 in 60 overs (G. S. Sobers 84, B. L. D'Oliveira 4–18)
Result: Worcestershire won by 18 runs.
Man of the Match: B. L. D'Oliveira.
Adjudicator: C. Washbrook.

1 AUGUST

Yorkshire v Lancashire at Headingley

Lancashire 205 in 59 overs (C. H. Lloyd 90, G. B. Stevenson 4–57, S. Oldham 3–45)
Yorkshire 173 in 54.3 overs (G. Boycott 39, J. H. Hampshire 37, P. Lever 4–17, J. Sullivan 3–42)
Result: Lancashire won by 32 runs.
Man of the Match: C. H. Lloyd.
Adjudicators: K. F. Barrington and I. Chappell (Australia).

SEMI-FINALS—14 AUGUST

Kent v Somerset at Canterbury

Somerset 154 in 58 overs (D. J. S. Taylor 49, Shepherd 3–30)
Kent 155–7 in 52.3 overs (Denness 35)
Result: Kent won by 3 wickets.
Man of the Match: A. P. E. Knott.
Adjudicator: K. F. Barrington.

15 AUGUST

Worcester v Lancashire at Worcester

Lancashire 236–7 in 60 overs (Wood 91, Brain 4–51)
Worcester 208 in 58.2 overs (Turner 47, Ormrod 47, Simmons 5–49)
Result: Lancashire won by 28 runs.
Man of the Match: B. Wood.
Adjudicator: W. J. Edrich.

GILLETTE CUP WINNERS	
1963 Sussex	1969 Yorkshire
1964 Sussex	1970 Lancashire
1965 Yorkshire	1971 Lancashire
1966 Warwickshire	1972 Lancashire
1967 Kent	1973 Gloucestershire
1968 Warwickshire	1974 Kent

THE GILLETTE CUP FINAL

KENT v LANCASHIRE

Played at Lord's, 9 September—Kent won by 4 wickets

LANCASHIRE

†D. Lloyd	c Woolmer b Graham	2
B. Wood	b Woolmer	17
H. Pilling	c Knott b Woolmer	9
C. H. Lloyd	run out	25
A. Kennedy	c Ealham b Johnson	9
‡F. M. Engineer	c Knott b Graham-Brown	15
D. P. Hughes	run out	15
J. Simmons	c Knott b Graham-Brown	3
K. Shuttleworth	run out	7
P. Lever	b Graham	3
P. Lee	not out	8
Extras (B1, LB4, W2, NB1)		8
Total (60 overs)		118

KENT

B. W. Luckhurst	b Lee	16
G. W. Johnson	b Wood	17
M. C. Cowdrey	b Simmons	7
†M. H. Denness	b Wood	1
A. G. E. Ealham	b Lee	17
J. N. Shepherd	c & b Wood	19
‡A. P. E. Knott	not out	18
R. A. Woolmer	not out	15
D. L. Underwood		
J. N. Graham	}did not bat	
J. Graham-Brown		
Extras (B3, LB1, W4, NB4)		12
Total (46.5 overs) (6 wkts)		122

BOWLING

KENT	O	M	R	W		Fall of Wickets	
Graham	11	6	14	2		L	K
Shepherd	9	2	16	0		1st	1st
Underwood	9	3	18	0	1st	10	37
Woolmer	12	2	20	2	2nd	30	52
Johnson	7	0	27	1	3rd	37	52
Graham-Brown	12	5	15	2	4th	68	53
LANCASHIRE					5th	72	75
Lever	12	3	39	0	6th	97	89
Shuttleworth	1	0	3	0	7th	98	—
Lee	12	3	30	2	8th	104	—
Simmons	6.5	3	14	1	9th	111	—
Wood	12	5	18	3	10th	118	—
Hughes	3	0	6	0			

Man of the Match: A. P. E. Knott.
Adjudicator: D. B. Close.

GILLETTE CUP
PRINCIPAL RECORDS

Highest innings total: 327-7 off 60 overs, Gloucestershire v Berkshire (Reading) 1966.

Highest innings total by a Minor County: 224-7 off 60 overs, Buckinghamshire v Cambridgeshire (Cambridge) 1972.

Highest innings total by side batting second: 272-9 off 60 overs, Middlesex v Surrey (Oval) 1970.

Highest innings total by side batting first and losing: 254-7 off 60 overs, Surrey v Somerset (Taunton) 1974.

Lowest innings total: 41 off 20 overs, Cambridgeshire v Buckinghamshire (Cambridge) 1972; 41 off 19.4 overs, Middlesex v Essex (Westcliff) 1972; 41 off 36.1 overs, Shropshire v Essex (Wellington) 1974.

Lowest innings total by side batting first and winning: 98 off 56.2 overs, Worcestershire v Durham (Chester-le-Street) 1968.

Highest individual innings: 146 G. Boycott, Yorks v Surrey (Lord's) 1965.

Highest individual innings by a Minor County player: 132 G. Robinson, Lincolnshire v Northumberland (Jesmond) 1971.

Record Wicket Partnerships

1st	227	R. E. Marshall & B. L. Reed, Hampshire v Bedfordshire (Goldington)	1968
2nd	204	B. W. Luckhurst & M. C. Cowdrey, Kent v Durham (Canterbury)	1974
3rd	157	R. B. Kanhai and M. J. K. Smith, Warwickshire v Lincolnshire (Birmingham)	1971
4th	169	M. J. Harris & G. S. Sobers, Nottinghamshire v Somerset (Nottingham)	1970
5th	135	J. F. Harvey & I. R. Buxton, Derbyshire v Worcestershire (Derby)	1972
6th	105	G. S. Sobers & R. A. White, Nottinghamshire v Worcestershire (Worcester)	1974
7th	107	D. R. Shepherd & D. A. Graveney, Gloucestershire v Surrey (Bristol)	1973
8th	55	B. S. V. Timms & A. T. Castell, Hampshire v Sussex (Hove)	1967
9th	87	M. A. Nash & A. E. Cordle, Glamorgan v Lincolnshire (Swansea)	1974
10th	45	A. T. Castell & D. W. White, Hampshire v Lancashire (Manchester)	1970

Hat-tricks: J. D. F. Larter, Northamptonshire v Sussex (Northampton) 1963

D. A. D. Sydenham, Surrey v Cheshire (Hoylake) 1964

R. N. S. Hobbs, Essex v Middlesex (Lord's) 1968

N. M. McVicker, Warwickshire v Lincolnshire (Birmingham) 1971

Seven wickets in an innings: 7-15 A. L. Dixon, Kent v Surrey (The Oval) 1967

P. J. Sainsbury (Hampshire) 7-30 in 1965 and R. D. Jackman (Surrey) 7-33 in 1970 have also achieved this feat.

Most 'Man of the Match' awards: 6 B. L. D'Oliveira (Worcestershire)
5 M. C. Cowdrey (Kent)

50 centuries have been scored in the competition.

SURREY WIN THE
BENSON AND HEDGES CUP

A low-scoring final

Surrey won a low-scoring final to win their first one-day competition. When Surrey were bowled out by Leicestershire for 170, Leicester looked as if they were on to a good thing, and although they lost Dudleston without a run having been scored, at 46 for 1, it still looked Leicester's Cup. But suddenly, 46 for 1 became 46 for 3, 50 for 4, and 65 for 5; from then on it was a grim struggle, with Leicester fighting what looked a losing battle. The Gold Award was given to John Edrich, for his 40 runs (which were the backbone of Surrey's uncertain batting), and for his leadership. But in the minds of a few, two Surrey bowlers might well have been rewarded. Arnold took 3 for 20 including the valuable wicket of Dudleston, and that of Illingworth at a time when the former England captain was successfully digging in. Pocock exhibited a priceless piece of off-spin bowling when he had precious few runs to play with, and was perhaps even more the cardinal figure. Still, Surrey won, and to their players that was what mattered. They have faltered so often in the past in one-day competitions that victory was all the sweeter. Edrich said afterwards, 'now for the Gillette Cup'; but hopes were swiftly to be dashed. Yet Surrey, the victors, did not head their zonal table: they were 3 points behind Kent. Nor, indeed, did Leicester head theirs; which was a neck and neck struggle with Worcester, Leicester, and Warwick all on 9 points. Eventually Warwick were eliminated on technical grounds – that their striking rate was less than the other two. Surrey's win in the semi-final at Old Trafford ran an almost identical course to the final. Edrich bore the brunt of the batting, and won the Gold Award, but a young quick-bowler, Alan Butcher, took 3 for 11, the bag being David Lloyd, Pilling, and Hayes; surely he must have run Edrich pretty close in the final reckoning.

SURREY v LEICESTERSHIRE

Played at Lord's, 20 July—Surrey won by 27 runs

SURREY

†J. H. Edrich	c & b Steele	40
L. E. Skinner	lbw b Higgs	0
G. P. Howarth	c Tolchard b Booth	22
Younis Ahmed	c Dudleston b Illingworth	43
G. R. J. Roope	b McKenzie	13
S. J. Storey	lbw b Illingworth	2
R. D. Jackman	c Tolchard b McKenzie	36
A. R. Butcher	c Tolchard b Higgs	7
P. I. Pocock	b Higgs	0
‡A. Long	c Tolchard b Higgs	0
G. G. Arnold	not out	7
Extras (LB5, NB2)		7
Total (54.1 overs)		170

LEICESTERSHIRE

B. Dudleston	lbw b Arnold	0
J. F. Steele	run out	18
M. E. J. C. Norman	lbw b Roope	24
B. F. Davison	c Howarth b Arnold	13
‡R. W. Tolchard	lbw b Roope	0
J. C. Balderstone	b Pocock	32
†R. Illingworth	b Arnold	23
N. M. McVicker	c Edrich b Pocock	10
G. D. McKenzie	st Long b Pocock	0
P. Booth	c Arnold b Jackman	5
K. Higgs	not out	8
Extras (B1, LB5, NB4)		10
Total (54 overs)		143

BOWLING

LEICESTERSHIRE	O	M	R	W	Fall of Wickets		
						S	L
						1st	*1st*
McKenzie	10.1	0	31	2			
Higgs	7	2	10	4			
Booth	8	1	30	1	1st	4	0
McVicker	8	1	25	0	2nd	36	46
Illingworth	11	2	36	2	3rd	99	46
Steele	10	0	31	1	4th	111	50
SURREY					5th	118	65
Arnold	10	4	20	3	6th	137	113
Jackman	11	1	34	1	7th	168	129
Roope	11	2	30	2	8th	168	129
Butcher	11	1	23	0	9th	168	131
Pocock	11	1	26	3	10th	170	143

Gold Award: J. H. Edrich.
Adjudicator: F. R. Brown.

BENSON & HEDGES CUP
PRINCIPAL RECORDS

Highest innings total: 327–4 off 55 overs, Leicestershire v Warwickshire (Coventry) 1972.

Highest innings total by side batting second: 282 off 50.5 overs, Gloucestershire v Hampshire (Bristol) 1974.

Highest innings total by side batting first and losing: 249–3 off 55 overs, Northamptonshire v Warwickshire (Northampton) 1974.

Lowest completed innings total: 68 off 36.5 overs, Glamorgan v Lancashire (Manchester) 1973.

Highest individual innings: 173* C. G. Greenidge, Hampshire v Minor Counties (South) (Amersham) 1973.

22 centuries have been scored in the competition.

Record Wicket Partnerships

1st	199	M. J. Harris & S. B. Hassan, Nottinghamshire v Yorkshire (Hull) 1973.
2nd	285*	C. G. Greenidge & D. R. Turner, Hampshire v Minor Counties (South) (Amersham) 1973.
3rd	227	M. E. J. C. Norman & B. F. Davison, Leicestershire v Warwickshire (Coventry) 1972.
	227	D. Lloyd & F. C. Hayes, Lancashire v Minor Counties (North) (Manchester) 1973.
4th	159	J. B. Bolus & A. J. Borrington, Derbyshire v Nottinghamshire (Nottingham) 1974.
5th	100	H. Pilling & J. Sullivan, Lancashire v Glamorgan (Manchester) 1973.
6th	103*	M. A. Nash & K. J. Lyons, Glamorgan v Minor Counties (South) (Chippenham) 1972.
7th	91	G. J. Saville & R. N. S. Hobbs, Essex v Middlesex (Lord's) 1972.
8th	73	E. E. Hemmings & S. J. Rouse, Warwickshire v Leicestershire (Birmingham) 1974.
9th	63	I. T. Botham & H. R. Moseley, Somerset v Hampshire (Taunton) 1974.
10th	31	J. F. Harvey & M. Hendrick, Derbyshire v Yorkshire (Chesterfield) 1974.

Hat-tricks: G. D. McKenzie, Leicestershire v Worcestershire (Worcester) 1972. K. Higgs, Leicestershire v Surrey (Lord's) 1974.

Six wickets in an innings: 6–27 A. G. Nicholson, Yorkshire v Minor Counties (North) (Middlesbrough) 1972.

Most 'Gold' awards: 6 B. Wood (Lancashire), 5 J. H. Edrich (Surrey).

Does perspiration make the new ball swing?

Some scientists insist that a cricket ball does not swing, despite the fact that a combination of polished leather, perspiration and humid weather has been known to play havoc with batting averages.

This does not mean that swing bowlers spend the day in a drench of perspiration—a quick spray with Right Guard keeps the most energetic cricketer dry right up to the Man-of-the-match presentation. But you'll never see a swing bowler spray Right Guard on his forehead—no matter what his views are on aerodynamics.

Right Guard Anti-Perspirant for dry comfort

LEICESTERSHIRE WIN THE JOHN PLAYER LEAGUE

Leicestershire who at one point had seemed likely to win the Benson and Hedges Cup, but failed in the end, did *not* fail in the John Player League – though their last match against Somerset was not without a certain amount of controversy. Leicester, however, were a good enough side to win something, and although of the four competitions this one is the least test of skill, Leicester will be happy with this rather than nothing. They thus became the fourth county to win the John Player League since its inception. Lancashire have won it twice, in 1969 and 1970, then Worcester, and then Kent, twice. Lancashire, joint 12th, and Worcester joint 8th, were well out of the running, but Kent still maintained their challenge, finishing third. Somerset gave Leicester a wonderful run for their money and will point to rain as their final handicap. But who knows what would have happened: in the history books, Leicester are the winners.

THE JOHN PLAYER AWARDS, 1974

Sixes (409 sixes were hit, each being worth £2.44): 19 D. B. Close (Somerset) (League record – won special £150 award for most sixes); 11 C. H. Lloyd (Lancashire), C. M. Old (Yorkshire), V. A. Richards (Somerset); 10 B. F. Davison (Leicester), P. W. Denning (Somerset); 9 J. A. Jameson (Warwickshire), L. G. Rowe (Derbyshire). Four wickets (59 instances, each share worth £16.95); 3 R. J. Clapp (Somerset), A. E. Cordle (Glamorgan), E. E. Hemmings (Warwickshire) (Share special £150 award for most 4 wickets); 2 K. D. Boyce (Essex), A. Buss (Sussex), A. M. E. Roberts (Hampshire), G. R. J. Roope (Surrey), P. E. Russell (Derbyshire), J. Sullivan (Lancashire), D. L. Williams (Glamorgan).

PRINCIPAL RECORDS

Highest innings total: 288–6 off 40 overs Sussex v Middlesex (Hove) 1969.
Highest innings total by side batting second: 254–7 off 39 overs Leics v Sussex (Leicester) 1969.
Highest innings total by side batting first and losing: 253–7 off 40 overs Sussex v Leics (Leicester) 1969.
Lowest completed innings total: 23 off 19.4 overs, Middlesex v Yorkshire (Leeds) 1974.
Highest individual innings: 155* B. A. Richards, Hampshire v Yorkshire (Hull) 1970.
63 centuries have been scored in the League.

Record Wicket Partnerships

1st 182 M. H. Denness & B. W. Luckhurst, Kent v Somerset (Weston-super-Mare) 1970.
  182 R. G. A. Headley & G. M. Turner, Worcestershire v Warwickshire (Birmingham) 1972.
2nd 179 B. W. Luckhurst & M. H. Denness, Kent v Somerset (Canterbury) 1973.
3rd 182 H. Pilling & C. H. Lloyd, Lancashire v Somerset (Manchester) 1970.
4th 175* M. J. K. Smith & D. L. Amiss, Warwickshire v Yorkshire (Birmingham) 1970.
5th 128 G. Barker & K. D. Boyce, Essex v Surrey (Oval) 1971.
6th 121 C. P. Wilkins & A. J. Borrington, Derbyshire v Warwickshire (Chesterfield) 1972.
7th 96* R. Illingworth & J. Birkenshaw, Leicestershire v Somerset (Leicester) 1971.
8th 88 B. A. Davis & M. A. Nash, Glamorgan v Kent (Swansea) 1970.
9th 86 D. P. Hughes & P. Lever, Lancashire v Essex (Leyton) 1973.
10th 57 D. A. Graveney & J. B. Mortimore, Gloucestershire v Lancashire (Tewkesbury) 1973.

Four wickets in four balls: A. Ward, Derbyshire v Sussex (Derby) 1970.
Hat-tricks (excluding above): R. Palmer, Somerset v Gloucestershire (Bristol) 1970, K. D. Boyce, Essex v Somerset (Westcliff) 1971, G. D. McKenzie, Leicestershire v Essex (Leicester) 1972, R. G. D. Willis, Warwickshire v Yorkshire (Birmingham) 1973, W. Blenkiron, Warwickshire v Derbyshire (Buxton) 1974, A. Buss, Sussex v Worcestershire (Hastings) 1974.
Eight wickets in an innings: 8-26 K. D. Boyce, Essex v Lancashire (Manchester) 1971.

JOHN PLAYER LEAGUE TABLE, 1974

1973 positions in brackets

		P	W	L	Rs	Tie	Pts
1	Leicestershire (5)	16	12	1	2	1	54
2	Somerset (11)	16	12	2	2	0	52
3	Kent (1)	16	10	4	2	0	44
4	Northamptonshire (17)	16	10	6	0	0	40
	Hampshire (3)	16	9	5	2	0	40
6	Sussex (7)	16	8	6	1	1	36
7	Yorkshire (2)	16	8	6	2	0	32
	Middlesex (8)	16	7	7	1	1	32
	Worcestershire (15)	16	7	7	2	0	32
10	Surrey (9)	16	7	8	1	0	30
	Warwickshire (16)	16	7	8	1	0	30
12	Lancashire (4)	16	5	9	1	1	24
	Gloucestershire (6)	16	4	8	4	0	24
14	Glamorgan (14)	16	5	10	1	0	22
15	Essex (10)	16	4	11	1	0	18
	Derbyshire (12)	16	4	11	1	0	18
17	Nottinghamshire (13)	16	3	13	0	0	12

WORCESTER ARE COUNTY CHAMPIONS
Hampshire just pipped

Worcestershire are the 1974 County Champions and though perhaps it is a little unfair to detract from their performance, it must be said that the dreadfully wet summer had an enormous bearing on the ultimate outcome of the title. The fact is that Hampshire (who were only two points behind Worcester in the end) would probably have won the Championship before the end of August if the weather had been kinder. They certainly had the better of a rain-ruined match against Lancashire, and would almost certainly have beaten Glamorgan by an innings, but for the loss of a considerable amount of play. Then the crowning iniquity was that rain spoilt the penultimate match against Somerset, and washed out all three days of the critical last match against Yorkshire at Bournemouth. It will be hard to convince any Hampshire player, or supporter, that given reasonable weather, Hampshire would not have repeated their success of 1973; in addition, they will point to the result of Hampshire's match against Worcester, which Hampshire won by an innings in two days. Worcester were bowled out for 94 and 98, Roberts achieving a match aggregate of 7 for 46. Hampshire thus cruised to an innings victory and took 16 points to Worcester's 4. After this match, it appeared to be odds-on Hampshire, but the weather, as it was with most cricket in 1974, became the final decider. Northants, who had been third the previous season, proved that this position was a true representation of their talents by repeating the procedure. It was a golden season for Roy Virgin, who hit seven centuries, scored nearly two thousand runs, and finished with a batting average in the Championship of 59.52. He was subsequently appointed captain for 1975, an honour well deserved on his 1974 performances. Bedi was the principal bowler, capturing 55 wickets at 18.12 apiece. Leicestershire rose five places from ninth to fourth, and Somerset, under the energetic leadership of Brian Close, improved considerably to finish fifth compared to 10th in the previous season. One of the biggest disappointments was Kent, who slipped from fourth to 10th, but they will point with some justification to the loss of their key players to Test matches. Surrey could say the same; they dropped from second to seventh. Derbyshire fell one place into last position with Glamorgan a few points ahead of them. But everyone will talk of what might have happened but for rain.

COUNTY CHAMPIONS

1873	{ Nottinghamshire	1899	Surrey	1937	Yorkshire
	Gloucestershire	1900	Yorkshire	1938	Yorkshire
1874	Derbyshire	1901	Yorkshire	1939	Yorkshire
1875	{ Nottinghamshire	1902	Yorkshire	1946	Yorkshire
	Lancashire	1903	Middlesex	1947	Middlesex
	Sussex	1904	Lancashire	1948	Glamorgan
1876	Gloucestershire	1905	Yorkshire	1949	{ Middlesex
1877	Gloucestershire	1906	Kent		Yorkshire
1878	Middlesex	1907	Nottinghamshire	1950	{ Lancashire
1879	{ Nottinghamshire	1908	Yorkshire		Surrey
	Lancashire	1909	Kent	1951	Warwickshire
1880	{ Nottinghamshire	1910	Kent	1952	Surrey
	Gloucestershire	1911	Warwickshire	1953	Surrey
1881	Lancashire	1912	Yorkshire	1954	Surrey
1882	{ Lancashire	1913	Kent	1955	Surrey
	Nottinghamshire	1914	Surrey	1956	Surrey
1883	Nottinghamshire	1919	Yorkshire	1957	Surrey
1884	Nottinghamshire	1920	Middlesex	1958	Surrey
1885	Nottinghamshire	1921	Middlesex	1959	Yorkshire
1886	Nottinghamshire	1922	Yorkshire	1960	Yorkshire
1887	Surrey	1923	Yorkshire	1961	Hampshire
1888	Surrey	1924	Yorkshire	1962	Yorkshire
1889	{ Nottinghamshire	1925	Yorkshire	1963	Yorkshire
	Lancashire	1926	Lancashire	1964	Worcestershire
	Surrey	1927	Lancashire	1965	Worcestershire
1890	Surrey	1928	Lancashire	1966	Yorkshire
1891	Surrey	1929	Nottinghamshire	1967	Yorkshire
1892	Surrey	1930	Lancashire	1968	Yorkshire
1893	Yorkshire	1931	Yorkshire	1960	Glamorgan
1894	Surrey	1932	Yorkshire	1970	Kent
1895	Surrey	1933	Yorkshire	1971	Surrey
1896	Yorkshire	1934	Lancashire	1972	Warwickshire
1897	Lancashire	1935	Yorkshire	1973	Hampshire
1898	Yorkshire	1936	Derbyshire	1974	Worcestershire

CHAMPIONSHIP TABLE, 1974

1973 positions in brackets

		P	W	L	D	Bonus Pts Bt	Bw	Pts
1	Worcestershire (6)	20	11	3	6	45	72	227
2	Hampshire (1)	20	10	3	6	55	70	225
3	Northamptonshire (3)	20	9	2	9	46	67	203
4	Leicestershire (9)	20	7	7	6	47	69	186
5	Somerset (10)	20	6	4	10	49	72	181
6	Middlesex (13)	20	7	5	8	45	56	171
	Surrey (2)	20	6	4	10	42	69	171
8	Lancashire (9)	20	5	0	15	47	66	163
9	Warwickshire (7)	20	5	5	10	44	65	159
10	Kent (4)	20	5	8	7	33	63	146
	Yorkshire (14)	20	4	7	8	37	69	146
12	Essex (8)	20	4	3	12	44	52	141
13	Sussex (15)	20	4	9	6	29	63	137
14	Gloucestershire (5)	20	4	9	6	29	55	124
15	Nottinghamshire (17)	20	1	9	10	42	66	118
16	Glamorgan (11)	20	2	7	10	28	56	104
17	Derbyshire (16)	20	1	6	13	23	62	95

2ND XI TABLE, 1974

	P	W	L	D	Bonus Pts Bt	Bw	Pts	Avge
Middlesex	14	7	2	5*	32	45	147	10.50
Essex	10	2	2	6	41	35	96	9.60
Surrey	13	3	4	6	34	53	117	9.00
Sussex	10	3	2	5	27	28	85	8.50
Lancashire	16	4	3	9	47	44	131	8.18
Hampshire	11	2	3	6*	30	34	84	7.63
Nottinghamshire	14	4	1	9*	31	35	106	7.57
Northamptonshire	17	3	2	12	38	59	127	7.47
Derbyshire	12	3	2	7	18	37	85	7.08
Kent	10	1	3	6	31	28	69	6.90
Glamorgan	17	3	5	9*	40	44	114	6.70
Warwickshire	20	3	8	9*	40	56	126	6.30
Worcestershire	16	3	3	10*	24	44	98	6.12
Gloucestershire	11	2	2	7*	16	21	57	5.17
Leicestershire	15	1	2	12	23	37	70	4.66

includes match/matches abandoned in which no play was possible.

SCORING OF POINTS IN THE COUNTY CHAMPIONSHIP

The scheme for scoring points in the County Championship is as follows:

(a) For a win, 10 points, plus any points scored in the first innings.

(b) In a tie, each side to score 5 points, plus any points scored in the first innings.

(c) If the scores are equal in a drawn match, the side batting in the fourth innings to score 5 points, plus any points scored in the first innings.

(d) First innings points awarded only for performances in the first 100 overs of each innings and retained whatever the result of the match.

    (i) A maximum of 4 batting points to be available as under: 150 to 199 runs—1 point; 200 to 249 runs—2 points; 250 to 299 runs—3 points; 300 runs or over—4 points.

    (ii) A maximum of 4 bowling points to be available as under: 3–4 wickets taken—1 point; 5–6 wickets taken—2 points; 7–8 wickets taken—3 points; 9–10 wickets taken—4 points.

(e) If play starts when less then 8 hours playing time remain and a one innings match is played, no first innings points shall be scored. The side winning on the one innings to score 10 points.

(f) The side which has the highest aggregate of points gained at the end of the season shall be the Champion County. Should any sides in the County Championship Table be equal on points, the side with most wins will have priority.

THE COUNTIES AND
THEIR PLAYERS

Compiled by Michael Fordham

Abbreviations

B	Born	HS	Highest score
RHB	Right-hand bat	HSUK	Highest score in this country
LHB	Left-hand bat		
RF	Right-arm fast	HSGC	Highest score Gillette Cup
RFM	Right-arm fast medium	HSJPL	Highest score John Player League
RM	Right-arm medium		
LF	Left-arm fast	HSBH	Highest score Benson & Hedges Cup
LFM	Left-arm fast medium		
LM	Left-arm medium	BB	Best bowling figures
OB	Off-break	BBUK	Best bowling figures in this country
LB	Leg-break		

DERBYSHIRE

Formation of present club: 1870.
Colours: Chocolate, amber, and pale blue.
Badge: Rose and crown.
County Champions (2): 1874 and 1936.
Gillette Cup finalists: 1969.
John Player League: Third in 1970.

Secretary: Major D. J. Carr, County Cricket Ground, Nottingham Road, Derby, DE2 6DA.
Captain: J. B. Bolus.

John Brian BOLUS (St Michael's College, Leeds) B Whitkirk (Leeds) 31/1/1934. RHB, LM. Debut for Yorkshire 1956. Cap 1960. Not re-engaged at end of 1962 season. Debut for Notts and cap 1963. Vice-captain from 1964 until 1967 and from 1969 to 1971. Benefit (£7,820) in 1971. County captain in 1972. Not re-engaged at end of season and joined Derbyshire as captain in 1973. Cap awarded on appointment. Tests: 7 in 1963 and 1963–64. Tour: India 1963–64. 1,000 runs (13)—2,190 runs (av 41.32) in 1963 and 2,143 runs (av 48.70) in 1970 best. Scored two centuries in match (147 and 101) Notts v Northants (Nottingham) 1969. Gillette Man of the Match awards: 2 HS: 202* Notts v Glamorgan (Nottingham) 1963. HSGC: 100* Notts v Yorks (Middlesbrough) 1963. HSJPL: 86 Notts v Surrey (Nottingham) 1969. HSBH: 71 v Notts (Nottingham) 1974. BB: 4–40 Yorks v Pakistanis (Bradford) 1962.

Anthony John (Tony) BORRINGTON (Spondon Park GS and Loughborough College) B Derby 8/12/1948. RHB, LB. Played for MCC Schools at Lord's in 1967. Played in one John Player League match in 1970. Debut 1971. Left staff after 1974 season and will only play occasionally in 1975. Benson and Hedges Gold awards: 1. HS: 75 v Yorks (Chesterfield) 1973. HSGC: 22 v Leics (Leicester) 1971. HSJPL: 84 v Glos (Derby) 1972. HSBH: 81 v Notts (Nottingham) 1974.

LBG	Leg-break and googly	BBGC	Best bowling figures
SLA	Slow left-arm orthodox		Gillette Cup
SLC	Slow left-arm 'chinaman'	BBJPL	Best bowling figures
WK	Wicket-keeper		John Player League
*	Not out or unfinished	BBBH	Best bowling figures
	stand		Benson & Hedges Cup

When a player is known by a name other than his first name, the name in question has been underlined.

All Test match appearances are complete to 31 October 1974.

The county of the cricketer's birth-place is given in the less obvious cases.

'Debut' denotes 'first-class debut' and 'Cap' means '1st XI county cap'.

'*Wisden 1973*' indicates that a player was selected as one of *Wisden's* Five Cricketers of the Year for his achievements in 1973.

Owing to the increasing number of privately arranged overseas tours of short duration, only those which may be regarded as major tours have been included.

Harold CARTWRIGHT B Halfway (Derbyshire) 12/5/1951. RHB. Played in John Player and Gillette Cup matches in 1971 and 1972. Debut 1973. HS: 63 v Middlesex (Burton-on-Trent) 1973. HSGC: 21 v Leics (Leicester) 1971. HSJPL: 76* v Middlesex (Chesterfield) 1973.

Ashley John HARVEY-WALKER (Strathallan School) B East Ham 21/7/1944. RHB, OB. Debut 1971, scoring 16 and 110* v Oxford U (Burton-on-Trent) in debut match, the first player ever to do so for the county. HS: 117 v Warwickshire (Birmingham) 1974. HSGC: 18 v Hants (Derby) 1974. HSJPL: 84 v Glos (Chesterfield) 1973. HSBH: 45 v Minor Counties (Derby) 1974. Plays hockey (CF) for Derbyshire 2nd XI.

Michael HENDRICK B Darley Dale (Derbyshire) 22/10/1948. RHB, RFM. Debut 1969. Cap 1972. Elected Best Young Cricketer of the Year in 1973 by the Cricket Writers Club. Tests: 5 in 1974. Tours: West Indies 1973–74, Australia and New Zealand 1974–75. Benson & Hedges Gold awards: 1. HS: 46 v Essex (Chelmsford) 1973. HSGC: 11 v Sussex (Chesterfield) 1973. HSJPL: 21 v Warwickshire (Buxton) 1974. HSBH: 32 v Notts (Chesterfield) 1973. BB: 8–45 v Warwickshire (Chesterfield) 1973. BBGC: 3–37 v Leics (Leicester) 1971. BBJPL: 6–7 v Notts (Nottingham) 1972. BBBH: 4–5 v Minor Counties (Derby) 1974.

Alan HILL (New Mills GS) B Buxworth (Derbyshire) 29/6/1950. RHB, OB. Joined staff 1970. Debut 1972. HS: 140* v Sussex (Derby) 1974. HSJPL: 54 v Glos (Chesterfield) 1973. HSBH: 21 v Notts (Nottingham) 1974.

Geoffrey MILLER (Chesterfield GS) B Chesterfield 8/9/1952. RHB, OB. Toured India 1970–71 and West Indies 1972 with England Young Cricketers. Won Sir Frank Worrell Trophy as Outstanding Boy Cricketer of 1972. Debut 1973. HS: 71 v Hants (Portsmouth) 1974. HSGC: 10 v Sussex (Chesterfield) 1973 and 10 v Hants (Derby) 1974. HSJPL: 44 v Kent (Chesterfield) 1973. HSBH: 18 v Yorks (Chesterfield) 1974. BB: 5–88 v Kent (Folkestone) 1974. BBJPL: 3–31 v Glamorgan (Ebbw Vale) 1974. Has played table tennis for county.

Alan MORRIS B Staveley (Derbyshire) 23/8/1953. RHB, LB. Debut 1974 (three matches). HS: 37 v Essex (Westcliff) 1974.

Michael Harry PAGE (Francis Askew HS, Hull) B Blackpool 17/6/1941. RHB, OB. Debut and cap 1964 scoring 990 runs (av 27.50) in debut season. Testimonial in 1975. 1,000 runs (5)—1,344 runs (av 40.72) in 1970 best. HS: 162 v Leics (Leicester) 1969. HSGC: 83 v Essex (Brentwood) 1965. HSJPL: 73* v Glamorgan (Swansea) 1970. HSBH: 47 v Minor Counties (Cheadle) 1973.

Lawrence George ROWE B Kingston (Jamaica) 8/1/1949. RHB, RM. Debut for Jamaica in Shell Shield tournament 1968–69. Played for International Cavaliers v Barbados (Scarborough) 1969 and also for Notts 2nd XI. Joined county in 1973 as a special overseas registration and made debut in 1974. Tests: 12 for West Indies between 1971–72 and 1973–74. Tours: Jamaica to England 1970, West Indies to England 1973, India and Pakistan 1974–75. Scored 1,059 runs (av 36.52) in 1974. Scored 1,117 runs (av 79.78) in 1973–74, the highest aggregate by a West Indian in West Indies. Scored four consecutive centuries all in Jamaica in 1971–72, including the unique achievement of 214 and 100* in Test debut v New Zealand. HS: 302 West Indies v England (Bridgetown) 1973–74. HSUK: 94 v Sussex (Derby) 1974. HSGC: 20 v Hants (Derby) 1974. HSJPL: 72 v Worcs (Ilkeston) 1974. HSBH: 13 v Lancs (Manchester) 1974.

Philip Edgar RUSSELL (Ilkeston GS) B Ilkeston 9/5/1944. RHB, RM/OB. Debut 1965. Not re-engaged after 1972 season, but rejoined staff in 1974. HS: 72 v Glamorgan (Swansea) 1970. HSJPL: 30 v Hants (Bournemouth) 1969. HSBH: 17* v Lancs (Manchester) 1972. BB: 6–61 v Glamorgan (Swansea) 1970. BBJPL: 5–54 v Notts (Nottingham) 1974. BBBH: 3–43 v Minor Counties (Derby) 1972.

Philip John (Phil) SHARPE (Worksop College) B Shipley (Yorks) 27/12/1936. RHB, OB. Outstanding slip field. Debut 1956 for Combined Services. Debut for Yorks 1958. Cap 1960. Elected Best Young Cricketer of the Year in 1962 by the Cricket Writers' Club. Wisden 1962. Benefit (£6,669) in 1971. Released by county after 1974 season and has joined Derbyshire for 1975. Tests: 12 between 1963 and 1969. Played in one match v Rest of World in 1970. Tour: India 1963–64. 1,000 runs (11)—2,252 runs (av 40.94) in 1962 best. Held 71 catches in 1962. Gillette Man of Match awards: 2. HS: 203* Yorks v Cambridge U (Cambridge) 1960. HSGC: 68 Yorks v Lancs (Manchester) 1969. HSJPL: 81 Yorks v Northants (Bradford) 1969. HSBH: 89* Yorks v Minor Counties (Middlesbrough) 1972. Good hockey player.

Keith STEVENSON (Bemrose GS, Derby) B Derby 6/10/1950. RHB, RM. Debut 1974. HS: 33 v Northants (Chesterfield) 1974. BB: 4–127 v Surrey (Chesterfield) 1974.

Frederick William (Fred) SWARBROOK B Derby 17/12/1950. LHB, SLA. Debut 1967 aged 16 years 6 months, youngest player ever to appear for county. Played for Griqualand West in 1972–73 and 1973–74 Currie Cup competitions. HS: 90 v Essex (Leyton) 1970. HSJPL: 12 v Worcs (Dudley) 1973. BB: 6–48 v Warwickshire (Coventry) 1970. Soccer for Derby County Juniors.

Robert William (Bob) TAYLOR B Stoke 17/7/1941. RHB, WK, RM. Played for Bignall End (N. Staffs and S. Cheshire League) when only 15 and for Staffordshire from 1958 to 1960. Debut 1960 for Minor Counties v South Africans (Stoke-on-Trent). Debut for county 1961. Cap 1962. Testimonial (£6,672) in 1973. Tests: 1 v New Zealand 1970–71. Tours: Australia and New Zealand 1970–71, 1974–75, Australia with Rest of the World team 1971–72, West Indies 1973–74. Withdrew from India, Sri Lanka, and Pakistan tour 1972–73. Dismissed 80 batsmen (77 ct 3 st) in 1962, 83 batsmen (81 ct 2 st) in 1963, and 86 batsmen (79 ct 7 st) in 1965. Dismissed 10 batsmen in match, all caught v Hants (Chesterfield) 1963 and 7 in innings, all caught v Glamorgan (Derby) 1966. Gillette Man of Match awards: 1. HS: 74* v Glamorgan (Derby) 1971. HSGC: 53* v Middlesex (Lord's) 1965. HSJPL: 43* v Glos (Burton-on-Trent) 1969. HSBH: 20 v Minor Counties (Cheadle) 1973.

Srinivasaraghavan VENKATARAGHAVAN B Madras 21/4/1946. RHB, OB. Close field. Debut for Madras in Ranji Trophy 1963–64. Debut for county as special overseas registration in 1973. Cap 1973. Tests: 26 for India between 1964–65 and 1974. Tours: India to England 1967, 1971 (vice-captain) and 1974 (vice-captain), West Indies 1970–71 (vice-captain). HS: 137 Tamil Nadu v Kerala (Tellicherry) 1970–71. HSUK: 57 Indians v Glamorgan (Cardiff) 1971. HSGC: 10 v Sussex (Chesterfield) 1973. HSJPL: 16 v Notts (Derby) 1973. BB: 9–93 Indians v Hampshire (Bournemouth) 1971. BBJPL: 3–31 v Notts (Derby) 1973.

Alan WARD B Dronfield (Derbyshire) 10/8/1947. RHB, RF. Debut 1966. Cap 1969. Elected Best Young Cricketer of the Year in 1969 by the Cricket Writers Club. Played for Border in 1971–72 Currie Cup competition. Was sent off the field for refusing to bowl against Yorks at Chesterfield in June 1973. Left staff afterwards, but rejoined in 1974. Tests: 4 in 1969 and 1971. Also played in 1 match v Rest of World in 1970. Tour: Australia 1970–71 returning home early owing to injury. Took 4 wickets in 4 balls in John Player League match v Sussex (Derby) 1970. Benson & Hedges Gold awards: 1. HS: 44 v Notts (Ilkeston) 1969. HSGC: 17 v Yorks (Lord's) 1969. HSJPL: 21* v Somerset (Buxton) 1969. BB: 7–42 v Glamorgan (Burton-on-Trent) 1974. BBGC: 3–31 v Yorks (Lord's) 1969. BBJPL: 5–11 v Sussex (Derby) 1970. BBBH: 4–14 v Lancs (Manchester) 1974.

John Michael WARD (Newcastle-under-Lyme HS and Oxford) B Sandon (Staffs) 14/9/1948. RHB. Played for Staffordshire 1969–70. Debut for Oxford U 1970. Blue 1971–73. Debut for county 1973. HS: 85 Oxford U v Warwickshire (Birmingham) 1973. HSJPL: 37 v Lancs (Chesterfield) 1974. HSBH: 54 Oxford U v Leics (Oxford) 1973. Has played rugby for Staffordshire.

NB The following players whose particulars appeared in the 1974 Annual are omitted: I. R. Buxton, R. L. Hanson, F. E. Rumsey, R. S. Swindell, and C. J. Tunnicliffe.
The career records of Swindell and Tunnicliffe will be found elsewhere in this Annual.

DERBYSHIRE

COUNTY AVERAGES
County Championship: Played 20; won 1, drawn 13, lost 6
All first-class matches: Played 22; won 2, drawn 13, lost 7

BATTING AND FIELDING

Cap		M	I	NO	Runs	HS	Avge	100	50	Ct	St
—	L. G. Rowe	17	30	1	1059	94	36.51	—	7	15	—
—	A. Hill	10	19	4	539	140*	35.93	2	2	3	—
1972	J. B. Bolus	22	38	6	892	112	27.87	1	5	4	—
—	A. J. Harvey-Walker	17	29	1	727	117	25.96	1	4	4	—
—	F. W. Swarbrook	20	32	11	490	65	23.33	—	2	18	—
—	A. Morris	3	6	1	113	37	22.60	—	—	1	—
1964	M. H. Page	18	29	6	645	91	22.24	—	4	14	—
1973	S. Venkataraghavan	8	11	2	181	33*	20.11	—	—	8	—
—	G. Miller	19	29	2	518	53	19.18	—	1	9	—
—	H. Cartwright	7	11	2	172	43*	19.11	—	—	5	—
1962	R. W. Taylor	20	31	3	479	54	17.10	—	1	49	3
—	A. J. Borrington	7	12	1	174	58	15.81	—	1	6	—
—	P. E. Russell	20	28	8	241	26*	12.05	—	—	19	—
—	J. M. Ward	10	16	0	170	37	10.62	—	—	3	—
—	K. Stevenson	9	10	2	83	33	10.37	—	—	2	—
1969	A. Ward	18	16	6	92	32	9.20	—	—	8	—
1972	M. Hendrick	12	12	6	43	6*	7.16	—	—	12	—
—	C. J. Tunnicliffe	4	6	0	18	14	3.00	—	—	—	—

Played in one match: R. S. Swindell 11*.

BOWLING

	Type	O	M	R	W	Avge	Best	5 wI	10 wM
M. Hendrick	RFM	305.1	84	669	39	17.15	5-13	1	—
A. Ward	RF	400.4	82	1174	56	20.96	7-42	5	1
G. Miller	OB	380	90	1020	42	24.28	5-88	1	—
S. Venk'van	OB	311.2	61	953	31	30.74	7-102	2	—
P. E. Russell	RM/OB	554.3	154	1413	44	32.11	5-75	1	—
K. Stevenson	RFM	171.2	16	654	18	36.33	4-127	—	—
F. W. Swarbrook	SLA	427.4	138	1168	21	55.61	4-51	—	—

Also bowled: A. J. Harvey-Walker 30-7-108-1; L. G. Rowe 27.4-7-84-1; R. S. Swindell 14-1-58-2; R. W. Taylor 3-0-9-0; C. J. Tunnicliffe 73-12-238-1.

County Records
First-class cricket

Highest innings totals:	For ...645 v Hampshire (Derby)	1898
	Agst...662 by Yorkshire (Chesterfield)	1898
Lowest innings totals:	For ... 16 v Nottinghamshire (Nottingham)	1879
	Agst... 23 by Hampshire (Burton-on-Trent)	1958
Highest individual innings:	For ...274 G. Davidson v Lancashire (Manchester)	1896
	Agst...343* P. A. Perrin for Essex (Chesterfield)	1904
Best bowling in an innings:	For ...10-40 W. Bestwick v Glamorgan (Cardiff)	1921
	Agst...10-47 T. F. Smailes for Yorkshire (Sheffield)	1939
Best bowling in a match:	For ...16-84 C. Gladwin v Worcs (Stourbridge)	1952
	Agst...16-101 G. Giffen for Australians (Derby)	1886

Most runs in a season:	2165 (av 48.11) D. B. Carr	1959
runs in a career:	20516 (av 31.41) D. Smith	1927–1952
100s in a season:	6 by L. F. Townsend	1933
100s in a career:	30 by D. Smith	1927–1952
wickets in a season:	168 (av 19.55) T. B. Mitchell	1935
wickets in a career:	1670 (av 17.11) H. L. Jackson	1947–1963

RECORD WICKET STANDS

1st	322	H. Storer & J. B. Bowden v Essex (Leyton)	1929
2nd	349	C. S. Elliott & J. D. Eggar v Nottinghamshire (Nottingham)	1947
3rd	246	J. Kelly & D. B. Carr v Leicestershire (Chesterfield)	1957
4th	328	P. Vaulkhard & D. Smith v Nottinghamshire (Nottingham)	1946
5th	203	C. P. Wilkins & I. R. Buxton v Lancashire (Manchester)	1971
6th	212	G. M. Lee & T. S. Worthington v Essex (Chesterfield)	1932
7th	241*	G. H. Pope & A. E. G. Rhodes v Hampshire (Portsmouth)	1948
8th	182	A. H. M. Jackson & W. Carter v Leicestershire (Leicester)	1922
9th	283	A. R. Warren & J. Chapman v Warwickshire (Blackwell)	1910
10th	93	J. Humphries & J. Horsely v Lancashire (Derby)	1914

One-day cricket

Highest innings totals:	Gillette Cup	250–9 v Hants (Bournemouth)	1963
	John Player League	260–6 v Glos (Derby)	1972
	Benson & Hedges Cup	225–6 v Notts (Nottingham)	1974
Lowest innings totals:	Gillette Cup	79 v Surrey (Oval)	1967
	John Player League	70 v Surrey (Derby)	1972
	Benson & Hedges Cup	108 v Yorks (Bradford)	1973
Highest individual innings:	Gillette Cup	83 M. H. Page v Essex (Brentwood)	1965
	John Player League	94 C. P. Wilkins v Warwickshire (Chesterfield)	1972
	Benson & Hedges Cup	81 A. J. Borrington v Notts (Nottingham)	1974
Best bowling figures:	Gillette Cup	6–18 T. J. P. Eyre v Sussex (Chesterfield)	1969
	John Player League	6–7 M. Hendrick v Notts (Nottingham)	1972
	Benson & Hedges Cup	4–5 M. Hendrick v Minor Counties (Derby)	1974

ESSEX

Formation of present club: 1876.
Colours: Blue, gold, and red.
Badge: Three scimitars with word 'Essex' underneath.
Best final position in Championship: Third in 1897.
Gillette Cup third round (5): 1966, 1969, 1971, 1972, and 1973.
John Player League runners-up: 1971.
Benson & Hedges Cup semi-finalists: 1973.

Secretary: S. R. Cox, The County Ground, New Writtle Street, Chelmsford CM2 0RW.
Captain: K. W. R. Fletcher.

David Laurence ACFIELD (Brentwood School & Cambridge) B Chelmsford 24/7/1947. RHB, OB. Debut 1966. Blue 1967–68. Cap 1970. HS: 42 Cambridge U v Leics (Leicester) 1967. BB: 7–36 v Sussex (Ilford) 1973. BBJPL: 5–14 v Northants (Northampton) 1970. Also obtained Blue for fencing (sabre). Has appeared in internationals in this sport and represented Great Britain in Olympic Games at Mexico City and Munich.

Keith David BOYCE B St Peter, Barbados 11/10/1943. RHB, RFM. Very good outfield. Debut for Barbados v Cavaliers in one match in 1964–65 and has played subsequently for Barbados in Shell Shield competitions. Joined county in 1965 and made debut in 1966. Cap 1967. *Wisden* 1973. Scored 910 runs (av 20.22) and took 81 wkts (av 27.24) in 1967. Scored 908 runs (av 20.63) and took 88 wkts (av 23.54) in 1968. Scored 1,023 runs (av 30.08) and took 82 wkts (av 20.20) in 1972. Tests: 12 for West Indies between 1971 and 1973–74. Tours: West Indies to England 1973, India and Pakistan 1974–75. Hat-trick v Warwickshire (Chelmsford) 1974 and in John Player League match v Somerset (Westcliff) 1971. Won single-wicket tournament at Lord's in 1969. Gillette Man of Match awards: 2. HS: 147* v Hants (Ilford) 1969. HSGC: 47 v Lancs (Chelmsford) 1971. HSJPL: 98 v Surrey (Oval) 1971. HSBH: 47 v Surrey (Oval) 1972. BB: 9–61 (13–108 match) v Cambridge U (Brentwood) 1966, in debut match for county. BBGC: 5–22 v Middlesex (Westcliff) 1972. BBJPL: 8–26 v Lancs (Manchester) 1971 (the record for the League). BBBH: 4–18 v Sussex (Chelmsford) 1974.

Robert Michael Oliver (Bob) COOKE B Adlington (Cheshire) 30/9/1943. LHB, LBG. Wears glasses. Played for Cheshire from 1969 to 1973. Has also played for Lancashire 2nd XI. Was professional for Stockport in Central Lancashire League 1969–70 and was subsequently professional for Fleetwood in Northern League. Debut for Minor Counties v Australians (Stoke-on-Trent) 1972. Debut for county 1973. Benson & Hedges Gold awards: 1 (for Minor Counties). HS: 139 v Sussex (Ilford) 1973. HSGC: 29* v Durham (Chester-le-Street) 1973. HSJPL: 83 v Northants (Westcliff) 1974. HSBH: 50* v Leics (Ilford) 1973.

Raymond Eric (Ray) EAST B Manningtree (Essex) 20/6/1947. RHB, SLA. Debut 1965. Cap 1967. Hat-trick, The Rest v MCC Tour XI (Hove) 1973. Benson & Hedges Gold awards: 2. HS: 89* v Worcs (Leyton)

68

1972. HSGC: 38* v Glos (Chelmsford) 1973. HSJPL: 22 v Kent
(Chelmsford) 1973. HSBH: 27 v Kent (Chelmsford) 1974. BB: 8–63
(15–115 match) v Warwickshire (Leyton) 1968. BBJPL: 6–18 v Yorks
(Hull) 1969. BBBH: 4–6 v Sussex (Hove) 1973.

Brian Ernest Arthur EDMEADES B Matlock (Derbyshire) 17/9/1941.
RHB, RM. Debut 1961. Cap 1965. 1,000 runs (4)—1,620 runs (av 35.21)
in 1970 best. Took 106 wkts (av 18.59) in 1966. Gillette Man of Match
awards: 1. Benson & Hedges Gold awards: 1. HS: 163 v Leics (Leyton)
1972. HSGC: 52 v Somerset (Westcliff) 1974. HSJPL: 45 v Notts
(Chelmsford) 1969. HSBH: 79 v Kent (Canterbury) 1973. BB: 7–37 v
Glamorgan (Leyton) 1966. BBGC: 4–71 v Glos (Chelmsford) 1973.
BBJPL: 4–17 v Kent (Blackheath) 1970. BBBH: 5–22 v Leics (Ilford)
1973.

Keith William Robert FLETCHER B Worcester 20/5/1944. RHB,
LB. Debut 1962. Cap 1963. Appointed county vice-captain in 1971 and
county captain in 1974. Benefit (£13,000) in 1973. *Wisden* 1973. Tests: 39
between 1968 and 1974. Also played in 4 matches v Rest of the World in
1970. Tours: Pakistan 1966–67, Ceylon and Pakistan 1968–69, Australia
and New Zealand 1970–71, 1974–75, India, Sri Lanka, and Pakistan
1972–73, West Indies 1973–74. 1,000 runs (11)—1,890 runs (av 41.08) in
1968 best. Gillette Man of Match awards: 1. HS: 228* v Sussex (Hastings)
1968. HSGC: 74 v Notts (Nottingham) 1969. HSJPL: 99* v Notts (Ilford)
1974. HSBH: 90 v Surrey (Oval) 1974. BB: 4–50 MCC under-25 v North
Zone (Peshawar) 1966–67.

Graham Alan GOOCH (Norlington Junior HS, Leyton) B Leytonstone
23/7/1953. RHB, RM. Toured West Indies with England Young
Cricketers 1972. Debut 1973. HS: 114* v Leics (Chelmsford) 1974. HSGC:
26 v Shropshire (Wellington) 1974. HSJPL: 27 v Northants (Northampton)
1973.

Brian Ross HARDIE (Larbert HS) B Stenhousemuir 14/1/1950. RHB,
RM. Has played for Stenhousemuir in East of Scotland League. Debut
for Scotland 1970. His father and elder brother K. M. Hardie have also
played for Scotland. Debut for Essex by special registration in 1973.
Cap 1974. Scored 1,168 runs (av 34.35) in 1974. Scored two centuries in
match for Scotland v MCC, Aberdeen 1971, a match not regarded as
first-class. HS: 133 v Warwickshire (Chelmsford) 1974. HSGC: 28 v
Shropshire (Wellington) 1974. HSJPL: 94 v Northants (Northampton)
1973. HSBH: 42* v Cambridge U (Cambridge) 1974.

Robin Nicholas Stuart HOBBS (Raine's Foundation School, Stepney)
B Chippenham (Wilts) 8/5/1942. RHB, LBG. Outstanding cover fielder.
Debut 1961. Cap 1964. Appointed county vice-captain in 1974. Benefit
1974. Tests: 7 between 1967 and 1971. Tours: South Africa 1964–65,
Pakistan 1966–67, West Indies 1967–68, Ceylon and Pakistan 1968–69.
100 wkts (2)—102 wkts (av 21.40) in 1970 best. Hat-trick v Middlesex
(Lord's) 1968 in Gillette Cup. Benson & Hedges Gold awards: 1. HS: 100
v Glamorgan (Ilford) 1968. HSGC: 34 v Lancs (Chelmsford) 1971.
HSJPL: 54* v Yorks (Colchester) 1970. HSBH: 40 v Middlesex (Lord's)
1972. BB: 8–63 (13–164 match) v Glamorgan (Swansea) 1966. BBGC:
4–55 v Wilts (Chelmsford) 1969. BBJPL: 6–22 v Hants (Harlow) 1973.

69

John Kenneth **LEVER** B Ilford 24/2/1949. RHB, LFM. Outfield.
Debut 1967. Cap 1970. Gillette Man of Match awards: 2. HS: 91 v
Glamorgan (Cardiff) 1970. HSJPL: 23 v Worcs (Worcester) 1974.
HSBH: 11* v Surrey (Oval) 1972 and 11 v Surrey (Chelmsford) 1973.
BB: 7–90 v Somerset (Leyton) 1971. BBGC: 5–8 v Middlesex (Westcliff)
1972. BBJPL: 5–18 v Warwickshire (Birmingham) 1972. BBBH: 4–32 v
Kent (Canterbury) 1973.

Kenneth Scott **McEWAN** (Queen's College, Queenstown) B Bedford,
Cape Province, South Africa 16/7/1952. RHB. Debut for Eastern Province
in 1972–73 Currie Cup competition. Played for T. N. Pearce's XI v West
Indians (Scarborough) 1973. Debut for county and cap 1974. Scored
1,056 runs (av 30.56) in 1974. Benson & Hedges Gold awards: 1. HS:
126 v Kent (Dartford) 1974. HSGC: 63 v Somerset (Westcliff) 1974.
HSJPL: 65 v Lancs (Southport) 1974. HSBH: 82 v Kent (Chelmsford)
1974.

Keith Rupert **PONT** B Wanstead 16/1/1953. Brother of Kelvin Pont
who was formerly on MCC staff at Lord's. RHB, RM. Debut 1970.
HS: 113 v Warwickshire (Birmingham) 1973. HSGC: 10 v Kent (Leyton)
1972. HSJPL: 41 v Somerset (Chelmsford) 1973. HSBH: 105 v Sussex
(Chelmsford) 1974. BB: 3–50 v Lancs (Manchester) 1974. Plays hockey
for Brentwood.

Graham John **SAVILLE** (Sir George Monoux GS, Walthamstow) B
Leytonstone 5/2/1944. RHB, LBG. Fine slip fielder. Debut 1963. Left staff
after 1966 season. Played for Norfolk from 1967 to 1969 and for Minor
Counties in 1968 and 1969. Rejoined staff and awarded cap 1970. Left
staff after 1973 season to become Assistant Secretary (Cricket). Played in
one match in 1974 v Lancs (Manchester). Scored 1,133 runs (av 29.81) in
1970. HS: 126* v Glamorgan (Swansea) 1972. HSGC: 73 Norfolk v
Cheshire (Macclesfield) 1968. HSJPL: 35 v Hants (Southampton) 1970.
HSBH: 85* v Middlesex (Lord's) 1972.

Neil **SMITH** (Ossett GS) B Dewsbury 1/4/1949. RHB, WK. Debut
for Yorks 1970. Debut for county by special registration in 1973. HS: 77 v
Hants (Chelmsford) 1974. HSJPL: 14 v Glos (Chelmsford) 1974.

Stuart **TURNER** B Chester 18/7/1943. RHB, RFM. Debut 1965. Cap
1970. Hat-trick v Surrey (Oval) 1971. HS: 121 v Somerset (Taunton)
1970. HSGC: 50 v Lancs (Chelmsford) 1971. HSJPL: 70 v Glos
(Chelmsford) 1974. HSBH: 36 v Sussex (Chelmsford) 1974. BB: 6–87 v
Sussex (Hove) 1974. BBGC: 3–16 v Glamorgan (Ilford) 1971. BBJPL:
4–14 v Hants (Portsmouth) 1969. BBBH: 3–21 v Kent (Canterbury) 1973.

NB The following player whose particulars appeared in the 1974
Annual has been omitted: B. Taylor.

COUNTY AVERAGES

County Championship: Played 20; won 4, drawn 12, lost 3, tied 1
All first-class matches: Played 21; won 4, drawn 13, lost 3, tied 1

BATTING AND FIELDING

Cap		M	I	NO	Runs	HS	Avge	100	50	Ct	St
1974	B. R. Hardie	21	36	2	1168	133	34.35	2	5	16	—
1970	S. Turner	21	32	4	951	118*	33.96	1	6	11	—
1974	K. S. McEwan	21	36	2	1040	126	30.58	2	4	11	—
—	G. A. Gooch	15	25	3	637	114*	28.95	1	2	4	—
—	R. M. O. Cooke	18	29	4	718	100	28.72	1	3	12	—
1967	R. E. East	21	31	6	544	64	21.76	—	4	16	—
1965	B. E. A. Edmeades	19	33	1	673	54*	21.03	—	2	3	—
1967	K. D. Boyce	12	16	0	335	75	20.93	—	1	7	—
1963	K. W. R. Fletcher	8	15	0	276	61	18.40	—	1	5	—
—	N. Smith	19	27	3	406	77	16.92	—	1	28	3
—	K. R. Pont	8	14	1	213	40	16.38	—	—	4	—
1970	J. K. Lever	19	19	3	91	19*	15.16	—	—	8	—
1970	D. L. Acfield	10	9	3	69	31	11.50	—	—	5	—
1964	R. N. S. Hobbs	18	23	8	145	22	9.66	—	—	9	—

Played in one match: G. J. Saville 1 & 41*.

BOWLING

	Type	O	M	R	W	Avge	Best	5 wI	10 wM
S. Turner	RFM	594.5	160	1265	69	18.33	6–87	4	—
K. D. Boyce	RFM	313.4	55	868	35	24.80	6–76	3	1
R. E. East	SLA	532.1	141	1314	47	27.95	5–27	1	—
R. N. S. Hobbs	LBG	325.1	87	907	32	28.34	5–73	1	—
B. E. A. Edmeades	RM	170.4	35	419	13	32.23	3–19	—	—
K. R. Pont	RM	91	20	229	7	32.71	3–50	—	—
D. L. Acfield	OB	258.2	74	575	16	35.93	5–52	1	—
J. K. Lever	LFM	449.2	73	1242	29	42.82	3–38	—	—

Also bowled: R. M. O. Cooke 20-1-90-1; K. W. R. Fletcher 3-0-18-0;
G. A. Gooch 56-11-153-3; B. R. Hardie 2-0-19-0; K. S. McEwan 0.2-0-0-1.

County Records

First-class cricket

Highest innings totals:	For ...692 v Somerset (Taunton)	1895
	Agst...803–4d by Kent (Brentwood)	1934
Lowest innings totals:	For ... 30 v Yorkshire (Leyton)	1901
	Agst... 31 by Derbyshire (Derby) and by Yorkshire (Huddersfield)	1914 & 1935
Highest individual innings:	For ...343* P. A. Perrin v Derbyshire (Chesterfield)	1904
	Agst...332 W. H. Ashdown for Kent (Brentwood)	1934
Best bowling in an innings:	For ...10–32 H. Pickett v Leicestershire (Leyton)	1895
	Agst...10–40 G. Dennett for Gloucestershire (Bristol)	1906
Best bowling in a match:	For ...17–119 W. Mead v Hampshire (Southampton)	1895
	Agst...17–56 C. W. L. Parker for Gloucestershire (Gloucester)	1925

71

ESSEX

Most runs in a season:	2308 (av 56.29) J. O'Connor	1934
runs in a career:	29162 (av 36.18) P. A. Perrin	1896–1928
100s in a season:	9 by J. O'Connor and D. J. Insole	1934 & 1955
100s in a career:	71 by J. O'Connor	1921–1939
wickets in a season:	172 (av 27.13) T. P. B. Smith	1947
wickets in a career:	1611 (av 26.26) T. P. B. Smith	1929–1951

RECORD WICKET STANDS
1st 270 A. V. Avery & T. C. Dodds v Surrey (The Oval) 1946
2nd 294 A. V. Avery & P. A. Gibb v Northampton (Northampton) 1952
3rd 343 P. A. Gibb & R. Horsfall v Kent (Blackheath) 1951
4th 298 A. V. Avery & R. Horsfall v Worcestershire (Clacton) 1948
5th 287 C. T. Ashton & J. O'Connor v Surrey (Brentwood) 1934
6th 206 J. W. H. T. Douglas & J. O'Connor v Gloucestershire (Cheltenham) 1923
    B. R. Knight & R. A. G. Luckin v Middlesex (Brentwood) 1962
7th 261 J. W. H. T. Douglas & J. Freeman v Lancashire (Leyton) 1914
8th 263 D. R. Wilcox & R. M. Taylor v Warwickshire (Southend) 1946
9th 251 J. W. H. T. Douglas & S. N. Hare v Derbyshire (Leyton) 1921
10th 218 F. H. Vigar & T. P. B. Smith v Derbyshire (Chesterfield) 1947

One-day cricket

Highest innings totals:	Gillette Cup	301–9 v Bedfordshire (Chelmsford)	1971
	John Player League	265–6 v Lancs (Chelmsford)	1969
	Benson & Hedges Cup	218 v Surrey (Chelmsford)	1973
Lowest innings totals:	Gillette Cup	100 v Derbyshire (Brentwood)	1965
	John Player League	69 v Derbyshire (Chesterfield)	1974
	Benson & Hedges Cup	123 v Kent (Canterbury)	1973
Highest individual innings:	Gillette Cup	101 B. Ward v Bedfordshire (Chelmsford)	1971
	John Player League	107 B. C. Francis v Lancs (Manchester)	1971
	Benson & Hedges Cup	90 K. W. R. Fletcher v Surrey (Oval)	1974
Best bowling figures:	Gillette Cup	5–8 J. K. Lever v Middlesex (Westcliff)	1972
	John Player League	8–26 K. D. Boyce v Lancs (Manchester)	1971
	Benson & Hedges Cup	5–22 B. E. A. Edmeades v Leics (Ilford)	1973

GLAMORGAN

Formation of present club: 1888.
Colours: Blue and gold.
Badge: Gold daffodil.
County Champions (2): 1948 and 1969.
Gillette Cup third round (3): 1964, 1969, and
1972.

Secretary: W. Wooller, 6 High Street, Cardiff,
CF1 2PW.
Captain: M. J. Khan.

Gregory de Lisle ARMSTRONG B St Michael, Barbados 11/5/1950.
RHB, RF. Debut 1973–74 for Barbados. Debut for county 1974. One
match v Pakistanis (Cardiff). Will be qualified for County Championship
and one-day competitions in 1975. HS: 15* Barbados v Jamaica
(Bridgetown) 1973–74 and 15* v Pakistanis (Cardiff) 1974. BB: 4–45
Barbados v Trinidad (Bridgetown) 1973–74.

Anthony Elton (Tony) CORDLE B St Michael, Barbados 21/9/1940.
RHB, RFM. Debut 1963. Cap 1967. HS: 81 v Cambridge U (Swansea)
1972. HSGC: 36 v Lincs (Swansea) 1974. HJJPL: 87 v Notts (Nottingham) 1971. HSBH: 14* v Somerset (Yeovil) 1973. BB: 9–49 (13–110
match) v Leics (Colwyn Bay) 1969. BBJPL: 4–16 v Somerset (Swansea)
1974. BBBH: 4–14 v Hants (Swansea) 1973.

Roger Clive DAVIS (Blundell's) B Cardiff 15/1/1946. Brother of F. J.
Davis who played for the county. RHB, OB. Debut 1964. Cap 1969.
Missed part of 1971 season owing to severe head injury, through being hit
by the ball whilst fielding at short leg. HS: 134 v Worcs (Cardiff) 1971.
HSGC: 26 v Northants (Northampton) 1972. HSJPL: 58 v Middlesex
(Lord's) 1974. HSBH: 46* v Glos (Swansea) 1972. BB: 6–82 v Glos
(Cheltenham) 1970. BBJPL: 4–48 v Essex (Swansea) 1969. BBBH: 3–39 v
Minor Counties (Swansea) 1973.

Robert David Louis DUDLEY-JONES (Millfield School) B Bridgend
26/5/1952. RHB, RM. Debut 1972. HS: 5 v Worcs (Cardiff) 1973. BB:
4–31 v Hants (Portsmouth) 1972. Played only in 2 Benson & Hedges Cup
matches in 1974. Trained as a teacher at Cardiff College of Education.

Geoffrey Phillip (Geoff) ELLIS (John Bright GS, Llandudno) B
Llandudno (Caernarvonshire) 24/5/1950. RHB, RM. Debut 1970. Benson
& Hedges Gold awards: 1. HS: 1,16 v Middlesex (Cardiff) 1974. HSGC:
16 v Glos (Cardiff) 1973. HSJPL: 28 v Notts (Nottingham) 1973. HSBH:
47* v Minor Counties (Swansea) 1973. BBJPL: 3–22 v Essex (Harlow)
1974. Trained as a teacher at Cardiff College of Education.

David Arthur FRANCIS (Cwmtawe Comprehensive School, Pontardawe)
B Clydach (Glamorgan) 29/11/1953. RHB, OB. Debut 1973 after playing
for 2nd XI in 1971 and 1972. HS: 52* v Leics (Cardiff) 1974. HSBH: 17 v
Hants (Southampton) 1974.

73

Stuart Charles HARRISON (Abersychan GTS) B Cwmbran (Monmouthshire) 21/9/1951. RHB, RM. Debut 1971. Played only in 1 Championship match, 2 John Player League matches and 1 Benson & Hedges Cup match in 1974. HS: 15 v Derbyshire (Derby) 1971. HSJPL: 20* v Middlesex (Cardiff) 1972. BB: 3–55 v Somerset (Cardiff) 1971. BBJPL: 3–47 v Derbyshire (Buxton) 1973. Trained as a teacher at Caerleon College of Education.

Leonard Winston (Len) HILL B Caerleon (Monmouthshire) 14/4/1942. RHB, occasional WK. Cover field. Debut 1964. Cap 1974. HS: 96* v Glos (Swansea) 1974. HSGC: 26 v Essex (Ilford) 1971. HSJPL: 34* v Notts (Swansea) 1974. Soccer (right-half) for Newport County and Swansea City.

John Anthony HOPKINS B Maesteg 16/6/1953. Younger brother of J. D. Hopkins, formerly on staff and who has appeared for Middlesex. RHB, WK. Debut 1970. HS: 88 v Glos (Colwyn Bay) 1971. HSJPL: 46* v Leics (Leicester) 1972. Is training as a teacher at Trinity College, Carmarthen.

Alan JONES B Swansea 4/11/1938. LHB, OB. Joined staff 1955. Debut 1957. Cap 1962. Played for Western Australia in 1963–64. Benefit (£10,000) in 1972. Played one match v Rest of World 1970. 1,000 runs (14) —1,865 runs (av 34.53) in 1966 and 1,862 runs (av 38.00) in 1968 best. Scored two centuries in match (187* and 105*) v Somerset (Glastonbury) 1963. Shared in record partnership for any wicket for county, 330 for 1st wkt with R. C. Fredericks v Northants (Swansea) 1972. Shared in 2nd wkt partnership record for county, 238 with A. R. Lewis v Sussex (Hastings) 1962. Has scored 32 centuries for county to equal record held by W. G. A. Parkhouse. HS: 187* v Somerset (Glastonbury) 1963. HSGC: 85 v Staffs (Stoke) 1971. HSJPL: 90 v Derbyshire (Buxton) 1973. HSBH: 65 v Somerset (Swansea) 1974.

Alan Lewis JONES (Ystalyfera GS and Cwmtawe Comprehensive School) B Alltwen (Glamorgan) 1/6/1957. No relation to A. and E. W. Jones. LHB. Played for 2nd XI in 1972. Debut 1973 at age of 16 years 3 months. HS: 54 v Essex (Swansea) 1974. HSJPL: 50 v Worcs (Cardiff) 1974.

Eifion Wyn JONES B Velindre (Glamorgan) 25/6/1942. Brother of A. Jones. RHB, WK. Debut 1961. Cap 1967. Benefit in 1975. Dismissed 94 batsmen (85 ct 9 st) in 1970. Dismissed 7 batsmen (6 ct 1 st) in innings v Cambridge U (Cambridge) 1970. HS: 146* v Sussex (Hove) 1968. HSGC: 67* v Herts (Swansea) 1969. HSJPL: 48 v Hants (Cardiff) 1971. HSBH: 31 v Somerset (Yeovil) 1973.

MAJID JAHANGIR KHAN (St Anthony's School and Aitchison College, Lahore, Punjab and Cambridge Universities) B Jullundur (India) 28/9/1946. Son of Dr Jahangir Khan, pre-war Indian Test cricketer and Cambridge Blue. RHB, RM/OB. Debut 1961–62 for Lahore B v Khairpur at age of 15 scoring 111* and taking 6–67 and has since played for various Lahore sides. Debut for county and age 1968. Wisden 1969. Blue 1970–72 (capt 1971–72). Appointed county captain in 1973. Played for Queensland in 1973–74 Sheffield Shield competition. Tests: 24 for Pakistan between 1964–65 and 1974, captaining country in 3 Tests. Tours: England 1963 with Pakistan Eaglets, followed by Australia and New

Zealand 1972–73. 1,000 runs (7)—2,074 runs (av 61.00) in 1972 best. Also scored 1,574 runs (av 60.53) in Australia and New Zealand 1972–73. Scored 147* in 89 minutes before lunch with 13 6's and 10 4's and hitting 30 runs off one over from R. C. Davis on third morning of match between Pakistanis and county at Swansea 1967. Scored 147 before lunch v West Indians (Swansea) and 114* before lunch v Worcs (Cardiff) in 1969. Hat-trick v Oxford U (Oxford) 1969. Gillette Man of Match awards: 1. HS: 241 Lahore Greens v Bahawalpur (Lahore) 1965–66. HSUK: 204 v Surrey (Oval) 1972. HSGC: 36 v Bucks (Amersham) 1972. HSJPL: 83 v Lancs (Ebbw Vale) 1972. HSBH: 83 v Hants (Southampton) 1974. BB: 6–67 in debut match. BBUK: 4–18 Pakistan Eaglets v Northants (Peterborough) 1963. BBGC: 5–24 v Northants (Northampton) 1969. BBJPL: 3–13 v Lancs (Manchester) 1971.

Michael John (Mike) LLEWELLYN B Clydach (Glamorgan) 27/11/1953. LHB, OB. Debut 1970. Benson & Hedges Gold awards: 1. HS: 112* v Cambridge U (Swansea) 1972. HSGC: 27 v Glos (Cardiff) 1973. HSJPL: 59 v Sussex (Hove) 1973. HSBH: 63 v Hants (Swansea) 1973. BB: 4–35 v Oxford U (Oxford) 1970.

Barry John LLOYD B Neath 6/9/1953. RHB, OB. Formerly on MCC groundstaff. Debut 1972. HS: 45* v Hants (Portsmouth) 1973. BB: 4–49 v Hants (Portsmouth) 1973. Is training as a teacher at Bangor Normal College.

Kevin James LYONS (Lady Mary's Boys High School, Cardiff) B Cardiff 18/12/1946. RHB, RM. Cover-point. Debut 1967. Appointed assistant coach after 1972 season. Reappeared in 1 John Player League match in both 1973 and 1974. HS: 92 v Cambridge U (Cambridge) 1972. HSGC: 16 v Cornwall (Truro) 1970. HSJPL: 56 v Notts (Nottingham) 1969. Soccer player.

Malcolm Andrew NASH (Wells Cathedral School) B Abergavenny (Monmouthshire) 9/5/1945. LHB, LM. Debut 1966. Cap 1969. Benson & Hedges Gold awards: 1. HS: 89 v Glos (Swansea) 1973. HSGC: 51 v Lincs (Swansea) 1974. HSJPL: 68 v Essex (Purfleet) 1972. HSBH: 92* v Minor Counties (Chippenham) 1972. BB: 7–15 v Somerset (Swansea) 1968. BBGC: 3–14 v Staffs (Stoke) 1971. BBJPL: 5–14 v Derbyshire (Buxton) 1973. BBBH: 4–25 v Minor Counties (Amersham) 1974. Plays hockey and has captained Welsh under-23 XI.

Kim Thomas NORKETT (Monmouth School) B British Military Hospital, Malta 24/12/1955. RHB, RFM. Played in one John Player League match v Hants (Basingstoke) in 1974 whilst still at school. Plays rugby for Newport.

Gwyn RICHARDS B Maesteg 29/11/1951. RHB, OB. Formerly on MCC staff. Debut 1971. HS: 61 v Northants (Swansea) 1974. HSJPL: 17* v Worcs (Worcester) 1973. HSBH: 28 v Glos (Neath) 1974.

John William SOLANKY B Dar-es-Salaam, Tanzania (formerly Tanganyika) 30/6/1942. RHB, RM/OB. Debut 1963–64 for East Africa v MCC (Kampala) and played for Coast Invitation XI v Pakistan International Airways (Mombasa) 1964. Played for Devon from 1967–69. Debut for county 1972. Cap 1973. Benson & Hedges Gold awards: 1.

HS: 71 v Leics (Cardiff) 1974. HSJPL: 45 v Glos (Cardiff) 1972. HSBH: 47 v Minor Counties (Amersham) 1974. BB: 5–37 v Notts (Cardiff) 1972. BBGC: 3–34 v Bucks (Amersham) 1972. BBJPL: 4–23 v Notts (Nottingham) 1973.

Richard James (Richie) THOMAS (West Monmouth GS, Pontypool) B Griffithstown (Monmouthshire) 18/6/1944. RHB, RM. Debut 1974. One match v Lancs (Liverpool) 1974.

David Lawrence WILLIAMS (Neath CGS) B Tonna, Neath 20/11/1946. LHB, RFM. Joined staff and made debut 1969 after playing for 2nd XI in 1967 and 1968. Cap 1971. Benson & Hedges Gold awards: 1. HS: 37* v Essex (Chelmsford) 1969. HSJPL: 10 v Kent (Swansea) 1973. BB: 7–60 v Lancs (Blackpool) 1970. BBGC: 3–15 v Essex (Ilford) 1971. BBJPL: 5–31 v Surrey (Byfleet) 1971. BBBH: 5–30 v Hants (Bournemouth) 1972. Rugby player.

NB The following players whose particulars appeared in the 1974 Annual have been omitted: T. C. Davies, K. M. V. Francis, and A. R. Lewis (retired). The career record of Lewis will be found elsewhere.

COUNTY AVERAGES

County Championship: Played 19; won 2, drawn 10, lost 7, abandoned 1
All first-class matches: Played 20; won 2, drawn 10, lost 8

BATTING AND FIELDING

Cap		M	I	NO	Runs	HS	Avge	100	50	Ct	St
1968	M. J. Khan	6	12	0	451	164	37.58	2	1	2	—
1974	L. W. Hill	14	24	4	718	96*	35.90	—	6	5	—
1962	A. Jones	20	36	1	1121	113	32.02	2	6	6	—
1969	R. C. Davis	19	34	3	752	73	24.25	—	6	9	—
1973	J. W. Solanky	15	25	5	452	71	22.60	—	3	2	—
—	G. P. Ellis	10	18	2	356	116	22.25	1	—	2	—
1960	A. R. Lewis	11	20	1	381	95	20.05	—	2	4	—
—	M. J. Llewellyn	9	17	0	318	61	18.70	—	1	7	—
1967	E. W. Jones	19	30	6	445	67	18.54	—	2	29	2
—	D. A. Francis	9	15	5	183	52*	18.30	—	1	5	—
—	G. Richards	15	28	2	436	61	16.76	—	1	4	—
—	A. L. Jones	4	7	0	108	54	15.42	—	1	—	—
—	J. A. Hopkins	9	15	2	183	39*	14.07	—	—	5	—
1967	A. E. Cordle	14	23	3	201	37	10.05	—	—	3	—
1969	M. A. Nash	17	25	5	220	46	10.00	—	—	7	—
1971	D. L. Williams	20	22	11	84	18	7.63	—	—	2	—
—	B. J. Lloyd	6	10	1	31	8*	3.44	—	—	4	—

Played in one match: G. L. Armstrong 15* & 1 (1 ct); S. C. Harrison did not bat; R. J. Thomas 8*.

BOWLING

	Type	O	M	R	W	Avge	Best	5 wI	10 wM
M. A. Nash	LM	539.5	124	1463	63	23.22	7–126	3	—
D. L. Williams	RFM	511	93	1586	55	28.83	5–67	2	—
A. E. Cordle	RFM	289	39	914	30	30.46	5–101	1	—
J. W. Solanky	RM/OB	290	59	880	24	36.66	5–78	1	—
B. J. Lloyd	OB	75.2	13	278	7	39.71	3–26	—	—
R. C. Davis	OB	444.5	136	956	22	43.45	4–92	—	—

Also bowled: G. L. Armstrong 20-2-101-2; G. P. Ellis 90-15-299-4; S. C. Harrison 14-2-65-1; G. Richards 8-1-33-0; R. J. Thomas 10.2-2-40-1.

County Records
First-class cricket

Highest innings totals:	For ...587–8d v Derbyshire (Cardiff)		1951
	Agst...653–6d by Gloucestershire (Bristol)		1928
Lowest innings totals:	For ... 22 v Lancashire (Liverpool)		1924
	Agst... 33 by Leicestershire (Ebbw Vale)		1965
Highest individual innings:	For ...287*E. Davies v Gloucestershire (Newport)		1939
	Agst...302* W. R. Hammond for Glos (Bristol)		1934
	302 W. R. Hammond for Glos (Newport)		1939
Best bowling in an innings:	For ...10–51 J. Mercer v Worcs (Worcester)		1936
	Agst...10–18 G. Geary for Leics (Pontypridd)		1929
Best bowling in a match:	For ...17–212 J. C. Clay v Worcs (Swansea)		1937
	Agst...16–96 G. Geary for Leics (Pontypridd)		1929
Most runs in a season:	2071 (av 49.30) W. G. A. Parkhouse		1959
runs in a career:	26104 (av 27.82) E. Davies	1924–1954	
100s in a season:	7 by W. G. A. Parkhouse		1950
100s in a career:	32 by W. G. A. Parkhouse	1948–1964	
	32 by A. Jones	1957–1974	
wickets in a season:	176 (av 17.34) J. C. Clay		1937
wickets in a career:	2174 (av 20.95) D. J. Shepherd	1950–1972	

RECORD WICKET STANDS
1st 330 A. Jones & R. C. Fredericks v Northamptonshire (Swansea) 1972
2nd 238 A. Jones & A. R. Lewis v Sussex (Hastings) 1962
3rd 313 E. Davies & W. E. Jones v Essex (Brentwood) 1948
4th 263 G. Lavis & C. Smart v Worcestershire (Cardiff) 1934
5th 264 M. Robinson & S. W. Montgomery v Hampshire (Bournemouth) 1949
6th 230 W. E. Jones & B. L. Muncer v Worcestershire (Worcester) 1953
7th 195* W. Wooller & W. E. Jones v Lancashire (Liverpool) 1947
8th 202 D. Davies & J. J. Hills v Sussex (Eastbourne) 1928
9th 203* J. J. Hills & J. C. Clay v Worcestershire (Swansea) 1929
10th 131* C. Smart & W. D. Hughes v South Africans (Cardiff) 1935

One-day cricket

Highest innings totals:	Gillette Cup	244–6 v Herts (Swansea)	1969
	John Player League	234–6 v Worcs (Cardiff)	1974
	Benson & Hedges Cup	208–9 v Hants (Bournemouth)	1972
Lowest innings totals:	Gillette Cup	76 v Northants (Northampton)	1968
	John Player League	65 v Surrey (Oval)	1969
	Benson & Hedges Cup	68 v Lancs (Manchester)	1973
Highest individual innings:	Gillette Cup	103* B. Hedges v Somerset (Cardiff)	1963
	John Player League	90 A. Jones v Derbyshire (Buxton)	1973
	Benson & Hedges Cup	92* M. A. Nash v Minor Counties (Chippenham)	1972
Best bowling figures:	Gillette Cup	5–21 P. M. Walker v Cornwall (Truro)	1970
	John Player League	6–36 G. C. Kingston v Derbyshire (Ebbw Vale)	1969
	Benson & Hedges Cup	5–30 D. L. Williams v Hants (Bournemouth)	1972

GLOUCESTERSHIRE

Formation of present club: 1871.
Colours: Blue, gold, brown, sky-blue, green, and red.
Badge: Coat of Arms of the City and County of Bristol.
County Champions (2): 1876 and 1877.
Joint Champions (2): 1873 and 1880.
Gillette Cup Winners: 1973.
Benson & Hedges Cup semi-finalists: 1972.

Secretary: G. W. Parker OBE, County Ground, Nevil Road, Bristol, BS7 9EJ.
Captain: A. S. Brown.

Andrew James BRASSINGTON B Bagnall (Staffordshire) 9/8/1954. RHB, WK. Debut 1974. HS: 8* v Notts (Cheltenham) 1974. Plays soccer as goalkeeper.

Anthony Stephen (Tony) BROWN (Fairfield GS, Bristol) B Bristol 24/6/1936. RHB, RM. Debut 1953. Cap 1957. Appointed county captain in 1969. Benefit 1969. Appointed assistant secretary in 1971. Scored 1,149 runs (av 20.15) in 1964. 100 wkts (2)—110 wkts (av 23.08) in 1959 and 110 wkts (av 26.40) in 1962. Hat-trick v Glamorgan (Swansea) 1973. Held 7 catches in innings v Notts (Nottingham) 1966 to equal world record held by M. J. Stewart (Surrey). Gillette Man of Match awards: 2. Benson & Hedges Gold awards: 1. HS: 116 v Somerset (Bristol) 1971. HSGC: 77* v Sussex (Lord's) 1973. HSJPL: 50 v Kent (Cheltenham) 1970. HSBH: 28* v Hants (Southampton) 1973. BB: 8–80 v Essex (Leyton) 1963. BBGC: 4–17 v Kent (Bristol) 1968. BBJPL: 4–24 v Somerset (Bristol) 1973. BBBH: 4–43 v Middlesex (Lord's) 1972.

Jack DAVEY (Tavistock GS) B Tavistock (Devon) 4/9/1944. LHB, LFM. Played for Devonshire in 1964 and 1965. Debut 1966. Cap 1971. HS: 37* v Indians (Gloucester) 1974. BB: 6–95 v Notts (Gloucester) 1967. BBGC: 4–35 v Essex (Chelmsford) 1973. BBJPL: 4–17 v Leics (Leicester) 1969. BBBH: 3–26 v Somerset (Taunton) 1972.

John Henry DIXON (Monkton Coombe School and Oxford) B Bournemouth 3/3/1954. Tall (6ft 5ins). RHB, RM. Played in University's first Benson & Hedges Cup match v Leics 1973. Debut for county against University 1973. HS: 7 v Warwickshire (Birmingham) 1974. BB: 5–51 v Oxford U (Oxford) 1973.

Malcolm Stephen Thomas DUNSTAN B Redruth (Cornwall) 14/10/1950. RHB, RM. Played for Cornwall from 1969 to 1972. Debut for county 1971. Joined staff by special registration in 1973. HS: 52 v Warwickshire (Birmingham) 1974. Scored 201* for 2nd XI v Glamorgan 2nd XI (Bristol) 1974.

James Clive (Jim) FOAT (Millfield School) B Salford Priors (Warwickshire) 21/11/1952. RHB, RM. Debut 1972. HS: 62* v Surrey (Oval) 1974. HSGC: 20 v Lancs (Bristol) 1974. HSJPL: 60 v Glamorgan (Bristol) 1973. HSBH: 10* v Middlesex (Lord's) 1972.

David Anthony GRAVENEY (Millfield School) B Bristol 2/1/1953. Son of J. K. Graveney. RHB, SLA. Debut 1972. HS: 50* v Leics (Leicester) 1974. HSGC: 44 v Surrey (Bristol) 1973. HSJPL: 28* v Essex (Gloucester) 1973. BB: 8–85 v Notts (Cheltenham) 1974. BBJPL: 4–22 v Hants (Lydney) 1974.

Alastair James HIGNELL (Denstone College and Cambridge) B Cambridge 4/9/1955. RHB, LB. Scored 117* and 78* for England Schools v All India Schools (Birmingham) 1973 and 133 for England Young Cricketers v West Indies Young Cricketers (Arundel) 1974. Debut 1974. HS: 27 v Notts (Cheltenham) 1974. Entered University 1974. Blue for rugby (full-back) 1974.

Roger David Verdon KNIGHT (Dulwich College and Cambridge) B Streatham 6/9/1946. LHB, RM. Debut for Cambridge U 1967. Blues 1967–70. Debut for Surrey 1968. Debut for Glos by special registration 1971. Cap 1971. 1,000 runs (5)—1,350 runs (av 38.57) in 1974 best. Gillette Man of Match awards: 3. Benson & Hedges Gold awards: 2. HS: 164* Cambridge U v Essex (Cambridge) 1970. HSGC: 75 v Glamorgan (Cardiff) 1973. HSJPL: 58 v Hants (Bristol) 1972. HSBH: 92 v Middlesex (Lord's) 1972. BB: 6–44 v Northants (Northampton) 1974. BBGC: 5–39 v Surrey (Bristol) 1971. BBJPL: 4–19 Surrey v Northants (Leatherhead) 1969. BBBH: 3–40 v Hants (Moreton-in-Marsh) 1972. Plays rugby.

Julian Thomas PAGE (Henbury Comprehensive School, Bristol and Cambridge) B Clifton, Bristol 1/5/1954. LHB, LM. Debut for University (two matches) 1974. Played in one John Player League match for county v Lancs (Manchester) 1974, but has yet to appear for county in a first-class match. HS: 11 Cambridge U v Notts (Cambridge) 1974.

Michael John (Mike) PROCTER (Hilton College, Natal) B Durban 15/9/1946. RHB, RF. Can also bowl OB. Vice-captain of South African Schools team to England 1963. Debut for county 1965 in one match v South Africans. Returned home to make debut for Natal in 1965–66 Currie Cup competition. Joined staff in 1968. Cap 1968. *Wisden* 1969. Transferred to Western Province for 1969–70 Currie Cup competition and Rhodesia in 1970–71. Appointed county vice-captain in 1971 and is captain of Rhodesia. Benefit in 1975. Tests: 7 for South Africa v Australia 1966–67 and 1969–70. Played in 5 matches for Rest of World v England in 1970. 1,000 runs (5)—1,786 runs (av 45.79) in 1971 best. Took 108 wkts (av 15.02) in 1969. Scored 6 centuries in 6 consecutive innings for Rhodesia 1970–71 to equal world record. Scored two centuries in match (114 and 131) for Rhodesia v International Wanderers (Salisbury) 1972–73. Hat-trick v Essex (Westcliff) 1972—all lbw—and also scored a century in the match. Gillette Man of Match awards: 2. Benson & Hedges Gold awards: 1. HS: 254 Rhodesia v Western Province (Salisbury) 1970–71. HSUK: 167 v Derbyshire (Chesterfield) 1971. HSGC: 107 v Sussex (Hove) 1971. HSJPL: 109* v Warwickshire (Cheltenham) 1972. HSBH: 154* v Somerset (Taunton) 1972. BB: 9–71 Rhodesia v Transvaal (Bulawayo) 1972–73. BBUK: 7–65 v Worcs (Worcester) 1969. BBGC: 3–20 v Sussex (Hove) 1971. BBJPL: 5–10 v Sussex (Arundel) 1972. BBBH: 5–26 v Somerset (Taunton) 1972. Plays rugby, hockey, tennis, golf, and squash rackets.

GLOUCESTERSHIRE

SADIQ MOHAMMAD B Junagadh (India) 3/5/1945. LHB, LBG. Youngest of family of five cricket-playing brothers which include Hanif and Mushtaq Mohammad. Debut in Pakistan 1959–60 at age of 14 years 9 months and has played subsequently for various Karachi sides and Pakistan International Airways. Played for Northants 2nd XI in 1967 and 1968, for Nelson in Lancs League in 1968, and subsequently for Polok, Glasgow in Scottish Western Union. Played for D. H. Robins' XI v Oxford U 1969 and for Essex v Jamaica XI in 1970. Debut for county 1972. Cap 1973. Tests: 18 for Pakistan between 1969–70 and 1974. Tours: Pakistan to England 1971 and 1974, Australia and New Zealand 1972–73. 1,000 runs (2)—1,586 runs (av 46.52) in 1974 best. Scored 1,169 runs (av 41.75) in Australia and New Zealand 1972–73. Benson & Hedges Gold awards: 3. HS: 184* v New Zealanders (Bristol) 1973. HSGC: 56 v Essex (Chelmsford) 1973. HSJPL: 93 v Hants (Bristol) 1972. HSBH: 128 v Minor Counties (Bristol) 1974. BB: 5–29 Pakistan International Airways v Dacca (Dacca) 1964–65 and 5–29 Karachi Blues v Lahore Greens (Karachi) 1970–71. BBUK: 5–37 v Kent (Bristol) 1973. BBJPL: 3–27 v Hants (Bristol) 1972. BBBH: 3–20 v Minor Counties (Bristol) 1972.

Julian Howard SHACKLETON (Millfield School) B Todmorden (Yorks) 29/1/1952. Son of D. Shackleton. RHB, RM. Debut 1971. HS: 18 v Oxford U (Oxford) 1973. BB: 4-38 v Surrey (Bristol) 1971.

David Robert SHEPHERD (Barnstaple GS) B Bideford (Devon) 27/12/1940. RHB, RM. Played for Devonshire from 1959 to 1964. Played for Minor Counties v Australians 1964. Debut 1965 scoring 108 in first match v Oxford U. Cap 1969. 1,000 runs (2)—1,079 runs (av 26.97) in 1970 best. Gillette Man of Match awards: 1. HS: 153 v Middlesex (Bristol) 1968. HSGC: 72* v Surrey (Bristol) 1973. HSJPL: 81 v Warwickshire (Cheltenham) 1973. HSBH: 81 v Hants (Bristol) 1974. Has played rugby for Bideford.

Andrew Willis STOVOLD (Filton HS) B Bristol 19/3/1951. RHB, WK. Toured West Indies with England Young Cricketers 1972. Played for 2nd XI since 1971. Debut 1973. HS: 102 v Notts (Cheltenham) 1974. HSGC: 18* v Worcs (Worcester) 1973. HSJPL: 60* v Northants (Bristol) 1973.

Philip Leslie THORN (Cotham GS) B Bristol 17/11/1951. RHB, SLA. Debut 1974. HS: 25 v Worcs (Cheltenham) 1974. Studied at Manchester University and Nottingham College of Education and is a teacher.

Syed ZAHEER ABBAS B Sialkot (Pakistan) 24/7/1947. RHB, OB. Wears glasses. Debut for Karachi Whites 1965–66, subsequently playing for Pakistan International Airways. *Wisden* 1971. Debut for county 1972. Tests: 15 for Pakistan between 1969–70 and 1974. Played in 5 matches for Rest of the World v Australia 1971–72. Tours: Pakistan to England 1971 and 1974, Australia and New Zealand 1972–73. Rest of the World to Australia 1971–72. 1,000 runs (3)—1,508 runs (av 55.85) in 1971 best. Scored 1,597 runs (av 84.05) in Pakistan 1973–74—the record aggregate for a Pakistan season. Scored 4 centuries in 4 consecutive innings in 1970–71. Was dismissed, hit the ball twice, for Pakistan International Airways v Karachi Blues (Karachi) 1969–70. HS: 274 Pakistan v England (Birmingham) 1971, sharing in record 2nd wkt partnership for

80

Pakistan first-class cricket 291 with Mushtaq Mohammad. HSGC: 45 v Essex (Chelmsford) 1973. HSJPL: 92 v Notts (Nottingham) 1972. HSBH: 24 v Hants (Southampton) 1973. BB: 4–54 Pakistan Public Works Department v Karachi (Karachi) 1968–69.

NB The following players whose particulars appeared in the 1974 Annual have been omitted: M. G. Heal, M. J. Hewett, C. A. Milton (retired), J. B. Mortimore (retired), R. B. Nicholls (retired) and R. Swetman (retired). The career records of Milton, Mortimore, Nicholls and Swetman will be found elsewhere in this Annual.

A. R. Windows re-appeared in two John Player League matches in 1974, but has not been included.

COUNTY AVERAGES

County Championship: Played 19; won 4, drawn 6, lost 9, abandoned
All first-class matches: Played 21; won 5, drawn 6, lost 10

BATTING AND FIELDING

Cap		M	I	NO	Runs	HS	Avge	100	50	Ct	St
1971	R. D. V. Knight	21	36	5	1273	144	41.06	4	4	12	—
1968	M. J. Procter	19	33	3	1033	157	34.43	2	6	10	—
1973	Sadiq Mohammad	5	8	0	271	88	33.87	—	2	7	—
—	Zaheer Abbas	5	7	0	207	112	29.57	1	—	2	—
1969	D. R. Shepherd	19	30	0	747	101	24.90	2	3	7	—
1957	R. B. Nicholls	13	23	2	512	68	24.38	—	6	2	—
—	A. W. Stovold	15	28	1	652	102	24.14	1	2	13	1
1949	C. A. Milton	12	19	1	413	76	22.94	—	2	17	—
1957	A. S. Brown	21	34	2	572	62	17.87	—	2	19	—
—	J. C. Foat	10	16	1	241	62*	16.06	—	1	7	—
—	M. S. T. Dunstan	6	9	0	143	52	15.88	—	1	1	—
1972	R. Swetman	6	8	4	63	14*	15.75	—	—	12	2
1971	J. Davey	14	20	11	137	37*	15.22	—	—	2	—
—	D. A. Graveney	18	25	3	282	50*	12.81	—	1	4	—
—	A. J. Hignell	8	14	1	161	27	12.38	—	—	9	—
1954	J. B. Mortimore	20	29	4	287	63	11.48	—	1	4	—
—	P. L. Thorn	4	6	2	45	25	11.25	—	—	4	—
—	J. H. Shackleton	6	8	4	34	11	8.50	—	—	3	—
—	A. J. Brassington	4	6	2	17	8*	4.25	—	—	4	1
—	J. H. Dixon	5	6	1	13	7	2.60	—	—	1	—

BOWLING

	Type	O	M	R	W	Avge	Best	5 wI	10 wM
M. J. Procter	RF	311.3	80	776	47	16.51	5–29	1	—
D. A. Graveney	SLA	384.5	105	1014	47	21.57	8–85	3	1
A. S. Brown	RM	346.4	86	925	35	26.42	5–49	1	—
J. Davey	LFM	286	46	812	26	31.23	3–49	—	—
Sadiq Mohammad	LBG	66	20	202	6	33.66	3–59	—	—
R.D.V. Knight	RM	343.3	78	999	29	34.44	6–44	1	—
J. B. Mortimore	OB	511.4	110	1403	30	46.76	4–26	—	—
J. H. Shackleton	RM	103	19	379	6	63.16	4–108	—	—

Also bowled: J. H. Dixon 82.4-11-323-4; R. B. Nicholls 3-0-12-0; D. R. Shepherd 5.5-2-12-0; P. L. Thorn 48-5-227-4.

County Records

First-class cricket

Highest innings totals:	For ...653–6d v Glamorgan (Bristol)	1928
	Agst...774–7d by Australians (Bristol)	1948
Lowest innings totals:	For ... 17 v Australians (Cheltenham)	1896
	Agst... 12 by Northamptonshire (Gloucester)	1907
Highest individual innings:	For ...318* W. G. Grace v Yorkshire (Cheltenham)	1876
	Agst...296 A. O. Jones for Notts (Nottingham)	1903
Best bowling in an innings:	For ...10–40 G. Dennett v Essex (Bristol)	1906
	Agst...10–66 A. A. Mailey for Aust (Cheltenham)	1921
	and K. Smales for Notts (Stroud)	1956
Best bowling in a match:	For ...17–56 C. W. L. Parker v Essex (Gloucester)	1925
	Agst...15–87 A. J. Conway for Worcestershire (Moreton-in-Marsh)	1914
Most runs in a season:	2860 (av 69.75) W. R. Hammond	1933
runs in a career:	33664 (av 57.05) W.R.Hammond	1920–1951
100s in a season:	13 by W. R. Hammond	1938
100s in a career:	113 by W. R. Hammond	1920–1951
wickets in a season:	222 (av 16.80 & 16.37) T. W. Goddard	1937 & 1947
wickets in a career:	3171 (av 19.43) C. W. L. Parker	1903–1935

RECORD WICKET STANDS

1st 395	D. M. Young & R. B. Nicholls v Oxford U (Oxford)	1962
2nd 256	C. T. M. Pugh & T. W. Graveney v Derbyshire (Chesterfield)	1960
3rd 336	W. R. Hammond & B. H. Lyon v Leicestershire (Leicester)	1933
4th 321	W. R. Hammond & W. L. Neale v Leicestershire (Gloucester)	1937
5th 261	W. G. Grace & W. O. Moberley v Yorkshire (Cheltenham)	1876
6th 320	G. L. Jessop & J. H. Board v Sussex (Hove)	1902
7th 248	W. G. Grace & E. L. Thomas v Sussex (Hove)	1896
8th 239	W. R. Hammond & A. E. Wilson v Lancashire (Bristol)	1938
9th 193	W. G. Grace & S. A. Kitcat v Sussex (Bristol)	1896
10th 131	W. R. Gouldsworthy & J. G. Bessant v Somerset (Bristol)	1923

One-day cricket

Highest innings totals:	Gillette Cup	327–7 v Berkshire (Reading)	1966
	John Player League	251–9 v Somerset (Bristol)	1974
	Benson & Hedges Cup	282 v Hants (Bristol)	1974
Lowest innings totals:	Gillette Cup	86 v Sussex (Hove)	1969
	John Player League	82 v Hants (Lydney)	1974
	Benson & Hedges Cup	70 v Hants (Moreton-in-Marsh)	1972
Highest individual innings:	Gillette Cup	127 R. B. Nicholls v Berks (Reading)	1966
	John Player League	127* D. M. Green v Hants (Bristol)	1970
	Benson & Hedges Cup	154* M. J. Procter v Somerset (Taunton)	1972

Best bowling figures:	Gillette Cup	5–39 R. D. V. Knight v Surrey (Bristol)	1971
	John Player League	5–10 M. J. Procter v Sussex (Arundel)	1972
	Benson & Hedges Cup	5–26 M. J. Procter v Somerset (Taunton)	1972

HAMPSHIRE

Formation of present club: 1863.
Colours: Blue, gold, and white.
Badge: Tudor rose and crown.
County Champions (2): 1961 and 1973.
Gillette Cup semi-finalists: 1966.
John Player League runners-up: 1969.

Secretary: E. D. R. Eagar, County Cricket
  Ground, Northlands Road, Southampton, SO9 2TY.
Captain: R. M. C. Gilliat.

Nigel Geoffrey COWLEY B Shaftesbury (Dorset) 1/3/1953. RHB. OB. Debut 1974. HS: 43 v Leics (Portsmouth) 1974. BB: 3–31 v Glamorgan (Southampton) 1974.

Richard Michael Charles GILLIAT (Charterhouse School and Oxford) B Ware (Herts) 20/5/1944. LHB, LB. Fine field in any position. Debut for Oxford U 1964. Blue 1964–67 (capt 1966). Debut for county 1966. Appointed assistant secretary in 1967, county vice-captain in 1969, and captain in 1971. Cap 1969. 1,000 runs (2)—1,386 runs (av 39.60) in 1969 best. HS: 223* v Warwickshire (Southampton) 1969. HSGC: 40 v Beds (Goldington) 1968. HSJPL: 65 v Lancs (Manchester) 1969. HSBH: 66* v Glamorgan (Southampton) 1974. Blue for soccer 1964–66 (capt in 1966).

Cuthbert Gordon GREENIDGE B St Peter, Barbados 1/5/1951. RHB, RM. Debut 1970. Cap 1972. Has subsequently played for Barbados. Tour: West Indies to India and Pakistan 1974–75. 1,000 runs (4)—1,656 runs (av 48.70) in 1973 best. Benson & Hedges Gold awards: 2. HS: 273* D. H. Robins' XI v Pakistanis (Eastbourne) 1974. HSGC: 100 v Kent (Canterbury) 1973. HSJPL: 102 v Sussex (Hove) 1974. HSBH: 173* v Minor Counties (Amersham) 1973—record for all one-day competitions—and shared in partnership of 285* for second wicket with D. R. Turner—the record partnership for all one-day competitions. BB: 5–49 v Surrey (Southampton) 1971.

Robert Stephen (Bob) HERMAN B Southampton 30/11/1946. Son of O. W. ('Lofty') Herman (former Hants player and first-class umpire). RHB, RFM. Debut for Middlesex 1965. Cap 1969. Not re-engaged after 1970 season, but recalled for 1971 after A. N. Connolly retired. Not re-engaged again after 1971 season and made debut for Hants in 1972. Cap 1972. Played for Border in 1972–73 Currie Cup competition. Benson & Hedges Gold awards: 1. HS: 56 v Worcs (Portsmouth) 1972. HSGC: 25 Middlesex v Essex (Lord's) 1968. HSJPL: 16* Middlesex v Sussex (Hove) 1969. HSBH: 11 v Somerset (Yeovil) 1972. BB: 8–42 v Warwickshire

(Portsmouth) 1972. BBGC: 6–42 Middlesex v Surrey (Lord's) 1968. BBJPL: 4–22 v Warwickshire (Birmingham) 1972. BBBH: 4–20 v Glos (Moreton-in-Marsh) 1972.

Michael John HILL (Abingdon School) B Harwell (Berks) 1/7/1951. LHB, WK. Played for Worcs and Hants 2nd XIs 1970. Joined county staff 1971. Debut 1973. One match v West Indians (Southampton) 1973. Did not play in 1974. HS: 17* v West Indians (Southampton) 1973.

Trevor Edward JESTY B Gosport 2/6/1948. RHB, RM. Good field in any position. Debut 1966. Cap 1971. Played for Border in 1973–74 Currie Cup competition. Gillette Man of Match awards: 1. Benson & Hedges Gold awards: 2. Took 3 wkts in 4 balls v Somerset (Portsmouth) 1969. HS: 90 v Kent (Basingstoke) 1974. HSGC: 62* v Notts (Nottingham) 1972. HSJPL: 62 v Lancs (Bournemouth) 1974. HSBH: 79 v Somerset (Taunton) 1974. BB: 5–24 v Lancs (Southport) 1973. BBGC: 4–32 v Notts (Nottingham) 1972. BBJPL: 4–11 v Glos (Portsmouth) 1969.

Richard Victor LEWIS (Peter Symond's School, Winchester) B Winchester 6/8/1947. RHB, LB. Useful field. Debut 1967. HS: 136 v Glos (Bristol) 1974. HSGC: 14 v Kent (Canterbury) 1973. HSJPL: 66 v Worcs (Dudley) and 66 v Somerset (Southampton) 1969. HSBH: 37* v Glos (Southampton) 1973. Plays soccer.

Thomas James (Tom) MOTTRAM (Quarry Bank Comprehensive School, Liverpool) B Liverpool 7/9/1945. Tall (6ft 4in). RHB, RM. Played in one John Player League match in 1971. Debut 1972. Did not play in 1974. HS: 15* v Notts (Bournemouth) 1973. BB: 6–63 v Warwickshire (Coventry) 1973. BBGC: 3–51 v Lancs (Bournemouth) 1972. BBJPL: 4–35 v Notts (Bournemouth) 1972. BBBH: 3–28 v Minor Counties (Amersham) 1973. Has studied at Edinburgh University and Loughborough College.

Andrew Joseph (Andy) MURTAGH (St Joseph's College, Beulah Hill, London) B Dublin 6/5/1949. RHB. Played for Surrey 2nd XI 1967–68 and for county 2nd XI since 1969. Debut 1973. Played for Eastern Province in 1973–74 Currie Cup competition. Did not play in 1974. HS: 47 v Sussex (Hove) 1973.

John Michael RICE (Brockley CGS, London) B Chandler's Ford (Hants) 23/10/1949. RHB, RM. On Surrey staff 1970, but not re-engaged. Debut 1971. HS: 29 v Sussex (Hove) 1974. HSJPL: 10* v Lancs (Bournemouth) 1972. BB: 4–64 v Sussex (Bournemouth) 1972. BBGC: 3–45 v Notts (Nottingham) 1972. BBJPL: 4–25 v Lancs (Manchester) 1971.

Barry Anderson RICHARDS (Durban HS) B Durban 21/7/1945. RHB, OB. Captain of South African Schools team to England 1963. Debut for Natal 1964–65. Appeared for Glos in one match in 1965 v South Africans, but decided not to qualify and returned home. Joined Hants in 1968 and scored 2,395 runs (av 47.90) in first full season, including over 2,000 runs in county Championship. Cap 1968. *Wisden* 1968. Played for South Australia in 1970–71. Tests: 4 for South Africa v Australia 1969–70. Played in 5 matches for Rest of World v England 1970. Scored two centuries in match (130 and 104*) v Northants (Northampton) 1968. 1,000 runs (7)—2,395 runs (av 47.90) in 1968 best. Has also scored over

1,000 runs in 1969–70, 1971–72, 1972-73 and 1973–74 seasons in South Africa—his aggregate of 1,285 runs (av 80.31) in 1973–74 being a record for a South African. Also scored 1,538 runs (av 109.86) in Australia 1970–71. Gillette Man of Match awards: 3. Benson & Hedges Gold awards: 2. HS: 356 South Australia v Western Australia (Perth) 1970–71 scoring 325* on first day of match. HSUK: 240 v Warwickshire (Coventry) 1973. HSGC: 129 v Lancs (Bournemouth) 1972. HSJPL: 155* v Yorks (Hull) 1970, record for the competition. HSBH: 129 v Glos (Bristol) 1974. BB: 7–63 v Rest of World (Bournemouth) 1968.

Anderson Montgomery Everton (Andy) ROBERTS B Urlings Village, Antigua 29/1/1951. RHB, RF. Debut for Leeward Islands v Windward Islands 1969–70 and has played subsequently for Combined Islands in Shell Shield competition. Debut 1973. Cap 1974. Tests: 1 West Indies v England 1973–74. Tours: West Indies to India and Pakistan 1974–75. Took 119 wkts (av 13.62) in 1974. Benson & Hedges Gold awards: 1. HS: 48* President's XI v MCC (Bridgetown) 1973–74. HSUK: 15* v Leics (Portsmouth) 1974. HSJPL: 21* v Surrey (Oval) 1974. BB: 8–47 v Glamorgan (Cardiff) 1974. BBJPL: 5–13 v Sussex (Hove) 1974. BBBH: 4–25 v Minor Counties (Portsmouth) 1974.

Peter James SAINSBURY B Southampton 13/6/1934. RHB, SLA, and good field anywhere. Debut 1954. Cap 1955. Benefit (£6,035) in 1965. Wisden 1973. Testimonial in 1974. Tour: Pakistan 1955–56. 1,000 runs (6)—1,533 runs (av 30.05) in 1961 best. 100 wkts (2)—107 wkts (av 17.51) in 1971 best, taking 60 wkts in last 8 matches of the season. Scored 959 runs in 1971 to miss double by 41 runs. Held 56 catches in 1957. Gillette Man of Match awards: 3. HS: 163 v Oxford U (Oxford) 1962. HSGC: 76 v Norfolk (Southampton) 1965. HSJPL: 42 v Essex (Portsmouth) 1974. HSBH: 42 v Somerset (Bournemouth) 1974. BB: 8–76 v Glos (Portsmouth) 1971. BBGC: 7–30 v Norfolk (Southampton) 1965. BBJPL: 4–20 v Glamorgan (Basingstoke) 1974. BBBH: 4–17 v Glos (Moreton-in-Marsh) 1972.

George Robert (Bob) STEPHENSON (Derby School) B Derby 19/11/1942. RHB, WK. Debut for Derbyshire 1967 following injury to R. W. Taylor. Joined Hants by special registration in 1969 following resignation of B. S. V. Timms. Cap 1969. Dismissed 80 batsmen (73 ct 7 st) in 1970. HS: 82 v Sussex (Bournemouth) 1970. HSGC: 29 v Notts (Nottingham) 1972. HSJPL: 20* v Warwickshire (Basingstoke) 1973. HSBH: 29* v Somerset (Taunton) 1974. Soccer for Derby County, Shrewsbury Town, and Rochdale.

Michael Norman Somerset TAYLOR (Amersham College) B Amersham (Bucks) 12/11/1942. Twin brother of D. J. S. Taylor of Somerset. RHB, RM. Close field. Played for Buckinghamshire in 1961–62. Debut for Notts 1964. Cap 1967. Not re-engaged after 1972 season and made debut for Hants in 1973. Cap 1973. Took 99 wkts (av 21.00) in 1968. Hat-trick Notts v Kent (Dover) 1965. Gillette Man of Match awards: 1. Benson & Hedges Gold awards: 1 (for Notts). HS: 105 Notts v Lancs (Nottingham) 1967. HSGC: 58 Notts v Hants (Nottingham) 1972. HSJPL: 44 v Worcs (Worcester) 1973. HSBH: 41 v Minor Counties (Portsmouth) 1974. BB: 7–53 v Glos (Bournemouth) 1973. BBGC: 4–31 Notts v Lancs (Nottingham) 1968. BBJPL: 4–20 Notts v Surrey (Nottingham) 1969. BBBH: 3–15 v Somerset (Taunton) 1974.

85

David Roy TURNER B Chippenham (Wilts) 5/2/1949. LHB, RM.
Fine field in any position. Played for Wiltshire in 1965. Debut 1966.
Cap 1970. 1,000 runs (3)—1,165 runs (av 32.36) in 1970 best. Benson &
Hedges Gold awards: 1. HS: 181* v Surrey (Oval) 1969. HSGC: 68 v
Yorks (Bradford) 1974. HSJPL: 99* v Glos (Bristol) 1972. HSBH: 123* v
Minor Counties (Amersham) 1973.

COUNTY AVERAGES

County Championship: Played 19; won 10, drawn 6, lost 3, abandoned 1
All first-class matches: Played 21; won 10, drawn 8, lost 3

BATTING AND FIELDING

Cap		M	I	NO	Runs	HS	Avge	100	50	Ct	St
1968	B. A. Richards	18	25	4	1297	225*	61.76	3	6	21	—
1969	R. M. C. Gilliat	21	29	3	977	106	37.57	1	8	18	—
1970	D. R. Turner	21	29	2	977	152	36.18	3	5	7	—
1955	P. J. Sainsbury	21	26	8	599	98	33.27	—	4	10	—
1972	C. G. Greenidge	21	31	1	804	120	26.80	1	6	22	—
1969	G. R. Stephenson	21	24	7	390	69*	22.94	—	2	61	1
1971	T. E. Jesty	21	28	2	571	90	21.96	—	3	16	—
1973	M. N. S. Taylor	21	24	2	479	68	21.77	—	3	12	—
—	N. G. Cowley	11	13	1	242	43	20.16	—	1	1	—
—	R. V. Lewis	10	15	1	250	136	17.85	1	—	9	—
—	J. M. Rice	3	4	1	51	29	17.00	—	—	3	—
1972	R. S. Herman	21	22	3	177	23	9.31	—	—	8	—
1974	A. M. E. Roberts	21	20	10	67	15*	6.70	—	—	2	—

BOWLING

	Type	O	M	R	W	Avge	Best	5 wI	10 wM
A.M.E. Roberts	RF	727.4	198	1621	119	13.62	8–47	6	—
M.N.S. Taylor	RM	541	147	1259	72	17.48	6–26	3	—
R. S. Herman	RFM	657.4	202	1426	73	19.53	6–15	3	—
P. J. Sainsbury	SLA	425.2	196	813	35	23.22	4–30	—	—
N. G. Cowley	OB	71	31	148	6	24.66	3–31	—	—
T. E. Jesty	RM	321.1	96	749	26	28.80	4–47	—	—

Also bowled: J. M. Rice 5-3-9-0; B. A. Richards 32-13-67-2.

County Records

First-class cricket

Highest innings totals:	For ...672–7d v Somerset (Taunton)	1899
	Agst...742 by Surrey (The Oval)	1909
Lowest innings totals:	For ... 15 v Warwickshire (Birmingham)	1922
	Agst... 23 by Yorkshire (Middlesbrough)	1965
Highest individual innings:	For ...316 R. H. Moore v Warwickshire (Bournemouth)	1937
	Agst...302*P. Holmes for Yorkshire (Portsmouth)	1920
Best bowling in an innings:	For ...9–25 R. M. H. Cottam v Lancs (Manchester)	1965
	Agst...9–21 L.B. Richmond for Notts (Nottingham)	1921
Best bowling in a match:	For ...16–88 J. A. Newman v Somerset (Weston-super-Mare)	1927
	Agst...17–119 W. Mead for Essex (Southampton)	1895

Most runs in a season: 2854 (av 79.27) C. P. Mead   1928
     runs in a career: 48892 (av 48.84) C. P. Mead   1905–1936
     100s in a season: 12 by C. P. Mead   1928
     100s in a career: 138 by C. P. Mead   1905–1936
     wickets in a season: 190 (av 15.61) A. S. Kennedy   1922
     wickets in a career: 2669 (av 18.22) D. Shackleton   1948–1969

RECORD WICKET STANDS

1st	249	R. E. Marshall & J. R. Gray v Middlesex (Portsmouth)	1960
2nd	321	G. Brown & E. I. M. Barrett v Gloucestershire (Southampton)	1920
3rd	344	C. P. Mead & G. Brown v Yorkshire (Portsmouth)	1927
4th	263	R. E. Marshall & D. A. Livingstone v Middlesex (Lord's)	1970
5th	235	G. Hill & D. F. Walker v Sussex (Portsmouth)	1937
6th	411	R. M. Poore & E. G. Wynyard v Somerset (Taunton)	1899
7th	325	G. Brown & C. H. Abercrombie v Essex (Leyton)	1913
8th	178	C. P. Mead & C. P. Brutton v Worcestershire (Bournemouth)	1925
9th	230	D. A. Livingstone & A. T. Castell v Surrey (Southampton)	1962
10th	192	A. Bowell & W. H. Livsey v Worcestershire (Bournemouth)	1921

NB A partnership of 334 for the first wicket by B. A. Richards, C. G. Greenidge, and D. R. Turner occurred against Kent at Southampton in 1973. Richards retired hurt after 241 runs had been scored and in the absence of any official ruling on the matter, it is a matter of opinion as to whether it should be regarded as the first-wicket record for the county.

One-day cricket

Highest innings totals:	Gillette Cup	321–4 v Bedfordshire (Goldington)	1968
	John Player League	251 v Glamorgan (Basingstoke)	1974
	Benson & Hedges Cup	321–1 v Minor Counties (Amersham)	1973
Lowest innings totals:	Gillette Cup	129 v Warwickshire (Birmingham)	1964
		129 v Warwickshire (Birmingham)	1965
	John Player League	43 v Essex (Basingstoke)	1972
	Benson & Hedges Cup	94 v Glamorgan (Swansea)	1973
Highest individual innings:	Gillette Cup	143* B. L. Reed v Bucks (Chesham)	1970
	John Player League	155* B. A. Richards v Yorks (Hull)	1970
	Benson & Hedges Cup	173* C. G. Greenidge v Minor Counties (Amersham)	1973
Best bowling figures:	Gillette Cup	7–30 P. J. Sainsbury v Norfolk (Southampton)	1965
	John Player League	5–13 A. M. E. Roberts v Sussex (Hove)	1974
	Benson & Hedges Cup	4–17 P. J. Sainsbury v Glos (Moreton-in-Marsh)	1972

87

KENT

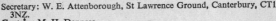

Formation of present club: 1859, reorganised 1870.
Colours: Red and white.
Badge: White horse.
County Champions (5): 1906, 1909, 1910, 1913, and 1970.
Gillette Cup winners (2): 1967 and 1974.
Gillette Cup finalists: 1971.
John Player League Champions (2): 1972 and 1973.
Benson & Hedges Cup winners: 1973.
Fenner Trophy winners (2): 1971 and 1973.

Secretary: W. E. Attenborough, St Lawrence Ground, Canterbury, CT1 3NZ.
Captain: M. H. Denness.

ASIF IQBAL RAZVI (Osmania University, Hyderabad, India) B Hyderabad 6/6/1943. Nephew of Ghulam Ahmed, former Indian off-break bowler and Test cricketer. RHB, RM. Good fielder. Debut 1959–60 for Hyderabad in Ranji Trophy. Migrated to Pakistan in 1961 and has since appeared for various Karachi teams and Pakistan International Airways. Captained Pakistan under-25 v England under-25 in 1966–67. Debut for county and cap 1968. *Wisden* 1967. Tests: 32 for Pakistan between 1964–65 and 1974. Tours: Pakistan to Australia and New Zealand 1964–65, 1972–73 (vice-captain), England 1967, 1971 (vice-captain) and 1974 (vice-captain), Pakistan Eaglets to England 1963, Pakistan 'A' to Ceylon 1964, Pakistan International Airways to East Africa 1964. 1,000 runs (4)—1,379 runs (av 39.40) in 1970 best. Scored 1,029 runs (av 41.16) in Australia and New Zealand 1972–73. Scored 146 v England (Oval) 1967 sharing in 9th wkt partnership of 190 with Intikhab Alam after Pakistan were 65–8—record 9th wkt stand in Test cricket. Gillette Man of Match awards: 2. Benson & Hedges Gold awards: 3. HS: 175 Pakistan v New Zealand (Dunedin) 1972–73. HSUK: 159 v Northants (Northampton) 1969. HSGC: 89 v Lancs (Lord's) 1971. HSJPL: 81 v Worcs (Canterbury) 1973. HSBH: 75 v Middlesex (Canterbury) 1973. BB: 6–45 Pakistan Eaglets v Cambridge U (Cambridge) 1963. BBJPL: 3–25 v Yorks (Dover) 1973. BBBH: 4–43 v Worcs (Lord's) 1973.

Grahame Selvey CLINTON (Chislehurst and Sidcup GS) B Sidcup 5/5/1953. LHB, RM. Toured West Indies v England Young Cricketers 1973. Debut 1974. One match v Pakistanis (Canterbury) 1974. HS: 20 v Pakistanis (Canterbury) 1974.

Michael Colin COWDREY (Tonbridge and Oxford) B Bangalore (India) 24/12/1932. RHB, LBG. Debut 1950. Cap 1951 (youngest Kent player to have received this award). Oxford Blue 1952–54 (captain 1954). Elected Best Young Cricketer of the Year in 1953 by the Cricket Writers' Club. *Wisden* 1955. County captain from 1957 to 1971. Awarded CBE in 1972 New Years Honours List. Tests: 109 between 1954–55 and 1971, captaining England in 27 Tests between 1959 and 1968–69. Played in 4 matches against Rest of the World in 1970. Has played more Tests and Test innings and held more catches than any other player. Shared in 4th wkt partnership of 411 with P. B. H. May v WI (Birmingham) 1957—

88

record 4th wkt stand in Test cricket and record stand for any wkt for England. Shared in 9th wkt partnership of 163* with A. C. Smith v NZ (Wellington) 1962–63, record 9th wkt stand for England in Test cricket. Tours: Australia and New Zealand 1954–55, 1958–59, 1962–63, 1965–66, 1970–71 (vice-captain on last four tours), 1974–75 (flown out as reinforcement), South Africa 1956–57, West Indies 1959–60 (vice-captain), 1967–68 (captain), India 1963–64 (withdrew from tour after selection as captain owing to injury but subsequently flown out as replacement and took over vice-captaincy from M. J. Stewart), Ceylon & Pakistan (captain) 1968–69. 1,000 runs (21)—2,093 runs (av 63.42) in 1965 best. Has also scored 1,000 runs on following tours (6): 1954–55, 1956–57, 1958–59, 1959–60, 1962–63 and 1965–66. Has scored two 100's in match on three occasions: 110 and 103 MCC v New South Wales (Sydney) 1954–55, 115* and 103* v Essex (Gillingham) 1955, and 149 and 121 v Australians (Canterbury) 1961. Scored 30,000th run of his career in Australia 1965–66 and 40,000th run and 100th century in 1973. Gillette Man of Match awards: 5. Benson & Hedges Gold awards: 1. HS: 307 MCC v South Australia (Adelaide) 1962–63. HSUK: 250 v Essex (Blackheath) 1959. HSGC: 116 v Suffolk (Ipswich) 1966. HSJPL: 67 v Sussex (Folkestone) 1969. HSBH: 107* v Middlesex (Lord's) 1972. BB: 4–22 v Surrey (Blackheath) 1951. Blues for rackets and tennis.

Michael Henry (Mike) DENNESS (Ayr Academy) B Bellshill (Lanarkshire) 1/12/1940. RHB, RM/OB. Debut for Scotland 1959. Debut for Kent 1962. Cap 1964. Appointed county captain in 1972. Benefit in 1974. Tests: 20 between 1969 and 1974, captaining England in 11 Tests in 1973–74 and 1974. Played in one match against Rest of the World in 1970. Tours: India, Sri Lanka, and Pakistan 1972–73 (vice-captain), West Indies 1973–74 (vice-captain), Australia and New Zealand 1974–75 (captain). Gillette Man of Match awards: 1. 1,000 runs (11)—1,606 runs (av 31.49) in 1966 best. HS: 188 England v Australia (Melbourne) 1975. HSGC: 85 v Leics (Leicester) 1971. HSJPL: 94* v Surrey (Tunbridge Wells) 1971. HSBH: 112* v Surrey (Oval) 1973.

Alan George Ernest EALHAM B Ashford (Kent) 30/8/1944. RHB, OB. Excellent outfield. Debut 1966. Cap 1970. Scored 1,363 runs (av 34.94) in 1971. Held 5 catches in innings v Glos (Folkestone) 1966, all in outfield off D. L. Underwood. HS: 105 v Somerset (Glastonbury) 1972. HSGC: 46 v Leics (Canterbury) 1974. HSJPL: 82 v Middlesex (Canterbury) 1971. HSBH: 48 v Essex (Canterbury) 1973.

Richard Burtenshaw ELMS (Bexley/Erith Technical HS) B Sutton (Surrey) 5/4/1949. RHB, LFM. Debut 1970. HS: 28* v Essex (Chelmsford) 1971. HSBH: 19 v Sussex (Hove) 1973. BB: 5–38 v Middlesex (Lord's) 1973. BBJPL: 3–27 v Derbyshire (Chesterfield) 1973. BBBH: 3–43 v Sussex (Hove) 1973.

John Norman GRAHAM (Queen Elizabeth GS, Hexham) B Hexham (Northumberland) 8/5/1943. Very tall (6ft 7½in). RHB, RM. Debut 1964. Cap 1967. Took 104 wkts (av 13.90) in 1967. HS: 23 v Cambridge U (Cambridge) 1968. HSJPL: 13 v Northants (Northampton) 1969. BB: 8–20 v Essex (Brentwood) 1969. BBGC: 4–19 v Essex (Brentwood) 1967. BBJPL: 3–6 v Northants (Brackley) 1973. BBBH: 3–45 v Hants (Southampton) 1973.

89

James Martin Hilary GRAHAM-BROWN (Sevenoaks School) B Thetford (Norfolk) 11/7/1951. RHB, RM. Great-nephew of L. B. Bluxland, former Derbyshire player. Debut 1974. HS: 29* v Derbyshire (Folkestone) 1974. BBJPL: 3–4 v Lancs (Manchester) 1974. Studied at University of Kent.

Richard William HILLS B Borough Green (Kent) 8/1/1951. RHB, RM. Played for 2nd XI since 1969. Debut 1973. HS: 36* v Lancs (Folkestone) 1973. HSJPL: 23* v Lancs (Maidstone) 1973. BB: 4–24 v Lancs (Folkestone) 1973.

Graham William JOHNSON (Shooters Hill GS and London School of Economics) B Beckenham 8/11/1946. RHB, OB. Debut 1965. Cap 1970. 1,000 runs (2)—1,438 runs (av 31.26) in 1973 best. Gillette Man of Match awards: 1. Benson & Hedges Gold awards: 1. HS: 158 v Warwickshire (Canterbury) 1974. HSGC: 120* v Bucks (Canterbury) 1974. HSJPL: 81 v Northants (Brackley) 1973. HSBH: 51 v Essex (Canterbury) 1973. BB: 6–35 (12–151 match) v Surrey (Blackheath) 1970. BBJPL: 5–26 v Surrey (Oval) 1974

Bernard Denis JULIEN (St Mary's College, Port of Spain) B Carenage, Trinidad 13/3/1950. RHB, LM/SLA/SLC. Debut for North Trinidad v South Trinidad (Pointe-a-Pierre) 1967–68. Has played subsequently for Trinidad in Shell Shield competition. Debut for county 1970. Cap 1972. Tests: 8 for West Indies in 1973 and 1973–74. Tours: West Indies to England 1973, India, Sri Lanka, and Pakistan 1974–75. Hat-trick for North Trinidad v South Trinidad (Port of Spain) 1968–69. Gillette Man of Match awards: 1. Benson & Hedges Gold awards: 2. HS: 127 West Indians v T. N. Pearce's XI (Scarborough) 1973. HSGC: 35 v Lancs (Manchester) 1972. HSJPL: 53 v Warwickshire (Birmingham) 1973. HSBH: 44 v Leics (Canterbury) 1974. BB: 7–63 North Trinidad v South Trinidad (Port of Spain) 1968–69. BBUK: 5–53 West Indians v Sussex (Hove) 1973. BBGC: 5–25 v Yorks (Canterbury) 1971. BBJPL: 4–28 v Northants (Northampton) 1972. BBBH: 5–21 v Surrey (Oval) 1973.

Alan Philip Eric KNOTT B Belvedere 9/4/1946. RHB, WK. Can bowl OB. Debut 1964. Cap 1965. Elected Best Young Cricketer of the Year in 1965 by Cricket Writers' Club. *Wisden* 1969. Played for Tasmania 1969–70 whilst coaching there. Tests: 61 between 1967 and 1974. Played in 5 matches against Rest of World in 1970. Tours: Pakistan 1966–67, West Indies, 1967–68 and 1973–74, Ceylon and Pakistan 1968–69, Australia and New Zealand 1970–71, 1974–75, India, Sri Lanka, and Pakistan 1972–73. 1,000 runs (2)—1,209 runs (av 41.68) in 1971 best. Scored two centuries in match (127* and 118*) v Surrey (Maidstone) 1972. Gillette Man of Match awards: 2. HS: 156 MCC v South Zone (Bangalore) 1972–73. HSUK: 128* v Surrey (Oval) 1971. HSGC: 27 v Leics (Leicester) 1971. HSJPL: 60 v Hants (Canterbury) 1969. HSBH: 49 v Surrey (Canterbury) 1974. Dismissed 84 batsmen (74 ct 10 st) in 1965. 81 batsmen (73 ct 8 st) in 1966, and 98 batsmen (90 ct 8 st) in 1967. Dismissed 7 batsmen (7 ct) on debut in Test cricket v Pakistan (Nottingham) 1967. Holds record for most catches in Test cricket.

Brian William LUCKHURST B Sittingbourne 5/2/1939. RHB, SLA. Joined staff 1954. Debut 1958. Cap 1963. *Wisden* 1970. Benefit (£18,231) in 1973. Tests: 19 between 1970–71 and 1973. Played in 5 matches against Rest of the World 1970. Tours: Australia and New Zealand 1970–71, 1974–75. 1,000 runs (13)—1,914 runs (av 47.85) in 1969 best. Scored 1,061 runs (av 46.13) in all limited-overs cricket in 1974—the first batsman to do so. Scored two centuries in match (113 and 100*) v Rest of World (Canterbury) 1968. Gillette Man of Match awards: 4. Benson & Hedges Gold awards: 1. HS: 215 v Derbyshire (Derby) 1973. HSGC: 129 v Durham (Canterbury) 1974. HSJPL: 142 v Somerset (Weston-super-Mare) 1970. HSBH: 111 v Leics (Canterbury) 1974. BB: 4–32 v Somerset (Gravesend) 1962. BBGC: 3–22 v Hants (Portsmouth) 1965.

David NICHOLLS (Gravesend GS) B East Dereham (Norfolk) 8/12/1943. LHB, reserve WK, LB. Debut 1960. Cap 1969. Scored 1,000 runs (av 32.25) in 1971. HS: 211 v Derbyshire (Folkestone) 1963. HSGC: 43 v Warwickshire (Canterbury) 1971. HSJPL: 64 v Glos (Gillingham) 1971. HSBH: 51 v Essex (Chelmsford) 1972.

Charles James Castell ROWE (King's School, Canterbury) B Hong Kong 27/11/1951. RHB, OB. Debut 1974. HS: 58* v Notts (Nottingham) 1974.

John Neil SHEPHERD (Alleyn's School, Barbados) B St Andrew, Barbados 9/11/1943. RHB, RM. Leg slip. Debut 1964–65 in one match for Barbados v Cavaliers and has played subsequently for Barbados in Shell Shield competition. Debut for county 1966. Cap 1967. Tests: 5 for West Indies in 1969 and 1970–71. Tour: West Indies to England 1969. Scored 1,157 runs (av 29.66) and took 96 wkts (av 18.72) in 1968. HS: 170 v Northants (Folkestone) 1968. HSGC: 77 v Sussex (Canterbury) 1967. HSJPL: 65 v Surrey (Oval) 1971. HSBH: 39 v Middlesex (Canterbury) 1973. BB: 8–40 West Indians v Glos (Bristol) 1969. BBGC: 4–23 v Essex (Leyton) 1972. BBJPL: 4–18 v Hants (Portsmouth) 1972. BBBH: 3–21 v Essex (Canterbury) 1973.

Christopher James TAVARE (Sevenoaks School and Oxford) B Orpington 27/10/1954. RHB, RM. Scored 124* for England Schools v All-India Schools (Birmingham) 1973. Debut 1974. HS: 31 v Yorks (Scarborough) 1974. HSJPL: 22 v Derbyshire (Maidstone) 1974. Entered University 1974.

Peter Aland TOPLEY (Simon Langton GS, Canterbury) B Canterbury 29/8/1950. RHB, SLA. Debut 1972. HS: 22 MCC v Kent (Canterbury) 1973.

Derek Leslie UNDERWOOD (Beckenham and Penge GS) B Bromley 8/6/1945. RHB, LM. Debut 1963, taking 100 wkts and becoming the youngest player ever to do so in debut season. Cap 1964 (second youngest Kent player to have received this award). Elected Best Young Cricketer of the Year in 1966 by the Cricket Writers' Club. *Wisden* 1968. Benefit in 1975. Took 1,000th wkt in first-class cricket in New Zealand 1970–71 at age of 25 years 264 days—only W. Rhodes (in 1902) and G. A. Lohmann (in 1890) have achieved the feat at a younger age. Tests: 47 between 1966 and 1974. Played in 3 matches against Rest of World in 1970. Tours: Pakistan 1966–67, Ceylon and Pakistan 1968–69, Australia and New Zealand 1970–71, 1974–75, India, Sri Lanka, and Pakistan 1972–73, West Indies

1973–74. 100 wkts (7)—157 wkts (av 13.80) in 1966 best. HS: 80 v Lancs (Manchester) 1969. HSGC: 28 v Sussex (Tunbridge Wells) 1963. HSJPL: 22 v Worcs (Dudley) 1969. HSBH: 17 v Essex (Canterbury) 1973. BB: 9–28 v Sussex (Hastings) 1964 and 9–37 v Essex (Westcliff) 1966. BBGC: 4–57 v Leics (Canterbury) 1974. BBJPL: 5–19 v Glos (Maidstone) 1972.

Robert Andrew (Bob) WOOLMER (Skinners' School, Tunbridge Wells) B Kanpur (India) 14/5/1948. RHB, RM. Debut 1968. Cap 1970. Played for Natal in 1973–74. Gillette Man of Match awards: 1. Benson & Hedges Gold awards: 1. HS: 112 v Derbyshire (Folkestone) 1974. HSGC: 39 v Glos (Canterbury) 1972. HSJPL: 46 v Surrey (Oval) 1972. HSBH: 29 v Sussex (Hove) 1973. BB: 7–47 v Sussex (Canterbury) 1969. BBGC: 4–37 v Leics (Leicester) 1971. BBJPL: 5–26 v Somerset (Canterbury) 1973. BBBH: 4–14 v Sussex (Tunbridge Wells) 1972.

NB The following player whose particulars appeared in the 1974 Annual has been omitted: D. A. Laycock (left staff).

COUNTY AVERAGES

County Championship: Played 20; won 5, drawn 7, lost 8
All first-class matches: Played 22; won 5, drawn 8, lost 9

BATTING AND FIELDING

Cap		I	M	NO	Runs	HS	Avge	100	50	Ct	St
1951	M. C. Cowdrey	21	30	3	1027	122	38.03	5	3	24	—
1963	B. W. Luckhurst	22	35	2	1067	148	32.33	2	4	23	—
1970	G. W. Johnson	22	35	2	1005	158	30.45	1	8	13	—
—	C. J. C. Rowe	14	16	8	237	58*	29.62	—	1	2	—
1970	R. A. Woolmer	22	32	4	802	112	28.64	3	1	14	—
1967	J. N. Shepherd	20	28	5	576	79	25.04	—	2	6	—
—	J.M.H. Graham-Brown	7	7	3	99	29*	24.75	—	—	2	—
1969	D. Nicholls	16	22	2	487	74	24.35	—	2	46	—
1964	M. H. Denness	7	11	1	229	56	22.90	—	1	7	—
1970	A. G. E. Ealham	22	33	3	686	73	22.86	—	4	12	—
1968	Asif Iqbal	4	8	0	164	80	20.50	—	1	2	—
—	C. J. Tavare	9	11	1	152	31	15.20	—	—	9	—
1972	B. D. Julien	4	8	0	78	28	9.75	—	1	1	—
1965	A. P. E. Knott	8	14	1	91	30*	7.00	—	—	19	—
—	R. B. Elms	15	16	5	68	13	6.18	—	—	3	—
1964	D. L. Underwood	8	10	4	27	11	4.50	—	—	4	—
1967	J. N. Graham	17	16	6	30	18*	3.00	—	—	1	—

Played in two matches: R. W. Hills 11 & 7.
Played in one match: G. S. Clinton 3 & 20; P. A. Topley did not bat.

BOWLING

	Type	O	M	R	W	Avge	Best	5 wI	10 wM
D. L. Underwood	LM	319.1	139	645	40	16.12	6–38	5	2
R.A. Woolmer	RM	446.4	135	1009	56	18.01	5–41	2	—
B.D. Julien	LM etc	93	21	266	12	22.16	5–91	1	—
G.W. Johnson	OB	460.2	139	1147	43	26.67	5–51	1	—
J.N. Graham	RM	465.3	107	1138	39	29.17	5–60	1	—
J.N. Shepherd	RM	613	145	1644	53	31.01	6–42	2	—
R. B. Elms	LFM	290.4	68	870	23	37.82	5–76	1	—
C.J.C. Rowe	OB	75.4	12	246	5	49.20	2–60	—	—

Also bowled: Asif Iqbal 1-0-5-0; G. S. Clinton 1-0-1-0; M. C. Cowdrey 15-0-54-2; J. M. H. Graham-Brown 30-7-77-1; R. W. Hills 10-1-30-1; A. P. E. Knott 0.2-0-4-0; B. W. Luckhurst 23-9-60-2; C. J. Tavare 1-0-6-0.

County Records
First-class cricket

Highest innings totals:	For ...803–4d v Essex (Brentwood)	1934
	Agst...676 by Australians (Canterbury)	1921
Lowest innings totals:	For ... 18 v Sussex (Gravesend)	1867
	Agst... 16 by Warwickshire (Tonbridge)	1913
Highest individual innings:	For ...332 W. H. Ashdown v Essex (Brentwood)	1934
	Agst...344 W. G. Grace for MCC (Canterbury)	1876
Best bowling in an innings:	For ...10–30 C. Blythe v Northamptonshire (Northampton)	1907
	Agst...10–48 C. H. G. Bland for Sussex (Tonbridge)	1899
Best bowling in a match:	For ...17–48 C. Blythe v Northamptonshire (Northampton)	1907
	Agst...17–106 T. W. Goddard for Gloucestershire (Bristol)	1939
Most runs in a season:	2894 (av 59.06) F. E. Woolley	1928
runs in a career:	48483 (av 42.05) F. E. Woolley	1906–1938
100s in a season:	10 by F. E. Woolley	1928 & 1934
100s in a career:	112 by F. E. Woolley	1906–1938
wickets in a season:	262 (av 14.74) A. P. Freeman	1933
wickets in a career:	3359 (av 14.45) A. P. Freeman	1914–1936

RECORD WICKET STANDS

1st 283	A. E. Fagg & P. R. Sunnucks v Essex (Colchester)	1938
2nd 352	W. H. Ashdown & F. E. Woolley v Essex (Brentwood)	1934
3rd 321	A. Hearne & J. R. Mason v Nottinghamshire (Nottingham)	1899
4th 297	H. T. W. Hardinge & A. P. F. Chapman v Hampshire (Southampton)	1926
5th 277	F. E. Woolley & L. E. G. Ames v New Zealanders (Canterbury)	1931
6th 284	A. P. F. Chapman & G. B. Legge v Lancashire (Maidstone)	1927
7th 248	A. P. Day & E. Humphreys v Somerset (Taunton)	1908
8th 157	A. L. Hilder & C. Wright v Essex (Gravesend)	1924
9th 161	B. R. Edrich & F. Ridgway v Sussex (Tunbridge Wells)	1949
10th 235	F. E. Woolley & A. Fielder v Worcestershire (Stourbridge)	1909

One-day cricket

Highest innings totals:	Gillette Cup	297–3 v Worcestershire (Canterbury)	1970
	John Player League	261–5 v Somerset (Weston-super-Mare)	1970
	Benson & Hedges Cup	268–5 v Surrey (Oval)	1973
Lowest innings totals:	Gillette Cup	110 v Gloucestershire (Bristol)	1968
	John Player League	84 v Gloucestershire (Folkestone)	1969

93

Highest individual innings:	Benson & Hedges Cup	172 v Surrey (Blackheath)	1972
	Gillette Cup	129 B. W. Luckhurst v Durham (Canterbury)	1974
	John Player League	142 B. W. Luckhurst v Somerset (Weston-super-Mare)	1970
	Benson & Hedges Cup	112* M. H. Denness v Surrey (Oval)	1973
Best bowling figures:	Gillette Cup	7–15 A. L. Dixon v Surrey (Oval)	1967
	John Player League	5–19 D. L. Underwood v Gloucestershire (Maidstone)	1972
	Benson & Hedges Cup	5–21 B. D. Julien v Surrey (Oval)	1973

LANCASHIRE

Formation of present club: 1864.
Colours: Red, green, and blue.
Badge: Red rose.
County Champions (8): 1881, 1897, 1904, 1926, 1927, 1928, 1930, and 1934.
Joint Champions (5): 1875, 1879, 1882, 1889, and 1950.
Gillette Cup winners (3): 1970, 1971, and 1972.
Gillette Cup finalists: 1974.
John Player League Champions (2): 1969 and 1970.
Benson & Hedges Cup semi-finalists (2): 1973 and 1974.
Secretary: A. K. James, Old Trafford, Manchester, M16 0PX.
Captain: D. Lloyd.

John **ABRAHAMS** (Heywood GS) B Cape Town, South Africa 21/7/1952. LHB, OB. Son of Cecil J. Abrahams, former professional for Milnrow and Radcliffe in Central Lancashire League. Has lived in this country since 1962. Debut 1973. HS: 78 Minor Counties v Pakistanis (Jesmond) 1974. HSJPL: 13* v Glos (Manchester) 1974.

Farokh Maneksha **ENGINEER** (Don Bosco HS, Bombay and Bombay University) B Bombay 25/2/1938. RHB, WK, LB. Debut for Combined Universities v West Indies 1958–59. Debut for Bombay in Ranji Trophy 1959–60 and played continuously for state and for West Zone in Duleep Trophy to 1967–68. Debut for county and cap 1968. Tests: 41 for India between 1961–62 and 1974. Played in 2 matches for Rest of World 1970 and 4 matches in 1971–72. Tours: Indian Starlets to Australia 1959–60, India to West Indies 1961–62, England 1967 and 1974, Australia and New Zealand 1967–68. Rest of World to Australia 1971–72. Scored 94* before lunch on recall to Indian team against West Indies (Madras) 1966–67. Scored century before lunch for West Zone v Central Zone in Duleep Trophy (Bombay) 1964–65. Scored 1,050 runs (av 47.72) in 1964–65 and 952 runs (av 32.82) in 1969. Dismissed 91 batsmen (86 ct 5 st) in 1970.

HS: 192 Rest of World v Combined XI (Hobart) 1971–72. HSUK: 141 v Derbyshire (Buxton) 1971. HSGC: 37* v Worcs (Worcester) 1971. HSJPL: 78* v Glamorgan (Southport) 1969. HSBH: 36 v Worcs (Manchester) 1973.

Antony John (Tony) GOOD (Worksop College) B in Ghana 10/11/1952. RHB, RFM. Played in schools matches at Lord's 1971–72 and toured West Indies with England Young Cricketers in 1972. Hat-trick for Public Schools v English Schools CA (Lord's) 1971. Debut 1973. One match v Glos (Manchester) and also played in one John Player League match. Did not play in 1974.

Keith GOODWIN B Oldham 21/6/1938. RHB, WK. Debut 1960. Cap 1965, gaining regular place in team following departure of G. Clayton. Became 2nd XI captain following signing of F. M. Engineer, but reappears occasionally through absence of Engineer. Benefit (£6,500) in 1973. Held 6 catches in John Player League match v Worcs (Worcester) 1969, the record for the League. HS: 23 v Glamorgan (Swansea) 1965.

Frank Charles HAYES (De La Salle College, Salford and Sheffield University) B Preston 6/12/1946. RHB, RM. Slip field. Debut 1970 scoring 94 and 99 in first two matches after scoring 203* for 2nd XI v Warwickshire 2nd XI (Birmingham). Cap 1972. Tests: 7 in 1973 and 1973–74, scoring 106* in second innings of his first Test v West Indies (Oval). Tour: West Indies 1973–74. 1,000 runs (2)—1,311 runs (av 35.43) in 1974 best. Gillette Man of Match awards: 1. Benson & Hedges Gold awards: 1. HS: 187 v Indians (Manchester) 1974. HSGC: 66* v Beds (Luton) 1973. HSJPL: 87* v Notts (Nottingham) 1974. HSBH: 102 v Minor Counties (Manchester) 1973. Amateur soccer player.

David Paul HUGHES (Newton-le-Willows GS) B Newton-le-Willows (Lancs) 13/5/1947. RHB, SLA. Good close field. Debut 1967. Cap 1970. Gillette Man of Match awards: 1. HS: 88* v Kent (Folkestone) 1973. HSGC: 42* v Middlesex (Lord's) 1974. HSJPL: 84 v Essex (Leyton) 1973. HSBH: 24 v Derbyshire (Manchester) 1973. BB: 7–24 v Oxford U (Oxford) 1970. BBGC: 4–61 v Somerset (Manchester) 1972. BBJPL: 5–26 v Hants (Bournemouth) 1970.

Andrew KENNEDY (Nelson GS) B Blackburn 4/11/1949. LHB, RM. Debut 1970. HS: 81 v Sussex (Manchester) 1974. HSGC: 36 v Worcs (Worcester) 1974. HSJPL: 68 v Warwickshire (Manchester) 1974.

Peter LEE B Arthingworth (Northants) 27/8/1945. RHB, RFM. Debut for Northants 1967. Joined Lancs in 1972. Cap 1972. Took 101 wkts (av 18.82) in 1973. HS: 26 Northants v Glos (Northampton) 1969. HSGC: 10* v Middlesex (Lord's) 1974. HSJPL: 27* Northants v Derbyshire (Chesterfield) 1971. BB: 8–53 v Sussex (Hove) 1973. BBGC: 3–23 v Middlesex (Lord's) 1974. BBJPL: 4–17 v Derbyshire (Chesterfield) 1972. BBBH: 4–32 v Worcs (Manchester) 1973.

Peter LEVER (Todmorden GS) B Todmorden (Yorks) 17/9/1940. RHB, RFM. Debut 1960. Cap 1965. Played for Tasmania in 1971–72 whilst coaching there. Testimonial (£7,000) in 1972. Tests: 12 between 1970–71 and 1972. Played in one match v Rest of World in 1970. Tours:

Australia and New Zealand 1970–71, 1974–75. Hat-trick v Notts (Manchester) 1969. Gillette Man of Match awards: 3. Benson & Hedges Gold awards: 1. HS: 88* England v India (Manchester) 1971. HSGC: 21 v Essex (Manchester) 1963. HSJPL: 23* v Essex (Leyton) 1973. HSBH: 10* v Derbyshire (Manchester) 1972. BB: 7–70 v Glamorgan (Manchester) 1972. BBGC: 5–30 v Hants (Manchester) 1970. BBJPL: 5–23 v Northants (Liverpool) 1970. BBBH: 5–21 v Minor Counties (Chester) 1972.

Clive Hubert LLOYD (Chatham HS, Georgetown) B Georgetown, Guyana 31/8/1944. Cousin of L. R. Gibbs. LHB, RM. Brilliant field. Wears contact lenses. Debut 1963–64 for British Guiana (now Guyana). Played for Haslingden in Lancashire League in 1967 and also for Rest of World XI in 1967 and 1968. Debut for county v Australians 1968. *Cap 1969. Wisden 1970.* Appointed county vice-captain in 1973. Tests: 36 for West Indies between 1966–67 and 1973–74. Played in 5 matches for Rest of World 1970 and 2 in 1971–72. Scored 118 on debut v England (Port of Spain) 1967–68, 129 on debut v Australia (Brisbane) 1968–69, and 82 and 78* on debut v India (Bombay) 1966–67. Tours: West Indies to India and Ceylon 1966–67, Australia and New Zealand 1968–69, England 1969 and 1973. Rest of World to Australia 1971–72 (returning early owing to back injury), India, Sri Lanka, and Pakistan 1974–75 (captain). 1,000 runs (5)—1,603 runs (av 47.14) in 1970 best. Also scored 1,000 runs in Australia and New Zealand 1968–69. Gillette Man of Match awards: 4. HS: 242* West Indies v India (Bombay) 1974–75. HSGC: 126 v Warwickshire (Lord's) 1972. HSJPL: 134* v Somerset (Manchester) 1970. HSBH: 73 v Notts (Manchester) 1974. BB: 4–48 v Leics (Manchester) 1970. BBGC: 3–39 v Somerset (Taunton) 1970. BBJPL: 4–33 v Middlesex (Lord's) 1971. BBBH: 3–23 v Derbyshire (Manchester) 1974.

David LLOYD (Accrington Secondary TS) B Accrington 18/3/1947. LHB, SLA. Short-leg field. Debut 1965. Cap 1968. Appointed county captain in 1973. Tests: 5 in 1974. Tour: Australia and New Zealand 1974–75. 1,000 runs (5)—1,510 runs (av 47.18) in 1972 best. Gillette Man of Match awards: 2. HS: 214* England v India (Birmingham) 1974. HSGC: 94 v Somerset (Taunton) 1971. HSJPL: 103* v Northants (Bedford) 1971. HSBH: 113 v Minor Counties (Manchester) 1973. BB: 7–38 v Glos (Lydney) 1966.

John LYON (St Helen's Central County Secondary School) B St Helens 17/5/1951. RHB, WK. Played for 2nd XI since 1971. Debut 1973. HS: 48 v Indians (Manchester) 1974. HSJPL: 14 v Hants (Bournemouth) 1974.

Harry PILLING (Ashton TS) B Ashton-under-Lyne (Lancs) 23/2/1943. 5ft 3in tall. RHB, OB. Debut 1962. Cap 1965. Testimonial (£9,500) 1974. 1,000 runs (7)—1,606 runs (av 36.50) in 1967 best. Scored two centuries in match (119* and 104*) v Warwickshire (Manchester) 1970. Gillette Man of Match awards: 2. Benson & Hedges Gold awards: 1. HS: 144 v Leics (Leicester) 1974. HSGC: 90 v Middlesex (Lord's) 1973. HSJPL: 85 v Sussex (Hove) 1970. HSBH: 109* v Glamorgan (Manchester) 1973.

Robert Malcolm RATCLIFFE B Accrington 29/11/1951. RHB, RM. Joined staff 1971. Debut 1972. HS: 12* v Leics (Liverpool) 1973 and 12 v Cambridge U (Cambridge) 1974. BB: 5–44 v Cambridge U (Cambridge) 1974. BBJPL: 3–9 v Glos (Manchester) 1974.

Bernard Wilfrid REIDY (St Mary's College, Blackburn) B Bramley Meade, Whalley (Lancs) 18/9/1953. LHB, SLA. Toured West Indies with England Young Cricketers 1972. Played for 2nd XI since 1971. Debut 1973. HS: 60 v Leics (Leicester) 1974.

Kenneth (Ken) SHUTTLEWORTH B St Helens 13/11/1944. RHB, RFM. Outfield. Debut 1964. Cap 1968. Tests: 5 in 1970–71 and 1971. Played in one match v Rest of World 1970. Tour: Australia and New Zealand 1970–71. HS: 71 v Glos (Cheltenham) 1967. HSGC: 23 v Somerset (Manchester) 1967. HSJPL: 19* v Notts (Manchester) 1969. HSBH: 12* v Derbyshire (Manchester) 1974. BB: 7–41 v Essex (Leyton) 1968. BBGC: 4–26 v Essex (Chelmsford) 1971. BBJPL: 5–13 v Notts (Nottingham) 1972. BBBH: 3–15 v Notts (Manchester) 1972.

Jack SIMMONS (Accrington Secondary TS and Blackburn TS) B Clayton-le-Moors (Lancs) 28/3/1941. RHB, OB. Debut for 2nd XI 1959. Played for Blackpool in Northern League as professional. Debut 1968. Cap 1971. Played for Tasmania from 1972–73 to 1974–75 whilst coaching there. HS: 112 v Sussex (Hove) 1970. HSGC: 33 v Essex (Chelmsford) 1971. HSJPL: 32 v Middlesex (Lord's) 1971. HSBH: 31 v Derbyshire (Manchester) 1974. BB: 7–64 v Hants (Southport) 1973. BBGC: 5–49 v Worcs (Worcester) 1974. BBJPL: 5–28 v Northants (Peterborough) 1972. BBBH: 3–5 v Glamorgan (Manchester) 1973. Has played soccer in Lancs Combination.

Kenneth Leslie (Ken) SNELLGROVE (Bootle GS) B Shepton Mallet (Somerset) 12/11/1941. RHB. Debut 1965. Cap 1971. Scored 991 runs (av 31.96) in 1971. Benson & Hedges Gold awards: 1. HS: 138 v Middlesex (Manchester) 1970. HSGC: 29 v Middlesex (Lord's) 1973. HSJPL: 76* v Kent (Maidstone) 1973. HSBH: 66 v Notts (Manchester) 1972. Former soccer player in Cheshire League.

John SULLIVAN B Ashton-under-Lyne (Lancs) 5/2/1945. RHB, RM. Outfield with very good throw. Debut 1963. Cap 1969. Played only in the one-day competitions in 1974. Former amateur boxer. Benson & Hedges Gold awards: 1. HS: 81* v Hants (Bournemouth) 1972. HSGC: 61 v Notts (Nottingham) 1968. HSJPL: 76* v Sussex (Hove) 1970. HSBH: 50 v Glamorgan (Manchester) 1973. BB: 4–19 v Yorks (Sheffield) 1973. BBGC: 3–42 v Yorks (Leeds) 1974. BBJPL: 5–22 v Leics (Leicester) 1969.

Barry WOOD B Ossett (Yorks) 26/12/1942. RHB, RM. Brother of R. Wood who played occasionally for Yorkshire some years ago. Debut for Yorks 1964. Joined Lancs by special registration, making debut for county in 1966. Cap 1968. Played for Eastern Province in Currie Cup in 1971–72 and 1973–74. Tests: 5 between 1972 and 1972–73. Tour: India, Pakistan, and Sri Lanka 1972–73. Scored centuries in both 'Roses' matches in 1970 against his native county. 1,000 runs (5)—1,492 runs (av 38.25) in 1971 best. Gillette Man of Match awards: 3. Benson & Hedges Gold awards: 6. HS: 186 v Leics (Leicester) 1972. HSGC: 91 v Worcs (Worcester) 1974. HSJPL: 67 v Sussex (Manchester) 1971 and 67 v Glamorgan (Ebbw Vale) 1972. HSBH: 77 v Yorks (Bradford) 1974. BB: 7–52 v Middlesex (Manchester) 1968. BBGC: 4–26 v Middlesex (Lord's) 1974. BBJPL: 5–19 v Kent (Manchester) 1971. BBBH: 4–34 v Derbyshire (Manchester) 1972.

COUNTY AVERAGES

County Championship: Played 20; won 5, drawn 15, lost 0
All first-class matches: Played 23; won 6, drawn 17, lost 0

BATTING AND FIELDING

Cap		M	I	NO	Runs	HS	Avge	100	50	Ct	St
1969	C. H. Lloyd	20	31	8	1458	178*	63.39	4	7	15	—
1968	D. Lloyd	9	13	0	552	186	42.46	2	2	9	—
1965	H. Pilling	18	26	6	777	144	38.85	2	2	6	—
—	B. W. Reidy	4	5	1	154	60	38.50	—	1	7	—
1972	F. C. Hayes	23	35	1	1283	187	37.73	3	7	17	—
1971	K. L. Snellgrove	11	17	4	454	75*	34.92	—	1	4	—
1971	J. Simmons	20	25	11	466	75	33.28	—	2	16	—
—	A. Kennedy	16	26	2	742	81	30.91	—	6	9	—
1968	B. Wood	22	35	1	893	101	26.26	1	4	10	—
1968	F. M. Engineer	6	9	1	180	66	22.50	—	1	9	—
1970	D. P. Hughes	22	29	7	399	62	18.13	—	2	16	—
1968	K. Shuttleworth	20	15	6	159	44	17.66	—	—	8	—
—	J. Abrahams	12	20	2	225	57	12.50	—	1	10	—
—	J. Lyon	16	16	2	170	48	12.14	—	—	29	1
1965	P. Lever	21	17	5	114	29	9.50	—	—	8	—
1972	P. Lee	11	7	6	5	2*	5.00	—	—	1	—

Played in one match: K. Goodwin 6*; R. M. Ratcliffe 12.

BOWLING

	Type	O	M	R	W	Avge	Best	5 wI	10 wM
R. M. Ratcliffe	RM	18	7	44	5	8.80	5–44	1	—
B. Wood	RM	405.4	136	892	43	20.74	6–33	3	—
D. Lloyd	SLA	60	19	156	7	22.28	4–36	—	—
P. Lever	RFM	562.1	142	1401	57	24.57	4–20	—	—
J. Simmons	OB	592.1	177	1467	58	25.29	5–79	2	—
K. Shuttleworth	RFM	566.1	162	1418	53	26.75	7–61	2	—
D. P. Hughes	SLA	591.3	196	1428	51	28.00	5–38	2	—
P. Lee	RFM	341.2	85	902	29	31.10	5–62	1	—

Also bowled: J. Abrahams 6-2-24-0; F. C. Hayes 1-0-1-0; C. H. Lloyd 23-9-47-2; H. Pilling 3-0-13-0; B. W. Reidy 5-0-20-0; K. L. Snellgrove 20-5-27-3.

County Records

First-class cricket

Highest innings totals:	For ...801 v Somerset (Taunton)	1895
	Agst...634 v Surrey (The Oval)	1895
Lowest innings totals:	For ... 25 v Derbyshire (Manchester)	1871
	Agst... 22 by Glamorgan (Liverpool)	1924
Highest individual innings:	For ...424 A. C. MacLaren v Somerset (Taunton)	1895
	Agst...315* T. Hayward for Surrey (The Oval)	1898
Best bowling in an innings:	For ...10–55 J. Briggs v Worcestershire (Manchester)	1900
	Agst...10–40 G. O. Allen for Middlesex (Lord's)	1929
Best bowling in a match:	For ...17–91 H. Dean v Yorkshire (Liverpool)	1913
	Agst...16–65 G. Giffen for Australians (Manchester)	1886

Most runs in a season: 2633 (av 56.02) J. T. Tyldesley   1901
   runs in a career: 34222 (av 45.20) E. Tyldesley   1909–1936
   100s in a season: 11 by C. Hallows   1928
   100s in a career: 90 by E. Tyldesley   1909–1936
   wickets in a season: 198 (av 18.55) E. A. McDonald   1925
   wickets in a career: 1816 (av 15.12) J. B. Statham   1950–1968

RECORD WICKET STANDS

1st 368 A. C. MacLaren & R. H. Spooner v Gloucestershire
       (Liverpool)   1903
2nd 371 F. Watson & E. Tyldesley v Surrey (Manchester)   1928
3rd 306 E. Paynter & N. Oldfield v Hampshire (Southampton)   1938
4th 324 A. C. MacLaren & J. T. Tyldesley v Nottinghamshire
       (Nottingham)   1904
5th 235* N. Oldfield & A. E. Nutter v Nottinghamshire
       (Manchester)   1939
6th 278 J. Iddon & H. R. W. Butterworth v Sussex (Manchester) 1932
7th 245 A. H. Hornby & J. Sharp v Leicestershire (Manchester)   1912
8th 150 A. Ward & C. R. Hartley v Leicestershire (Leicester)   1900
9th 142 L. O. S. Poidevin & A. Kermode v Sussex (Eastbourne)   1907
10th 173 J. Briggs & R. Pilling v Surrey (Liverpool)   1885

One-day cricket

Highest innings totals:	Gillette Cup	304–9 v Leicestershire (Manchester)	1963
	John Player League	255–5 v Somerset (Manchester)	1970
	Benson & Hedges Cup	275–5 v Minor Counties (Manchester)	1973
Lowest innings totals:	Gillette Cup	59 v Worcestershire (Worcester)	1963
	John Player League	76 v Somerset (Manchester)	1972
	Benson & Hedges Cup	82 v Yorks (Bradford)	1972
Highest individual innings:	Gillette Cup	126 C. H. Lloyd v Warwicks (Lord's)	
	John Player League	134* C. H. Lloyd v Somerset (Manchester)	1972 / 1970
	Benson & Hedges Cup	113 D. Lloyd v Minor Counties (Manchester)	1973
Best bowling figures:	Gillette Cup	5–28 J. B. Statham v Leics (Manchester)	1963
	John Player League	5–13 K. Shuttleworth v Notts (Nottingham)	1972
	Benson & Hedges Cup	5–21 P. Lever v Minor Counties (Chester)	1972

LEICESTERSHIRE

Formation of present club: 1879.
Colours: Scarlet and dark green.
Badge: Running fox (gold) on green background.
Best final position in Championship: Third (2), 1953 and 1967.
Gillette Cup third round (5): 1968, 1969, 1971, 1973 and 1974.
John Player League Champions: 1974.
Benson & Hedges Cup winners: 1972.
Benson & Hedges Cup finalists: 1974.

Secretary: F. M. Turner, County Ground, Grace Road, Leicester, LE2 8AD.
Captain: R. Illingworth CBE.

John Christopher (Chris) BALDERSTONE B Huddersfield 16/11/1940. RHB, SLA. Played for Yorks from 1961 to 1970. Specially registered and made debut for Leics in 1971. Cap 1973. Scored 1,222 runs (av 42.13) in 1973. Gillette Man of Match awards: 1. Benson & Hedges Gold awards: 1. HS: 140 v Northants (Northampton) 1974. HSGC: 119* v Somerset (Taunton) 1973. HSJPL: 65* v Essex (Leicester) 1973. HSBH: 63* v Middlesex (Leicester) 1974. BB: 6–84 v Derbyshire (Leicester) 1971. BBJPL: 3–29 v Worcs (Leicester) 1971. Soccer for Huddersfield Town and Carlisle United.

Jack BIRKENSHAW (Rothwell GS) B Rothwell (Yorks) 13/11/1940. LHB, OB. Played for Yorks 1958 to 1960. Specially registered and made debut for Leics in 1961. Cap 1965. Benefit in 1974. Scored 951 runs (av 30.67) in 1969. Tests: 5 in 1972–73 and 1973–74. Tours: India, Pakistan, and Sri Lanka 1972–73, West Indies 1973–74. 100 wkts (2)—111 wkts (av 21.41) in 1967 best. Hat-tricks (2): v Worcs (Worcester) 1967 and v Cambridge U (Cambridge) 1968. Shared in 7th wkt partnership record for county, 206 with B. Dudleston v Kent (Canterbury) 1969. HS: 131 v Surrey (Guildford) 1969. HSGC: 45 v Kent (Canterbury) 1974. HSJPL: 61 v Hants (Leicester) 1970. HSBH: 35* v Worcs (Worcester) 1972. BB: 8–94 v Somerset (Taunton) 1972. BBGC: 3–19 v Somerset (Leicester) 1968. BBJPL: 4–27 v Surrey (Oval) 1969.

Peter BOOTH (Whitcliffe Mount GS, Cleckheaton) B Shipley (Yorks) 2/11/1952. RHB, RFM. Played for MCC Schools at Lord's 1970 and 1971. Toured West Indies with England Youth Team 1972. Debut 1972. HS: 57 v Derbyshire (Derby) 1974. HSJPL: 15* v Worcs (Leicester) 1973. BB: 4–18 v Oxford U (Oxford) 1972. Trained as a teacher at Loughborough College.

Nigel Edwin BRIERS (Lutterworth GS) B Leicester 15/1/1955. RHB. Cousin of N. Briers who played once for county in 1967. Debut 1971 at age of 16 years 104 days. Youngest player ever to appear for county. One match v Cambridge U 1971 and one match v Oxford U 1972. Did not play in 1973 or 1974. HS: 12* v Cambridge U (Cambridge) 1971.

Brian Fettes DAVISON (Gifford Technical HS, Rhodesia) B Bulawayo, Rhodesia 21/12/1946. RHB, RM. Debut for Rhodesia 1967–68 in Currie Cup competition. Debut for county 1970 after having played for International Cavaliers. Cap 1971. 1,000 runs (4)—1,670 runs (av 46.38) in 1974 best. Gillette Man of Match awards: 1. Benson & Hedges Gold awards: 4. HS: 142 v Sussex (Hove) 1974. HSGC: 82 v Kent (Canterbury) 1974. HSJPL: 85* v Glamorgan (Cardiff) 1974. HSBH: 158* v Warwickshire (Coventry) 1972. BB: 5–52 Rhodesia v Griqualand West (Bulawayo) 1967–68. BBUK: 4–99 v Northants (Leicester) 1970. BBJPL: 4–29 v Glamorgan (Neath) 1971. Has played hockey for Rhodesia.

Barry DUDLESTON (Stockport School) B Bebington (Cheshire) 16/7/1945. RHB, SLA. Short leg field. Debut 1966. Cap 1969. 1,000 runs (6)—1,374 runs (av 31.22) in 1970 best. Benson & Hedges Gold awards: 2. HS: 171* v Kent (Canterbury) 1969, sharing in 7th wkt partnership record for county, 206 with J. Birkenshaw. HSGC: 46 v Kent (Leicester) 1971. HSJPL: 109* v Glos (Gloucester) 1974. HSBH: 90 v Warwickshire (Leicester) 1973. BB: 4–6 v Surrey (Leicester) 1972.

Kenneth (Ken) HIGGS B Kidsgrove (Staffordshire) 14/1/1937. LHB, RFM. Played for Staffordshire 1957. Debut for Lancs 1958. Cap 1959. *Wisden* 1967. Benefit (£8,390) in 1968. Retired after 1969 season. Reappeared for Leics in 1972. Cap 1972. Tests: 15 between 1965 and 1968. Shared in 10th wkt partnership of 128 with J. A. Snow v WI (Oval) 1966— 2 runs short of then record 10th wkt partnership in Test cricket. Tours: Australia and New Zealand 1965–66, West Indies 1967–68. 100 wkts (5)— 132 wkts (av 19.42) in 1960 best. Hat-tricks (2): Lancs v Essex (Blackpool) 1960 and Lancs v Yorks (Leeds) 1968. Hat-trick also in Benson & Hedges Cup Final v Surrey (Lord's) 1974. Benson & Hedges Gold awards: 1. HS: 63 England v WI (Oval) 1966. HSGC: 25 Lancs v Somerset (Taunton) 1966. HSJPL: 15* Lancs v Surrey (Manchester) 1969. BB: 7–19 Lancs v Leics (Manchester) 1965. BBGC: 4–10 Lancs v Cheshire (Macclesfield) 1966. BBJPL: 6–17 v Glamorgan (Leicester) 1973. BBBH: 4–10 v Surrey (Lord's) 1974. Soccer (half-back) for Port Vale.

David John HUMPHRIES B Alveley (Shropshire) 6/8/1953. LHB, WK. Played for Shropshire 1971–73. Debut 1974. HS: 60 v Lancs (Leicester) 1974.

Raymond (Ray) ILLINGWORTH B Pudsey 8/6/1932. RHB, OB. Debut for Yorks 1951. Cap 1955. *Wisden* 1959. Benefit (£6,604) in 1965. Left Yorks after 1968 season and joined Leics by special registration in 1969 being appointed county captain. Cap 1969. Awarded CBE in the 1973 New Years Honours list. Tests: 61 between 1958 and 1973 captaining England in 31 Test matches between 1969 and 1973. Played in 5 matches as captain against Rest of World in 1970. Tours: West Indies 1959–60, Australia and New Zealand 1962–63, 1970–71 (captain). 1,000 runs (8)— 1,726 runs (av 46.64) in 1959 best. 100 wkts (10)—131 wkts (av 14.36) in 1968 best. Doubles (6): 1957, 1959–62 and 1964. Had match double of 100 runs and 10 wkts Yorks v Kent (Dover) 1964 (135 and 14–101). Gillette Man of Match awards: 1 (for Yorks). Benson & Hedges Gold awards: 2. HS: 162 Yorks v Indians (Sheffield) 1959. HSGC: 59 v Notts (Leicester)

LEICESTERSHIRE

1970. HSJPL: 79 v Yorks (Leicester) 1970. HSBH: 41 v Oxford U (Oxford) 1973. BB: 9–42 Yorks v Worcs (Worcester) 1957. BBGC: 5–29 Yorks v Surrey (Lord's) 1965. BBJPL: 4–5 v Worcs (Dudley) 1972. BBBH: 5–20 v Somerset (Leicester) 1974.

George Alan KNEW (Wyggeston GS, Leicester) B Leicester 5/3/1954. RHB. Debut 1972. Did not play in 1974. HS: 25 v Derbyshire (Derby) 1973. HSJPL: 42* v Surrey (Leicester) 1973.

Graham Douglas McKENZIE (John Curtin HS, Fremantle) B Cottesloe, Perth, Western Australia 24/6/1941. RHB, RFM. Debut for Western Australia 1959–60. Debut for county and cap 1969. Tests: 60 for Australia between 1961 and 1970–71. Played in 3 matches for Rest of World 1970 and 2 matches for Australia v Rest of World 1971–72. Tours: Australia to England 1961, 1964 and 1968, India and Pakistan 1964–65, West Indies 1964–65, South Africa 1966–67, India and South Africa 1969–70. Took 200th wkt in Test cricket against West Indies in 1968–69 and is youngest ever bowler to achieve targets of 100, 150 and 200 wkts in Tests. His 100 wkts achieved in second fastest time of 3 years 165 days. Hat-tricks v Worcs (Worcester) 1972 in Benson & Hedges Cup and v Essex (Leicester) 1972 in John Player League. HS: 76 Australia v South Africa (Sydney) 1963–64. HSUK: 55 v Derbyshire (Leicester) 1972. HSGC: 12* v Warwickshire (Birmingham) 1972 and 12 v Northants (Leicester) 1974. HSJPL: 41* v Lancs (Manchester) 1970. BB: 8–71 Australia v West Indies (Melbourne) 1968–69. BBUK: 7–8 v Glamorgan (Leicester) 1971. BBGC: 3–30 v Derbyshire (Leicester) 1971. BBJPL: 5–15 v Essex (Leicester) 1972. BBBH: 5–34 v Kent (Canterbury) 1974.

Norman Michael McVICKER (Strand GS, Whitefield, Manchester) B Radcliffe (Lancs) 4/11/1940. RHB, RFM. Played for Lincolnshire from 1963 to 1968, and was captain in 1967–68. Debut for Minor Counties v South Africans (Jesmond) 1965. Debut for Warwickshire 1969. Cap 1971. Debut for Leics 1974. Cap 1974. Hat-trick Warwickshire v Lincs (Birmingham) 1971 in Gillette Cup competition. Gillette Man of Match awards: 2. HS: 65* Warwickshire v Lancs (Manchester) 1972 and 65 Warwickshire v Lancs (Blackpool) 1973. HSGC: 42 Warwickshire v Glamorgan (Birmingham) 1972. HSJPL: 45 Warwickshire v Notts (Birmingham) 1971. HSBH: 23 Warwickshire v Leics (Leicester) 1972. BB: 7–29 Warwickshire v Northants (Birmingham) 1969. BBGC: 5–26 Warwickshire v Lincs (Birmingham) 1971. BBJPL: 4–28 Warwickshire v Middlesex (Lord's) 1969. BBBH: 5–32 Warwickshire v Oxford U (Oxford) 1973.

Michael Eric John Charles (Mick) NORMAN (Northampton GS) B Northampton 19/1/1933. RHB, RM. Debut for Northants 1952. Cap 1960. Left staff after 1965 season. Debut and cap for Leics 1966. Left staff after 1969 season to become a teacher and is only available for one-day matches and in school holidays. Testimonial in 1975. 1,000 runs (8)—1,964 runs (av 33.86) in 1960 best. Gillette Man of Match awards: 1. HS: 221* v Cambridge U (Cambridge) 1967. HSGC: 52 v Somerset (Leicester) 1968. HSJPL: 90* v Warwickshire (Birmingham) 1970. HSBH: 86 v Warwickshire (Coventry) 1972.

102

Martin SCHEPENS (Rawlins School, Quorn) B Barrow-upon-Soar (Leics) 12/8/1955. RHB, LB. Played for 2nd XI since 1971. Debut 1973 aged 17 years 8 months. One match v Cambridge U (Cambridge) in 1973 and one match v Pakistanis (Leicester) 1974. HS: 11 v Pakistanis (Leicester) 1974.

Charles Terry SPENCER B Leicester 18/8/1931. RHB, RM. Debut and cap 1952. Test trial 1953. Benefit (£3,500) in 1964. Took 123 wkts (av 19.56) in 1961. Retired after 1969 season, but reappeared in John Player League in 1970 and regularly since 1971. HS: 90 v Essex (Leicester) 1964, sharing in 8th wkt partnership record for county, 164 with M. R. Hallam. HSJPL: 18* v Notts (Leicester) 1969. BB: 9–63 v Yorks (Huddersfield) 1954. BBGC: 4–28 v Warwickshire (Birmingham) 1972. BBJPL: 5–13 v Somerset (Weston-Super-Mare) 1969. BBBH: 4–20 v Oxford U (Oxford) 1973.

John Frederick STEELE B Stafford 23/7/1946. Younger brother of D. S. Steele of Northants. RHB, SLA. Debut 1970. Was 12th man for England v Rest of World (Lord's) a month after making debut. Cap 1971. Played for Natal in 1973–74 Currie Cup competition. 1,000 runs (3)—1,347 runs (av 31.32) in 1972 best. Gillette Man of Match awards: 1. Benson & Hedges Gold awards: 3. HS: 195 v Derbyshire (Leicester) 1971. HSGC: 85* v Northants (Leicester) 1974. HSJPL: 92 v Essex (Leicester) 1973. HSBH: 91 v Somerset (Leicester) 1974. BB: 7–29 Natal B v Griqualand West (Umzinto) 1973–74. BBUK: 5–15 v Northants (Leicester) 1971. BBJPL: 4–27 v Derbyshire (Burton-on-Trent) 1973. BBBH: 3–17 v Cambridge U (Leicester) 1972.

Terry Kevin STRETTON B Cosby (Leics) 23/5/1953. RHB, RM. Debut 1972. HS: 3* v Pakistanis (Leicester) 1974.

Jeffrey Graham (Jeff) TOLCHARD (Malvern College) B Torquay 17/3/1944. Brother of R. W. Tolchard. RHB, RM. Good cover point. Played for Devon in 1963 and from 1966 to 1969. Debut 1970. HS: 66 v Warwickshire (Leicester) 1972. HSGC: 18 v Kent (Canterbury) 1974. HSJPL: 12* v Somerset (Leicester) 1972. HSBH: 28 v Oxford U (Oxford) 1973. Studied at Loughborough College. Has played soccer for Torquay United and Exeter City.

Roger William TOLCHARD (Malvern College) B Torquay 15/6/1946. RHB, WK. Played for Devon in 1963 and 1964. Also played for Hants 2nd XI and Public Schools v Combined Services (Lord's) in 1964. Debut 1965. Cap 1966. Appointed vice-captain in 1970. Relinquished appointment in 1973. Tour: India, Pakistan, and Sri Lanka 1972–73. Scored 998 runs (av 30. 24) in 1970. Benson & Hedges Gold awards: 2. HS: 126* v Cambridge U (Cambridge) 1970. HSGC: 16 v Sussex (Hove) 1969. HSJPL: 103 v Middlesex (Lord's) 1972 and was dismissed obstructing the field. HSBH: 63* v Northants (Leicester) 1972. Has had soccer trial for Leicester City.

NB The following players whose particulars appeared in the 1974 Annual have been omitted: P. R. Haywood and R. B. Matthews.

103

COUNTY AVERAGES

County Championship: Played 20; won 7, drawn 6, lost 7
All first-class matches: Played 24; won 9, drawn 6, lost 9

BATTING AND FIELDING

Cap		M	I	NO	Runs	HS	Avge	100	50	Ct	St
1971	B. F. Davison	24	39	3	1670	142	46.38	4	11	22	—
1969	B. Dudleston	24	41	5	1337	135	37.13	4	4	21	—
1973	J. C. Balderstone	14	23	2	775	140	36.90	1	6	9	—
1966	R. W. Tolchard	23	33	9	728	103	30.33	1	3	46	7
1971	J. F. Steele	24	41	5	953	116*	26.47	1	5	28	—
1969	R. Illingworth	21	27	8	448	67	23.57	—	2	7	—
1965	J. Birkenshaw	22	28	6	516	70*	23.45	—	1	16	—
1974	N. M. McVicker	24	25	5	438	64	21.90	—	3	6	—
—	J. G. Tolchard	19	26	3	419	64*	18.21	—	2	5	—
1966	M. E. J. C. Norman	12	20	3	265	40*	15.58	—	—	5	—
—	D. J. Humphries	3	6	1	74	60	14.80	—	1	3	1
1969	G. D. McKenzie	21	20	4	214	50	13.37	—	1	7	—
—	P. Booth	7	7	0	70	57	10.00	—	1	1	—
1972	K. Higgs	20	15	9	22	10*	3.66	—	—	14	—
1952	C. T. Spencer	3	1	0	1	1	1.00	—	—	—	—

Played in two matches: T. K. Stretton 3*, 0; 6*, 4 (1 ct).
Played in one match: M. Schepens 4, 11 (1 ct).

BOWLING

	Type	O	M	R	W	Avge	Best	5 wI	10 wM
R. Illingworth	OB	535.1	204	1014	57	17.78	7–18	4	—
J.C. Balderstone	SLA	134.4	33	351	19	18.47	4–19	—	—
G.D. McKenzie	RFM	531.3	131	1345	71	18.94	5–36	4	—
N.M. McVicker	RFM	511.1	113	1357	61	22.24	6–19	2	—
J. Birkenshaw	OB	478.2	130	1127	45	25.04	7–56	4	—
K. Higgs	RFM	421.1	107	996	39	25.53	5–53	2	—
P. Booth	RFM	124.5	17	380	14	27.14	3–57	—	—
J. F. Steele	SLA	397.5	136	866	30	28.86	4–38	—	—

Also bowled: B. F. Davison 47.3-14-113-4; B. Dudleston 23-3-72-2;
C. T. Spencer 36-5-112-0; T. K. Stretton 54-16-136-3.

County Records

First-class cricket

Highest innings totals:	For ...701-4d v Worcestershire (Worcester)	1906
	Agst...739-7d by Nottinghamshire (Nottingham)	1903
Lowest innings totals:	For ... 25 v Kent (Leicester)	1912
	Agst... 24 by Glamorgan (Leicester)	1971
Highest individual innings:	For ...252* S. Coe v Northants (Leicester)	1914
	Agst...341 G. H. Hirst for Yorkshire (Leicester)	1905
Best bowling in an innings:	For ...10-18 G. Geary v Glamorgan (Pontypridd)	1929
	Agst...10-32 H. Pickett for Essex (Leyton)	1895
Best bowling in a match:	For ...16-96 G. Geary v Glamorgan (Pontypridd)	1929
	Agst...16-102 C. Blythe for Kent (Leicester)	1909

Most runs in a season:	2446 (av 52.04) L. G. Berry	**1937**
runs in a career:	30143 (av 30.32) L. G. Berry	1924–1951
100s in a season:	7 by L. G. Berry and	
	W. Watson	1937 and 1959
100s in a career:	45 by L. G. Berry	1924–1951
wickets in a season:	170 (av 18.96) J. E. Walsh	1948
wickets in a career:	2130 (av 23.19) W. E. Astill	1906–1939

RECORD WICKET STANDS

1st 380	C. J. B. Wood & H. Whitehead v Worcestershire	
	(Worcester)	1906
2nd 287	W. Watson & A. Wharton v Lancashire (Leicester)	1961
3rd 316*	W. Watson & A. Wharton v Somerset (Taunton)	1961
4th 270	C. S. Dempster & G. S. Watson v Yorkshire (Hull)	1937
5th 226*	R. MacDonald & F. Geeson v Derbyshire (Glossop)	1901
6th 262	A. T. Sharpe & G. H. S. Fowke v Derbyshire	
	(Chesterfield)	1911
7th 206	B. Dudleston & J. Birkenshaw v Kent (Canterbury)	1969
8th 164	M. R. Hallam & C. T. Spencer v Essex (Leicester)	1964
9th 160	W. W. Odell & R. T. Crawford v Worcestershire	
	(Leicester)	1902
10th 157	W. E. Astill & W. H. Marlow v Gloucestershire	
	(Cheltenham)	1933

One-day cricket

Highest innings totals:	Gillette Cup	229 v Kent (Canterbury) 1974
	John Player League	262–6 v Somerset (Frome) 1970
	Benson & Hedges Cup	327–4 v Warwickshire
		(Coventry) 1972
Lowest innings totals:	Gillette Cup	56 v Northamptonshire
		(Leicester) 1964
	John Player League	36 v Sussex (Leicester) 1973
	Benson & Hedges Cup	143 v Surrey (Lord's) 1974
Highest individual innings:	Gillette Cup	119* J. C. Balderstone
		v Somerset (Taunton) 1973
	John Player League	109* B. Dudleston v Glos
		(Gloucester) 1974
	Benson & Hedges Cup	158* B. F. Davison v
		Warwicks (Coventry) 1972
Best bowling figures:	Gillette Cup	4–26 P. T. Marner v Kent
		(Leicester) 1969
		4–26 N. M. McVicker v
		Northants (Leicester) 1974
	John Player League	6–17 K. Higgs v
		Glamorgan (Leicester) 1973
	Benson & Hedges Cup	5–20 R. Illingworth v
		Somerset (Leicester) 1974

MIDDLESEX

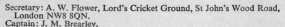

Formation of present club: 1863.
Colours: Blue
Badge: Three Seaxes.
County Champions (5): 1878, 1903, 1920, 1921, and 1947.
Joint Champions: 1949.
Gillette Cup semi-finalists (3): 1965, 1968, and 1973.

Secretary: A. W. Flower, Lord's Cricket Ground, St John's Wood Road, London NW8 8QN.
Captain: J. M. Brearley.

Graham Derek **BARLOW** (Ealing GS) B Folkestone 26/3/1950. LHB, RM. Cover field. Played in MCC Schools matches at Lord's 1968. Debut 1969. HS: 70 v Worcs (Worcester) 1974. HSJPL: 43 v Lancs (Lord's) 1974. Studied at Loughborough College for whom he played rugby.

John Michael (Mike) BREARLEY (City of London School and Cambridge) B Harrow 28/4/1942. RHB. Occasional WK. Debut 1961 scoring 1,222 runs (av 35.94) in first season. Blue 1961–64 (capt 1963–64). Cap 1964. Elected Best Young Cricketer of the Year in 1964 by the Cricket Writers' Club. Did not play in 1966 or 1967, but reappeared in latter half of each season between 1968 and 1970. Appointed county captain in 1971. Holds record for most runs scored for Cambridge U (4,310 runs, av 38.48). Tours: South Africa 1964–65, Pakistan 1966–67 (captain). 1,000 runs (5)— 2,178 runs (av 44.44) in 1964 best. Benson & Hedges Gold awards: 1. HS: 312* MCC under-25 v North Zone (Peshawar) 1966–67. HSUK: 173* v Glamorgan (Cardiff) 1974. HSGC: 60 v Surrey (Oval) 1965. HSJPL: 75* v Glamorgan (Lord's) 1974. HSBH: 87* v Leics (Leicester) 1974.

Roland Orlando BUTCHER B East Point, St Philip, Barbados 14/10/1953. RHB, RM. Debut 1974. HS: 53* v Surrey (Lord's) 1974. HSJPL: 33 v Northants (Lord's) 1974.

Phillippe Henri (Phil) EDMONDS (Gilbert Rennie HS, Lusaka, Skinners' School, Tunbridge Wells, Cranbrook School and Cambridge) B Lusaka, Northern Rhodesia (now Zambia) 8/3/1951. RHB, SLA. Debut for Cambridge U and county 1971. Blue 1971–73 (capt 1973). Cap 1974. Elected Best Young Cricketer of the Year in 1974 by the Cricket Writers' Club. HS: 76 Cambridge U v Notts (Nottingham) 1973. HSJPL: 28 v Hants (Southampton) 1974. HSBH: 40* Cambridge U v Leics (Leicester) 1972. BB: 7–38 v Kent (Canterbury) 1974. BBJPL: 3–19 v Leics (Lord's) 1973. Has also played rugby for University and narrowly missed obtaining Blue.

John Ernest EMBUREY B Peckham 20/8/1952. RHB, OB. Played for Surrey Young Cricketers 1969–70. Joined county staff 1972. Debut 1973. BB: 3–50 v Derbyshire (Burton-on-Trent) 1973.

Norman George (Smokey) FEATHERSTONE (King Edward VII High School, Johannesburg) B Que Que, Rhodesia 20/8/1949. RHB, **OB**. Member of South African Schools Team to England 1967. Debut for Transvaal B 1967–68 in Currie Cup competition. Debut for county 1968. Cap 1971. Asked to be released from contract after 1972 season, but subsequently changed his decision. Scored 1,096 runs (av 28.10) in 1970. HS: 125 v Sussex (Lord's) 1974. HSGC: 50 v Derbyshire (Lord's) 1970. HSJPL: 71 v Glos (Lydney) 1970. HSBH: 33 v Worcs (Lord's) 1974. BB: 3–32 v Notts (Worksop) 1971. BBJPL: 4–33 v Derbyshire (Derby) 1971.

Hilary Angelo (Larry) GOMES B Arima, Trinidad 13/7/1953. LHB, RM. Toured England with West Indian schoolboys team 1970. Debut for Trinidad v New Zealanders 1971–72. Joined county staff 1972. Debut for county 1973. HS: 123 East Trinidad v South Trinidad (California) 1972–73. HSUK: 85 v Hants (Lord's) 1974. HSGC: 22 v Notts (Lord's) 1973. HSJPL: 58 v Hants (Southampton) 1974. HSBH: 67 v Leics (Leicester) 1974. BB: 4–22 v Yorks (Bradford) 1973.

Hon. Timothy Michael LAMB (Shrewsbury School and Oxford) B Hartford (Cheshire) 24/3/1953. Younger son of Lord Rochester. RHB, RM. Debut for Oxford U 1973. Blue 1973–74. Debut for county 1974. HS: 40* v Surrey (Lord's) 1974. BB: 5–57 Oxford U v Notts (Oxford) 1974.

Dennis Alston MARRIOTT B Annotto Bay, Jamaica 29/11/1939. RHB, LM. Debut for Surrey 1965. Not re-engaged after 1967 season. Reappeared for Middlesex 1972. Cap 1973. HS: 24* Surrey v Leics (Leicester) 1967. BB: 5–71 v Notts (Nottingham) 1973. BBGC: 3–42 v Lancs (Lord's) 1973. BBJPL: 5–13 v Glos (Lydney) 1973.

John Thomas MURRAY B Kensington 1/4/1935. RHB, WK. Can bowl RM. Debut 1952. Cap 1956. Benefit (£8,010) in 1966. *Wisden* 1966. Second benefit in 1975. Tests: 21 between 1961 and 1967. Tours: New Zealand 1960–61, India and Pakistan 1961–62, Australia and New Zealand 1962–63 and 1965–66, Pakistan with Commonwealth team 1963–64, South Africa 1964–65, Ceylon and Pakistan 1968–69. 1,000 runs (6)— 1,160 runs (av 28.29) in 1965 best. Achieved wicket-keeper's 'double' in 1957 with 1,025 runs and 104 dismissals (82 ct 22 st): only L. E. G. Ames had previously recorded this feat. Dismissed 102 batsmen (95 ct 7 st) in 1960. Dismissed 6 batsmen (6 ct) in innings v India (Lord's) 1967, to equal record for a wicket-keeper in a Test Match. Dismissed 9 batsmen (8 ct 1 st) in match v Hants (Lord's) 1965. Gillette Man of Match awards: 2. HS: 142 MCC v NE Transvaal (Pretoria) 1964–65. HSUK: 133* v Oxford U (Oxford) 1963. HSGC: 63 v Norfolk (Lord's) 1970. HSJPL: 75* v Derbyshire (Chesterfield) 1973. HSBH: 45 v Northants (Lord's) 1974.

John Sidney Ernest PRICE (St Marylebone GS) B Harrow 22/7/1937. LHB, RFM. Debut 1961. Cap 1963. Benefit (£9,810) in 1972. Tests: 15 between 1963–64 and 1972. Left staff after 1972 season and will only play occasionally in future. Tours: India 1963–64, South Africa 1964–65. Took 94 wkts (av 18.74) in 1966. Gillette Man of Match awards: 2. HS: 53* D. H. Robins' XI v West Indians (Eastbourne) 1969. HSGC: 14 v Surrey (Oval) 1971. HSJPL: 12* v Glamorgan (Swansea) 1973. HSBH: 12* v

Essex (Harlow) 1973. BB: 8–48 v Derbyshire (Lord's) 1966. BBGC: 6–34 v Surrey (Oval) 1971. BBJPL: 4–27 v Sussex (Hove) 1974. BBBH: 3–49 v Surrey (Lord's) 1973.

Clive Thornton **RADLEY** (King Edward VI GS, Norwich) B Hertford 13/5/1944. RHB, LB. Debut 1964. Cap 1967. 1,000 runs (8)—1,414 runs (av 38.21) in 1969 and 1,413 runs (av 41.55) in 1972 best. Shared in 6th wkt partnership record for county, 227 with F. J. Titmus v South Africans (Lord's) 1965. HS: 139 v Sussex (Hove) 1967. HSGC: 44 v Surrey (Oval) 1970. HSJPL: 133* v Glamorgan (Lord's) 1969. HSBH: 63 v Glos (Lord's) 1972.

Nigel Patrick Dorai **ROSS** B Chelsea 5/4/1953. RHB, WK. Debut 1973 HS: 30 v Glos (Bristol) 1974. HSJPL: 37 v Warwickshire (Birmingham) 1974.

Michael Walter William (Mike) **SELVEY** (Battersea GS and Manchester and Cambridge Universities) B Chiswick 25/4/1948. RHB, RFM. Debut for Surrey 1968. Debut for Cambridge U and Blue 1971. Debut for Middlesex 1972. Cap 1973. Played for Orange Free State in 1973–74 Currie Cup competition. Benson & Hedges Gold awards: 1. HS: 42 Cambridge U v Pakistanis (Cambridge) 1971. HSJPL: 14* v Northants (Lord's) 1973. HSBH: 27* v Surrey (Lord's) 1973. BB: 6–43 v Sussex (Lord's) 1972. BBJPL: 4–21 v Lancs (Manchester) 1972. BBBH: 5–39 v Glos (Lord's) 1972. Played soccer for University.

Michael John (Mike) **SMITH** (Enfield GS) B Enfield 4/1/1942. RHB, SLA. Debut 1959. Cap 1967. 1,000 runs (7)— 1,705 runs (av 39.65) in 1970 best. Gillette Man of Match awards: 1. HS: 181 v Lancs (Manchester) 1967. HSGC. 90 v Lancs (Lord's) 1973. HSJPL: 110 v Lancs (Lord's) 1971. HSBH: 82 v Surrey (Lord's) 1973. BB: 4–13 v Glos (Lord's) 1961.

Frederick John (Fred) **TITMUS** (The William Ellis School, Highgate) B St Pancras 24/11/1932. RHB, OB. Debut 1949 (aged 16). Cap 1953. *Wisden* 1962. Benefit (£6,833) in 1963. Appointed county captain in 1965, but resigned post during 1968 season. Appointed vice-captain in 1971. Second benefit (£6,196) in 1973. Won single-wicket tournament at Lord's in 1966. Tests: 49 between 1955 and 1967-68. Tours: Pakistan 1955–56, Australia and New Zealand 1962–63, 1965–66 (Australia only), 1974–75, India 1963–64, South Africa 1964–65, West Indies 1967–68 (vice-captain), returning home early through loss of four toes in accident. 1,000 runs (8)—1,703 runs (av 37.02) in 1961 best. 100 wkts (16)—191 wkts (av 16.31) in 1955 best. Has taken more wickets (2,214) for Middlesex than any other bowler. Doubles (8): 1955 to 1957, 1959 to 1962, 1967. Missed double by 62 runs in 1963 and by 76 runs in 1968. Shared in 6th wkt partnership record for county, 227 with C. T. Radley v South Africans (Lord's) 1965. Hat-trick v Somerset (Weston-super-Mare) 1966. Took 4 wkts in 6 balls for England v New Zealand (Leeds) 1965. Gillette Man of Match awards: 3. HS: 137* MCC v South Australia (Adelaide) 1962–63. HSUK: 120* v Sussex (Hove) 1961. HSGC: 41 v Sussex (Lord's) 1973. HSJPL: 28 v Warwickshire (Lord's) 1973. HSBH: 17* v Worcs (Lord's) 1974. BB: 9–52 v Cambridge U (Cambridge) 1962 and 9–57 v Lancs (Lord's) 1964. BBGC: 5–26 v Derbyshire (Lord's) 1970. BBJPL: 5–25 v Essex (Lord's) 1971. Soccer (IL) for Watford and Hendon.

Martin Jeffrey VERNON B Middlesex Hospital, St Marylebone 4/7/1951. RHB, RFM. On MCC staff from 1966–72. Debut 1974. HS: 27 v Sussex (Hove) 1974. BB: 6–58 v Somerset (Taunton) 1974. BBJPL: 3–13 v Yorks (Leeds) 1974.

NB The following players whose particulars appeared in the 1974 Annual have been omitted: C. J. R. Black (left staff) and K. V. Jones (left staff).

The career record of Jones will be found elsewhere in this Annual.

COUNTY AVERAGES

County Championship: Played 20; won 7, drawn 8, lost 5
All first-class matches: Played 21; won 7, drawn 8, lost 6

BATTING AND FIELDING

Cap		M	I	NO	Runs	HS	Avge	100	50	Ct	St
—	T. M. Lamb	5	3	2	60	40*	60.00	—	—	—	—
1967	M. J. Smith	18	32	4	1235	170*	44.10	3	6	9	—
1964	J. M. Brearley	21	36	5	1324	173*	42.70	2	7	20	—
1967	C. T. Radley	21	35	5	1047	111*	34.90	3	4	32	—
1971	N. G. Featherstone	21	34	4	928	125	30.93	2	3	19	—
1956	J. T. Murray	20	27	3	584	82*	24.33	—	3	37	12
—	G. D. Barlow	12	21	2	457	70	24.05	—	4	2	—
—	R. O. Butcher	5	8	1	150	53*	21.42	—	1	3	—
1953	F. J. Titmus	21	26	6	366	81*	18.30	—	1	6	—
1974	P. H. Edmonds	20	27	4	393	57	17.08	—	1	19	—
1971	K. V. Jones	14	17	2	251	52	16.73	—	1	1	—
—	N. P. D. Ross	6	11	1	137	30	13.70	—	1	1	—
1963	J. S. E. Price	7	3	1	26	15	13.00	—	—	3	—
—	M. J. Vernon	10	12	4	99	27	12.37	—	—	1	—
—	L. A. Gomes	12	19	1	222	85	12.33	—	1	2	—
1973	M. W. W. Selvey	15	16	7	102	37*	11.33	—	—	2	—

Played in two matches: D. A. Marriott 1, 1*; 7.
Played in one match: J. E. Emburey 4* (2 ct).

BOWLING

	Type	O	M	R	W	Avge	Best	5 wI	10 wM
J. S. E. Price	RFM	153	33	451	21	21.47	6–54	1	—
F. J. Titmus	OB	901.2	302	1851	85	21.77	7–39	6	2
P. H. Edmonds	SLA	752.5	248	1704	73	23.34	7–38	3	1
N. G. Featherstone	OB	42.5	9	132	5	26.40	2–14	—	—
K. V. Jones	RM	278.5	69	778	27	28.81	5–78	1	—
M. J. Vernon	RFM	155	19	586	20	29.30	6–58	2	1
M.W.W. Selvey	RFM	414.3	82	1246	35	35.60	6–109	2	—
L. A. Gomes	RM	105	24	308	6	51.33	2–21	—	—
T. M. Lamb	RM	94	21	270	5	53.80	3–55	—	—

Also bowled: J. E. Emburey 21-2-74-0; D. A. Marriott 38-9-91-4.

County Records
First-class cricket

Highest innings totals:	For ...642–3d v Hampshire (Southampton)		1923
	Agst...665 by West Indians (Lord's)		1939
Lowest innings totals:	For ... 20 v MCC (Lord's)		1864
	Agst... 31 by Gloucestershire (Bristol)		1924
Highest individual innings:	For ...331* J. D. Robertson v Worcs (Worcester)		1949
	Agst...316* J. D. Hobbs for Surrey (Lord's)		1926
Best bowling in an innings:	For ...10–40 G. O. Allen v Lancs (Lord's)		1929
	Agst... 9–38 R. C. Robertson-Glasgow for Somerset (Lord's)		1924
Best bowling in a match:	For ...16–114 { G. Burton v Yorks (Sheffield)		1888
	{ J. T. Hearne v Lancs (Manchester)		1898
	Agst...C. W. L. Parker for Glos (Cheltenham)		1930
Most runs in a season:	2650 (av 85.48) W. J. Edrich		1947
runs in a career:	40302 (av 49.81) E. H. Hendren		1907–1937
100s in a season:	13 by D. C. S. Compton		1947
100s in a career:	119 by E. H. Hendren		1907–1937
wickets in a season:	158 (av 14.63) F. J. Titmus		1955
wickets in a career:	2214 (av 21.3) F. J. Titmus		1949–1974

RECORD WICKET STANDS

1st 310 W. E. Russell & M. J. Harris v Pakistanis (Lord's) 1967
2nd 380 F. A. Tarrant & J. W. Hearne v Lancashire (Lord's) 1914
3rd 424* W. J. Edrich & D. C. S. Compton v Somerset (Lord's) 1948
4th 325 J. W. Hearne & E. H. Hendren v Hampshire (Lord's) 1919
5th 338 R. S. Lucas & T. C. O'Brien v Sussex (Hove) 1895
6th 227 C. T. Radley & F. J. Titmus v South Africans (Lord's) 1965
7th 271* E. H. Hendren & F. T. Mann v Nottinghamshire (Nottingham) 1925
8th 182* M. H. C. Doll & H. R. Murrell v Nottinghamshire (Lord's) 1913
9th 160* E. H. Hendren & T. J. Durston v Essex (Leyton) 1927
10th 230 R. W. Nicholls & W. Roche v Kent (Lord's) 1899

One-day cricket

Highest innings totals:	Gillette Cup	280–8 v Sussex (Lord's)	1965
	John Player League	241–6 v Worcestershire (Lord's)	1970
	Benson & Hedges Cup	235–7 v Kent (Lord's)	1972
Lowest innings totals:	Gillette Cup	41 v Essex (Westcliff)	1972
	John Player League	23 v Yorkshire (Leeds)	1974
	Benson & Hedges Cup	122 v Sussex (Lord's)	1973
Highest individual innings:	Gillette Cup	123 W. E. Russell v Surrey (Lord's)	1968
	John Player League	133* C. T. Radley v Glamorgan (Lord's)	1969
	Benson & Hedges Cup	110 P. H. Parfitt v Essex (Lord's)	1972
Best bowling figures:	Gillette Cup	6–28 K. V. Jones v Lancashire (Lord's)	1974
	John Player League	6–6 R. W. Hooker v Surrey (Lord's)	1969
	Benson & Hedges Cup	5–39 M. W. W. Selvey v Gloucestershire (Lord's)	1972

NORTHAMPTONSHIRE

Formation of present club: 1820, reorganised 1878.
Colours: Maroon.
Badge: Tudor Rose.
County Championship runners-up (3):
 1912, 1957, and 1965.
Gillette Cup semi-finalists: 1963.

Secretary: K. C. Turner, County Ground, Wantage Rd, Northampton,
NN1 4TJ.
Captain: R. T. Virgin.

Bishen Singh BEDI (St Francis HS, Amritsar and Punjab University).
B Amritsar, India 25/9/1946. RHB, SLA. Debut for Northern Punjab
in Ranji Trophy 1961–62, aged 15½ years, subsequently transferring to
Delhi. Debut for county and cap 1972. Tests: 35 for India between 1966–67
and 1974. Played in 5 matches for Rest of World v Australia 1971–72.
Tours: India to England 1967, 1971 and 1974, Australia and New Zealand
1967–68, West Indies 1970–71, Rest of World to Australia 1971–72. 100
wkts (2)—112 wkts (av 24.64) in 1974 best. Hat-trick Delhi v Punjab
(Delhi) 1968–69. HS: 61 Delhi v Jammu and Kashmir (Srinagar) 1970–71
and 61 v Glos (Northampton) 1974. HSJPL: 14 v Warwickshire
(Birmingham) 1972. HSBH: 11 v Leics (Northampton) 1973. BB: 7–19
North Zone v South Zone (Madras) 1969–70. BBUK: 7–34 v Essex
(Chelmsford) 1972. BBJPL: 4–35 v Glos (Northampton) 1974.

Geoffrey (Geoff) COOK B Middlesbrough 9/10/1951. RHB, SLA.
Debut 1971. HS: 122* v Sussex (Hove) 1971. HSGC: 23 v Glamorgan
(Northampton) 1972. HSJPL: 55 v Hants (Northampton) 1974. HSBH:
54 v Cambridge U (Cambridge) 1972.

Robert Michael Henry (Bob) COTTAM B Cleethorpes (Lincolnshire)
16/10/1944. RHB, RFM. Debut for Hampshire 1963. Cap 1965. Elected
Best Young Cricketer of the Year in 1968 by the Cricket Writers' Club.
Left Hants after 1971 season and made debut for Northants in 1972. Cap
1972. Tests: 4 in 1968–69 and 1972–73. Tours: Ceylon and Pakistan
1968–69, India, Pakistan, and Sri Lanka 1972–73. 100 wkts (3)—130 wkts
(av 17.56) in 1968 best. Gillette Man of Match awards: 1 (for Hants).
Benson & Hedges Gold awards: 1. HS: 62* v Glos (Northampton) 1974.
HSGC: 15 Hants v Warwickshire (Birmingham) 1964. HSJPL: 15*
Hants v Essex (Southampton) 1970 and 15 v Warwickshire (Birmingham)
1972.BB: 9–25 Hants v Lancs (Manchester) 1965 (the best bowling figures
ever in an innings for Hants). BBGC: 4–9 Hants v Wilts (Chippenham)
1964. BBJPL: 4–17 v Notts (Kettering) 1972. BBBH: 4–28 v Warwickshire
(Coventry) 1973.

John Cooper James DYE B Gillingham 24/7/1942. RHB, LFM. Plays
in contact lenses. Debut for Kent 1962. Cap 1966. Not re-engaged after
1971 season and made debut for Northants in 1972. Cap 1972. Played
for Eastern Province in 1972–73 Currie Cup competition. HS: 29* v
Worcs (Northampton) 1972. HSJPL: 10* v Notts (Luton) 1973. BB: 7–45

v Essex (Westcliff) 1973. BBGC: 3–39 v Glamorgan (Northampton) 1972. BBJPL: 4–18 Kent v Somerset (Bath) 1969 and 4–18 v Kent (Canterbury) 1974. BBBH: 3–21 v Warwickshire (Coventry) 1973.

Brian James GRIFFITHS B Wellingborough 13/6/1949. RHB, RM. Debut 1974. HS: 6 v Somerset (Taunton) 1974. BB: 3–54 v Oxford U (Oxford) 1974. BBJPL: 4–45 v Warwickshire (Peterborough) 1974.

Alan HODGSON (Annfield Plain GTS) B Moorside Consett, County Durham 27/10/1951. Tall (6ft 4½in). LHB, RFM. Joined staff 1969. Debut 1970. HS: 41 v New Zealanders (Northampton) 1973. HSGC: 20 v Kent (Canterbury) 1971. HSJPL: 26 v Middlesex (Lord's) 1973. HSBH: 13 v Worcs (Worcester) 1973. BB: 5–36 v Essex (Leyton) 1974. BBJPL: 4–34 v Surrey (Northampton) 1971.

Wayne LARKINS B Roxton (Beds) 22/11/1953. RHB. Joined staff 1969. Debut 1972. HS: 109 v Cambridge U (Cambridge) 1973. HSJPL: 45 v Yorks (Huddersfield) 1974. HSBH: 34 v Warwickshire (Coventry) 1973.

MUSHTAQ MOHAMMAD B Junagadh, India 22/11/1943. RHB, LBG. Fourth of family of five cricket-playing brothers which includes Hanif Mohammad. Debut 1956–57 at age of 13 years 41 days for Karachi Whites v Hyderabad (Hyderabad) scoring 87 and taking 5–28. Made Test debut v West Indies 1958–59 at age of 15 years 124 days and youngest player ever to do so. Scored two Test centuries before the age of 19, the only player ever to have scored a Test century under this age. *Wisden* 1962. Joined Northants in 1964. Won single-wicket tournament at Lord's in 1965. Qualified for county championship in 1966. Cap 1967. Tests: 36 for Pakistan between 1958–59 and 1974. Played in 2 matches for Rest of World in 1970. Tours: Pakistan to India 1960–61, England 1962 and also in 1963 with Pakistan Eaglets, Australia and New Zealand 1972–73. 1,000 runs (9)—1,949 runs (av 59.06) in 1972 best. Scored 1,112 runs (av 61.77) in 1961–62. Scored two centuries in match (128* and 123) for D. H. Robins' XI v West Indians (Eastbourne) 1969. Gillette Man of Match awards: 1. HS: 303* Karachi Blues v Karachi University (Karachi) 1967–68. HSUK: 176 Pakistanis v Cambridge U (Cambridge) 1962. HSGC: 68 v Notts (Northampton) 1967. HSJPL: 89 v Surrey (Tolworth) 1973. HSBH: 58 v Leics (Leicester) 1974. BB: 7–18 Karachi Whites v Khairpur (Karachi) 1963–64. BBUK: 7–59 Pakistanis v Middlesex (Lord's) 1974. BBGC: 3–31 v Beds (Luton) 1967. BBJPL: 4–30 v Lancs (Northampton) 1974.

SARFRAZ NAWAZ (Government College, Lahore) B Lahore, Pakistan 1/12/1948. RHB, RFM. Debut 1967–68 for West Pakistan Governor's XI v Punjab University at Lahore and subsequently played for various Lahore sides. Debut for county 1969. Not re-engaged after 1971 season, but rejoined staff in 1974. Tests: 11 for Pakistan between 1968–69 and 1974. Tours: Pakistan to England 1971 and 1974, Australia and New Zealand 1972–73. HS: 59 Punjab University v Lahore (Lahore) 1970–71. HSUK: 53 Pakistanis v England (Leeds) 1974. HSJPL: 40* v Glos (Brackley) 1971. HSBH: 24 v Middlesex (Lord's) 1974. BB: 8–27 Pakistanis v Notts (Nottingham) 1974. BBJPL: 4–17 v Leics (Kettering) 1971.

George SHARP B West Hartlepool 12/3/1950. RHB, WK. Can also bowl LM. Debut 1968. Cap 1973. HS: 76* v Sussex (Hove) 1972. HSGC: 30 v Kent (Canterbury) 1971. HSJPL: 47 v Sussex (Hove) 1974. HSBH: 36 v Warwickshire (Coventry) 1973. England Boys Table Tennis player.

David Stanley STEELE B Stoke-on-Trent 29/9/1941. Cousin of B.S. Crump, former Northants player, and brother of J. F. Steele of Leics. RHB, SLA. Short-leg field. Played for Staffordshire from 1958 to 1962. Debut for Northants 1963. Cap 1965. Benefit in 1975. 1,000 runs (7)—1,618 runs (av 52.19) in 1972 best. HS: 140* v Worcs (Worcester) 1971. HSGC: 60 v Sussex (Northampton) 1973. HSJPL: 76 v Sussex (Hove) 1974. HSBH: 69 v Warwickshire (Northampton) 1974. BB: 8–29 v Lancs (Northampton) 1966.

Alan TAIT B Washington, County Durham 27/12/1953. LHB. Debut 1971. HS: 99 v Lancs (Blackpool) 1974. HSGC: 39 v Glamorgan (Northampton) 1972. HSJPL: 102* v Warwickshire (Peterborough) 1974. HSBH: 51 v Worcs (Northampton) 1972.

Roy Thomas VIRGIN (Huish's GS, Taunton) B Taunton 26/8/1939. RHB, LB. Occasional WK. Debut for Somerset 1957. Cap 1960. Testimonial (£4,000) in 1969. Wisden 1970. Left Somerset after 1972 season and made debut for Northants by special registration in 1973. Cap 1974. Appointed county captain for 1975. Played for Western Province in 1972–73 Currie Cup competition. 1,000 runs (10)—2,223 runs (av 47.29) in 1970 best. Scored two centuries in match (124 and 125*) Somerset v Warwickshire (Birmingham) 1965. Held 42 catches in 1966, a Somerset record. Gillette Man of Match awards: 2 (for Somerset). HS: 179* Somerset v Lancs (Manchester) 1971. HSGC: 105* Somerset v Lancs (Taunton) 1971. HSJPL: 123* Somerset v Surrey (Oval) 1970. HSBH: 59 v Warwickshire (Northampton) 1974.

Patrick James (Jim) WATTS (Stratton School, Biggleswade) B Henlow (Beds) 16/6/1940. Brother of P. D. Watts who also played for county. LHB, RM. Debut 1959, scoring 1,118 runs (av 26.66) in his first season. Cap 1962. Left staff after 1966 season, but rejoined staff in 1970. Appointed county captain in 1971. Benefit in 1974. Left staff after 1974 season to train as a teacher, but will be available for one-day matches in 1975 and in latter part of season. Appointed vice-captain for 1975. 1,000 runs (7)—1,798 runs (av 43.85) in 1962 best. Benson & Hedges Gold awards: 1. HS: 145 v Hants (Bournemouth) 1962. HSGC: 40 v Glamorgan (Northampton) 1972. HSJPL: 83 v Lancs (Bedford) 1971. HSBH: 40 v Middlesex (Lord's) 1974. BB: 6–18 v Somerset (Taunton) 1965. BBGC: 4–48 v Warwickshire (Northampton) 1964. BBJPL: 5–24 v Notts (Peterborough) 1971. BBBH: 4–11 v Middlesex (Lord's) 1974.

Peter WILLEY B Sedgefield (County Durham) 6/12/1949. RHB, RM. Debut 1966 aged 16 years 5 months scoring 78 in second innings of first match v Cambridge U (Cambridge). Cap 1971. Scored 923 runs (av 28.84) in 1970. HS: 158* v Oxford U (Oxford) 1971. HSGC: 20 v Glamorgan (Northampton) 1968 and 20 v Sussex (Northampton) 1973. HSJPL: 102 v Sussex (Hove) 1971. SHBH: 58 v Warwickshire (Northampton) 1974. BB: 5–14 v Middlesex (Lord's) 1970. BBGC: 3–42 v Somerset (Northampton) 1967. BBJPL: 4–59 v Kent (Northampton) 1971.

NORTHAMPTONSHIRE

Richard Grenville WILLIAMS (Ellesmere Port GS) B Bangor (Caernarvonshire) 10/8/1957. RHB, OB. Debut for 2nd XI in 1972, aged 14 years 11 months. Debut 1974, aged 16 years 10 months. One match v Oxford U (Oxford). HS: 64 v Oxford U (Oxford) 1974.

NB The following players whose particulars appeared in the 1974 Annual have been omitted: R. R. Bailey (left staff), N. Maltby, and C. Milburn. In addition, J. W. Swinburne who re-appeared in three matches has not been included as he is unlikely to play again.

The career records of Maltby, Milburn, and Swinburne will be found elsewhere in this Annual.

COUNTY AVERAGES

County Championship: Played 20; won 9, drawn 9, lost 2
All first-class matches: Played 23; won 9, drawn 11, lost 3

BATTING AND FIELDING

Cap		M	I	NO	Runs	HS	Avge	100	50	Ct	St
1974	R. T. Virgin	23	39	5	1936	144*	56.74	7	10	24	—
1962	P. J. Watts	21	33	7	1040	104*	40.00	1	7	13	—
1965	D. S. Steele	21	36	3	1022	104	30.96	1	7	20	—
—	Sarfraz Nawaz	6	9	3	156	38	26.00	—	—	2	—
1971	P. Willey	23	37	3	790	100*	23.23	1	2	11	—
—	G. Cook	23	37	4	746	85	21.31	—	2	33	—
—	A. Tait	16	26	0	545	99	20.96	—	4	3	—
—	N. Maltby	4	6	2	83	59	20.75	—	1	1	—
1972	B. S. Bedi	10	11	3	158	61	19.75	—	1	1	—
1973	G. Sharp	23	32	7	443	48	17.72	—	—	44	6
1967	Mushtaq Mohammad	6	11	0	187	46	17.00	—	—	5	—
1963	C. Milburn	12	17	4	167	39*	12.84	—	—	4	—
—	A. Hodgson	13	15	4	128	30	11.63	—	—	4	—
1972	R. M. H. Cottam	14	10	2	88	62*	11.00	—	1	8	—
—	W. Larkins	9	12	3	71	15	7.88	—	—	4	—
1972	J. C. J. Dye	20	15	8	47	11*	6.71	—	—	5	—
—	J. W. Swinburne	3	3	1	5	4*	2.50	—	—	2	—
—	B. J. Griffiths	5	7	2	6	6	1.20	—	—	2	—

Played in one match: R. G. Williams 15 & 64.

BOWLING

								5	10
	Type	O	M	R	W	Avge	Best	wI	wM
B. S. Bedi	SLA	456.3	152	999	55	18.16	7–75	3	1
Sarfraz Nawaz	RFM	232.2	62	582	31	18.77	5–73	1	—
R.M.H. Cottam	RFM	454	113	1101	56	19.66	6–88	4	—
J. W. Swinburne	OB	80	20	219	10	21.90	5–22	1	—
J. C. J. Dye	LFM	541.1	110	1512	69	21.91	5–54	2	—
A. Hodgson	RFM	284.2	67	751	31	24.22	5–36	1	—
Mushtaq Mohammad	LBG	124	43	353	14	25.21	4–71	—	—
C. Milburn	RM	146	29	353	12	29.41	3–25	—	—
D. S. Steele	SLA	161	59	405	13	13.15	3–68	—	—
B. J. Griffiths	RM	110	23	385	10	38.50	3–54	—	—
P. Willey	RM	238.1	69	595	15	39.66	3–94	—	—

Also bowled: W. Larkins 7-2-27-0; N. Maltby 10-1-42-0; R. T. Virgin 1-1-0-0; P. J. Watts 65.1-25-119-1; R. G. Williams 22-5-76-2.

County Records
First-class cricket

Highest innings totals:	For ...557–6d v Sussex (Hove)		1914
	Agst...670–9d by Sussex (Hove)		1921
Lowest innings totals:	For ... 12 v Gloucestershire (Gloucester)		1907
	Agst... 43 by Leicestershire (Peterborough)		1968
Highest individual innings:	For ...300 R. Subba Row v Surrey (The Oval)		1958
	Agst...333 K. S. Duleepsinhji for Sussex (Hove)		1930
Best bowling in an innings:	For ...10–127 V. W. C. Jupp v Kent (Tunbridge Wells)		1932
	Agst...10–30 C. Blythe for Kent (Northampton)		1907
Best bowling in a match:	For ...15–31 G. E. Tribe v Yorkshire (Northampton)		1958
	Agst...17–48 C. Blythe for Kent (Northampton)		1907
Most runs in a season:	2198 (av 51.11) D. Brookes		1952
runs in a career:	28980 (av 36.13) D. Brookes		1934–1959
100s in a season:	8 by R. Haywood		1921
100s in a career:	67 by D. Brookes		1934–1959
wickets in a season:	175 (av 18.70) G. E. Tribe		1955
wickets in a career:	1097 (av 21.31) E. W. Clark		1922–1947

RECORD WICKET STANDS

1st 361	N. Oldfield & V. Broderick v Scotland (Peterborough)	1953
2nd 307*	T. L. Livingston & D. Barrick v Sussex (Northampton)	1953
3rd 320	T. L. Livingston & F. Jakeman v South Africans (Northampton)	1951
4th 232	G. J. Thompson & S. G. Smith v Hampshire (Portsmouth)	1910
5th 347	D. Brookes & D. Barrick v Essex (Northampton)	1952
6th 376	R. Subba Row & A. Lightfoot v Surrey (The Oval)	1958
7th 229	W. W. Timms & F. A. Walden v Warwickshire (Northampton)	1926
8th 155	F. R. Brown & A. E. Nutter v Glamorgan (Northampton)	1952
9th 156	R. Subba Row & S. Starkie v Lancashire (Northampton)	1955
10th 148	R. Bellamy & V. Murdin v Glamorgan (Northampton)	1925

One-day cricket

Highest innings totals:	Gillette Cup	248 v Sussex (Hove)	1968
	John Player League	239–3 v Kent (Dover)	1970
	Benson & Hedges Cup	249–3 v Warwickshire (Northampton)	1974
Lowest innings totals:	Gillette Cup	62 v Leics (Leicester)	1974
	John Player League	41 v Middlesex (Northampton)	1972
	Benson & Hedges Cup	113 v Worcs (Northampton)	1974
Highest individual innings:	Gillette Cup	84 C. Milburn v Middlesex (Lord's)	1963
	John Player League	115* H. M. Ackerman v Kent (Dover)	1970
	Benson & Hedges Cup	69 D. S. Steele v Warwickshire (Northampton)	1974

Best bowling figures:	Gillette Cup	5–24 J. D. F. Larter v Leicestershire (Leicester)	1964
	John Player League	6–22 R. R. Bailey v Hants (Portsmouth)	1972
	Benson & Hedges Cup	4–11 P. J. Watts v Middlesex (Lord's)	1974

NOTTINGHAMSHIRE

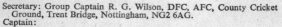

Formation of present club: 1841, reorganised 1866.
Colours: Green and gold.
Badge: County Badge of Nottinghamshire.
County Champions (6): 1883, 1884, 1885, 1886, 1907, and 1929.
Joint Champions (6): 1873, 1875, 1879, 1880, 1882, and 1889.
Gillette Cup semi-finalists: 1969.

Secretary: Group Captain R. G. Wilson, DFC, AFC, County Cricket Ground, Trent Bridge, Nottingham, NG2 6AG.
Captain:

John Dennis BIRCH B Nottingham 18/6/1955. RHB, RM. Debut 1973. HS: 26 v Worcs (Worcester) 1973. HSJPL: 13 v Sussex (Eastbourne) 1974. BB: 3–45 v Worcs (Newark) 1974.

Charles John COOK B Retford 5/6/1946. RHB, OB. Debut 1974. One match v Indians (Nottingham). Also played in nine John Player League matches and one Gillette Cup match. HSJPL: 17 v Glamorgan (Swansea) 1974. BBJPL: 4–19 v Surrey (Nottingham) 1974.

Peter John HACKER B Lenton Abbey, Nottingham 16/7/1952. RHB, LFM. Debut 1974. One match v Pakistanis (Nottingham). Also played in one John Player League match.

William Henry (Dusty) HARE (Magnus GS, Newark) B Newark 29/11/1952. RHB. Debut 1971. Left staff after 1974 season and will play only occasionally in future. HS: 36 v Warwickshire (Coventry) 1974. Plays rugby (full-back) for Newark and East Midlands and appeared for England v Wales 1973–74.

Michael John (Mike, Pasty) HARRIS B St Just-in-Roseland (Cornwall) 25/5/1944. RHB, LBG. Occasional WK. Debut for Middlesex 1964. Cap 1967. Left staff after 1968 season and joined Notts by special registration in 1969. Cap 1970. Played for Eastern Province in 1971–72 Currie Cup competition. 1,000 runs (7)—2,238 runs (av 50.86) in 1971 best. Scored 9 centuries in 1971 to equal county record. Scored two centuries in match twice in 1971, 118 and 123 v Leics (Leicester) and 107 and 131* v Essex (Chelmsford). Shared in 1st wkt partnership record for Middlesex,

312 with W. E. Russell v Pakistanis (Lord's) 1967. Benson & Hedges Gold awards: 2. HS: 201* v Glamorgan (Nottingham) 1973. HSGC: 101 v Somerset (Nottingham) 1970. HSJPL: 104* v Hants (Nottingham) 1970. HSBH: 101 v Yorks (Hull) 1973. BB: 4–16 v Warwickshire (Nottingham) 1969.

Basharat HASSAN (City HS, Nairobi) B Nairobi (Kenya) 24/3/1944. RHB, RM, occasional WK. Debut for East Africa Invitation XI v MCC 1963–64. Played for Coast Invitation XI v Pakistan International Airways 1964. Also played for Kenya against these and other touring sides. Debut for county 1966. Cap 1970. 1,000 runs (3)—1,395 runs (av 32.44) in 1970 best. HS: 125* v Pakistanis (Nottingham) 1971. HSGC: 78 v Middlesex (Nottingham) 1969. HSJPL: 86* v Warwickshire (Birmingham) 1972. HSBH: 98* v Minor Counties (Nottingham) 1973. BBGC: 3–20 v Durham (Chester-le-Street) 1967. Plays hockey.

Peter David JOHNSON (Nottingham HS and Cambridge) B Nottingham 12/11/1949. RHB, LBG. Debut for D. H. Robins' XI v Oxford U (Eastbourne) 1969 whilst still at school. Debut for University and county 1970. Blue 1970–72. Did not play in 1973 or 1974, but has joined staff for 1975. HS: 82 Cambridge U v Leics (Cambridge) 1970. BB: 3–34 Cambridge U v Glamorgan (Cambridge) 1970. Plays rugby.

Harry Chand LATCHMAN (Christopher Wren Comprehensive, Shepherd's Bush, London) B Kingston, Jamaica 26/7/1943. RHB, LBG. Debut for Middlesex 1965. Cap 1968. Not re-engaged after 1973 season and made debut for Notts in 1974. Testimonial for Middlesex in 1974. HS: 96 Middlesex v Worcs (Kidderminster) 1972. HSGC: 15 Middlesex v Surrey (Oval) 1970. HSJPL: 45* Middlesex v Somerset (Bath) 1970. HSBH: 26 v Yorks (Nottingham) 1974. BB: 7–91 Middlesex v Pakistanis (Lord's) 1967. BBJPL: 3–26 v Warwickshire (Birmingham) 1974.

Nirmal NANAN B Preysal Village, Couva, Trinidad 19/8/1951. RHB, LBG. Toured England with West Indian schoolboy team 1970. Debut 1969–70 for South Trinidad v North Trinidad (Pointe-a-Pierre). Debut for county 1971. HS: 72 v Oxford U (Oxford) 1971. HSJPL: 58 v Somerset (Torquay) 1972. BB: 3–12 v Oxford U (Oxford) 1971.

Derek William RANDALL B Retford 24/2/1951. RHB, RM. Played in one John Player League match in 1971. Debut 1972. Cap 1973. Scored 1,013 runs (av 27.37) in 1973. Benson & Hedges Gold awards: 1. HS: 107 v Worcs (Worcester) 1973. HSGC: 17 v Warwickshire (Birmingham) 1974. HSJPL: 93 v Somerset (Nottingham) 1974. HSBH: 56 v Lancs (Nottingham) 1973.

Clive Edward Butler RICE (St John's College, Johannesburg) B Johannesburg 23/7/1949. RHB, RFM. Debut for Transvaal 1969–70. Played for D. H. Robins' XI v West Indians 1973 and v Pakistanis 1974. Has joined county for 1975. HS: 81 Transvaal B v North-Eastern Transvaal (Pretoria) 1969–70 in debut match, scoring 64 in second innings. HSUK: 34* D. H. Robins' XI v West Indians (Eastbourne) 1973. BB: 5–65 Transvaal B v Orange Free State (Bloemfontein) 1972–73.

Michael John (Mike) SMEDLEY (Woodhouse GS, Sheffield) B Maltby (Yorks) 28/10/1941. RHB, OB. Very good fielder, particularly cover point. Played for Yorkshire 2nd XI 1960 to 1962. Debut 1964. Cap 1966. Appointed county vice-captain in 1973. Benefit in 1975. 1,000 runs in season (7)—1,718 runs (av 38.17) in 1971 best. Scored two centuries in match (119 and 109) v Lancs (Manchester) 1971. Shared in 7th wkt partnership record for county, 204 with R. A. White v Surrey (Oval) 1967. Gillette Man of Match awards: 1. Benson & Hedges Gold awards: 1. HS: 149 v Glamorgan (Cardiff) 1970. HSGC: 75 v Glos (Nottingham) 1968. HSJPL: 61 v Yorks (Sheffield) 1970. HSBH: 66 v Minor Counties (Nottingham) 1973.

Barry STEAD B Leeds 21/6/1939. LHB, LFM. Debut for Yorks 1959, taking 7–76 v Indians (Bradford) in his first match. Played for Combined Services in 1960 and 1961. Debut for Notts 1962. Cap 1969. Took 98 wkts (av 20.38) in 1972. Hat-trick v Somerset (Nottingham) 1972. HS: 58 v Glos (Bristol) 1972. HSGC: 24 v Worcs (Worcester) 1974. HSJPL: 33 v Worcs (Nottingham) 1974. HSBH: 22* v Lancs (Manchester) and 22 v Yorks (Nottingham) 1974. BB: 8–44 v Somerset (Nottingham) 1972. BBGC: 5–44 v Worcs (Worcester) 1974. BBJPL: 4–24 v Somerset (Torquay) 1972. BBBH: 3–19 v Derbyshire (Chesterfield) 1973.

William (Bill) TAYLOR B Manchester 24/1/1947. RHB, RFM. Played for Lancs 2nd XI 1964–65. Professional for Leek in North Staffs and South Cheshire League 1967–70. Debut 1971. Benson & Hedges Gold awards: 1. HS: 26* v Leics (Nottingham) 1972. HSGC: 11* v Hants (Portsmouth) 1971. HSJPL: 13* v Warwickshire (Birmingham) 1974. HSBH: 17* v Derbyshire (Chesterfield) 1973. BB: 6–42 v Warwickshire (Nottingham) 1972. BBJPL: 4–11 v Sussex (Nottingham) 1972. BBBH: 4–25 v Derbyshire (Chesterfield) 1973.

Paul Adrian TODD B Morton (Notts) 12/3/1953. RHB, RM. Debut 1972. HS: 66* v Warwickshire (Nottingham) 1972 in debut match retiring hurt with hairline fracture of jaw. HSGC: 41 v Middlesex (Lord's) 1973. HSJPL: 58 v Glamorgan (Nottingham) 1973.

Howard Trevor TUNNICLIFFE (Malvern College) B Derby 4/3/1950. RHB, RM. Debut 1973. Is training as a teacher and will only be available for one-day matches until July. HS: 87 v Derbyshire (Nottingham) 1974. HSGC: 27 v Warwickshire (Birmingham) 1974. HSJPL: 22 v Northants (Nottingham), 22* v Leics (Leicester) and 22 v Glamorgan (Swansea) 1974. HSBH: 17 v Yorks (Nottingham) 1974. BB: 3–55 v Lancs (Manchester) 1974.

Robert Arthur (Bob) WHITE (Chiswick GS) B Fulham 6/10/1936. LHB, OB. Debut for Middlesex 1958. Cap 1963. Debut for Notts after special registration in 1966 and developed into useful off-break bowler. Cap 1966. Benefit in 1974. Scored 1,355 runs (av 33.87) in 1963. HS: 116* v Surrey (Oval) 1967, sharing in 7th wkt partnership record for county, 204 with M. J. Smedley. HSGC: 39 v Worcs (Worcester) 1966, HSJPL: 86* v Surrey (Guildford) 1973. HSBH: 52* v Worcs (Worcester) 1973. BB: 7–41 v Derbyshire (Ilkeston) 1971. BBGC: 3–43 v Worcs (Worcester) 1968. BBJPL: 4–48 v Kent (Canterbury) 1970. BBBH: 3–31 v Minor Counties (Cleethorpes) 1972.

Philip Alan WILKINSON B Hucknall (Notts) 23/8/1951. RHB, RM. Debut 1971. Cap 1974. HS: 28* v Cambridge U (Cambridge) 1974. HSBH: 14* v Derbyshire (Nottingham) 1974. BB: 4–46 v Surrey (Guildford) 1974. BBJPL: 3–20 v Warwickshire (Birmingham) 1974. BBBH: 3–31 v Minor Counties (Lakenham) 1974.

NB The following players whose particulars appeared in the 1974 Annual have been omitted: J. D. Bond (retired), D. R. Doshi (not re-engaged), G. Edwards, C. Forbes, D. A. Pullan (left staff), and G. S. Sobers (retired). The career records of Bond, Doshi, Pullan, and Sobers will be found elsewhere in this Annual.

COUNTY AVERAGES

County Championship: Played 20; won 1, drawn 10, lost 9
All first-class matches: Played 24; won 2, drawn 12, lost 10

BATTING AND FIELDING

Cap		M	I	NO	Runs	HS	Avge	100	50	Ct	St
1968	G. S. Sobers	15	27	4	1110	132*	48.26	4	6	17	—
1970	M. J. Harris	23	41	3	1690	133	44.47	6	7	24	5
1966	M. J. Smedley	23	41	6	1134	118*	32.40	1	6	26	—
1970	B. Hassan	22	42	6	1009	83*	28.02	—	9	22	—
—	H. T. Tunnicliffe	11	19	5	357	87	25.50	—	2	2	—
1973	D. W. Randall	21	40	4	763	105	21.19	1	4	12	—
1966	R. A. White	23	38	3	563	83	16.08	—	3	9	—
—	H. C. Latchman	20	29	7	302	78	13.72	—	1	13	—
—	P. A. Todd	10	18	1	232	37	13.64	—	1	4	—
1974	J. D. Bond	17	24	4	245	65*	12.25	—	1	3	—
—	W. H. Hare	5	9	1	92	36	11.50	—	—	4	—
1974	P. A. Wilkinson	15	21	8	148	28*	11.38	—	—	2	—
1971	D. A. Pullan	6	10	4	58	25	9.66	—	—	12	5
1969	B. Stead	23	30	2	257	32*	9.17	—	—	6	—
—	J. D. Birch	6	10	1	76	21	8.44	—	—	7	—
—	N. Nanan	5	10	0	83	35	8.30	—	—	4	—
—	W. Taylor	14	13	5	51	14*	6.37	—	—	4	—
—	D. R. Doshi	3	3	0	6	2	2.00	—	—	1	—

Played in one match: C. J. Cook 1 (1 ct); P. J. Hacker 0 & 0 (1ct).

BOWLING

	Type	O	M	R	W	Avge	Best	5 wI	10 wM
R. A. White H. C.	OB	704.4	197	1909	79	24.16	6–41	4	1
Latchman	LBG	351.3	66	1158	47	24.63	6–31	3	—
W. Taylor	RFM	303	58	885	34	26.02	5–83	1	—
B. Stead	LFM	620	146	1686	61	27.63	6–65	1	1
G. S. Sobers	LFM etc	350.4	79	925	29	31.89	4–48	—	—
D. R. Doshi	SLA	130	39	327	10	32.70	2–49	—	—
J. D. Birch P. A.	RM	45	5	169	5	33.80	3–45	—	—
Wilkinson H. T.	RM	377.1	98	953	28	34.03	4–46	—	—
Tunnicliffe	RM	72	11	255	7	36.42	3–55	—	—

Also bowled: C. J. Cook 35-7-105-1; P. J. Hacker 7-1-31-0; W. H. Hare 4-0-18-0; M. J. Harris 4-0-24-0; B. Hassan 3-0-14-0; N. Nanan 5-0-10-1; D. W. Randall 3-0-22-0.

County Records
First-class cricket

Highest innings totals:	For ...739–7d by Leicestershire (Nottingham)	1903
	Agst...706–4d by Surrey (Nottingham)	1947
Lowest innings totals:	For ...13 v Yorkshire (Nottingham)	1901
	Agst...16 by Derbyshire (Nottingham) and Surrey (The Oval)	1879 & 1880
Highest individual innings:	For ...312* W. W. Keeton v Middlesex (The Oval)	1939
	Agst...345 C.G. Macartney for Australians (Nottm)	1921
Best bowling in an innings:	For ...10–66 K. Smales v Gloucestershire (Stroud)	1956
	Agst...10–10 H. Verity for Yorkshire (Leeds)	1932
Best bowling in a match:	For ...17–89 F.C.L. Matthews v Northants (Nottm)	1923
	Agst...17–89 W. G. Grace for Glos (Cheltenham)	1877
Most runs in a season:	2620 (av 53.46) W. W. Whysall	1929
runs in a career:	31327 (av 36.71) G. Gunn	1902–1932
100s in a season:	9 by W. W. Whysall and M. J. Harris	1928 1971
100s in a career:	62 by J. Hardstaff	1930–1955
wickets in a season:	181 (av 14.96) B. Dooland	1954
wickets in a career:	1653 (av 20.40) T. Wass	1896–1914

RECORD WICKET STANDS

1st 391	A. O. Jones & A. Shrewsbury v Gloucestershire (Bristol)	1899
2nd 398	W. Gunn & A. Shrewsbury v Sussex (Nottingham)	1890
3rd 369	J. Gunn & W. Gunn v Leicestershire (Nottingham)	1903
4th 361	A. O. Jones & J. Gunn v Essex (Leyton)	1905
5th 266	A. Shrewsbury & W. Gunn v Sussex (Hove)	1884
6th 303*	H. Winrow & P. F. Harvey v Derbyshire (Nottingham)	1947
7th 204	M. J. Smedley & R. A. White v Surrey (Oval)	1967
8th 220	G. F. H. Heane & R. Winrow v Somerset (Nottingham)	1933
9th 167	W. McIntyre & G. Wootton v Kent (Nottingham)	1869
10th 152	E. Alletson & W. Riley v Sussex (Hove)	1911

One-day cricket

Highest innings totals:	Gillette Cup	271 v Gloucestershire (Nottingham)	1968
	John Player League	252–5 v Warwickshire (Birmingham)	1971
	Benson & Hedges Cup	226–5 v Minor Counties (Nottingham)	1973
Lowest innings totals:	Gillette Cup	123 v Yorkshire (Scarborough)	1969
	John Player League	66 v Yorks (Bradford)	1969
	Benson & Hedges Cup	95 v Lancashire (Manchester)	1972
Highest individual innings:	Gillette Cup	107 M. Hill v Somerset (Taunton)	1964
	John Player League	116* G. St. A. Sobers v Worcestershire (Newark)	1971
	Benson & Hedges Cup	101 M. J. Harris v Yorks (Hull)	1973

Best bowling figures:	Gillette Cup	5–44 B. Stead v Worcestershire (Worcester)	1974
	John Player League	5–23 C. Forbes v Glos (Bristol)	1969
	Benson & Hedges Cup	4–25 W. Taylor v Derbys (Chesterfield)	1973

SOMERSET

Formation of present club: 1875, reorganised 1885.
Colours: Black, white, and maroon.
Badge: Wessex Wyvern.
Best final position in Championship: Third (4), 1892, 1958, 1963, and 1966.
Gillette Cup finalists: 1967.
John Player League runners-up: 1974.
Benson & Hedges Cup semi-finalists: 1974.

Secretary: R. Stevens, County Cricket Ground, St James's Street, Taunton, TA1 1JT.
Captain: D. B. Close.

Ian Terence BOTHAM B Heswall (Cheshire) 24/11/1955. RHB, RM. Played for 2nd XI in 1971. On MCC staff 1972–73. Played for county in last two John Player League matches of 1973. Debut 1974. Benson & Hedges Gold awards: 1. HS: 59 v Middlesex (Taunton) 1974. HSGC: 19 v Kent (Canterbury) 1974. HSJPL: 30 v Worcs (Worcester) 1974. HSBH: 45* v Hants (Taunton) 1974. BB: 5–59 v Leics (Weston-super-Mare) 1974. Plays soccer in Somerset Senior League.

Dennis BREAKWELL (Ounsdale Comprehensive School, Wombourne, Wolverhampton) B Brierly Hill (Staffs) 2/7/1948. LHB, SLA. Debut for Northants 1969 after being on staff for some years. Left county after 1972 season and joined Somerset by special registration in 1973. HS: 97 Northants v Derbyshire (Chesterfield) 1970. HSGC: 19* v Essex (Westcliff) 1974. HSJPL: 29 Northants v Notts (Peterborough) 1971 and 29 Northants v Warwickshire (Birmingham) 1972. HSBH: 17 v Glos (Bristol) 1973. BB: 8–39 Northants v Kent (Dover) 1970. BBJPL: 4–10 Northants v Derbyshire (Northampton) 1970.

Graham Iefvion BURGESS (Millfield School) B Glastonbury 5/5/1943. RHB, RM. Debut 1966. Cap 1968. Gillette Man of Match awards: 1. HS: 129 v Glos (Taunton) 1973. HSGC: 73 v Leics (Taunton) 1967. HSJPL: 66* v Glos (Bristol) 1971. HSBH: 58 v Hants (Yeovil) 1972. BB: 6–51 (12–125 match) v Glos (Bath) 1971. BBGC: 3–54 v Essex (Westcliff) 1974. BBJPL: 6–25 v Glamorgan (Glastonbury) 1972. BBBH: 4–12 v Glamorgan (Pontypridd) 1972. Plays soccer.

SOMERSET

Thomas William (Tom) CARTWRIGHT (Foxford School, Coventry) B Coventry 22/7/1935. RHB, RM. Debut for Warwickshire 1952, scoring 82 and 22* v Notts (Nottingham) in first match. Cap 1958. Benefit (£9,592) in 1968. Left county staff after 1969 season to take post as coach at Millfield School. Debut for Somerset by special registration and cap 1970. Testimonial in 1975. Tests: 5 between 1964 and 1965. Bowled 77 and 62 overs in Australia's two completed innings in his two Tests in 1964. Tour: South Africa 1964–65. 1,000 runs (3)—1,668 runs (av 30.88) in 1961 best. 100 wkts (8)—147 wkts (av 15.52) in 1967 best. Double in 1962. Hat-trick Warwickshire v Somerset (Birmingham) 1969. Benson & Hedges Gold awards: 2. HS: 210 Warwickshire v Middlesex (Nuneaton) 1962. HSGC: 37 Warwickshire v Lancs (Manchester) 1964. HSJPL: 61 v Middlesex (Lord's) 1972. HSBH: 34 v Hants (Bournemouth) 1973. BB: 8–39 Warwickshire v Somerset (Weston-super-Mare) 1962. Had match analysis of 15–89 Warwickshire v Glamorgan (Swansea) 1967. BBGC: 3–16 Warwickshire v Worcs (Lord's) 1966. BBJPL: 4–7 Warwickshire v Northants (Birmingham) 1971. BBBH: 3–12 v Glamorgan (Pontypridd) 1972 and 3–12 v Minor Counties (Taunton) 1974.

Robert John (Bob) CLAPP B Weston-super-Mare 12/12/1948. RHB, RM. Debut 1972. Is a schoolteacher and plays mostly in one-day matches. Took 51 wickets (av 15.90) in one-day matches in 1974 and is the only bowler to take 50 wkts in these matches in one season. BBJPL: 5–38 v Worcs (Worcester) 1974. BBBH: 4–32 v Glos (Taunton) 1974.

Dennis Brian CLOSE (Aireborough GS, Yeadon, Yorks) B Rawdon, Leeds 24/2/1931. LHB, RM/OB. Good short-leg field. Debut for Yorks and cap 1949. Benefit (£8,154) in 1961. Appointed county captain in 1963. *Wisden* 1963. Testimonial (£6,540) in 1970. Engagement terminated after 1970 season and made debut for Somerset in 1971. Cap 1971. Appointed county captain in 1972. Tests: 19 between 1949 and 1967 captaining England in 7 Test matches. Also captained England in one-day internationals v Australia 1972. Made Test debut v New Zealand at age of 18 years 149 days—youngest player ever to appear for England. Tours: Australia 1950–51, Pakistan 1955–56. 1,000 runs (18)—1,985 runs (av 35.44) in 1961 best. 100 wkts (2)—114 wkts (av 24.08) in 1952 best. Doubles (2): 1949 (debut season) and 1952 (next full season after National Service). Only three wkts short in 1955. Shared in 4th wkt partnership record for county, 226 with D. J. S. Taylor v Glamorgan (Swansea) 1974. Gillette Man of Match awards: 1 (for Yorks). Benson & Hedges Gold awards: 1. HS: 198 Yorks v Surrey (Oval) 1960. HSGC: 96 Yorks v Surrey (Oval) 1969. HSJPL: 131 v Yorks (Bath) 1974. HSBH: 88 v Hants (Yeovil) 1972. BB: 8–41 Yorks v Kent (Leeds) 1959. BBGC: 4–60 Yorks v Sussex (Hove) 1963. BBJPL: 4–9 v Glamorgan (Taunton) 1973. BBBH: 3–59 v Glos (Bristol) 1973. Played soccer for Leeds United, Arsenal, and Bradford City.

Peter William DENNING (Millfield School) B Chewton Mendip (Somerset) 16/12/1949. LHB, OB. Debut 1969. Cap 1973. Gillette Man of Match awards: 2. Benson & Hedges Gold awards: 2. HS: 85* v New Zealanders (Taunton) 1974. HSGC: 112 v Surrey (Taunton) 1974. HSJPL: 100 v Northants (Brackley) 1974. HSBH: 87 v Glos (Taunton) 1974. Trained as a teacher at St Luke's College, Exeter.

Brian Anthony LANGFORD (Dr Morgan's School, Bridgwater) B Birmingham 17/12/1935. RHB, OB. Debut 1953. Took 26 wkts for 308 runs in first three matches (all at Bath), including 8–96 (14–156 match) v Kent in his second match. Cap 1957. Testimonial (£4,250) in 1966. County captain from 1969 to 1971. Second testimonial (£2,250) in 1971. 100 wkts (5)—116 wkts (av 18.28) in 1958 best. HS: 68* v Sussex (Hove) 1960, 68 v Kent (Gillingham) 1963 and 68* v Glamorgan (Taunton) 1972. HSGC: 56 v Glamorgan (Cardiff) 1963. HSJPL: 24 v Glamorgan (Glastonbury) 1970. BB: 9–26 (15–54 match) v Lancs (Weston-super-Mare) 1958. BBGC: 3–17 v Notts (Taunton) 1965. BBJPL: 4–73 v Lancs (Manchester) 1970.

Hallam Reynold MOSELEY B Christchurch, Barbados 28/5/1948. RHB, RFM. Toured England with Barbados team in 1969 and made debut v Notts (Nottingham). Has played for Barbados in Shell Shield since 1969–70. Joined county in 1970 and made debut in1971. Cap 1972. HS: 67 v Leics (Taunton) 1972. HSGC: 15 v Lancs (Manchester) 1972. HSJPL: 24 v Notts (Torquay) 1972. HSBH: 33 v Hants (Bournemouth) 1973. BB: 5–24 v Essex (Westcliff) 1974. BBGC: 4–31 v Surrey (Taunton) 1974. BBJPL: 5–30 v Middlesex (Lord's) 1973. BBBH: 3–24 v Minor Counties (Taunton) 1974.

James Michael (Jim) PARKS (Hove County GS) B Haywards Heath (Sussex) 21/10/1931. Son of J. H. Parks. RHB, LB, WK. Debut for Sussex 1949. Cap 1951. Acted as wicket-keeper for some matches in 1958 and took over the position regularly in 1959. Benefit (£9,400) in 1964. Appointed county captain in 1967, but resigned post during 1968 season. *Wisden* 1967. Joint testimonial (£5,000 each) with K. G. Suttle in 1972. Left staff after 1972 season and made debut for Somerset in 1973 on 3-year contract. Cap 1973. Will play only in one-day cricket in future. Tests: 46 between 1954 and 1967–68. Tours: Pakistan 1955–56, South Africa 1956–57 (returned home ill after first match) and 1964–65(New Zealand 1960–61, India 1963–64, Australia and New Zealand 1965–66, West Indies 1967–68. 1,000 runs (20)—2,314 runs (av 42.07) in 1955 and 2,313 runs (av 51.40) in 1959 best. Scored century in each innings (101 and 100*), Sussex v Worcs (Worcester) 1957. Completed 30,000 runs in 1968. Dismissed 93 batsmen (86 ct 7 st) in 1959 and also (89 ct 4 st) in 1961. Gillette Man of Match awards: 2 (for Sussex). Benson & Hedges Gold awards: 1. HS: 205* Sussex v Somerset (Hove) 1955. HSGC: 102* Sussex v Durham (Hove) 1964. HSJPL: 96* Sussex v Somerset (Hove) 1970. HSBH: 69 v Glamorgan (Yeovil) 1973. BB: 3–23 Sussex v Cambridge U (Hove) 1956. Played soccer for Haywards Heath.

Isaac Vivian Alexander (Viv) RICHARDS (Antigua Grammar School) B St John's, Antigua 7/3/1952. RHB, OB. Debut 1971–72 for Leeward Islands v Windward Islands and subsequently played for Combined Islands in Shell Shield tournament. Debut for county and cap 1974. Tour: West Indies to India, Sri Lanka, and Pakistan 1974–75. Scored 1,223 runs (av 33.05) in 1974. Benson & Hedges Gold awards:1. HS: 192* West Indies v India (New Delhi) 1974–75. HSUK: 107 v Yorks (Bath) 1974. HSGC: 18 v Kent (Canterbury) 1974. HSJPL: 108* v Notts (Nottingham) 1974. HSBH: 81* v Glamorgan (Swansea) 1974. BB: 3–49 Combined Islands v Trinidad (Port of Spain) 1972–73.

123

Peter James ROBINSON B Worcester 9/2/1943. Nephew of R. O. Jenkins. LHB, SLA. Slip field. Debut for Worcs 1963. Left staff after 1964 season and made debut for Somerset in 1965. Cap 1966. Became opening batsman in 1967 and scored 917 runs (av 26.20), but has subsequently reverted to 'middle order' position. Testimonial in 1974. Played in only one match in 1974. Scored 1,158 runs (av 26.93) in 1970. HS: 140 v Northants (Northampton) 1970. HSGC: 67 v Leics (Taunton) 1973. HSJPL: 71* v Warwickshire (Birmingham) 1973. HSBH: 15 v Minor Counties (Taunton) 1973. BB: 7–10 v Notts (Nottingham) 1966. BBBH: 3–17 v Minor Counties (Plymouth) 1972. Soccer as amateur for Worcester City.

Peter Michael ROEBUCK (Millfield School and Cambridge) B Oxford 6/3/1956. RHB. Played for 2nd XI in 1969 at age of 13. Debut 1974 (two matches). HS: 46 v Warwickshire (Weston-super-Mare) 1974. Entered University in 1974.

Brian Charles ROSE (Weston-super-Mare GS) B Dartford (Kent) 4/6/1950. LHB, LM. Played for English Schools CA at Lord's 1968. Debut 1969. Played in one match and one John Player League match in 1974. HS: 125 v Kent (Glastonbury) 1972. HSGC: 28 v Derbyshire (Taunton) 1969. HSJPL: 65* v Derbyshire (Weston-super-Mare) 1973. HSBH: 34* v Glamorgan (Yeovil) 1973. Trained as a teacher at Borough Road College, Isleworth.

Derek John Somerset TAYLOR (Amersham College) B Amersham (Bucks) 12/11/1942. Twin brother of M. N. S. Taylor of Hants. RHB, WK. Debut for Surrey 1966. Cap 1969. Left staff after 1969 season and made debut for Somerset in 1970. Cap 1971. Played for Griqualand West in Currie Cup competition 1970–71 and 1971–72. Scored 994 runs (av 28.40) in 1974. Shared in 4th wkt partnership record for county, 226 with D. B. Close v Glamorgan (Swansea) 1974. HS: 179 v Glamorgan (Swansea) 1974. HSGC: 49 v Kent (Canterbury) 1974. HSJPL: 28 v Middlesex (Taunton) 1974. HSBH: 33 v Minor Counties (Taunton) 1974. Has played soccer for Corinthian Casuals.

NB The following players whose particulars appeared in the 1974 Annual have been omitted: A. A. Jones (emigrated to Rhodesia), M. J. Kitchen (left staff), and S. G. Wilkinson (left staff). The career records of all these players will be found elsewhere in this Annual.

COUNTY AVERAGES

County Championship: Played 20; won 6, drawn 10, lost 4
All first-class matches: Played 23; won 6, drawn 12, lost 5

BATTING AND FIELDING

Cap		M	I	NO	Runs	HS	Avge	100	50	Ct	St
1966	M. J. Kitchen	13	24	2	819	88	37.22	—	7	2	—
1971	D. B. Close	23	28	7	1099	114*	35.45	1	5	23	—
1974	I. V. A. Richards	23	38	1	1223	107	33.05	2	6	18	—
1971	D. J. S. Taylor	23	40	5	994	179	28.40	1	5	45	5
—	S. G. Wilkinson	3	4	1	84	32*	28.00	—	—	—	—
—	D. Breakwell	19	28	7	585	67	27.85	—	2	9	—
1973	J. M. Parks	22	36	5	717	66	23.12	—	2	18	—

124

Cap		M	I	NO	Runs	HS	Avge	100	50	Ct	St
1970	T. W. Cartwright	7	8	0	185	68	23.12	—	1	5	—
1973	P. W. Denning	21	35	1	641	60	18.85	—	2	13	—
1968	G. I. Burgess	21	33	0	588	90	17.81	—	4	19	—
—	I. T. Botham	18	29	3	441	59	16.96	—	1	15	—
1972	A. A. Jones	21	24	11	103	27	7.92	—	—	4	—
1972	H. R. Moseley	20	25	9	120	36*	7.50	—	—	9	—
1957	B. A. Langford	14	21	7	97	18	6.92	—	—	4	—

Played in two matches: P. M. Roebuck 46, 0; 0, 8.
Played in one match: R. J. Clapp 0; P. J. Robinson 1 (3 ct); B. C. Rose 14, 7.

BOWLING

	Type	O	M	R	W	Avge	Best	5 wI	10 wM
H.R. Moseley	RFM	661.5	198	1420	81	17.53	5–24	3	—
D. B. Close	RM/OB	97	30	255	13	19.61	5–70	1	—
B.A. Langford	OB	412.1	153	937	42	22.30	5–51	3	—
T. W. Cartwright	RM	273	130	493	22	22.40	4–45	—	—
A. A. Jones	RFM	565	122	1539	67	22.97	6–37	5	—
I. T. Botham	RM	309	76	779	30	25.96	5–59	1	—
G. I. Burgess	RM	437.1	114	1140	41	27.80	3–18	—	—
D. Breakwell	SLA	346.1	109	957	27	35.44	4–56	—	—
I. V. A. Richards	OB	95	31	273	6	45.50	2–53	—	—

Also bowled: R. J. Clapp 7-1-24-0; P. W. Denning 4-1-4-1; P. J. Robinson 4-0-19-0; J. M. Parks 5.3-3-21-0.

County Records

First-class cricket

Highest innings totals:	For ...675–9d v Hampshire (Bath)		1924
	Agst... 811 by Surrey (The Oval)		1899
Lowest innings totals:	For ... 25 v Gloucestershire (Bristol)		1947
	Agst... 22 by Gloucestershire (Bristol)		1920
Highest individual innings:	For ...310 H. Gimblett v Sussex (Eastbourne)		1948
	Agst...424 A. C. MacLaren for Lancs (Taunton)		1895
Best bowling in an innings:	For ...10–49 E. J. Tyler v Surrey (Taunton)		1895
	Agst...10–35 A. Drake for Yorkshire (Weston-super-Mare)		1914
Best bowling in a match:	For ...16–83 J. C. White v Worcestershire (Bath)		1919
	Agst...17–137 W. Brearley for Lancashire (Manchester)		1905
Most runs in a season:	2761 (av 56.82) W. E. Alley		1961
runs in a career:	21108 (av 37.09) H. Gimblett		1935–1954
100s in a season:	10 by W. E. Alley		1961
100s in a career:	49 by H. Gimblett		1935–1954
wickets in a season:	169 (av 19.24) A. W. Wellard		1938
wickets in a career:	2153 (av 18.10) J. C. White		1909–1937

RECORD WICKET STANDS

1st 346	H. T. Hewett & L. C. H. Palairet v Yorkshire (Taunton)	1892
2nd 286	J. C. W. MacBryan & M. D. Lyon v Derbyshire (Buxton)	1924
3rd 300	G. Atkinson & P. B. Wight v Glamorgan (Bath)	1960

4th 226	D. J. S. Taylor & D. B. Close v Glamorgan (Swansea)		1974
5th 235	J. C. White & C. C. C. Case v Gloucestershire (Taunton)		1927
6th 265	W. E. Alley & K. E. Palmer v Northamptonshire (Northampton)		1961
7th 240	S. M. J. Woods & V. T. Hill v Kent (Taunton)		1898
8th 143*	E. F. Longrigg & C. J. P. Barnwell v Gloucestershire (Bristol)		1938
9th 183	C. Greetham & H. W. Stephenson v Leicestershire (Weston-super-Mare)		1963
10th 143	J. J. Bridges & H. Gibbs v Surrey (Weston-super-Mare)		1919

One-day cricket

Highest innings totals:	Gillette Cup	257–5 v Surrey (Taunton)	1974
	John Player League	262–3 v Gloucestershire (Bristol)	1974
	Benson & Hedges Cup	265–8 v Gloucestershire (Taunton)	1974
Lowest innings totals:	Gillette Cup	63 v Yorkshire (Taunton)	1965
	John Player League	61 v Hampshire (Bath)	1973
	Benson & Hedges Cup	121 v Glamorgan (Pontypridd)	1972
Highest individual innings:	Gillette Cup	116 M. J. Kitchen v Lancashire (Manchester)	1972
	John Player League	131 D. B. Close v Yorkshire (Bath)	1974
	Benson & Hedges Cup	95 R. C. Cooper v Minor Counties (Plymouth)	1972
Best bowling figures:	Gillette Cup	5–18 R. Palmer v Lancashire (Taunton)	1966
	John Player League	6–25 G. I. Burgess v Glamorgan (Glastonbury)	1972
	Benson & Hedges Cup	4–12 G. I. Burgess v Glamorgan (Pontypridd)	1972

SURREY

Formation of present club: 1845.
Colours: Chocolate.
Badge: Prince of Wales' Feathers.
County Champions (17): 1887, 1888, 1890, 1891, 1892, 1894, 1895, 1899, 1914, 1952, 1953, 1954, 1955, 1956, 1957, 1958, and 1971.
Joint Champions (2): 1889 and 1950.
Gillette Cup finalists: 1965.
Benson & Hedges Cup winners: 1974.
Secretary: Lt-Col W. H. Sillitoe, Kennington Oval, London, SE11 5SS.
Captain: J. H. Edrich.

Geoffrey Graham (Geoff) ARNOLD B Earlsfield (Surrey) 3/9/1944. RHB, RFM. Debut 1963. Cap 1967. *Wisden* 1971. Tests: 27 between 1967 and 1974. Tours: Pakistan 1966–67, India, Pakistan, and Sri Lanka 1972–73, West Indies 1973–74, Australia and New Zealand 1974–75. Took 109 wkts (av 18.22) in 1967. Hat-trick v Leics (Leicester) 1974. Gillette Man of Match awards: 2. HS: 73 MCC under-25 v Central Zone (Sahiwal) 1966–67. HSUK: 63 v Warwickshire (Birmingham) 1968. HSGC: 15 v Sussex (Oval) 1970 and 15 v Worcs (Worcester) 1972. HSJPL: 24* v Notts (Nottingham) 1971. HSBH: 11* v Kent (Oval) 1973. BB: 8–41 (13–128 match) v Glos (Oval) 1967. BBGC: 5–9 v Derbyshire (Oval) 1967. BBJPL: 5–11 v Glamorgan (Oval) 1969. BBBH: 3–20 v Leics (Lord's) 1974. Soccer for Corinthian Casuals.

Christopher John (Chris) AWORTH (Tiffin School, Kingston and Cambridge) B Wimbledon 19/2/1953. LHB, SLA. Debut for Cambridge U 1973. Debut for county 1974. Blue 1973–74. University captain for 1975. HS: 97 Cambridge U v Warwickshire (Cambridge) 1974. HSJPL: 24 v Sussex (Byfleet) 1974. HSBH: 23 Cambridge U v Kent (Cambridge) 1974.

Raymond Paul (Ray) BAKER (Wallington HS) B Carshalton (Surrey) 9/4/1954. RHB, RM. Played for 2nd XI since 1971. Debut 1973. HS: 5 v New Zealanders (Oval) 1973. BB: 6–29 v Essex (Ilford) 1974. BBJPL: 4–42 v Kent (Oval) 1974.

Alan Raymond BUTCHER (Heath Clark GS, Croydon) B Croydon 7/1/1954. LHB, LM. Played in two John Player League matches in 1971. Debut 1972. HS: 57 v Middlesex (Lord's) 1974. HSJPL: 12 v Somerset (Oval) 1973. BB: 6–48 v Hants (Guildford) 1972. BBJPL: 3–28 v Lancs (Oval) 1972. BBBH: 3–11 v Lancs (Manchester) 1974.

John Hugh EDRICH B Blofield (Norfolk) 21/6/1937. LHB, RM. Played for Norfolk in 1954 and Surrey 2nd XI in 1955. Debut 1956 for Combined Services. Debut for Surrey 1958. Cap 1959. *Wisden* 1965. Benefit (£10,551) in 1968. Appointed county captain in 1973. Testimonial in 1975. Tests: 65 between 1963 and 1974. Scored century (120) on debut v Australia at Lord's 1964. Tours: India 1963–64, Australia and New Zealand 1965–66, 1970–71 and 1974–75 (vice-captain), West Indies 1967–68, Ceylon and Pakistan 1968–69. 1,000 runs (16)—2,482 runs (av 51.70) in 1962 best. Also scored 1,060 runs (av 44.16) on 1965–66 tour and 1,136 runs (av 56.80) in 1970–71. Scored 1,799 runs (av 52.91) in 1959 in first full season, despite absence through injury for a few matches. Scored two centuries in match v Notts (Nottingham) 1959 (112 and 124) & Worcs (Worcester) 1970 (143 and 113*) and v Warwickshire (Oval) 1971 (111 and 124). Scored 1,311 runs in 9 consecutive innings all over 50 including three consecutive centuries, in 1965. Completed 30,000 runs in 1971. Gillette Man of Match awards: 2. Benson & Hedges Gold awards: 5. HS: 310* England v New Zealand (Leeds) 1965 sharing in 2nd wkt partnership of 369 with K. F. Barrington. HSGC: 96 v Glos (Oval) 1964. HSJPL: 108* v Derbyshire (Derby) 1972. HSBH: 83* v Sussex (Oval) 1973.

Geoffrey Philip (Geoff) HOWARTH (Auckland GS) B Auckland 29/3/1951. Younger brother of H. J. Howarth, New Zealand Test cricketer. RHB, OB. Debut for New Zealand under-23 XI v Auckland (Auckland) 1968–69. Joined Surrey staff 1969. Debut 1971. Cap 1974. HS: 159 v Kent

127

(Maidstone) 1973. HSGC: 19 v Lincs (Lincoln) and 19 v Somerset (Taunton) 1974. HSJPL: 62 v Derbyshire (Oval) 1974. HSBH: 80 v Yorks (Oval) 1974. BB: 5–32 Auckland v Central Districts (Auckland) 1973–74.

INTIKHAB ALAM B Hoshiarpur, India 28/12/1941. RHB, LBG. Debut for Karachi 1957–58 aged 16 years 9 months and has played continuously for various Karachi sides and Pakistan International Airways since. Professional for West of Scotland Club in Scottish Western Union for some seasons. Debut for county and cap 1969. Tests: 41 for Pakistan between 1959–60 and 1974, captaining country in 15 Tests. Played in 5 matches for Rest of World in 1970 and 5 in 1971–72. Took wkt of C. C. McDonald with first ball he bowled in Test cricket. Tours: Pakistan to India 1960–61, England 1962, 1967, 1971 and 1974 (captain on last two tours), Ceylon 1964, Australia and New Zealand 1964–65, 1972–73 (captain), Pakistan Eaglets to England 1963, Pakistan International Airways to East Africa 1964, Rest of World to Australia 1971–72 (vice-captain). Took 104 wkts (av 28.36) in 1971. Hat-trick v Yorks (Oval) 1972. HS: 182 Karachi Blues v Pakistan International Airways B (Karachi) 1970–71. HSUK: 139 v Glos (Oval) 1973. HSGC: 25* v Middlesex (Oval) 1970. HSJPL: 62 v Northants (Tolworth) 1973. HSBH: 32 v Middlesex (Lord's) 1973. BB: 8–54 Pakistanis v Tasmania (Hobart) 1972–73. BBUK: 8–61 Pakistanis v Minor Counties (Swindon) 1967. BBJPL: 6–25 v Derbyshire (Oval) 1974. BBBH: 3–42 v Essex (Chelmsford) 1973.

Robin David JACKMAN (St Edmund's School, Canterbury) B Simla (India) 13/8/1945. RHB, RFM. Debut 1966. Cap 1970. Played for Western Province in 1971–72 and Rhodesia in 1972–73 and 1973–74 Currie Cup competitions. Hat-tricks (3): v Kent (Canterbury) 1971, Western Province v Natal (Pietermaritzburg) 1971–72 and v Yorks (Leeds) 1973. Gillette Man of Match awards: 1. HS: 92* v Kent (Oval) 1974. HSGC: 12 v Glos (Bristol) 1973. HSJPL: 41 v Yorks (Oval) 1974. HSBH: 36 v Leics (Lord's) 1974. BB: 8–40 Rhodesia v Natal (Durban) 1972–73. BBUK: 7–36 v Yorks (Oval) 1973. BBGC: 7–33 v Yorks (Harrogate) 1970. BBJPL: 6–34 v Derbyshire (Derby) 1972. BBBH: 4–31 v Kent (Canterbury) 1974.

Arnold LONG (Wallington CGS) B Cheam 18/12/1940. LHB, WK. Joined staff 1959. Debut 1960. Cap 1962. Benefit (£10,353) in 1971. Appointed county vice-captain in 1973. Dismissed 7 batsmen in innings and 11 in match (all ct) v Sussex (Hove) 1964, world record for most catches in match and only one short of record for most dismissals in match. Dismissed 89 batsmen (72 ct 17 st) in 1962. HS: 92 v Leics (Leicester) 1970. HSGC: 42 v Sussex (Oval) 1970. HSJPL: 71 v Warwickshire (Birmingham) 1971. HSBH: 46 v Kent (Oval) 1973. Soccer for Corinthian Casuals.

Dudley Richard OWEN-THOMAS (King's College School, Wimbledon and Cambridge) B Mombasa, Kenya 20/9/1948. RHB, OB. Played for 2nd XI from 1967 to 1969. Debut for Cambridge U 1969. Blues 1969–72. Debut for county 1970. Elected Best Young Cricketer of the Year in 1972 by Cricket Writers' Club. Scored 1,065 runs (av 34.35) in 1971. HS: 182* Cambridge U v Middlesex (Cambridge) 1969. HSGC: 66 v Lincs (Lincoln) 1974. HSJPL: 52 v Northants (Tolworth) 1973. HSBH: 46 Cambridge U v Warwickshire (Birmingham) 1972. BB: 3–20 Cambridge U v Worcs (Halesowen) 1969.

128

Patrick Ian (Pat) POCOCK (Wimbledon Technical School) B Bangor (Caernarvonshire) 24/9/1946. RHB, OB. Debut 1964. Cap 1967. Played for Northern Transvaal in 1971–72 Currie Cup competition. Tests: 15 between 1967–68 and 1973–74. Tours: Pakistan 1966–67, West Indies 1967–68 and 1973–74, Ceylon and Pakistan 1968–69, India, Pakistan, and Sri Lanka 1972–73. Took 112 wkts (av 18.22) in 1967. Took 4 wkts in 4 balls, 5 in 6, 6 in 9, and 7 in 11 (the last two being first-class records) v Sussex (Eastbourne) 1972. Hat-tricks (2): as above and v Worcs (Guildford) 1971. Benson & Hedges Gold awards: 1. HS: 75* v Notts (Oval) 1968. HSGC: 11* v Somerset (Taunton) 1974. HSJPL: 22 v Notts (Nottingham) 1971. HSBH: 19 v Middlesex (Oval) 1972. BB: 7–57 v Essex (Romford) 1968. BBGC: 3–44 v Lincs (Lincoln) 1974. BBJPL: 4–27 v Essex (Chelmsford) 1974. BBBH: 3–24 v Essex (Oval) 1974.

Graham Richard James ROOPE (Bradfield College) B Fareham (Hants) 12/7/1946. RHB, RM. Played for Public Schools XI v Comb. Services (Lord's) 1963 and 1964. Played for Berkshire 1963 scoring century against Wiltshire. Joined county staff and debut 1964. Cap 1969. Played for Griqualand West in 1973–74 Currie Cup competition. Tests: 8 between 1972–73 and 1973. Tour: India, Pakistan, and Sri Lanka 1972–73. 1,000 runs (5)—1,641 runs (av 44.35) in 1971 best. Scored two centuries in match (109 and 103*) v Leics (Leicester) 1971. Held 59 catches in 1971. Benson & Hedges Gold awards: 3. HS: 171 v Yorks (Oval) 1971. HSGC: 36 v Middlesex (Lord's) 1968. HSJPL: 120* v Worcs (Byfleet) 1973. HSBH: 115 v Essex (Chelmsford) 1973. BB: 5–14 v West Indians (Oval) 1969. BBGC: 5–23 v Derbyshire (Oval) 1967. BBJPL: 4–31 v Glamorgan (Oval) 1974. Soccer (goalkeeper) for Corinthian Casuals, Wimbledon, and Guildford City.

Lonsdale Ernest SKINNER (Hillcroft Comprehensive School, Tooting) B Plaisance, British Guiana 7/9/1950. RHB, WK. Joined staff 1969. Debut 1971. HS: 84 v Sussex (Oval) 1974. HSGC: 32 v Somerset (Taunton) 1974. HSJPL: 70 v Warwickshire (Birmingham) 1974.

David Mark SMITH (Battersea GS) B Balham 9/1/1956. LHB, RM. Played for 2nd XI in 1972. Debut 1973 aged 17 years 4 months, whilst still at school. Played in one John Player League match only in 1974. HSJPL: 12 v Derbyshire (Derby) 1973.

Alan Otto Charles VERRINDER (Windsor GS) B Henley-on-Thames (Oxfordshire) 28/7/1955. RHB, RFM. Debut 1974. One match v Middlesex (Lord's). Also played in two John Player League matches.

Mohammad YOUNIS AHMED (Moslem HS, Lahore) B Jullundur Pakistan 20/10/1947. LHB, LM/SLA. Younger step-brother of Saeed Ahmed, who has played for county 2nd XI. Debut 1961–62 for Pakistan Inter Board Schools XI v South Zone at age of 14 years 4 months. Debut for Surrey 1965. Cap 1969. Played for South Australia in 1972–73 Sheffield Shield competition. Tests: 2 for Pakistan v New Zealand 1969–70. 1,000 runs (4)—1,760 runs (av 47.56) in 1969 best. Benson & Hedges Gold awards: 1. HS: 155* v Warwickshire (Oval) 1973. HSGC: 87 v Middlesex (Oval) 1970. HSJPL: 96 v Leics (Oval) 1970. HSBH: 101* v Kent (Canterbury) 1974. BB: 3–12 The Rest v Pakistan XI (Sahiwal) 1969–70.

NB The following players whose particulars appeared in the 1974 Annual have been omitted: M. J. Edwards (retired) and S. J. Storey (retired). The career records of both these players will be found elsewhere in this Annual.

COUNTY AVERAGES

County Championship: Played 20; won 6, drawn 10, lost 4
All first-class matches: Played 21; won 6, drawn 10, lost 5

BATTING AND FIELDING

Cap		M	I	NO	Runs	HS	Avge	100	50	Ct	St
1959	J. H. Edrich	9	14	1	578	152*	44.46	1	3	5	—
1964	S. J. Storey	17	23	4	744	111	39.15	2	3	14	—
1969	G. R. J. Roope	21	33	6	907	119	33.59	1	4	28	—
1969	Younis Ahmad	19	33	4	907	116	31.27	1	4	17	—
1974	G. P. Howarth	17	30	2	751	98	26.82	—	4	7	—
1970	R. D. Jackman	19	25	4	474	92*	22.57	—	5	10	—
1969	Intikhab Alam	7	10	1	202	62	22.44	—	2	2	—
—	C. J. Aworth	6	9	2	149	35	21.28	—	—	3	—
—	L. E. Skinner	10	18	0	364	84	20.22	—	2	5	—
1967	G. G. Arnold	8	7	3	73	23	18.25	—	—	2	—
1966	M. J. Edwards	15	27	2	402	63	16.08	—	2	8	—
—	A. R. Butcher	15	16	3	207	57	15.92	—	1	3	—
—	D. R. Owen-Thomas	16	25	4	328	35	15.61	—	—	8	—
1967	P. I. Pocock	21	25	6	289	41	15.21	—	—	16	—
1962	A. Long	21	22	6	232	42	14.50	—	—	41	5
—	R. P. Baker	9	9	6	7	3*	2.33	—	—	5	—

Played in one match: A. O. C. Verrinder 0, 0 (1 ct).

BOWLING

	Type	O	M	R	W	Avge	Best	5 wI	10 wM
G. G. Arnold	RFM	275.1	92	515	51	10.09	6–32	4	1
R. P. Baker	RM	207.1	48	511	27	18.92	6–29	1	—
R. D. Jackman	RFM	638.1	141	1660	81	20.49	6–58	4	—
S. J. Storey	RM	180	48	401	16	25.06	3–2	—	—
P. I. Pocock	OB	628.5	192	1576	60	26.26	5–30	3	—
A. R. Butcher	LM	191	42	478	18	26.55	3–31	—	—
G. R. J. Roope	RM	315.2	76	857	32	26.78	3–5	—	—
Intikhab Alam	LBG	160.3	44	465	14	33.21	5–60	1	—

Also bowled: C. J. Aworth 8–1–25–0; G. P. Howarth 37–7–132–0; A. O. C. Verrinder 6–1–18–1; Younis Ahmad 6–2–11–0.

County Records

First-class cricket

Highest innings totals:	For ...811 v Somerset (The Oval)	1899
	Agst...705-8d by Sussex (Hastings)	1902
Lowest innings totals:	For ... 16 v Nottinghamshire (The Oval)	1880
	Agst... 15 by MCC (Lord's)	1839
Highest individual innings:	For ...357* R. Abel v Somerset (The Oval)	1899
	Agst...300* F. Watson for Lancashire (Manchester)	1928
	300 R. Subba Row for Northamptonshire (The Oval)	1958

Best bowling in an innings:	For ...10–43 T. Rushby v Somerset (Taunton)	1921
	Agst...10–28 W. P. Howell for Australians (The Oval)	1899
Best bowling in a match:	For ...16–83 G. A. R. Lock v Kent (Blackheath)	1956
	Agst...15–57 W. P. Howell for Australians (The Oval)	1899
Most runs in a season:	3246 (av 72.13) T. Hayward	1906
runs in a career:	43703 (av 49.77) J. B. Hobbs	1905–1934
100s in a season:	13 by T. Hayward	1906
	J. B. Hobbs	1925
100s in a career:	144 by J. B. Hobbs	1905–1934
wickets in a season:	250 (av 14.06) T. Richardson	1895
wickets in a career:	1775 (av 17.91) T. Richardson	1892–1905

RECORD WICKET STANDS

1st	428	J. B. Hobbs & A. Sandham v Oxford U (The Oval)	1926
2nd	371	J. B. Hobbs & E. G. Hayes v Hampshire (The Oval)	1909
3rd	353	A. Ducat & E. G. Hayes v Hampshire (Southampton)	1919
4th	448	R. Abel & T. R. Hayward v Yorkshire (The Oval)	1899
5th	308	J. N. Crawford & F. C. Holland v Somerset (The Oval)	1908
6th	298	A. Sandham & H. S. Harrison v Sussex (The Oval)	1913
7th	200	T. F. Shepherd & J. W. Hitch v Kent (Blackheath)	1921
8th	204	T. Hayward & L. C. Braund v Lancashire (The Oval)	1898
9th	168	E. R. T. Holmes & E. W. Brookes v Hampshire (The Oval)	1936
10th	173	A. Ducat & A. Sandham v Essex (Leyton)	1921

One-day cricket

Highest innings totals:	Gillette Cup	280–5 v Middlesex (Oval)	1970
	John Player League	231–3 v Leicestershire (Leicester)	1973
	Benson & Hedges Cup	234–8 v Essex (Chelmsford)	1973
Lowest innings totals:	Gillette Cup	106 v Worcestershire (Worcester)	1972
	John Player League	82 v Lancashire (Manchester)	1971
	Benson & Hedges Cup	125 v Sussex (Hove)	1972
Highest individual innings:	Gillette Cup	101 M. J. Stewart v Durham (Chester-le-Street)	1972
	John Player League	120* G. R. J. Roope v Worcestershire (Byfleet)	1973
	Benson & Hedges Cup	115 G. R. J. Roope v Essex (Chelmsford)	1973
Best bowling figures:	Gillette Cup	7–33 R. D. Jackman v Yorkshire (Harrogate)	1970
	John Player League	6–25 Intikhab Alam v Derbyshire (Oval)	1974
	Benson & Hedges Cup	4–31 R. D. Jackman v Kent (Canterbury)	1974

SUSSEX

Formation of present club: 1839, reorganised 1857.
Colours: Dark blue, light blue, and gold.
Badge: County Arms of six martlets (in shape of
  inverted pyramid).
Joint Champions: 1875.
County Championship runners-up (6): 1902,
  1903, 1932, 1933, 1934, and 1953.
Gillette Cup winners (2): 1963 and 1964.
Gillette Cup finalists (3): 1968, 1970, and 1973.

Secretary: Lt-Cmdr I. M. Stoop, DFC, County Ground, Eaton Road
Hove, BN3 3AN.
Captain: A. W. Greig.

John Robert Troutbeck BARCLAY (Eton College) B Bonn, West
Germany 22/1/1954. RHB, OB. Debut 1970 age 16¼, whilst still at school.
Was in XI at school from age of 14 and scored the record number of runs
for school in a season in 1970. Played in MCC Schools matches at Lord's
in 1969–71. Vice-captain of English Schools Cricket Association team to
India 1970–71. Captain of England Young Cricketers team to West Indies
1972. HS: 52 v Somerset (Taunton) 1973. HSJPL: 48 v Derbyshire (Derby)
1974. BB: 5–28 v Oxford U (Oxford) 1973.

Antony (Tony) BUSS (Bexhill GS) B Brightling (Sussex) 1/9/1939.
RHB, RFM. Joined county staff 1955. Debut 1958. Cap 1963. Benefit
(£8,000) in 1971. Appointed county vice-captain in 1973. 100 wkts (3)—
120 wkts (av 20.30) in 1965 and 120 wkts (av 22.55) in 1966 best. Hat-
tricks (2): v Cambridge U (Cambridge) and Derbyshire (Hove) in 1965.
Also obtained hat-trick in John Player League match v Worcs (Hastings)
1974. Gillette Man of Match awards: 1. HS: 83 v Northants (Hove) 1969.
HSGC: 28 v Somerset (Taunton) 1968. HSJPL: 20 v Derbyshire (Derby)
1970. BB: 8–23 v Notts (Hove) 1966. BBGC: 4–22 v Derbyshire (Hove)
1968. BBJPL: 5–53 v Kent (Hove) 1970.

Michael Alan (Mike) BUSS B Brightling (Sussex) 24/1/1944. Brother
of A. Buss. LHB, LM. Debut 1961. Developed into opening batsman in
1966, and changed bowling style from SLA to LM in 1967. Cap 1967.
Played for Orange Free State in 1972–73 and 1973–74 Currie Cup
competitions. Tour: Pakistan 1966–67, flown out as replacement for R. N.
Abberley. 1,000 runs (4)—1,379 runs (av 37.27) in 1970 best. Gillette Man
of Match awards: 2. Benson & Hedges Gold awards: 1. HS: 159 v
Glamorgan (Swansea) 1967. HSGC: 72 v Essex (Chelmsford) 1970.
HSJPL: 121 v Notts (Worksop) 1971. HSBH: 78 v Middlesex (Hove)
1972. BB: 7–58 v Hants (Bournemouth) 1970. BBGC: 4–14 v Glos (Hove)
1969. BBJPL: 6–14 v Lancs (Hove) 1973.

Robert Giles Lenthall CHEATLE (Stowe School) B London 31/7/1953.
LHB, SLA. Debut 1974. One match v Surrey (Oval).

132

Mark James Julian FABER (Eton College and Oxford) B Horsted Keynes (Sussex) 15/8/1950. RHB, RM. Grandson of Rt Hon Harold Macmillan. Debut for Oxford U 1970. Blue 1972. Debut for county 1973. HS: 112* v Middlesex (Hove) 1974. HSJPL: 86 v Leics (Hove) 1974. HSBH: 29 v Cambridge U (Hove) 1974.

Peter John GRAVES (Hove Manor School) B Hove 19/5/1946. LHB, SLA. Close field. Debut 1965. Cap 1969. Played for Orange Free State in 1969–70, 1970–71 (captain) and 1973–74 Currie Cup competitions whilst appointed as coach. 1,000 runs (3)—1,282 runs (av 38.84) in 1974 best. Gillette Man of Match awards: 1. Benson & Hedges Gold awards: 1. HS: 145* v Glos (Gloucester) 1974. HSGC: 84* v Derbyshire (Chesterfield) 1973. HSJPL: 101* v Middlesex (Eastbourne) 1972. HSBH: 114* v Cambridge U (Hove) 1974. BB: 3–69 Orange Free State v Australians (Bloemfontein) 1969–70. BBUK: 3–75 v Glos (Cheltenham) 1965. Soccer player.

Geoffrey Alan (Geoff) GREENIDGE B Bridgetown, Barbados 26/5/1948. RHB, LBG. Debut 1966–67 for Barbados in Shell Shield tournament. Debut for county 1968. Cap 1970. Tests: 5 for West Indies between 1971–72 and 1972–73. 1,000 runs (5)—1,334 runs (av 26.68) in 1971 and 1,331 runs (av 35.97) in 1973 best. HS: 205 Barbados v Jamaica (Bridgetown) 1966–67. HSUK: 172 v Middlesex (Hove) 1970. HSGC: 76 v Glos (Lord's) 1973. HSJPL: 79 v Essex (Hove) and 79 v Northants (Hove) 1974. HSBH: 56 v Kent (Hove) 1973. BB: 7–124 Barbados v Jamaica (Bridgetown) 1966–67.

Anthony William (Tony) GREIG (Queen's College, Queenstown) B Queenstown, South Africa 6/10/1946. Very tall (6ft 7½in). RHB, RM. Good field in any position. Debut for Border in 1965–66 Currie Cup competition. Debut for Sussex 1966. Cap 1967. Elected Best Young Cricketer of the Year in 1967 by the Cricket Writers' Club. Transferred to Eastern Province in 1970–71. Appointed county captain in 1973. Tests: 30 between 1972 and 1974. Played in 3 matches against Rest of World in 1970 and 5 matches for Rest of World v Australia 1971–72. Tours: Rest of World to Australia 1971–72, India, Pakistan, and Sri Lanka 1972–73, West Indies 1973–74 (vice-captain), Australia and New Zealand 1974–75. 1,000 runs (6)—1,305 runs (av 26.10) in 1968 best. Scored two centuries in match for L. C. Stevens' XI v Cambridge U (Eastbourne) 1966—a match not regarded as first-class. Hat-trick, Eastern Province v Natal (Port Elizabeth) 1971–72. Took 3 wkts in 4 balls v Hants (Hove) 1967. Gillette Man of Match awards: 4. HS: 167* MCC v Western Australia (Perth) 1974–75. HSUK: 156 v Lancs (Hove) 1967 in debut match in championship. HSGC: 61 v Middlesex (Lord's) 1973. HSJPL: 75 v Lancs (Manchester) 1971 and 75* v Derbyshire (Derby) 1974. HSBH: 103 v Cambridge U (Hove) 1974. BB: 8–25 v Glos (Hove) 1967. BBGC: 5–42 v Kent (Canterbury) 1970. BBJPL: 6–28 v Middlesex (Hove) 1971. BBBH: 3–15 v Yorks (Bradford) 1972.

Jeremy Jonathan (Jerry) GROOME (Seaford College) B Bognor Regis 7/4/1955. RHB, RM. Debut 1974. HS: 59 v Kent (Hove) 1974. HSJPL: 64 v Worcs (Worcester) 1974. HSBH: 35 v Kent (Canterbury) 1974.

SUSSEX

Alan William MANSELL B Redhill 19/5/1951. RHB, WK. Debut 1969. HS: 72* v Somerset (Hove) 1974. HSJPL: 28 v Yorks (Bradford) 1974.

Roger Philip Twells MARSHALL (Charterhouse) B Horsham 28/2/1952. RHB, LFM. Wears glasses. Debut 1973. HS: 26 v Surrey (Oval) 1974. BB: 4–37 v Glamorgan (Hove) 1973.

Gehan Dixon MENDIS (St Thomas College, Colombo and Brighton, Hove and Sussex GS) B Colombo, Ceylon 20/4/1955. RHB. Played for 2nd XI since 1971. Played in one John Player League match in 1973. Debut 1974. One match v Worcs (Hastings). HSJPL: 15* v Glamorgan (Hove) 1973.

Jeremy Dennis (Jerry) MORLEY B Newmarket (Suffolk) 20/10/1950. LHB. Formerly on MCC groundstaff. Debut 1971. Cap 1973. HS: 127 v Warwickshire (Hove) 1973. HSGC: 36 v Northants (Northampton) 1973. HSJPL: 50 v Northants (Wellingborough) 1973. HSBH: 28 v Surrey (Hove) 1974.

Austin Edward Werring PARSONS (Avondale College, Auckland) B Glasgow 9/1/1949. RHB, LB. Debut for New Zealand under-23 XI v Otago 1971–72 and played for Auckland in 1973–74 Plunket Shield competition. Debut for county 1974 after playing for Kent 2nd XI in 1973. One match v Pakistanis (Hove). HS: 78 Auckland v Northern Districts (Rotorua) 1974–75. HSUK: 39* v Pakistanis (Hove) 1974.

Christopher Paul PHILLIPSON (Ardingly College) B Brindaban, India 10/2/1952. RHB, RM. Debut 1970. HS: 11* v Surrey (Hove) 1973. BB: 6–56 v Notts (Hove) 1972. BBJPL: 4–25 v Middlesex (Eastbourne) 1972. Trained as a teacher at Loughborough College of Education.

John Augustine SNOW (Christ's Hospital, Horsham) B Peopleton (Worcs) 13/10/1941. RHB, RF. Debut 1961. Cap 1964. Wisden 1972. Benefit in 1974. Tests: 42 between 1965 and 1973. Played in 5 matches v Rest of World 1970. Shared in 10th wkt partnership of 128 with K. Higgs v West Indies (Oval) 1966—2 runs short of then record 10th wkt partnership in Test cricket. Tours: West Indies 1967–68, Ceylon and Pakistan 1968–69, Australia 1970–71. 100 wkts (2)—126 wkts (av 19.09) in 1966 best. Gillette Man of Match awards: 1. Benson & Hedges Gold awards: 2. HS: 73 England v India (Lord's) 1971. HSGC: 19 v Worcs (Hove) 1974. HSJPL: 31* v Hants (Hove) 1969. HSBH: 25 v Essex (Chelmsford) 1972. BB: 7–29 v West Indians (Hove) 1966. BBGC: 4–35 v Surrey (Oval) 1970. BBJPL: 5–15 v Surrey (Hove) 1972. BBBH: 5–30 v Kent (Canterbury) 1974.

John SPENCER (Brighton, Hove and Sussex GS, and Cambridge) B Brighton 6/10/1949. RHB, RM. Debut 1969. Blues 1970–72. Cap 1973. Benson & Hedges Gold awards: 1. HS: 55 Cambridge U v Glamorgan (Swansea) 1972. HSGC: 14 v Glos (Hove) 1971. HSJPL: 30* v Surrey (Byfleet) 1974. HSBH: 18 Cambridge U v Warwickshire (Birmingham) 1972. BB: 6–19 v Glos (Gloucester) 1974. BBGC: 4–25 v Derbyshire (Chesterfield) 1973. BBJPL: 4–16 v Somerset (Hove) 1973. BBBH: 4–29 Cambridge U v Worcs (Cambridge) 1972.

Christopher Edward (Chris) WALLER B Guildford 3/10/1948. RHB, SLA. Debut for Surrey 1967. Cap 1972. Left staff after 1973 season and made debut for Sussex in 1974. HS: 74 Surrey v Pakistanis (Oval) 1971. BB: 7–64 Surrey v Sussex (Oval) 1971. BBJPL: 3–28 v Kent (Hove) 1974. BBBH: 3–17 v Cambridge U (Hove) 1974.

NB The following players whose particulars appeared in the 1974 Annual have been omitted: J. Denman (left staff), M. G. Griffith (left staff), and U. C. Joshi (not re-engaged). In addition, Nicholas Wisdom, RHB, RM. son of the comedian Norman Wisdom, who appeared in two matches has not been included as he has left the staff. The career records of Griffith, Joshi, and Wisdom will be found elsewhere in this Annual.

COUNTY AVERAGES

County Championship: Played 20; won 4, drawn 7, lost 8, tied 1
All first-class matches: Played 22; won 5, drawn 7, lost 9, tied 1

BATTING AND FIELDING

Cap		M	I	NO	Runs	HS	Avge	100	50	Ct	St
1969	P. J. Graves	21	39	6	1282	145*	38.84	3	7	13	—
1970	G. A. Greenidge	21	42	3	1187	147	30.43	2	4	16	—
1967	M. G. Griffith	11	20	3	408	121*	24.00	1	2	7	—
—	M. J. J. Faber	15	28	3	593	112*	23.72	1	2	9	—
1973	J. D. Morley	22	43	2	864	85	21.07	—	6	10	1
1967	A. W. Greig	10	19	0	399	70	21.00	—	3	9	—
1964	J. A. Snow	21	33	3	543	63	18.10	—	1	8	—
—	A. W. Mansell	20	33	6	470	72*	17.40	—	1	32	2
1971	U. C. Joshi	6	8	5	51	20	17.00	—	—	4	—
1963	A. Buss	4	5	2	42	15	14.00	—	—	1	—
1967	M. A. Buss	16	25	3	260	31	11.81	—	—	11	—
1973	J. Spencer	18	26	5	243	37	11.57	—	—	9	—
—	J. J. Groome	9	16	0	181	59	11.31	—	1	3	—
—	J. R. T. Barclay	11	21	0	237	28	11.28	—	—	10	—
—	C. E. Waller	20	29	4	182	25	7.28	—	—	11	—
—	C. P. Philipson	10	9	5	23	6	5.75	—	—	2	—

Played in two matches: R. P. T. Marshall 26, 16*; 11*, 19*; N. Wisdom 31* ;4.

Played in one match: R. G. L. Cheatle 0*; G. D. Mendis 1; A. E. W. Parsons 39*, 4.

BOWLING

	Type	O	M	R	W	Avge	Best	5 wI	10 wM
J. A. Snow	RF	535.1	116	1426	73	19.53	6–14	6	2
M. A. Buss	LM	350	122	797	32	24.90	6–74	2	—
J. Spencer	RM	464.3	112	1243	47	26.44	6–19	3	—
C. P. Philipson	RM	189	50	439	16	27.43	5–30	1	—
A. W. Greig	LBG	340.5	67	1119	35	31.97	6–50	1	—
U. C. Joshi	OB	182	54	431	13	33.15	4–79	—	—
C. E. Waller	SLA	582.5	151	1580	47	33.61	5–69	2	—
J. R. T. Barclay	OB	96	22	272	8	34.00	3–41	—	—
A. Buss	RFM	93.2	30	219	5	43.80	2–27	—	—

Also bowled: R. G. L. Cheatle 14-3-53-0; M. J. J. Faber 9.4-3-17-1; P. J. Graves 1-0-6-0; G. A. Greenidge 7-0-45-0; M. G. Griffith 1-0-8-0; R. P. T. Marshall 41-3-128-2; J. D. Morley 1-1-0-0; A. E. W. Parsons 0.2-0-4-0; N. Wisdom 13.5-3-33-2.

County Records
First-class cricket

Highest innings totals:	For ...705–8d v Surrey (Hastings)	1902
	Agst...726 by Nottinghamshire (Nottingham)	1895
Lowest innings totals:	For ... 19 v Surrey (Godalming)	1830
	19 v Nottinghamshire (Hove)	1873
	Agst... 18 by Kent (Gravesend)	1867
Highest individual innings:	For ...333 K. S. Duleepsinhji v Northants (Hove)	1930
	Agst...322 E. Paynter for Lancashire (Hove)	1937
Best bowling in an innings:	For ...10–48 C. H. G. Bland v Kent (Tonbridge)	1899
	Agst... 9–11 A. P. Freeman for Kent (Hove)	1922
Best bowling in a match:	For ...17–106 G. R. Cox v Warwicks (Horsham)	1926
	Agst...17–67 A. P. Freeman for Kent (Hove)	1922
Most runs in a season:	2850 (av 64.77) John Langridge	1949
runs in a career:	34152 (av 37.69) John Langridge	1928–1955
100s in a season:	12 by John Langridge	1949
100s in a career:	76 by John Langridge	1928–1955
wickets in a season:	198 (av 13.45) M. W. Tate	1925
wickets in a career:	2223 (av 16.34) M. W. Tate	1912–1937

RECORD WICKET STANDS

1st 490	E. H. Bowley & John Langridge v Middlesex (Hove)	1933
2nd 385	E. H. Bowley & M. W. Tate v Northamptonshire (Hove)	1921
3rd 298	K. S. Ranjitsinhji & E. H. Killick v Lancashire (Hove)	1901
4th 326*	G. Cox & James Langridge v Yorkshire (Leeds)	1949
5th 297	J. H. Parks & H. W. Parks v Hampshire (Portsmouth)	1937
6th 255	K. S. Duleepsinhji & M. W. Tate v Northamptonshire (Hove)	1930
7th 344	K. S. Ranjitsinhji & W. Newham v Essex (Leyton)	1902
8th 229*	C. L. A. Smith & G. Brann v Kent (Hove)	1902
9th 178	H. W. Parks & A. F. Wensley v Derbyshire (Horsham)	1930
10th 156	G. R. Cox & H. R. Butt v Cambridge U (Cambridge)	1908

One-day cricket

Highest innings totals:	Gillette Cup	314–7 v Kent (Tunbridge Wells)	1963
	John Player League	288–6 v M'sex (Hove)	1969
	Benson & Hedges Cup	280–5 v Cambridge U (Hove)	1974
Lowest innings totals:	Gillette Cup	49 v Derbyshire (Chesterfield)	1969
	John Player League	63 v Derbyshire (Hove)	1969
	Benson & Hedges Cup	85 v Yorks (Bradford)	1972
Highest individual innings:	Gillette Cup	115 E. R. Dexter v Northants (Northampton)	1963
	John Player League	121 M. A. Buss v Notts (Worksop)	1971
	Benson & Hedges Cup	114* P. J. Graves v Cambridge U (Hove)	1974
Best bowling figures:	Gillette Cup	6–30 D. L. Bates v Glos (Hove)	1968
	John Player League	6–14 M. A. Buss v Lancashire (Hove)	1973
	Benson & Hedges Cup	5–30 J. A. Snow v Kent (Canterbury)	1974

WARWICKSHIRE

Formation of present club: 1884.
Colours: Blue, yellow, and white.
Badge: Bear and ragged staff.
County Champions (3): 1911, 1951, and 1972.
Gillette Cup winners(2): 1966 and 1968.
Gillette Cup finalists (2): 1964 and 1972.
Benson & Hedges Cup semi-finalists: 1972.

Secretary: L. T. Deakins, County Ground, Edgbaston, Birmingham, B5 7QU
Captain:

Robert Neal ABBERLEY (Saltley GS) B Birmingham 22/4/1944. RHB, OB. Good outfield. Debut 1964. Cap 1966. Tour: Pakistan 1966-67 (returning home early owing to injury). 1,000 runs (3)—1,315 runs (av 28.58) in 1966 best. HS: 117* v Essex (Birmingham) 1966. HSGC: 47 v Lincs (Birmingham) 1971. HSJPL: 76 v Glamorgan (Birmingham) 1974. HSBH: 91 v Worcs (Worcester) 1974.

Dennis Leslie AMISS B Birmingham 7/4/1943. RHB, LM/SLA. Joined county staff 1958. Debut 1960. Cap 1965. Benefit in 1975. Tests: 32 between 1966 and 1974. Played in one match v Rest of World 1970. Tours: Pakistan 1966-67, India, Pakistan, and Sri Lanka 1972-73, West Indies 1973-74, Australia and New Zealand 1974-75. 1,000 runs (10)—1,850 runs (av 54.41) in 1967 best. Also scored 1,120 runs (av 74.66) in West Indies 1973-74. Gillette Man of Match awards: 2. Benson & Hedges Gold awards: 1. HS: 262* England v West Indies (Kingston) 1973-74. HSUK: 195 v Middlesex (Birmingham) 1974. HSGC: 113 v Glamorgan (Swansea) 1966. HSJPL: 110 v Surrey (Birmingham) 1974. HSBH: 71* v Oxford U (Oxford) 1973. BB: 3-21 v Middlesex (Lord's) 1970.

William Anderson (Bill) BOURNE (Harrison College, Barbados) B Clapham, Barbados 15/11/1952. RHB, RFM. Toured England with West Indian schoolboys team 1970. Debut for Barbados 1970-71 in last match of Shell Shield competition. Joined staff 1971. Debut for county 1973. HS: 84 v Oxford U (Birmingham) 1973. HSJPL: 18* v Hants (Birmingham) 1974. BB: 3-31 v Oxford U (Oxford) 1974. BBJPL: 4-24 v Glamorgan (Birmingham) 1974.

David John (Dave) BROWN (Queen Mary GS, Walsall) B Walsall 30/1/1942. RHB, RFM. Tall (6ft 4in). Debut 1961. Cap 1964. Benefit (£21,109) in 1973. Tests: 26 between 1965 and 1969. Played in 2 matches v Rest of World 1970. Tours: South Africa 1964-65, Australia and New Zealand 1965-66, Pakistan 1966-67 (vice-captain), West Indies 1967-68, Ceylon and Pakistan 1968-69. Gillette Man of Match awards: 1. HS: 79 v Derbyshire (Birmingham) 1972. HSGC: 24 v Somerset (Birmingham) 1967. HSJPL: 38* v Worcs (Birmingham) 1972. HSBH: 20* v Northants (Coventry) 1973. BB: 8-64 v Sussex (Birmingham) 1964. BBGC: 5-18 v Glamorgan (Swansea) 1966. BBJPL: 5-13 v Worcs (Birmingham) 1970. BBBH: 3-25 v Northants (Northampton) 1972.

WARWICKSHIRE

Maxwell Nicholas **FIELD** (Bablake School, Coventry, London and Cambridge Universities) B Coventry 23/3/1950. RHB, RM. Debut for 2nd XI in 1967. Debut for both University and county in 1974. Blue 1974. HS: 39* Cambridge U v Warwickshire (Cambridge) 1974. BB: 4–76 Cambridge U v Oxford U (Lord's) 1974.

Barrie Keith **GARDOM** (Bishop Vesey's GS, Sutton Coldfield) B Birmingham 31/12/1952. RHB, LB. Debut for 2nd XI in 1970. Toured West Indies with England Young Cricketers in 1972. Debut 1973. HS: 79* v Surrey (Birmingham) 1974. BB: 6–139 v Essex (Chelmsford) 1974.

Edward Ernest (Eddie) **HEMMINGS** (Campion School, Leamington Spa) B Leamington Spa 20/2/1949. RHB, RM/OB. Debut 1966. Cap 1974. HS: 80 v Worcs (Worcester) 1971. HSGC: 20 v Worcs (Birmingham) 1973. HSJPL: 44* v Kent (Birmingham) 1971. HSBH: 61* v Leics (Birmingham) 1974. BB: 7–57 v Lancs (Birmingham) 1974. BBJPL: 5–22 v Northants (Birmingham) 1974.

Geoffrey William (Geoff) **HUMPAGE** (Golden Hillock Comprehensive School, Birmingham) B Birmingham 24/4/1954. RHB, WK. Debut 1974 (two matches). HS: 13 v Oxford U (Oxford) 1974.

John Alexander **JAMESON** (Taunton School) B Bombay 30/6/1941. RHB, RM/OB. Good field in covers. Can keep wicket. Debut 1960. Cap 1964. Benefit in 1974. Tests: 4 in 1971 and 1973–74. Tour: West Indies 1973–74. 1,000 runs (10)—1,948 runs (av 48.70) in 1973 and 1,932 runs (av 48.30) in 1974 best. Scored two centuries in match (110 & 111) D. H. Robins' XI v Indians (Eastbourne) 1974. Hat-trick v Glos (Birmingham) 1965. Gillette Man of Match awards: 1. Benson & Hedges Gold awards: 1. HS: 240* v Glos (Birmingham) 1974, sharing in world record 2nd wkt partnership—465* with R. B. Kanhai. HSGC: 100* v Hants (Birmingham) 1964. HSJPL: 123* v Notts (Nottingham) 1973. HSBH: 75 v Middlesex (Coventry) 1974. BB: 4–22 v Oxford U (Oxford) 1971. BBJPL: 5–60 v Kent (Folkestone) 1974. Plays rugby, soccer, and hockey.

Alvin Isaac (Kalli) **KALLICHARRAN** B Port Mourant, Berbice, Guyana 21/3/1949. LHB, LBG. 5ft 4in tall. Debut 1966–67 for Guyana in Shell Shield competition. Debut for county 1971. Cap 1972. Tests: 15 for West Indies between 1971–72 and 1973–74, scoring 100* and 101 in first two innings in Tests v New Zealand. Tours: West Indies to England 1973, India, Sri Lanka, and Pakistan 1974–75. 1,000 runs (3)—1,309 runs (av 35.37) in 1974 best. HS: 197 Guyana v Jamaica (Kingston) 1973–74. HSUK: 164 v Notts (Coventry) 1972. HSGC: 88 v Glamorgan (Birmingham) 1972. HSJPL: 101* v Derbyshire (Chesterfield) 1972. HSBH: 57 v Worcs (Birmingham) 1973.

Rohan Babulal **KANHAI** B Port Mourant, Berbice, Guyana 26/12/1935. RHB, RM. Former WK. Debut for British Guiana (now Guyana) 1954–55. Played for Western Australia in Sheffield Shield competition in 1961–62. Played league cricket for Aberdeenshire, Blackpool, and Ashington. Debut for county and cap 1968. Played for Tasmania 1969–70 whilst coaching there. Tests: 79 for West Indies between 1957 and 1973–74, 61 of them consecutive from 1st Test v England 1957 to 1968–69, sequence being broken by his returning to England at end of Australian tour to undergo cartilage operation. Captained country in 13 Tests. Played in 5 matches for Rest of World against England 1970 and 3 against Australia 1971–72. Tours: West Indies to England 1957, 1963, 1966, and 1973 (captain), India and Pakistan 1958–59, Australia 1960–61, India and Ceylon 1966–67, Australia 1968–69, Rest of World to Australia 1971–72. 1,000 runs (9)—1,894 runs (av 57.39) in 1970 best. Also scored over 1,000 runs in India and Pakistan 1958–59 and in Australia 1960–61. Scored two centuries in Test match (117 and 115) v Australia (Adelaide) 1960–61. Scored 8 centuries in 1972 to equal county record. Gillette Man of Match awards: 3. Benson & Hedges Gold awards: 3. HS: 256 West Indies v India (Calcutta) 1958–59. HSUK: 253 v Notts (Nottingham) 1968 sharing in record partnership for county for 4th wkt, 402 with K. Ibadulla. Also shared in world record partnership for 2nd wkt—465* with J. A. Jameson v Glos (Birmingham) 1974. HSGC: 126 v Lincs (Birmingham) 1971. HSJPL: 120 v Leics (Birmingham) 1972. HSBH: 102* v Northants (Birmingham) 1974.

Deryck Lance MURRAY (Queen's Road College, Port of Spain, and Cambridge and Nottingham Universities) B Port of Spain, Trinidad 20/5/1943. RHB, WK. Can bowl LBG. Debut for Trinidad 1960–61. Debut for Cambridge U 1965. Blue 1965–66 (captain in 1966). Debut for Notts 1966. Cap 1967. Left county after 1969 season and made debut for Warwickshire in 1972. Cap 1972. Tours: West Indies to England 1963 and 1973, India and Ceylon 1966–67. India, Sri Lanka and Pakistan 1974–75 (vice-captain). Tests: 22 for West Indies between 1963 and 1973–74. Played in 3 matches for Rest of World against England in 1970. 1,000 runs (3)—1,358 runs (av 30.17) in 1966 best. Benson & Hedges Gold awards: 2. HS: 166* Notts v Surrey (Oval) 1966. HSGC: 72* v Notts (Birmingham) 1974. HSJPL: 65* v Kent (Folkestone) 1974. HSBH: 82 v Worcs (Worcester) 1972. Dismissed 24 batsmen (22 ct 2 st) in 1963 Test series.

Stephen Peter PERRYMAN (Sheldon Heath Comprehensive School) B Yardley, Birmingham 22/10/1955. RHB, RM. Debut 1974. One match v Cambridge U (Nuneaton).

Stephen John (Mic) ROUSE (Moseley County School) B Merthyr Tydfil (Glamorgan) 20/1/1949. LHB, LM. Debut 1970. Cap 1974. Benson & Hedges Gold awards: 1. HS: 55 v Yorks (Sheffield) 1974. HSJPL : 23 v Notts (Birmingham) 1974. HSBH: 25 v Leics (Birmingham) 1974. BB: 5–47 v Lancs (Manchester) 1972. BBGC: 4–42 v Worcs (Birmingham) 1973. BBJPL: 4–42 v Hants (Southampton) 1971. BBBH: 5–21 v Worcs (Worcester) 1974. Plays rugby, hockey, and basketball.

Kenneth David SMITH (Heaton GS) B Jesmond, Newcastle-upon-Tyne 9/7/1956. RHB. Son of Kenneth D. Smith, former Northumberland and Leics player. Played for 2nd XI 1972. Debut 1973. Played in two matches in 1973 and one match in 1974. HS: 49 v Oxford U (Birmingham) 1973.

Michael John Knight (Mike) SMITH (Stamford School and Oxford) B Broughton Astley (Leics) 30/6/1933. RHB. Good close field. Plays in glasses. Debut for Leicestershire 1951. Cap 1955. Blues 1954–56 (captain in 1956). Created record by scoring three centuries in University match including 201* in 1954. Debut for Warwicks 1956. Cap 1957. County captain from 1957 to 1967. Retired after 1967 season but returned to play regularly in 1970. *Wisden* 1959. Tests: 50 between 1958 and 1972 captaining England in 25 Test matches. Tours: West Indies 1959–60, India and Pakistan 1961–62 (vice-captain), India 1963–64 (captain), South Africa 1964–65 (captain), Australia and New Zealand 1965–66 (captain). 1,000 runs (19)—3,245 runs (av 57.94) in 1959 best. Also scored 1,000 runs (1,079 runs, av 46.91) in Australia and New Zealand 1965–66. Scored 1,209 runs in July 1959. Held 6 catches in innings v Leics (Hinckley) 1962. Held 52 catches for Warwicks in 1961—county record. Gillette Man of Match awards: 3. Blue and England cap for rugby. HS: 204 Commonwealth XI v Natal (Durban) 1960–61. HSUK: 201* Oxford U v Cambridge U (Lord's) 1954. HSGC: 88* v Lincs (Birmingham) 1971 and 88 v Hants (Birmingham) 1964. HSJPL: 97* v Northants (Birmingham) 1973. HSBH: 62* v Worcs (Birmingham) 1973.

John WHITEHOUSE (King Edward VI School, Nuneaton and Bristol University) B Nuneaton 8/4/1949. RHB, OB. Played for county against Scotland in 1970, a match no longer counted as first-class. Debut 1971, scoring 173 v Oxford U (Oxford) in first innings of debut match, in 167 minutes with 35 4's. Elected Best Young Cricketer of the Year in 1971 by Cricket Writers' Club. Cap 1973. Did not play in 1974 as he was taking accountancy examinations. Scored 1,295 runs (av 38.08) in 1971. HS as above. HSGC: 68 v Lancs (Lord's) 1972. HSJPL: 80* v Worcs (Birmingham) 1973. HSBH: 43 v Worcs (Worcester) 1972.

Robert George Dylan (Bob) WILLIS (Guildford RGS) B Sunderland 30/5/1949. RHB, RF. Debut for Surrey 1969. Left staff after 1971 season and made debut for Warwickshire in 1972. Cap 1972. Tests: 11 between 1970–71 and 1974. Tours: Australia and New Zealand 1970–71 (flown out as replacement for A. Ward) and 1974–75, West Indies 1973–74. Hat-trick v Derbyshire (Birmingham) 1972 and also in John Player League v Yorks (Birmingham) 1973. Gillette Man of Match awards: 1 (for Surrey). HS: 34 D. H. Robins' XI v Combined B Section XI (Pretoria) 1972–73. HSUK: 33 Surrey v Kent (Canterbury) 1971. HSGC: 12* Surrey v Sussex (Oval) 1970. HSJPL: 24 Surrey v Worcs (Oval) 1971. BB: 8–44 v Derbyshire (Birmingham) 1972. BBGC: 6–49 Surrey v Middlesex (Oval) 1970. BBJPL: 4–12 v Middlesex (Lord's) 1973. BBBH: 3–41 v Middlesex (Coventry) 1974. Has played soccer (goalkeeper) for Guildford City.

NB The following players whose particulars appeared in the 1974 Annual have been omitted: W. Blenkiron (left staff to take league engagement), A. K. C. Jones, P. J. Lewington (left staff), J. I. McDowall, A. C. Smith (retired) and W. N. Tidy (left staff). The career records of Blenkiron, Lewington, Smith, and Tidy will be found elsewhere in this Annual.

COUNTY AVERAGES

County Championship: Played 20; won 6, drawn 10, lost 4
All first-class matches: Played 24; won 7, drawn 13, lost 4

BATTING AND FIELDING

Cap		M	I	NO	Runs	HS	Avge	100	50	Ct	St
1968	R. B. Kanhai	14	22	4	936	213*	52.00	3	4	3	—
1964	J. A. Jameson	23	40	2	1711	240*	45.02	4	7	22	—
1965	D. L. Amiss	9	16	2	625	195	44.64	2	1	4	—
1957	M. J. K. Smith	23	38	8	1159	105	38.63	1	8	23	—
1972	A. I. Kallicharran	24	39	2	1309	132	35.37	3	7	10	—
1972	R. G. D. Willis	16	20	15	134	23*	26.80	—	—	9	—
1974	S. J. Rouse	9	13	3	242	55	24.20	—	1	5	—
1974	E. E. Hemmings	23	32	5	645	74	23.88	—	3	12	—
1966	R. N. Abberley	13	21	0	467	99	22.23	—	1	13	—
1972	D. L. Murray	22	34	2	707	78	22.09	—	2	47	3
—	B. K. Gardom	14	20	2	374	79*	20.77	—	2	6	—
1961	A. C. Smith	18	23	4	368	39	19.36	—	—	5	—
—	W. A. Bourne	12	16	2	210	29	15.00	—	—	12	—
—	P. J. Lewington	5	2	1	12	8	12.00	—	—	2	—
1969	W. Blenkiron	12	15	1	147	28	10.50	—	—	2	—
1964	D. J. Brown	20	20	7	123	21*	9.46	—	—	7	—

Played in two matches: M. N. Field 1*; G. W. Humpage 13; 0 (5 ct).
Played in one match: S. P. Perryman did not bat; K. D. Smith 14;
W. N. Tidy did not bat.

BOWLING

	Type	O	M	R	W	Avge	Best	5 wI	10 wM
S. J. Rouse	LM	164.5	34	489	27	18.11	4-26	—	—
D. J. Brown	RFM	495	134	1143	56	20.41	5-45	1	—
R.G.D. Willis	RF	375	72	1083	53	20.43	5-85	1	—
E. E. Hemmings	RM/OB	738	213	1855	84	22.08	7-57	6	1
A. C. Smith	RM	291.4	70	729	26	28.03	4-49	—	—
W. Blenkiron	RFM	160.4	34	473	15	31.53	5-45	1	—
W. A. Bourne	RFM	166	29	578	17	34.00	3-31	—	—
B.K. Gardom	LB	195.2	31	696	17	40.94	6-139	1	—
J.A. Jameson	RM/OB	202.5	41	632	12	52.66	4-47	—	—

Also bowled: D. L. Amiss 6-1-17-1; M. N. Field 11-1-45-0; A. I.
Kallicharran 34-4-119-2; R. B. Kanhai 3-0-9-0; P. J. Lewington
90-29-227-4; D. L. Murray 7-3-23-0; M. J. K. Smith 1-1-0-0.

County Records

First-class cricket

Highest innings totals:	For ...657–6d v Hampshire (Birmingham)	1899
	Agst...887 by Yorkshire (Birmingham)	1896
Lowest innings totals:	For ... 16 v Kent (Tonbridge)	1913
	Agst... 15 by Hampshire (Birmingham)	1922
Highest individual innings:	For ...305* F. R. Foster v Worcestershire (Dudley)	1914
	Agst...316 R. H. Moore for Hants (Bournemouth)	1937
Best bowling in an innings:	For ...10–41 J. D. Bannister v Combined Services (Birmingham)	1959
	Agst...10–36 H. Verity for Yorkshire (Leeds)	1931

141

Best bowling in a match:	For ...15–76 S. Hargreave v Surrey (The Oval)	1903
	Agst...17–92 A. P. Freeman for Kent (Folkestone)	1932
Most runs in a season:	2417 (av 60.42) M. J. K. Smith	1959
runs in a career:	34172 (av 35.31) W. G. Quaife	1894–1928
100s in a season:	8 by R. E. S. Wyatt	1937
	and R. B. Kanhai	1972
100s in a career:	71 by W. G. Quaife	1894–1928
wickets in a season:	180 (av 15.13) W. E. Hollies	1946
wickets in a career:	2201 (av 20.45) W. E. Hollies	1932–1957

RECORD WICKET STANDS

1st 377*	N. F. Horner & K. Ibadulla v Surrey (The Oval)	1960
2nd 465*	J. A. Jameson & R. B. Kanhai v Gloucestershire (Birmingham)	1974
3rd 327	S. P. Kinneir & W. G. Quaife v Lancashire (Birmingham)	1901
4th 402	R. B. Kanhai & K. Ibadulla v Notts (Nottingham)	1968
5th 268	W. Quaife & W. G. Quaife v Essex (Leyton)	1900
6th 220	H. E. Dollery & J. Buckingham v Derbyshire (Derby)	1938
7th 250	H. E. Dollery & J. S. Ord v Kent (Maidstone)	1953
8th 228	A. J. Croom & R. E. S. Wyatt v Worcestershire (Dudley)	1925
9th 154	G. W. Stephens & A. J. Croom v Derbyshire (Birmingham)	1925
10th 128	F. R. Santall & W. Sanders v Yorkshire (Birmingham)	1930

One-day cricket

Highest innings totals:	Gillette Cup	307–8 v Hampshire (Birmingham)	1964
	John Player League	249–6 v Worcestershire (Birmingham)	1972
	Benson & Hedges Cup	250–5 v Northants (Northampton)	1974
Lowest innings totals:	Gillette Cup	109 v Kent (Canterbury)	1971
	John Player League	85 v Glamorgan (Swansea)	1972
		85 v Gloucestershire (Cheltenham)	1973
	Benson & Hedges Cup	96 v Leics (Leicester)	1972
Highest individual innings:	Gillette Cup	126 R. B. Kanhai v Lincs (Birmingham)	1971
	John Player League	123* J. A. Jameson v Notts (Nottingham)	1973
	Benson & Hedges Cup	102* R. B. Kanhai v Northants (Northampton)	1974
Best bowling figures:	Gillette Cup	6–32 K. Ibadulla v Hants (Birmingham)	1965
	John Player League	5–13 D. J. Brown v Worcs (Birmingham)	1970
	Benson & Hedges Cup	5–21 S. J. Rouse v Worcestershire (Worcester)	1974

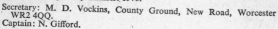

Formation of present club: 1865.
Colours: Dark green and black.
Badge: Shield, *Argent* bearing *Fess* between three *Pears Sable.*
County Champions (3): 1964, 1965 and 1974.
Gillette Cup finalists (2): 1963 and 1966.
John Player League Champions: 1971.
Benson & Hedges Cup finalists: 1973.

Secretary: M. D. Vockins, County Ground, New Road, Worcester WR2 4QQ.

Captain: N. Gifford.

Brian Maurice BRAIN (King's School, Worcester) B Worcester 13/9/1940. RHB, RFM. Debut 1959. Left staff in 1960. Rejoined staff in 1963 and reappeared in 1964. Cap 1966. Left staff in 1971, but rejoined in 1973. Gillette Man of Match awards: 1. HS: 38 v Glos (Cheltenham) 1964. HSGC: 21* v Sussex (Worcester) 1967. HSJPL: 15 v Northants (Northampton) 1974. HSBH: 12 v Lancs (Manchester) 1973. BB: 6–32 v Somerset (Bath) 1973. BBGC: 4–13 v Durham (Chester-le-Street) 1968. BBJPL: 4–27 v Somerset (Taunton) 1970. BBBH: 3–25 v Leics (Worcester) 1974.

George Rodney CASS B Overton (Yorks) 23/4/1940. LHB, WK. Joined Essex staff in 1963 and made debut in 1964. Left staff after 1967 season and joined Worcs. Debut for county 1969. Cap 1970. Played for Tasmania from 1970–71 to 1972–73 whilst coaching there. HS: 104* Essex v Warwickshire (Birmingham) 1967. HSGC: 43* v Derbyshire (Derby) 1969, 43 v Kent (Canterbury) 1970 and 43 v Sussex (Hove) 1974. HSJPL: 63 v Essex (Harlow) 1969. HSBH: 56* v Warwickshire (Worcester) 1974.

James (Jimmy) CUMBES (Didsbury Secondary Technical School) B East Didsbury (Lancs) 4/5/1944. RHB, RFM. Outfield. Debut for Lancs 1963. Not re-engaged at end of 1967 season and made debut for Surrey in 1968. Not re-engaged after 1970 season and rejoined Lancs in 1971. Made debut for Worcs in 1972 by special registration. HS: 25* Surrey v West Indians (Oval) 1969. BB: 6–35 Surrey v Oxford U (Oxford) 1968. BBGC: 4–23 v Sussex (Hove) 1974. BBJPL: 3–18 Surrey v Lancs (Manchester) 1969. Soccer (goalkeeper) for Tranmere Rovers, West Bromwich Albion, and Aston Villa.

Basil Lewis D'OLIVEIRA B Cape Town 4/10/1931. RHB, RM/OB. Played for Middleton in Central Lancashire League from 1960 to 1963. Made first-class debut in Commonwealth tour of 1961–62 playing in two matches in Rhodesia. Took part in further tour of Rhodesia in 1962–63. Toured Pakistan with Commonwealth XI 1963–64. Joined Worcestershire staff, becoming eligible for Championship matches in 1965. Cap 1965. *Wisden* 1966. Played for Kidderminster in Birmingham League whilst qualifying. Awarded OBE in 1969 Birthday Honours list. Benefit in 1975. Tests: 44 between 1966 and 1972. Played in 4 matches against Rest of

World 1970. Tours: West Indies 1967–68, Ceylon and Pakistan 1968–69, Australia and New Zealand 1970–71. 1,000 runs (7)—1,691 runs (av 43.35) in 1965 best. Gillette Man of Match awards: 6. Benson & Hedges Gold awards: 2. HS: 227 v Yorks (Hull) 1974. HSGC: 102 v Sussex (Hove) 1974. HSJPL: 100 v Surrey (Byfleet) 1971. HSBH: 84 v Middlesex (Lord's) 1974. BB: 6–29 v Hants (Portsmouth) 1968. BBGC: 4-18 v Notts (Worcester) 1974. BBJPL: 5–26 v Glos (Lydney) 1972. BBBH: 3–13 v Northants (Northampton) 1972.

Norman **GIFFORD** B Ulverston (Lancs) 30/3/1940. LHB, SLA. Joined staff 1958 and made debut 1960. Cap 1961. Appointed county captain in 1971 after being vice-captain since 1969. Benefit in 1974. Tests: 15 between 1964 and 1973. Played in one match for Rest of World v Australia 1971–72. Tours: Rest of World to Australia 1971–72, India, Pakistan, and Sri Lanka 1972–73. 100 wkts (3)—133 wkts (av 19.66) in 1961 best. Hattrick v Derbyshire (Chesterfield) 1965. Took 4 wkts in 6 balls v Cambridge U (Cambridge) 1972. Gillette Man of Match awards: 1. Benson & Hedges Gold awards: 1. HS: 89 v Oxford U (Oxford) 1963. HSGC: 38 v Warwickshire (Lord's) 1966. HSJPL: 29 v Essex (Worcester) 1974. HSBH: 33 v Kent (Lord's) 1973. BB: 8–28 v Yorks (Sheffield) 1968. BBGC: 4–7 v Surrey (Worcester) 1972. BBJPL: 4–18 v Middlesex (Worcester) 1974. BBBH: 5–32 v Northants (Worcester) 1973.

Ronald George Alphonso (Ron) **HEADLEY** B Kingston, Jamaica 29/6/1939. Son of George Headley, leading West Indian batsman before the war. LHB, LB. Debut 1958. Cap 1961. Played for Jamaica in Shell Shield competition in 1965–66 and 1973–74. Benefit (£10,014) in 1972. Tests: 2 for West Indies in 1973. Tour: West Indies to England 1973 as replacement for G. S. Camacho. 1,000 runs (13)—2,040 runs (av 31.87) in 1961 best. Scored two centuries in match (187 and 108) v Northants (Worcester) 1971. Shared in century partnership for first wicket of each innings of a match twice with P. J. Stimpson in 1971. Gillette Man of Match awards: 1. Benson & Hedges Gold awards: 2. HS: 187 v Northants (Worcester) 1971. HSGC: 83 v Surrey (Worcester) 1963. HSJPL: 112* v Kent (Worcester) 1974. HSBH: 132 v Oxford U (Worcester) 1973. BB: 4–40 v Glamorgan (Worcester) 1963.

Edward John Orton (Ted) **HEMSLEY** (Bridgnorth GS) B Norton, Stoke-on-Trent 1/9/1943. RHB, RM. Cover point. Debut 1963. Cap 1969. Benson & Hedges Gold awards: 2. HS: 138* v Oxford U (Oxford) 1969. HSGC: 73 v Sussex (Hove) 1972. HSJPL: 72 v Notts (Nottingham) 1969. HSBH: 73 v Warwickshire (Birmingham) 1973. BB: 3–5 v Warwickshire (Worcester) 1971. BBJPL: 4–42 v Essex (Worcester) 1971. Soccer (winghalf) for Shrewsbury Town and Sheffield United.

Vanburn Alonza (Van) **HOLDER** B St Michael, Barbados 8/10/1945. RHB, RFM. Debut 1966–67 for Barbados in one match in Shell Shield tournament. Debut for county 1968. Cap 1970. Tests: 16 for West Indies between 1969 and 1974. Tours: West Indies to England 1969 and 1973, India, Sri Lanka, and Pakistan 1974–75. HS: 122 Barbados v Trinidad (Bridgetown) 1973–74. HSUK: 52 v Glos (Dudley) 1970. HSGC: 25* v Notts (Worcester) 1974. HSJPL: 35* v Middlesex (Lord's) 1970. HSBH: 15* v Leics (Leicester) 1973. BB: 7–40 v Glamorgan (Cardiff) 1974.

BBGC: 3–14 v Oxfordshire (Cowley) 1970. BBJPL: 6–33 v Middlesex (Lord's) 1972. BBBH: 5–12 v Northants (Northampton) 1974.

IMRAN KHAN NIAZI (Aitchison College and Cathedral School, Lahore, Worcester RGS and Oxford) B Lahore, Pakistan 25/11/1952. RHB, RFM. Cousin of Majid Jahangir Khan. Debut for Lahore A 1969–70 and has played subsequently for various Lahore teams. Debut for county 1971. Played only in one-day matches for county in 1974. Blue 1973–74 (capt in 1974). Tests: 4 for Pakistan v England in 1971 and 1974. Tours: Pakistan to England 1971 and 1974. Scored 1,016 runs (av 36.28) in 1974. Scored two centuries in match (117* & 106), Oxford U v Notts (Oxford) 1974. HS: 170 Oxford U v Northants (Oxford) 1974. HSGC: 20 v Glos (Worcester) 1973. HSJPL: 56 v Hants (Worcester) 1973. HSBH: 26 Oxford U v Warwickshire (Oxford) 1973. BB: 6–54 Lahore Greens v Railways (Lahore) 1970–71. BBUK: 6–63 Oxford U v Warwickshire (Birmingham) 1973. BBJPL: 5–29 v Leics (Leicester) 1973.

John Darling INCHMORE (Ashington GS) B Ashington (Northumberland) 22/2/1949. RHB, RFM. Played for Northumberland in 1970. Played for both Warwickshire and Worcs 2nd XIs in 1972 and for Stourbridge in Birmingham League. Debut 1973. HS: 113 v Essex (Worcester) 1974. HSJPL: 10* v Glamorgan (Cardiff) 1974. BB: 5–50 v Middlesex (Worcester) 1974. BBGC: 3–40 v Leics (Worcester) 1973. BBJPL: 3–38 v Yorks (Bradford) 1974.

Ivan Nicholas JOHNSON (Malvern College) B Nassau, Bahamas 27/6/1953. LHB, SLA. Played in MCC Schools matches at Lord's 1970–71. Toured West Indies with England Young Cricketers team 1972. Debut 1972. HS: 55 v Glos (Worcester) 1973. HSGC: 23 v Warwickshire (Birmingham) 1973. HSJPL: 36* v Notts (Dudley) 1973. HSBH: 26 v Lancs (Manchester) 1973. BB: 4–61 v Oxford U (Oxford) 1974. BBGC: 3–30 v Warwickshire (Birmingham) 1974.

Joseph Alan ORMROD (Kirkcaldy HS) B Ramsbottom (Lancs) 22/12/1942. RHB, OB. Slip field. Debut 1962. Cap 1966. Tour: Pakistan 1966–67. 1,000 runs (7)—1,466 runs (av 30.54) in 1968 best. HS: 204* v Kent (Dartford) 1973. HSGC: 50 v Essex (Worcester) 1966. HSJPL: 92 v Glamorgan (Cardiff) 1974. HSBH: 63* v Northants (Northampton) 1972. BB: 5–27 v Glos (Bristol) 1972. BBJPL: 3–51 v Hants (Worcester) 1972.

John Morton PARKER (Mahurangi College, Warkworth, New Zealand) B Dannevirke, Hawke's Bay, New Zealand 21/2/1951. RHB, LBG. Has two elder brothers who have played first-class cricket in New Zealand. Debut 1971. Subsequently returned to New Zealand and played in Plunket Shield competitions. Cap 1974. Tests: 10 for New Zealand between 1972–73 and 1973–74. Tours: New Zealand to England 1973, Australia 1973–74. Scored~1,182 runs (av 32.83) in 1973. HS: 195 Northern Districts v Canterbury (Whangarei) 1972–73. HSUK: 140 v Essex (Worcester) 1974. HSJPL: 73 v Glamorgan (Worcester) 1973. HSBH: 42 v Lancs (Worcester) 1974.

WORCESTERSHIRE

Alan Paul PRIDGEON B Wall Heath (Staffs) 22/2/1954. RHB, RM. Joined staff 1971. Debut 1972. Played one match v Oxford U and three John Player League matches in 1974. HS: 18* v Surrey (Worcester) 1973. HSJPL: 13* v Hants (Worcester) 1973. BB: 3–50 v Leics (Worcester) 1972. BBJPL: 4–17 v Essex (Worcester) 1974. Plays amateur soccer.

Christopher Paul ROBERTS (Clee Humberstone Foundation School, Cleethorpes) B Cleethorpes 12/10/1951. RHB, RM. 6ft 4in tall. Played for both Lincolnshire and county 2nd XI in 1971 and 1972. Joined staff 1973. Debut 1974. One match v Glamorgan (Worcester). Also played in one John Player League match. Trained as a teacher at Borough Road College of Education.

Ravindera SENGHERA B Delhi 25/1/1947. RHB, OB. Has lived in UK since June 1964 and has played for Smethwick in Birmingham League. Debut 1974. BB: 5–81 v Oxford U (Oxford) 1974.

Glenn Maitland TURNER (Otago Boys' HS) B Dunedin (New Zealand) 26/5/1947. RHB, OB. Slip or cover field. Debut for Otago in Plunket Shield competition 1964–65 whilst still at school. Debut for county 1967. Cap 1968. *Wisden* 1970. Tests: 27 for New Zealand between 1968–69 and 1973–74. Tours: New Zealand to England 1969 and 1973 (vice-captain), India and Pakistan 1969–70, Australia 1969–70 and 1973–74 (vice-captain), West Indies 1971–72. 1,000 runs (7)—2,416 runs (av 67.11) in 1973 best, including 1,018 runs (av 78.30) by 31 May—the first occasion since 1938. Scored 1,284 runs (av 85.60) in West Indies and Bermuda 1971–match (122 and 128*) v Warwickshire (Birmingham) 1972, (101 and 110*) New Zealand v Australia (Christchurch) 1973–74 and also for Otago v both Northern Districts and Central Districts 1974–75. Benson & Hedges Gold awards: 1. HS: 259 twice in successive innings, New Zealanders v Guyana and New Zealand v West Indies (Georgetown) 1971–72. HSUK: 202* v Cambridge U (Cambridge) 1974. HSGC: 117* v Lancs (Worcester) 1971. HSJPL: 129* v Glamorgan (Worcester) 1973. HSBH: 89 v Cambridge U (Cambridge) 1972. BB: 3–18 v Pakistanis (Worcester) 1967. Has played hockey for Worcs and had trial for Midlands.

Howard Gordon WILCOCK (Giggleswick School, Settle, Yorks) B New Malden (Surrey) 26/2/1950. RHB, WK. Joined staff 1969. Debut 1971. HS: 50 v Warwickshire (Worcester) 1974. HSGC: 11 v Lancs (Worcester) 1974. HSJPL: 30 v Hants (Bournemouth) 1974.

Keith William WILKINSON B Stoke-on-Trent 15/1/1950. LHB, LM. Debut 1969. HS: 141 v Oxford U (Oxford) 1974. HSGC: 95 v Notts (Worcester) 1974. HSJPL: 60 v Sussex (Worcester) 1973. HSBH: 19 v Lancs (Manchester) 1973. BB: 5–60 v Sussex (Worcester) 1971. BBBH: 3–20 v Cambridge U (Cambridge) 1972.

Thomas James (Jim) YARDLEY (King Charles I GS, Kidderminster) B Chaddesley Corbett (Worcs) 27/10/1946. LHB, RM. Occasional WK. Outfield. Debut 1967. Cap 1972. Scored 1,066 runs (av 30.45) in 1971. HS: 135 v Notts (Worcester) 1973. HSGC: 52 v Warwickshire (Birmingham) 1972 and 52* v Warwickshire (Birmingham) 1973. HSJPL: 57* v Sussex (Worcester) 1973. HSBH: 75* v Warwickshire (Worcester) 1972.

146

NB The following players whose particulars appeared in the 1974 Annual have been omitted: R. J. Lanchbury (not re-engaged) and A. Shutt (not re-engaged).

The career record of Lanchbury will be found elsewhere in this Annual.

COUNTY AVERAGES

County Championship: Played 20; won 9, drawn 7, lost 4
All first-class matches: Played 23; won 11, drawn 8, lost 4

BATTING AND FIELDING

Cap		M	I	NO	Runs	HS	Avge	100	50	Ct	St
1968	G. M. Turner	20	31	9	1332	202*	60.54	3	5	13	—
1965	B. L. D'Oliveira	18	26	3	1026	227	44.60	2	4	4	—
—	K. W. Wilkinson	4	7	0	296	141	42.28	1	1	5	—
1961	R. G. A. Headley	19	31	2	1064	137	36.68	3	5	9	—
1969	E. J. O. Hemsley	10	15	2	442	120*	34.00	1	2	9	—
—	R. J. Lanchbury	3	6	2	130	50*	32.50	—	1	1	—
1974	J. M. Parker	17	27	1	760	140	29.23	2	3	12	1
1972	T. J. Yardley	22	31	8	656	66*	28.52	—	5	34	—
—	I. N. Johnson	3	3	2	28	22	28.00	—	1	1	—
1966	J. A. Ormrod	22	34	2	673	82	21.03	—	3	31	—
—	H. G. Wilcock	14	19	3	302	44	18.87	—	40	1	
—	J. D. Inchmore	16	16	4	181	113	15.08	1	—	9	—
1970	G. R. Cass	8	9	1	105	39	13.12	—	23	—	
1961	N. Gifford	22	27	6	270	30	12.85	—	17	—	
1970	V. A. Holder	21	23	4	204	29	10.73	—	7	—	
1966	B. M. Brain	22	22	7	154	35	10.26	—	8	—	
—	J. Cumbes	8	6	3	14	10	4.66	—	1	—	

Played in two matches: R. Senghera did not bat.

Played in one match: A. P. Pridgeon did not bat; C. P. Roberts 0*.

BOWLING

	Type	O	M	R	W	Avge	Best	5 wI	10 wM
R. Senghera	OB	79	29	152	13	11.69	5–81	1	—
V. A. Holder	RFM	659	146	1493	94	15.88	7–40	5	1
B. L. D'Oliveira	RM/OB	345.3	105	697	40	17.42	5–49	1	—
N. Gifford	SLA	617	197	1333	69	19.31	7–15	3	—
I. N. Johnson	SLA	51	16	98	5	19.60	4–61	—	—
B. M. Brain	RFM	633.1	121	1752	84	20.85	6–58	2	—
J.D. Inchmore	RFM	283.2	55	858	39	22.00	5–50	1	—
J. Cumbes	RFM	243.5	49	595	21	28.33	4–25	—	—

Also bowled: E. J. O. Hemsley 40.4-10-121-4; J. M. Parker 1-0-1-0; A. P. Pridgeon 26-7-61-2; C. P. Roberts 21-4-40-1.

County Records

First-class cricket

Highest innings totals:	For ...633 v Warwickshire (Worcester)	1906
	Agst...701–4d by Leicestershire (Worcester)	1906
Lowest innings totals:	For ... 24 v Yorkshire (Huddersfield)	1903
	Agst... 30 by Hampshire (Worcester)	1903
Highest individual innings:	For ...276 F. L. Bowley v Hampshire (Dudley)	1914
	Agst...331* J. D. Robertson for Middx (Worcester)	1949

147

Best bowling in an innings:	For ...9–23 C. F. Root v Lancashire (Worcester)	1931
	Agst...10–51 J. Mercer for Glamorgan (Worcester)	1936
Best bowling in a match:	For ...15–87 A. J. Conway v Gloucestershire (Moreton-in-Marsh)	1914
	Agst...17–212 J. C. Clay for Glamorgan (Swansea)	1937
Most runs in a season:	2654 (av 52.03) H. H. I. H. Gibbons	1934
runs in a career:	34490 (av 34.04) D. Kenyon	1946–1967
100s in a season:	10 by G. M. Turner	1970
100s in a career:	70 by D. Kenyon	1946–1967
wickets in a season:	207 (av 17.52) C. F. Root	1925
wickets in a career:	2143 (av 23.73) R. T. D. Perks	1930–1955

RECORD WICKET STANDS

1st	309	F. L. Bowley & H. K. Foster v Derbyshire (Derby)	1901
2nd	274	H. H. I. H. Gibbons & Nawab of Pataudi v Kent (Worcester)	1933
		H. H. I. H. Gibbons & Nawab of Pataudi v Glamorgan (Worcester)	1934
3rd	315	W. V. Fox & L. G. Crawley v Northamptonshire (Worcester)	1923
4th	277	H. H. I. H. Gibbons & B. W. Quaife v Middlesex (Worcester)	1931
5th	393	E. G. Arnold & W. B. Burns v Warwickshire (Birmingham)	1909
6th	195	G. N. Foster & J. A. Cuffe v Leicestershire (Worcester)	1913
7th	197	H. H. I. H. Gibbons & R. Howorth v Surrey (The Oval)	1938
8th	145*	F. Chester & W. H. Taylor v Essex (Worcester)	1914
9th	181	J. A. Cuffe & R. O. Burrows v Gloucestershire (Worcester)	1907
10th	119	W. B. Burns & G. A. Wilson v Somerset (Worcester)	1906

One-day cricket

Highest innings totals:	Gillette Cup	259–9 v Sussex (Hove)	1974
	John Player League	258–4 v Sussex (Dudley)	1972
	Benson & Hedges Cup	274–8 v Oxford U (Worcester)	1973
Lowest innings totals:	Gillette Cup	98 v Durham (Chester-le-Street)	1968
	John Player League	86 v Yorkshire (Leeds)	1969
	Benson & Hedges Cup	146 v Leics (Worcester)	1972
Highest individual innings:	Gillette Cup	117* G. M. Turner v Lancashire (Worcester)	1971
	John Player League	129* G. M. Turner v Glamorgan (Worcester)	1973
	Benson & Hedges Cup	132 R. G. A. Headley v Oxford U (Worcester)	1973
Best bowling figures:	Gillette Cup	6–14 J. A. Flavell v Lancs (Worcester)	1963
	John Player League	6–33 V. A. Holder v Middlesex (Lord's)	1972
	Benson & Hedges Cup	5–12 V. A. Holder v Northants (Northampton)	1974

YORKSHIRE

Formation of present club: 1863, reorganised 1891.
Colours: Oxford blue, Cambridge blue, and gold.
Badge: White Rose.
County Champions (29): 1893, 1896, 1898, 1900,
1901, 1902, 1905, 1908, 1912, 1919, 1922,
1923, 1924, 1925, 1931, 1932, 1933, 1935,
1937, 1938, 1939, 1946, 1959, 1960, 1962,
1963, 1966, 1967, and 1968.
Joint Champions (1): 1949.
Gillette Cup winners (2): 1965 and 1969.
John Player League runners-up: 1973.
Benson & Hedges Cup finalists: 1972.

Secretary: J. Lister, Headingley Cricket Ground, Leeds, LS6 3BU.
Captain: G. Boycott.

David Leslie (Blue) BAIRSTOW (Hanson GS, Bradford) B Bradford
1/9/1951. RHB, WK. Debut 1970 whilst still at school. Played for MCC
Schools at Lord's in 1970. Cap 1973. Dismissed 70 batsmen (64 ct 6 st)
in 1971, including 9 in match and 6 in innings (all ct) v Lancs (Manchester).
HS: 79 v Somerset (Bath) 1974. HSGC: 21 v Warwickshire (Leeds) 1972.
HSJPL: 50 v Glamorgan (Hull) 1974. HSBH: 15 v Derbyshire
(Chesterfield) 1974. Soccer for Bradford City.

Michael Kenneth (Mike) BORE B Hull 2/6/1947. RHB, LM. Debut
1969. HS: 37* v Notts (Bradford) 1973. HSJPL: 15 v Kent (Dover) 1973.
BB: 6–63 v Glos (Sheffield) 1971. BBGC: 3–35 v Kent (Canterbury) 1971.
BBJPL: 4–21 v Sussex (Middlesbrough) 1970 and 4–21 v Worcs
(Worcester) 1970. BBBH: 3–29 v Minor Counties (Leeds) 1974.

Geoffrey (Geoff) BOYCOTT (Hemsworth GS) B Fitzwilliam (Yorks)
21/10/1940. RHB, RM. Plays in contact lenses. Debut 1962. Cap 1963.
Elected Best Young Cricketer of the Year in 1963 by the Cricket Writers'
Club. *Wisden* 1964. Appointed county captain in 1971. Played for
N. Transvaal in 1971–72. Benefit (£20,639) in 1974. Tests: 63 between 1964
and 1974. Played in 2 matches against Rest of World in 1970. Tours:
South Africa 1964–65, Australia and New Zealand 1965–66 and 1970–71
(returned home early through broken arm injury), West Indies 1967–68
and 1973–74. 1,000 runs (11)—2,503 runs (av 100.12) in 1971 best. Only
English batsman ever to have an average of 100 for a season. Also scored
1,000 runs in South Africa 1964–65 (1,135 runs, av 56.75), West Indies
1967–68 (1,154 runs, av 82.42), Australia 1970–71 (1,535 runs av 95.93).
Scored two centuries in match (103 and 105) v Notts (Sheffield) 1966
and (160* and 116) England v The Rest (Worcester) 1974. Gillette Man of
Match awards: 1. Benson & Hedges Gold awards: 2. HS: 261* MCC v
President's XI (Bridgetown) 1973–74. HSUK: 260* v Essex (Colchester)
1970. HSGC: 146 v Surrey (Lord's) 1965 (record for competition) sharing
in partnership of 192 for 2nd wkt with D. B. Close. HSJPL: 108* v
Northants (Huddersfield) 1974. HSBH: 83* v Minor Counties (Chester-
le-Street) 1973. BB: 3–47 England v South Africa (Cape Town) 1964–65.

149

Philip (Phil) CARRICK B Armley, Leeds 16/7/1952. RHB, SLA. Debut 1970. HS: 46 v Derbyshire (Chesterfield) 1974. HSGC: 18 v Durham (Harrogate) 1973. HSJPL: 8–33 v Cambridge U (Cambridge) 1973.

Howard Pennett COOPER (Buttershaw Comprehensive School, Bradford) B Bradford 17/4/1949. LHB, RM. Debut 1971. Played for Northern Transvaal in 1973–74 Currie Cup competition. Played in only one match and two Benson & Hedges Cup matches in 1974. HS: 47 v Surrey (Scarborough) 1972. HSGC: 10* v Warwickshire (Leeds) 1972 and 10* v Durham (Harrogate) 1973. HSJPL: 20* v Lancs (Leeds) 1973. BB: 4–37 v Hants (Southampton) 1972. BBJPL: 4–27 v Warwickshire (Birmingham) 1973. BBBH: 3–22 v Minor Counties (Leeds) 1974.

Geoffrey Alan (Geoff) COPE (Temple Moor School, Leeds) B Leeds 23/2/1947. RHB, OB. Wears glasses. Debut 1966. Cap 1970. Suspended from playing in second half of 1972 season by TCCB, owing to unsatisfactory bowling action. Action cleared in 1973 by TCCB subcommittee after watching film of him bowling. Hat-trick v Essex (Colchester) 1970. HS: 66 v Northants (Northampton) 1970. HSJPL: 16* v Sussex (Bradford) 1974. BB: 7–36 v Essex (Colchester) 1970. BBJPL: 3–24 v Northants (Bradford) 1969.

John Harry (Jackie) HAMPSHIRE (Oakwood Technical HS, Rotherham) B Thurnscoe (Yorks) 10/2/1941. RHB, LB. Debut 1961. Cap 1963. Played for Tasmania v Indians 1967–68 and v West Indies 1968–69 whilst on coaching engagement in Tasmania. Tests: 7 between 1969 and 1972. Scored 107 in his first Test v West Indies (Lord's) and is only English player to have scored a century on debut in Test cricket when this has occurred at Lord's. Tour: Australia and New Zealand 1970–71. 1,000 runs (10)—1,513 runs (av 32.19) in 1965 best. Gillette Man of Match awards: 2. HS: 183* v Sussex (Hove) 1971. HSGC: 87* v Hants (Bradford) 1974. HSJPL: 119 v Leics (Hull) 1971. HSBH: 41* v Notts (Hull) 1973. BB: 7–52 v Glamorgan (Cardiff) 1963.

Colin JOHNSON (Pocklington School) B Pocklington (Yorks) 5/9/1947. RHB, OB. Played in MCC Schools matches at Lord's 1966. Debut 1969. HS: 107 v Somerset (Sheffield) 1973. HSGC: 44 v Durham (Harrogate) 1973. HSJPL: 54 v Worcs (Bradford) 1974. HSBH: 20 v Leics (Lord's) 1972.

Barrie LEADBEATER B Harehills, Leeds 14/8/1943. RHB, RM. Distant cousin of E. Leadbeater who played for county from 1949 to 1956 and subsequently for Warwickshire. Debut 1966. Cap 1969. Gillette Man of Match awards: 1 (in 1969 final). HS: 99* v Kent (Scarborough) 1974. HSGC: 76 v Derbyshire (Lord's) 1969. HSJPL: 86* v Northants (Sheffield) 1972. HSBH: 90 v Lancs (Bradford) 1974.

Richard Graham LUMB (Percy Jackson GS, Doncaster and Mexborough GS) B Doncaster 27/2/1950. RHB, RM. Played in MCC Schools matches at Lord's 1968. Debut 1970 after playing in one John Player League match in 1969. Cap 1974. Scored 1,004 runs (av 28.68) in 1974. HS: 123* v Northants (Northampton) 1974. HSGC: 31 v Hants (Bradford) 1974. HSJPL: 65 v Notts (Scarborough) 1974. HSBH: 55* v Notts (Nottingham) 1974.

Anthony George (Tony) NICHOLSON (Wheelwright GS, Dewsbury) B Dewsbury 25/6/1938. RHB, RM. Former policeman in Rhodesia. Debut 1962. Cap 1963. Selected to tour South Africa 1964–65 but had to withdraw owing to back injury. Benefit (£13,214) in 1973. 100 wkts (2)— 113 wkts (av 15.50) in 1966 best. Benson & Hedges Gold awards: 1. HS: 50 v Middlesex (Lord's) 1974. HSGC: 15* v Warwickshire (Birmingham) 1968. HSJPL: 13* v Northants (Bradford) 1971. BB: 9–62 v Sussex (Eastbourne) 1967. BBGC: 3–11 v Cambridgeshire (Castleford) 1967. BBJPL: 6–36 v Somerset (Sheffield) 1972. BBBH: 6–27 v Minor Counties (Middlesbrough) 1972 (record for the competition).

Christopher Middleton (Chris) OLD (Acklam Hall Secondary GS, Middlesbrough) B Middlesbrough 22/12/1948. LHB, RFM. Good field in any position. Debut 1966. Cap 1969. Elected Best Young Cricketer of the Year in 1970 by the Cricket Writers' Club. Tests: 18 between 1972–73 and 1974. Played in 2 matches against Rest of World 1970. Tours: India, Pakistan, and Sri Lanka 1972–73, West Indies 1973–74, Australia and New Zealand 1974–75. Benson & Hedges Gold awards: 1. HS: 116 v Indians (Bradford) 1974. HSGC: 29 v Lancs (Leeds) 1974. HSJPL: 82 v Somerset (Bath) 1974. HSBH: 52* v Notts (Nottingham) 1974. BB: 7–20 v Glos (Middlesbrough) 1969. BBGC: 4–32 v Lancs (Manchester) 1967. BBJPL: 5–33 v Sussex (Hove) 1971. BBBH: 4–17 v Derbyshire (Bradford) 1973.

Stephen (Steve) OLDHAM B High Green, Sheffield 26/7/1948. RHB, RFM. Debut 1974. BB: 3–7 v Glos (Harrogate) 1974. BBGC: 3–45 v Lancs (Leeds) 1974. BBJPL: 4–21 v Notts (Scarborough) 1974.

Arthur Leslie (Rocker) ROBINSON B Brompton (Yorks) 17/8/1946. LHB, LFM. Debut 1971. Hat-trick v Notts (Worksop) 1974. HS: 28* v Surrey (Leeds) 1973. HSGC: 18* v Lancs (Leeds) 1974. HSJPL: 14 v Surrey (Oval) 1971. BB: 6–61 v Surrey (Oval) 1974. BBJPL: 4–25 v Surrey (Oval) 1974. BBBH: 3–20 v Notts (Nottingham) 1974.

Dennis SCHOFIELD B Holmfirth 9/10/1947. RHB, RM. Debut 1970. Played one match in both 1970 and 1971. Re-appeared in one match in 1974. HS: 6* v Notts (Worksop) 1974. BB: 5–42 v Notts (Worksop) 1974.

Arnold SIDEBOTTOM (Broadway GS, Barnsley) B Barnsley 1/4/1954. RHB, RM. Played for 2nd XI since 1971 and in Schools matches at Lord's in that year. Debut 1973. Played in only one-day matches in 1974. HSJPL: 12* v Glamorgan (Hull) 1974. BB: 3–61 v Glos (Gloucester) 1973. BBJPL: 4–40 v Lancs (Manchester) 1974.

Peter John SQUIRES (Ripon GS) B Ripon 4/8/1951. RHB. Played in one John Player League match in 1971. Debut 1972. HS: 67 v Surrey (Oval) 1974. HSJPL: 52 v Lancs (Manchester) 1974. HSBH: 14 v Lancs (Bradford) 1974. Trained as a teacher at St John's College, York. Plays rugby for Harrogate and Yorkshire and won 8 caps for England in 1972–73 and 1973–74 seasons. Toured South Africa with England rugby team 1973, missing last month of cricket season.

Graham Barry STEVENSON (Minsthorpe GS) B Ackworth (Yorks) 16/12/1955. RHB, RM. Played for 2nd XI in 1972. Debut 1973. HS: 18 v Essex (Leyton) 1974. HSJPL: 27 v Kent (Leeds) 1974. BBGC: 4–57 v Lancs (Leeds) 1974. BBJPL: 3–29 v Derbyshire (Chesterfield) 1974.

151

YORKSHIRE

Richard Andrew John TOWNSLEY (Rothwell GS) B Castleford 24/6/1952. LHB, RM. Appeared for 2nd XI in 1972. Debut 1974. One match v Essex (Leyton).

NB The following players whose particulars appeared in the 1974 Annual have been omitted: S. P. Coverdale, R. P. Hodson (not re-engaged), R. A. Hutton (emigrated to South Africa), D. Wilson (retired) and J. D. Woodford.

The career records of Coverdale, Hutton, and Wilson will be found elsewhere in this Annual. P. J. Sharpe, who was released after the 1974 season, has joined Derbyshire and his particulars will be found under that County.

COUNTY AVERAGES

County Championship: Played 19; won 4, drawn 8, lost 7
All first-class matches: Played 22; won 6, drawn 9, lost 7

BATTING AND FIELDING

Cap		M	I	NO	Runs	HS	Avge	100	50	Ct	St
1963	G. Boycott	18	30	5	1478	149*	59.12	4	8	6	—
1963	J. H. Hampshire	14	23	6	901	158	53.00	2	3	10	—
1969	B. Leadbeater	19	31	4	804	99*	29.77	—	5	10	—
1974	R. G. Lumb	18	31	2	763	123*	26.31	2	2	14	—
1969	C. M. Old	11	15	0	387	116	25.80	1	1	8	—
—	P. Carrick	12	13	3	196	46	19.60	—	—	11	—
1963	A. G. Nicholson	16	16	8	153	50	19.12	—	1	3	—
1964	R. A. Hutton	17	25	5	376	102*	18.80	1	—	15	—
1973	D. L. Bairstow	22	31	2	533	79	18.37	—	4	51	11
—	P. J. Squires	13	21	3	329	67	18.27	—	2	6	—
1960	P. J. Sharpe	17	29	2	474	83	17.55	—	2	17	—
1970	G. A. Cope	22	24	7	275	43	16.17	—	—	1	—
—	C. Johnson	8	12	1	173	60*	15.72	—	1	5	—
—	A. L. Robinson	16	9	4	43	17*	8.60	—	—	6	—
1960	D. Wilson	8	12	4	64	22	8.00	—	—	1	—
—	G. B. Stevenson	4	4	0	25	18	6.25	—	—	4	—

Played in two matches: M. K. Bore 0, 1 (1 ct); S. Oldham 5* (1 ct).
Played in one match: H. P. Cooper 8* (1 ct); D. Schofield 6*; R. A. J. Townsley 0, 2.

BOWLING

	Type	O	M	R	W	Avge	Best	5 wI	10 wM
D. Schofield	RM	21.2	3	52	5	10.40	5–42	1	—
C. M. Old	RFM	330	103	736	46	16.00	5–30	2	—
P. Carrick	SLA	405.4	167	840	47	17.87	6–43	2	1
A. L. Robinson	LFM	375.5	103	880	43	20.46	6–61	2	—
G. A. Cope	OB	742.5	260	1681	77	21.83	7–101	5	1
A. G. Nicholson	RM	471	152	1100	44	25.00	5–74	1	—
R. A. Hutton	RFM	259.2	70	620	24	25.83	6–85	1	—
D. Wilson	SLA	157.4	39	469	17	-27.58	5–36	1	—

Also bowled: M. K. Bore 44.1-17-129-0; H. P. Cooper 21-8-54-2; J. H. Hampshire 11-7-6-0; C. Johnson 4-2-6-0; S. Oldham 20.5-5-69-4; G. B. Stevenson 29-9-88-2.

152

County Records
First-class cricket

Highest innings totals:	For ...887 v Warwickshire (Birmingham)		1896
	Agst...630 by Somerset (Leeds)		1901
Lowest innings totals:	For ... 23 v Hampshire (Middlesbrough)		1965
	Agst... 13 by Nottinghamshire (Nottingham)		1901
Highest individual innings:	For ...341 G. H. Hirst v Leicestershire (Leicester)		1905
	Agst...318*W. G. Grace for Glos (Cheltenham)		1876
Best bowling in an innings:	For ...10–10 H. Verity v Nottinghamshire (Leeds)		1932
	Agst...10–37 C. V. Grimmett for Australians (Sheffield)		1930
Best bowling in a match:	For ...17–91 H. Verity v Essex (Leyton)		1933
	Agst...17–91 H. Dean for Lancashire (Liverpool)		1913
Most runs in a season:	2883 (av 80.08) H. Sutcliffe		1932
runs in a career:	38561 (av 50.21) H. Sutcliffe	1919–1945
100s in a season:	12 by H. Sutcliffe		1932
100s in a career:	112 by H. Sutcliffe	1919–1945
wickets in a season:	240 (av 12.72) W. Rhodes		1900
wickets in a career:	3608 (av 16.00) W. Rhodes	1898–1930

RECORD WICKET STANDS

1st 555	P. Holmes & H. Sutcliffe v Essex (Leyton)	1932
2nd 346	W. Barber & M. Leyland v Middlesex (Sheffield)	1932
3rd 323*	H. Sutcliffe & M. Leyland v Glamorgan (Huddersfield)	1928
4th 312	G. H. Hirst & D. Denton v Hampshire (Southampton)	1914
5th 340	E. Wainwright & G. H. Hirst v Surrey (The Oval)	1899
6th 276	M. Leyland & E. Robinson v Glamorgan (Swansea)	1926
7th 254	D. C. F. Burton & W. Rhodes v Hampshire (Dewsbury)	1919
8th 292	Lord Hawke & R. Peel v Warwickshire (Birmingham)	1896
9th 192	G. H. Hirst & S. Haigh v Surrey (Bradford)	1898
10th 148	Lord Hawke & D. Hunter v Kent (Sheffield)	1898

One-day cricket

Highest innings totals:	Gillette Cup	317–4 v Surrey (Lord's)	1965
	John Player League	235–6 v Nottinghamshire (Sheffield)	1970
	Benson & Hedges Cup	209–2 v Nottinghamshire (Hull)	1973
Lowest innings totals:	Gillette Cup	76 v Surrey (Harrogate)	1970
	John Player League	74 v Warwickshire (Birmingham)	1972
	Benson & Hedges Cup	125 v Lancashire (Manchester)	1973
Highest individual innings:	Gillette Cup	146 G. Boycott v Surrey (Lord's)	1965
	John Player League	119 J. H. Hampshire v Leicestershire (Hull)	1971
	Benson & Hedges Cup	90 B. Leadbeater v Lancashire (Bradford)	1974
Best bowling figures:	Gillette Cup	6–15 F. S. Trueman v Somerset (Taunton)	1965
	John Player League	7–15 R. A. Hutton v Worcestershire (Leeds)	1969
	Benson & Hedges Cup	6–27 A. G. Nicholson v Minor Counties (Middlesbrough)	1972

THE FIRST-CLASS UMPIRES FOR 1975

NB The abbreviations used are identical with those used in 'The Counties and their Players'.

William Edward (Bill) ALLEY B Sydney (Australia) 3/2/1919. LHB, RM. Played for New South Wales 1945–46 to 1947–48. Subsequently came to England to play League cricket and then for Somerset from 1957 to 1968. *Wisden* 1961. Testimonial (£2,700) in 1961. Tours: India and Pakistan 1949–50, Pakistan 1963–64 with Commonwealth team. Scored 3,019 runs (av 56.96) in 1961 including 2,761 runs and 10 centuries for county, both being records. Won Man of the Match award in Gillette Cup Competition on three occasions. HS: 221* v Warwickshire (Nuneaton) 1961. BB: 8–65 v Surrey (Oval) 1962. Career record: 19,612 runs (av 31.88), 31 centuries, 768 wkts (av 22.68). Appointed 1969. Umpired in 2 Tests in 1974.

Ronald (Ron) ASPINALL B Almondbury (Yorks) 26/10/1918. RHB, RFM. Played for Yorkshire from 1946 to 1950 (retiring early through injury) and for Durham from 1951 to 1957. HS: 75* v Notts (Nottingham) 1948. BB: 8–42 v Northants (Rushden) 1949. Career record: 763 runs (av 19.07), 131 wkts (av 20.38). Appointed 1960.

Robert Ernest BARNARD B Greenwich, London 28/6/1925. Has not played first-class cricket. On Minor Counties list since 1970. Appointed 1975.

Harold Denis BIRD B Barnsley 19/4/1933. RHB, RM. Played for Yorks from 1956 to 1959 and for Leics from 1960 to 1964. Has since been professional at Paignton CC. HS: 181* Yorks v Glamorgan (Bradford) 1959. Career record: 3,315 runs (av 20.71), 2 centuries. Appointed 1970. Umpired in 5 Tests in 1973 and 1974.

William Lloyd BUDD B Hawkley (Hants) 20/10/1913. RHB, RFM. Played for Hampshire from 1934 to 1946. HS: 77* v Surrey (Oval) 1937. BB: 4–22 v Essex (Southend) 1937. Career record: 941 runs (av 11.47), 64 wkts (av 39.15). Was on Minor Counties list for some years. Appointed 1969.

David John CONSTANT B Bradford-on-Avon (Wilts) 9/11/1941. LHB, SLA. Played for Kent from 1961 to 1963 and for Leics from 1965 to 1968. HS: 80 v Glos (Bristol) 1966. Career record: 1,517 runs (av 19.20), 1 wkt (av 36.00). Appointed 1969. Umpired in 8 Tests between 1971 and 1974.

Cecil (Sam) COOK B Tetbury (Glos) 23/8/1921. RHB, SLA. Played for Gloucestershire from 1946 to 1964. Benefit (£3,067) in 1957. Took wicket with first ball in first-class cricket. Tests: 1 v SA 1947. HS: 35* v Sussex (Hove) 1957. BB: 9–42 v Yorks (Bristol) 1947. Career record: 1,964 runs (av 5.39), 1,782 wkts (av 20.52). Appointed 1971, after having withdrawn from appointment in 1966.

John Frederick (Jack) CRAPP B St Columb (Cornwall) 14/10/1912. LHB. Played for Gloucestershire from 1936 to 1956 captaining county in 1953 and 1954. Benefit (£3,611) in 1951. Tests: 7 in 1948 and 1948-49. Tours: South Africa 1948-49, India 1953-54 with Commonwealth Team. HS: 175 v Cambridge U (Cambridge) 1947. Career record: 23,615 runs (av 35.03), 38 centuries, 6 wkts (av 51.00). Appointed 1957. Umpired in 4 Tests in 1964 and 1965.

David Gwilliam Lloyd EVANS B Lambeth (London) 27/7/1933. RHB, WK. Played for Glamorgan from 1956 to 1969. Benefit (£3,500) in 1969. HS: 46* v Oxford U (Oxford) 1961. Career record: 2,875 runs (av 10.53), 558 dismissals (502 ct 56 st). Appointed 1971.

Arthur Edward FAGG B Chartham (Kent) 15/6/1915. Opening RHB, slip field. Played for Kent from 1932 to 1957. Benefit (£3,456) in 1951. Tests: 5 between 1936 and 1939. Tour: Australia 1936-37 returning home early through illness. Holds world record of two double-centuries in match (244 and 202*) v Essex (Colchester) 1938. HS: 269* v Notts (Nottingham) 1953. Career record: 27,291 runs (av 36.05), 58 centuries. Appointed 1959. Has umpired in 16 Tests between 1967 and 1974. Also umpired in 4 matches between England and Rest of World in 1970.

Henry HORTON B Colwall (Herefordshire) 18/4/1923. RHB. Played for Worcs from 1946 to 1949 and for Hants from 1953 to 1967. Benefit (£5,900) in 1964. HS: 160* v Yorks (Scarborough) 1961. Career record: 21,669 runs (av 32.83), 32 centuries, 3 wkts (av 64.66).   Soccer for Blackburn Rovers, Southampton and Hereford United. Appointed 1973.

Arthur JEPSON B Selston (Notts) 12/7/1915. RHB, RFM. Played for Notts from 1938 to 1959. Benefit (£2,000) in 1951. HS: 130 v Worcs (Nottingham) 1950. BB: 8-45 v Leics (Nottingham) 1958. Career record: 6,369 runs (av 14.31), 1 century, 1,051 wkts (av 29.08). Soccer (goalkeeper) for Port Vale, Stoke City and Lincoln City. Appointed 1960. Umpired in 4 Tests between 1966 and 1969.

Raymond (Ray) JULIAN B Cosby (Leics) 23/8/1936. RHB, WK. Played for Leicestershire from 1953 (debut at age of 16) to 1971, but lost regular place in side to R. W. Tolchard in 1966. HS: 51 v Worcs (Worcester) 1962. Career record: 2,581 runs (av 9.73), 421 dismissals (382 ct 39 st). Appointed 1972.

John George LANGRIDGE B Chailey (Sussex) 10/2/1910. Younger brother of late James Langridge. Opening RHB and outstanding slip field. Played for Sussex from 1928 to 1955. *Wisden* 1949. Shared joint benefit (£1,930) with H. W. Parks in 1948. Testimonial (£3,825) in 1953. Scored more runs and centuries in first-class cricket than any other player who never appeared in a Test match. Only F. E. Woolley, W. G. Grace, W. R. Hammond, and G. A. R. Lock have held more catches than his total of 786. HS: 250* v Glamorgan (Hove) 1933. Career record: 34,380 runs (av 37.45), 76 centuries, 44 wkts (av 42.00). Appointed 1956. Umpired in 7 Tests between 1960 and 1963.

Barrie John MEYER B Bournemouth 21/8/1932. RHB, WK. Played for Gloucestershire from 1957 to 1971. Benefit 1971. HS: 63 v Indians (Cheltenham) 1959, v Oxford U (Bristol) 1962 and v Sussex (Bristol) 1964. Career record: 5,367 runs (av 14.19), 826 dismissals (707 ct 119 st). Soccer for Bristol Rovers, Plymouth Argyle, Newport County, and Bristol City. Appointed 1973.

Donald Osmund OSLEAR B Cleethorpes (Lincs) 3/3/29. Has not played first-class cricket. Played soccer for Grimsby Town, Hull City, and Oldham Athletic. Also played ice hockey. Has umpired in county second XI matches since 1972. Appointed in 1975.

Kenneth Ernest (Ken) PALMER B Winchester 22/4/1937. RHB, RFM. Played for Somerset from 1955 to 1969. Testimonial (£4,000) in 1968. Tour: Pakistan with Commonwealth team 1963–64. Coached in Johannesburg 1964–65 and was called upon by MCC to play in final Test v South Africa owing to injuries to other bowlers. Tests (1): 1 v SA 1964–65. HS: 125* v Northants (Northampton) 1961. BB: 9–57 v Notts (Nottingham) 1963. Career record: 7,771 runs (av 20.66), 2 centuries, 866 wkts (av 21. 34). Appointed 1972.

Cecil George (Cec) PEPPER B Forbes, New South Wales (Australia) 15/9/1918. RHB, LBG. Played for New South Wales 1938–39 to 1940–41, Australian Services 1945 and 1945–46. Returned to England to play in League cricket from 1947 and appeared in the Hastings Festivals in 1956 and 1957. Tours: India and Ceylon 1945–46 with Australian Services Team and India and Pakistan 1949–50 with Commonwealth Team. HS: 168 Australian Services v H. D. G. Leveson-Gower's XI (Scarborough) 1945. BB: 6–33 Commonwealth XI v Holkar Cricket Association (Indore) 1949–50. Career record: 1,927 runs (av 29.64), 1 century, 169 wkts (av 29.31). Appointed 1964.

William Edward (Eddie) PHILLIPSON B North Reddish (Lancs) 3/12/1910. RHB, RFM. Played for Lancashire from 1933 to 1948. Grant (£1,750) in 1948. Tour: New Zealand with Sir Julian Cahn's Team 1938–39. HS: 113 v Glamorgan (Preston) 1939. BB: 8–100 v Kent (Dover) 1934. Career record: 4,096 runs (av 25.76), 2 centuries, 555 wkts (av 24.72). Appointed 1956. Umpired in 12 Tests between 1958 and 1965.

Albert Ennion Growcott (Dusty) RHODES B Tintwhistle (Cheshire) 10/10/1916. Father of H. J. Rhodes, RHB, LBG. Played for Derbyshire from 1937 to 1954. Testimonial (£2,096) in 1952. Tour: India 1951–52 returning home early owing to injury. Achieved 5 hat-tricks. HS: 127 v Somerset (Taunton) 1949. BB: 8–162 v Yorks (Scarborough) 1947. Career record: 7,363 runs (av 18.97), 3 centuries, 661 wkts (av 28.22). Appointed 1959. Has umpired in 8 Tests between 1963 and 1973. Also umpired in 2 matches between England and Rest of World 1970.

Peter ROCHFORD B Halifax 27/8/1928. RHB, WK. On Yorkshire staff 1951. Played for Gloucestershire from 1952 to 1957. HS: 31* v Oxford U (Oxford) 1956. Career record: 479 runs (av 5.26), 152 dismissals (118ct 34st). Appointed 1975.

Thomas William (Tom) SPENCER B Deptford 22/3/1914. RHB, RM. Played for Kent from 1935 to 1946. HS: 96 v Sussex (Tunbridge Wells) 1946. Career record: 2,152 runs (av 20.11), 1 wkt (av 19.00). Appointed 1950 (longest serving umpire on list). Has umpired in 10 Tests between 1954 and 1974.

Alan Geoffrey Thomas WHITEHEAD B Butleigh (Somerset) 28/10/1940. LHB, SLA. Played for Somerset from 1957 to 1961. HS: 15 v Hants (Southampton) 1959 and 15 v Leics (Leicester) 1960. BB: 6–74 v Sussex (Eastbourne) 1959. Career record: 137 runs (av 5.70), 67 wkts (av 34.41). Served on Minor Counties list in 1969. Appointed 1970.

Peter Bernard WIGHT B Georgetown (British Guiana) 25/6/1930. RHB, OB. Played for British Guiana in 1950–51 and for Somerset from 1953 to 1965. Benefit (£5,000) in 1963. HS: 222* v Kent (Taunton) 1959. BB: 6–29 v Derbyshire (Chesterfield) 1957. Career record: 17,773 runs (av 33.09), 28 centuries, 68 wkts (av 33.26). Appointed 1966.

NB The Test Match panel for 1975 is W. E. Alley, H. D. Bird, D. Constant. A. E. Fagg, and T. W. Spencer.

Does long hair disguise leg spin?

Is it cricket to expect a batsman to spot the wrong-un when it is delivered out of a bush of billowing shoulder-length barnet? The MCC aren't saying. But there is a solution. A quick spray of The Dry Look, when the bowler isn't looking, will hold every hair in place. And, because it's non-greasy, it's undetectable. The Dry Look comes in two grades, for normal hair and difficult hair: to be on the safe side, batsmen should carry both.

**The Dry Look
natural hair control**

FIRST-CLASS AVERAGES 1974

The following averages are published in alphabetical order and include everyone who appeared in first-class matches during the season.

†*Indicates left-handed batsman.*

BATTING AND FIELDING

	Cap	M	I	NO	Runs	HS	Avge	100	50	Ct	St
Abberley R. N. (Wa/DHR)	1966	14	23	0	567	99	24.65	—	2	13	—
Abid Ali S. (Ind)	—	14	22	4	470	71	26.11	—	4	5	—
†Abrahams J. (La/MCo)	—	13	22	2	304	78	15.20	—	2	10	—
Acfield D.L. (Ex/MCC)	1970	12	9	3	69	31	11.50	—	—	5	—
Aftab Baloch (Pak)	—	7	8	4	101	42*	25.25	—	—	4	—
Aftab Gul (Pak)	—	6	10	0	293	112	29.30	1	1	1	—
Amiss D. L. (E/Wa/EXI/MCC/DHR)	1965	18	31	3	1510	195	53.92	5	4	6	—
Anderson I. J. (Ire)	—	1	2	0	3	3	1.50	—	—	2	—
Armstrong G. D. (Gm)	—	1	2	1	16	15*	16.00	—	—	1	—
Arnold G. G. (E/Sy/MCC)	1967	14	12	3	102	23	11.33	—	—	6	—
Asif Iqbal (Pak/K)	1968	16	24	2	611	80	27.77	—	4	8	—
Asif Masood (Pak)	—	12	5	4	25	17*	25.00	—	—	3	—
†Aworth C. J. (Sy/CU)	—	17	29	2	767	97	28.40	—	6	8	—
Bailey D. (MCo)	—	1	2	0	85	60	42.50	—	1	—	—
Bairstow D. L. (Y/MCC)	1973	23	32	3	533	79	18.37	—	4	51	11
Baker R. K. (CU)	—	11	20	0	364	51	18.20	—	1	19	1
Baker R. P. (Sy)	—	9	9	6	7	3*	2.33	—	—	5	—
Balderstone J. C. (Le)	1973	14	23	2	775	140	36.90	1	6	9	—
Barclay J. R. T. (Sx)	—	11	21	0	237	28	11.28	—	—	10	—
Barker P. D. (OU)	—	1	2	0	15	14	7.50	—	—	—	—
†Barlow G. D. (M)	—	12	21	2	457	70	24.05	—	4	2	—
Bedi B. S. (Ind/No/TNP)	1972	24	23	6	253	61	14.88	—	1	7	—
Birch J. D. (Nt)	—	6	10	1	76	21	8.44	—	—	7	—
†Birkenshaw J. (Le/Res)	1965	23	29	7	530	70*	24.09	—	1	16	—
Blenkiron W. (Wa)	1969	12	15	1	147	28	10.50	—	—	2	—
Bolus J. B. (D)	1972	22	38	6	892	112	27.87	1	5	4	—
Bond J. D. (Nt)	1974	17	24	4	245	65*	12.25	—	1	3	—
Booth P. (Le)	—	7	7	0	70	57	10.00	—	1	1	—
Bore M. K. (Y)	—	2	2	0	1	1	0.50	—	—	1	—
Borrington A. J. (D)	—	7	12	1	174	58	15.81	—	1	6	—
Bose G. (Ind)	—	9	18	0	328	66	18.22	—	2	4	—
Botham I. T. (So)	—	18	29	3	441	59	16.96	—	1	15	—
†Botton N. D. (OU)	—	10	20	4	249	38*	15.56	—	—	8	—
Bourne W. A. (Wa)	—	12	16	2	210	29	15.00	—	—	12	—
Boyce K. D. (Ex)	1967	12	16	0	335	75	20.93	—	1	7	—
Boycott G. (E/Y/EXI/MCC)	1963	21	36	6	1783	160*	59.43	6	8	7	—
Bradley P. (MCo)	—	1	2	1	9	9*	9.00	—	—	—	—
Brain B. M. (Wo)	1966	22	22	7	154	35	10.26	—	—	8	—
Brassington A. J. (Gs)	—	4	6	2	17	8*	4.25	—	—	4	1

159

	Cap	M	I	NO	Runs	HS	Avge	100	50	Ct	St
†Breakwell D. (So)	—	19	28	7	585	67	27.85	—	2	9	—
Brearley J. M. (M)	1964	21	36	5	1324	173*	42.70	2	7	20	—
Brooker M. E. W. (CU)	—	4	7	4	8	4*	2.66	—	1	1	—
Brown A. S. (Gs)	1957	21	34	2	572	62	17.87	—	2	19	—
†Brown D. B. S. (So)	—	1	2	0	34	25	17.00	—	—	1	—
Brown D. J. (Wa)	1964	20	20	7	123	21*	9.46	—	—	7	—
Burgess G. I. (So)	1968	21	33	0	588	90	17.81	—	4	19	—
Buss A. (Sx)	1963	4	5	2	42	15	14.00	—	—	1	—
†Buss M. A. (Sx)	1967	16	25	3	260	31	11.81	—	—	11	—
†Butcher A. R. (Sy)	—	15	16	3	207	57	15.92	—	1	3	—
Butcher R. O. (M)	—	5	8	1	150	53*	21.42	—	1	3	—
Carrick P. (Y)	—	12	13	3	196	46	19.60	—	—	11	—
Cartwright H. (D)	—	7	11	2	172	43*	19.11	—	—	5	—
Cartwright T. W. (So)	1970	7	8	0	185	68	23.12	—	1	5	—
†Cass G. R. (Wo)	1970	8	9	1	105	39	13.12	—	—	23	—
Chandrasekhar B. S. (Ind)	—	10	5	3	2	2*	1.00	—	—	7	—
†Cheatle R. G. L. (Sx)	—	1	1	1	0	0*	0.00	—	—	—	—
Clapp R. J. (So)	—	1	1	0	0	0	0.00	—	—	—	—
Clark J. (Sc)	—	1	2	1	0	0*	0.00	—	—	2	—
†Clinton G. S. (K)	—	1	2	0	23	20	11.50	—	—	—	—
†Close D. B. (So/DHR)	1971	24	40	9	1153	114*	37.19	1	5	25	—
Colhoun O. D. (Ire)	—	1	2	1	0	0*	0.00	—	—	1	—
Collyer F. E. (MCo)	—	1	2	0	6	6	3.00	—	—	5	—
Cook C. J. (Nt)	—	1	1	0	1	1	1.00	—	—	1	—
Cook G. (No)	—	23	37	2	746	85	21.31	—	2	33	—
†Cooke R. M. O. (Ex)	—	18	29	4	718	100	28.72	1	3	12	—
†Cooper H. P. (Y)	—	1	1	1	8	8*	—	—	—	1	—
Cope G. A. (Y)	1970	22	24	7	275	43	16.17	—	—	1	—
Cordle A. E. (Gm)	1967	14	23	3	201	37	10.05	—	—	3	—
Corlett S. C. (Ire)	—	1	2	0	17	10	8.50	—	—	4	—
Cottam R. M. H. (No)	1972	14	10	2	88	62*	11.00	—	1	8	—
Coverdale S. P. (CU)	—	10	18	0	250	52	13.88	—	2	5	—
Cowdrey M. C. (K)	1951	21	30	3	1027	122	38.03	5	3	24	—
Cowley N. G. (H)	—	11	13	1	242	43	20.16	—	—	1	—
Cumbes J. (Wo)	—	8	6	3	14	10	4.66	—	—	1	—
†Davey J. (Gs)	1971	14	20	11	137	37*	15.22	—	—	2	—
Davis R. C. (Gm)	1969	19	34	3	752	73	24.25	—	6	9	—
Davison B. F. (Le)	1971	24	39	3	1670	142	46.38	4	11	22	—
Denness M. H. (E/K/EXI/MCC)	1964	15	21	2	760	118	40.00	3	1	13	—
†Denning P. W. (So)	1973	21	35	1	641	60	18.85	—	2	13	—
Dixon J. H. (Gs)	—	5	6	1	13	7	2.60	—	—	1	—
Docwra E. D. (OU)	—	1	2	0	26	20	13.00	—	—	—	—
D'Oliveira B. L. (Wo)	1965	18	26	3	1026	227	44.60	2	4	4	—
†Doshi D. R. (Nt)	—	3	3	0	6	2	2.00	—	—	1	—
Dudleston B. (Le)	1969	24	41	5	1337	135	37.13	4	4	21	—
Dunstan M. S. T. (Gs)	—	4	7	0	143	52	15.88	—	1	1	—
Dye J. C. J. (No)	1972	20	15	8	47	11*	6.71	—	—	5	—
Ealham A. G. E. (K)	1970	22	33	3	686	73	22.86	—	4	12	—
East R. E. (Ex/Res)	1967	22	31	6	544	64	21.76	—	4	16	—
Edmeades B.E.A. (Ex)	1965	19	33	1	673	54*	21.03	—	2	3	—

	Cap	M	I	NO	Runs	HS	Avge	100	50	Ct	St
Edmonds P. H. (M/MCC)	1974	22	31	7	453	57	18.87	—	1	24	—
†Edrich J. H. (E/Sy/Res)	1959	16	23	2	1126	152*	53.61	3	6	7	—
Edwards M. J. (Sy)	1966	15	27	2	402	63	16.08	—	2	8	—
Elder J. W. G. (Ire)	—	1	1	0	0	0	0.00	—	—	3	—
Ellis G. P. (Gm)	—	10	18	2	356	116	22.25	1	—	2	—
†Ellis R. (Sc)	—	1	2	0	4	3	2.00	—	—	1	—
Elms R. B. (K)	—	15	16	5	68	13	6.18	—	—	3	—
Emburey J. E. (M)	—	1	1	1	4	4*	—	—	—	1	—
Engineer F.M. (Ind/La)	1968	15	26	5	680	108	32.38	1	4	26	1
Faber M. J. (Sx)	—	15	28	3	593	112*	23.72	1	2	9	—
Featherstone N. G. (M/TNP)	1971	22	35	4	996	125	32.12	2	4	19	—
Field M. N. (Wa/CU)	—	10	15	5	122	39*	12.20	—	—	1	—
Fisher P. B. (OU)	—	7	13	1	136	29	11.33	—	—	13	—
Fleming R. C. J. (CU)	—	9	15	7	60	13*	7.50	—	—	5	—
Fletcher K. W. R. (E/Ex/EXI/MCC)	1963	16	25	4	809	123*	38.52	3	3	10	—
Foat J. C. (Gs)	—	10	16	1	241	62*	16.06	—	1	7	—
Francis D. A. (Gm)	—	9	15	5	183	52*	18.30	—	1	5	—
Fursdon E. D. (OU)	—	11	18	5	239	55	18.38	—	1	1	—
Gardom B. K. (Wa)	—	14	20	2	374	79*	20.77	—	2	6	—
Gavaskar S. M. (Ind)	—	14	26	2	993	136	41.37	3	4	6	—
†Gifford N. (Wo)	1961	22	27	6	270	30	12.85	—	—	17	—
†Gilliat R. M. C. (H)	1969	21	29	3	977	106	37.57	1	8	18	—
Glover T. R. (OU)	—	5	10	1	262	103*	29.11	1	—	3	—
Goddard G. F. (Sc)	—	1	2	0	4	2	2.00	—	—	1	—
†Gomes L. A. (M)	—	12	19	1	222	85	12.33	—	1	2	—
Gooch G. A. (Ex)	—	15	25	3	637	114*	28.95	1	2	4	—
Goodwin K. (La)	1965	1	1	0	6	6*	—	—	—	—	—
Graham J. N. (K)	1967	17	16	6	30	18*	3.00	—	—	2	—
Graham-Brown J.M.H. (K)	—	7	7	3	99	29*	24.75	—	—	2	—
Graveney D. A. (Gs)	—	18	25	3	282	50*	12.81	—	1	4	—
†Graves P. J. (Sx)	1969	21	39	6	1282	145*	38.84	3	7	13	—
Greenidge C. G. (H/DHR)	1972	22	33	2	1093	273*	35.25	2	6	23	—
Greenidge G. A. (Sx)	1970	21	42	3	1187	147	30.43	2	4	16	—
Greig A. W. (E/Sx/EXI/MCC)	1967	18	28	1	669	106	24.77	1	4	24	—
Griffith M. G. (Sx)	1967	11	20	3	408	121*	24.00	1	2	7	—
Griffiths B. J. (No)	—	5	7	2	6	6	1.20	—	—	—	—
Groome J. J. (Sx)	—	9	16	0	181	59	11.31	—	1	3	—
Hacker P. J. (Nt)	—	1	2	0	0	0	0.00	—	—	1	—
Hampshire J. H. (Y)	1963	14	23	6	901	158	53.00	2	3	10	—
Hanley R. W. (DHR)	—	1	—	—	—	—	—	—	—	—	—
Hardie B. R. (Ex)	1974	21	36	2	1168	133	34.35	2	5	16	—
Hardie K. M. (Sc)	—	1	2	1	17	14*	17.00	—	—	—	—
Hare W. H. (Nt)	—	5	9	1	92	36	11.50	—	—	4	—
Harris M. J. (Nt)	1970	23	41	3	1690	133	44.47	6	7	24	5
Harrison J. (Ire)	—	1	2	0	1	1	0.50	—	—	—	—
Harrison S. C. (Gm)	—	1	—	—	—	—	—	—	—	—	—
Harvey-Walker A. J. (D)	—	17	29	1	727	117	25.96	1	4	4	—

	Cap	M	I	NO	Runs	HS	Avge	100	50	Ct	St
Hassan B. (Nt)	1970	23	43	6	1009	83*	27.27	—	9	23	—
Hayes F. C. (La/Res/DHR)	1972	25	39	2	1311	187	35.43	3	7	19	—
Hayes P. J. (CU)	—	5	8	1	61	21*	8.71	—	—	—	—
†Headley R.G.A. (Wo)	1961	19	31	2	1064	137	36.68	3	5	9	—
Hemmings E. E. (Wa)	1974	23	32	5	645	74	23.88	—	3	12	—
Hemsley E. J. O. (Wo)	1969	10	15	2	442	120*	34.00	1	2	9	—
Hendrick M. (E/D/EXI/MCC)	1972	20	15	8	51	9	7.28	—	—	19	—
Herman R. S. (H)	1972	21	22	3	177	23	9.31	—	—	8	—
†Higgs K. (Le)	1972	20	15	9	22	10*	3.66	—	—	14	—
Hignell A. J. (Gs)	—	8	14	1	161	27	12.38	—	—	9	—
Hill A. (D)	—	10	19	4	539	140*	35.93	2	2	3	—
Hill L. W. (Gm)	1974	14	24	4	718	96*	35.90	—	6	5	—
Hills R. W. (K)	—	2	2	0	18	11	9.00	—	—	—	—
Hobbs R. N. S. (Ex/DHR)	1964	19	23	8	145	22	9.66	—	—	9	—
†Hodgson A. (No)	—	13	15	4	128	30	11.63	—	—	4	—
Holder V. A. (Wo)	1970	21	23	4	204	29	10.73	—	—	7	—
Hopkins J. A. (Gm)	—	9	15	2	183	39*	14.07	—	—	5	—
Howarth G. P. (Sy)	1974	17	30	2	751	98	26.82	—	4	7	—
Howick N. K. (OU)	—	5	10	0	51	14	5.10	—	—	1	—
Hughes D. P. (La)	1970	22	29	7	399	62	18.13	—	2	16	—
Humpage G. W. (Wa)	—	2	2	0	13	13	6.50	—	—	5	—
†Humphries D. J. (Le)	—	3	6	1	74	60	14.80	—	1	3	1
Hutton R. A. (Y/TNP)	1964	18	25	5	376	102*	18.80	1	—	15	—
Illingworth R. (Le)	1969	21	27	8	448	67	23.57	—	2	7	—
Imran Khan (Pak/OU)	—	19	31	3	1016	170	36.28	4	1	10	—
Inchmore J. D. (Wo)	—	16	14	4	181	113	15.08	1	—	9	—
Intikhab Alam (Pak/Sy)	1969	20	28	3	525	62	21.00	—	5	6	—
Jackman R. D. (Sy/MCC)	1970	20	27	6	481	92*	22.90	—	5	10	—
Jackson E. J. W. (CU)	—	10	18	3	203	33	13.53	—	—	—	—
Jameson J. A. (Wa/DHR)	1964	24	42	2	1932	240*	48.30	6	7	24	—
Jarrett D. W. (OU)	—	7	13	0	138	51	10.61	—	1	7	—
Jarrett G. M. (MCo)	—	1	2	0	6	6	3.00	—	—	—	—
Jesty T. E. (H)	1971	21	28	2	571	90	21.96	—	3	16	—
Johnson A. A. (MCo)	—	1	2	0	16	12	8.00	—	—	—	—
Johnson C. (Y)	—	8	12	1	173	60*	15.72	—	1	5	—
Johnson G. W. (K/MCC)	1970	23	37	2	1029	158	29.40	1	8	14	—
†Johnson I. N. (Wo)	—	3	3	2	28	22	28.00	—	—	1	—
†Jones A. (Gm)	1962	20	36	1	1121	113	32.02	2	6	6	—
Jones A. A. (So)	1972	21	24	11	103	27	7.92	—	—	4	—
†Jones A. L. (Gm)	—	4	7	0	108	54	15.42	—	1	—	—
Jones E. W. (Gm)	1967	19	30	6	445	67	18.54	—	2	29	2
Jones K. V. (M)	1971	14	17	2	251	52	16.73	—	1	1	—
Joshi U. C. (Sx)	1971	6	8	5	51	20	17.00	—	—	4	—
Julien B. D. (K)	1972	4	8	0	78	28	9.75	—	—	1	—
†Kallicharran A. I. (Wa)	1972	24	39	2	1309	132	35.37	3	7	10	—
Kanhai R. B. (Wa)	1968	14	22	4	936	213*	52.00	3	4	3	—

	Cap	M	I	NO	Runs	HS	Avge	100	50	Ct	St
†Kennedy A. (La)	—	16	26	2	742	81	30.91	—	6	9	—
Kerslake R. C. (MCo)	—	1	2	0	64	64	32.00	—	1	—	—
Khan M. J. (Pak/Gm)	1968	20	35	3	1451	164	45.34	5	6	21	—
Kirmani S.M.H. (Ind)	—	9	10	1	144	46*	48.00	—	—	12	7
†Kitchen M. J. (So)	1966	13	24	2	819	88	37.22	—	7	2	—
†Knight R. D. V. (Gs/Res/MCC)	1971	23	40	5	1350	144	38.57	4	4	16	—
Knott A. P. E. (E/K/EXI)	1965	15	21	1	254	83	12.70	—	1	41	4
Laing J. G. B. (Sc)	—	1	2	0	21	18	10.50	—	—	2	—
†Laing J. R. (Sc)	—	1	2	0	35	34	17.50	—	—	1	—
Lamb T. M. (M/OU)	—	12	12	6	101	40*	16.83	—	—	—	—
Lanchbury R. J. (Wo)	—	3	6	2	130	50*	32.50	—	1	1	—
Langford B. A. (So)	1957	14	21	7	97	18	6.92	—	—	4	—
Larkins W. (No)	—	9	12	3	71	15	7.88	—	—	4	—
Latchman H. C. (Nt)	—	20	29	7	302	78	13.72	—	1	13	—
Leadbeater B. (Y)	1969	19	31	4	804	99*	29.77	—	5	10	—
Lee P. (La)	1972	11	7	6	5	2*	5.00	—	—	1	—
Lee R. J. (OU)	—	3	6	0	151	82	25.16	—	1	—	—
Lever J. K. (Ex/Res/DHR)	1970	21	19	13	91	19*	15.16	—	—	8	—
Lever P. (La)	1965	21	17	5	114	29	9.50	—	—	8	—
Lewington P. J. (Wa)	—	5	2	1	12	8	12.00	—	—	2	—
Lewis A. R. (Gm/Res/MCC)	1960	13	23	1	477	95	21.68	—	3	5	—
Lewis R. V. (H)	—	10	15	1	250	136	18.75	1	—	9	—
Linehan A. J. (Ire)	—	1	2	0	13	13	6.50	—	—	—	—
†Llewellyn M. J. (Gm)	—	9	17	0	318	61	18.70	—	1	7	—
Lloyd B. J. (Gm)	—	6	10	1	31	8*	3.44	—	—	4	—
†Lloyd C. H. (La)	1969	20	31	8	1458	178*	63.39	4	7	15	—
†Lloyd D. (E/La/EXI)	1968	15	22	2	958	214*	47.90	3	3	14	—
Lloyd M. F. D. (OU)	—	5	9	0	65	36	7.22	—	—	2	—
†Loney J. K. (CU)	—	2	2	0	4	2	2.00	—	—	—	—
†Long A. (Sy)	1962	21	22	6	232	42	14.50	—	—	41	5
Luckhurst B. W. (K)	1963	22	35	2	1067	148	32.33	2	4	23	—
Lumb R. G. (Y)	1974	18	31	2	763	123*	26.31	2	2	14	—
Lyon J. (La)	—	16	16	2	170	48	12.14	—	—	29	1
McEwan K. S. (Ex/TNP)	1974	22	37	2	1056	126	30.17	2	4	11	—
McKenzie G. D. (Le)	1969	21	20	4	214	50	13.37	—	1	7	—
McVicker N. M. (Le)	1974	24	25	5	438	64	21.90	—	3	6	—
Madan Lal Sharma (Ind)	—	12	18	6	399	79*	33.25	—	2	11	—
†Maltby N. (No)	—	4	6	2	83	59	20.75	—	1	1	—
Mankad A. V. (Ind)	—	13	22	6	611	66*	38.18	—	4	5	—
Mansell A. W. (Sx)	—	20	33	6	470	72*	17.40	—	1	32	2
Marriott D. A. (M)	1973	2	3	1	9	7	4.50	—	—	—	—
Marshall R. P. T. (Sx)	—	2	4	3	72	26	72.00	—	—	4	—
Maslin M. (MCo)	—	1	2	0	23	23	11.50	—	—	—	—
Mazullah Khan (Pak)	—	4	2	1	1	1	1.00	—	—	3	—
Mendis G. D. (Sx)	—	1	1	0	1	1	1.00	—	—	—	—
Milburn C. (No)	1963	12	17	4	167	39*	12.84	—	—	4	—
Miller G. (D)	—	19	29	2	518	53	19.18	—	1	9	—

	Cap	M	I	NO	Runs	HS	Avge	100	50	Ct	St
Milton C. A. (Gs)	1949	12	19	1	413	76	22.94	—	2	17	—
Mitchell S. (Ire)	—	1	2	0	29	27	14.50	—	—	1	—
Mitra A. (OU)	—	4	8	0	104	30	13.00	—	—	2	—
Mohammad Nazir (Pak)	—	6	4	3	9	9*	9.00	—	—	3	—
Monteith J. D. (Ire)	—	1	2	0	46	30	23.00	—	—	2	—
More H. K. (Sc)	—	1	2	0	40	32	20.00	—	—	4	—
†Morley J. D. (Sx)	1973	22	43	2	864	85	21.07	—	6	10	1
Morris A. (D)	—	3	6	1	113	37	22.60	—	—	1	—
Mortimore J. B. (Gs/TNP)	1954	21	30	4	308	63	11.84	—	1	4	—
Moseley H. R. (So)	1972	20	25	9	120	36*	7.50	—	—	9	—
†Moses G. H. (CU)	—	3	4	2	37	24*	18.50	—	—	—	—
Murray D. L. (Wa)	1972	22	34	2	707	78	22.09	—	2	47	3
Murray J. T. (M/DHR/TNP)	1956	22	28	4	654	82*	24.33	—	4	37	14
Murrills T. J. (CU)	—	11	20	0	334	43	16.70	—	—	8	—
Mushtaq Mohammad (Pak/No/DHR)	1967	21	34	3	973	101*	31.38	1	6	12	—
Naik S. S. (Ind)	—	11	21	3	730	135	40.55	2	4	3	—
Nanan N. (Nt)	—	5	10	0	83	35	8.30	—	—	4	—
Naseer Malik (Pak)	—	7	5	1	48	21	12.00	—	—	4	—
†Nash M. A. (Gm)	1969	17	25	3	220	46	10.00	—	—	7	—
†Nicholls D. (K)	1969	16	22	2	487	77	24.35	—	2	46	—
Nicholls R. B. (Gs)	1957	13	23	2	512	68	24.38	—	6	2	—
Nicholson A. G. (Y)	1963	16	16	8	153	50	19.12	—	1	3	—
Norman M.E.J.C. (Le)	1966	12	20	1	265	40*	15.58	—	—	5	—
Northcote-Grenn S.R. (OU)	—	3	6	0	38	20	6.33	—	—	2	—
†Old C. M. (E/Y/EXI)	1969	18	22	2	529	116	26.45	1	2	12	—
Oldham S. (Y)	—	2	1	1	5	5*	—	—	—	—	—
Ormrod J. A. (Wo)	1966	22	34	2	673	82	21.03	—	3	31	—
Owen-Thomas D. R. (Sy)	—	16	25	4	328	35	15.61	—	—	8	—
†Page J. T. (CU)	—	2	4	0	31	11	7.75	—	—	—	—
Page M. H. (D)	1964	18	29	0	645	91	22.24	—	4	14	—
Parker J. M. (Wo)	1974	17	27	1	760	140	29.23	2	3	12	1
Parks J. M. (So)	1973	22	36	5	717	66	23.12	—	2	18	—
Parsons A. E. W. (Sx)	—	1	2	1	43	39*	43.00	—	—	—	—
Patel B. P. (Ind)	—	14	22	3	511	107	26.89	2	1	6	—
Paver R. G. L. (OU)	—	3	5	0	62	34	12.40	—	—	8	—
Perryman S. P. (Wa)	—	1	—	—	—	—	—	—	—	—	—
Phillipson C. P. (Sx)	—	10	9	5	23	6	5.75	—	—	2	—
Pigot D. R. (Ire)	—	1	2	0	13	7	6.50	—	—	2	—
Pilling H. (La/MCC)	1965	19	28	7	869	144	41.38	2	3	6	—
Pocock P. I. (Sy)	1967	21	25	6	289	41	15.21	—	—	16	—
Pont K. R. (Ex)	—	8	14	1	213	40	16.38	—	—	4	—
Porteous T. W. (Sc)	—	1	2	0	0	0	0.00	—	—	—	—
Prasanna E.A.S. (Ind)	—	13	13	3	52	13	5.20	—	—	4	—
Prentice C.N.R. (OU)	—	1	2	0	23	19	11.50	—	—	—	—
†Price J. S. E. (M)	1963	7	3	1	26	15	13.00	—	—	3	—
Pridgeon A. P. (Wo)	—	1	—	—	—	—	—	—	—	—	—
Procter M. J. (Gs)	1968	19	33	3	1033	157	34.43	2	6	10	—

164

	Cap	M	I	NO	Runs	HS	Avge	100	50	Ct	St
Pullan D. A. (Nt)	1971	6	10	4	58	25	9.66	—	—	12	5
Radley C. T. (M/Res/MCC/TNP)	1967	24	40	5	1231	111*	35.17	3	5	34	—
Randall D. W. (Nt/MCC)	1973	22	42	4	804	105	21.15	1	4	14	—
Ratcliffe R. M. (La)	—	1	1	0	12	12	12.00	—	—	1	—
†Reidy B. W. (La)	—	4	5	1	154	60	38.50	—	1	7	—
Rice C. E. B. (DHR)	—	1	1	1	28	28*	—	—	—	1	—
Rice J. M. (H)	—	3	4	1	51	29	17.00	—	—	3	—
Richards B. A. (H/DHR)	1968	19	27	4	1406	225*	61.13	4	6	23	—
Richards G. (Gm)	—	15	28	2	436	61	16.76	—	1	4	—
Richards I. V. A. (So)	1974	23	38	1	1223	107	33.05	2	6	18	—
Roberts A. M. E. (H)	1974	21	20	10	67	15*	6.70	—	—	2	—
Roberts C. P. (Wo)	—	1	1	1	0	0*	—	—	—	—	—
Robertson F. (Sc)	—	1	2	0	5	5	2.50	—	—	—	—
†Robinson A. L. (Y)	—	16	9	4	43	17*	8.60	—	—	6	—
†Robinson P. J. (So)	1966	1	1	0	1	1	1.00	—	—	1	—
Roebuck P. M. (So)	—	2	4	0	54	46	13.50	—	—	—	—
Roope G. R. J. (Sy)	1969	21	33	6	907	119	33.59	1	4	28	—
†Rose B. C. (So)	—	1	2	0	21	14	10.50	—	—	—	—
Ross N. P. D. (M)	—	6	11	1	137	30	13.70	—	—	1	—
†Rouse S. J. (Wa)	1974	9	13	3	242	55	24.20	—	1	5	—
Rowe C. J. C. (K)	—	14	16	8	237	58*	29.62	—	1	2	—
Rowe L. G. (D)	—	17	30	1	1059	94	36.51	—	7	15	—
Russell D. P. (CU)	—	8	16	1	291	56*	19.40	—	2	2	—
Russell P. E. (D)	—	20	28	8	241	26*	12.05	—	—	18	—
†Sadiq Mohammad (Pak/Gs)	1973	19	32	2	1278	106	42.60	2	10	24	—
Sainsbury P. J. (H)	1955	21	26	8	599	98	33.27	—	4	10	—
Sarfraz Nawaz (Pak/No)	—	17	21	7	317	53	22.64	—	1	8	—
Saville G. J. (Ex)	1970	1	2	1	42	41*	42.00	—	—	2	—
Schepens M. (Le)	—	1	2	0	15	11	7.50	—	—	1	—
Schofield D. (Y)	—	1	1	1	6	6*	—	—	—	—	—
Selvey M. W. W. (M)	1973	15	16	7	102	37*	11.33	—	—	2	—
Senghera R. (Wo/DHR)	—	3									
Shackleton J. H. (Gs)	—	6	8	4	34	11	8.50	—	—	3	—
Shafiq Ahmed (Pak)	—	7	12	3	451	100*	50.11	1	3	5	—
Sharp G. (No)	1973	23	32	7	443	48	17.72	—	—	44	6
Sharpe P. J. (Y)	1960	17	29	2	474	83	17.55	—	2	17	—
Shepherd D. R. (Gs)	1969	19	30	0	747	101	24.90	2	3	7	—
Shepherd J. N. (K/DHR)	1967	21	30	6	609	79	25.37	—	2	6	—
Short J. F. (Ire)	—	1	2	0	72	48	36.00	—	—	—	—
Shuttleworth K. (La)	1968	20	15	6	159	44	17.66	—	—	8	—
Simmons J. (La)	1971	20	25	11	466	75	33.28	—	2	16	—
Siviter K. (OU)	—	2	4	1	31	26	10.33	—	—	—	—
Skinner L. E. (Sy)	—	10	18	0	364	84	20.22	—	2	5	—
Smedley M. J. (Nt)	1966	23	41	6	1134	118*	32.40	1	6	26	—
Smith A. C. (Wa)	1961	18	23	4	368	39	19.36	—	—	5	—
Smith A. J. S. (DHR)	—	1	2	1	30	29*	30.00	—	—	1	—

	Cap	M	I	NO	Runs	HS	Avge	100	50	Ct	St
Smith K. D. (Wa)	—	1	1	0	14	14	14.00	—	—	—	—
Smith M. J. (M/Res/MCC/DHR/TNP)	1967	22	38	4	1468	170*	43.17	3	7	9	—
Smith M. J. K. (Wa)	1957	23	38	8	1159	105	38.63	1	8	23	—
Smith N. (Ex)	—	19	27	3	406	77	16.92	—	1	28	3
Smyth R. I. (CU)	—	10	20	0	438	61	21.90	—	3	2	—
Snellgrove K. L. (La)	1971	11	17	4	454	75*	34.92	—	1	4	—
Snow J. A. (Sx/Res)	1964	22	34	3	552	63	17.80	—	1	8	—
Snowden W. (CU)	—	11	20	0	253	52	12.65	—	1	3	—
†Sobers G. S. (Nt)	1968	15	27	4	1110	132*	48.26	4	6	17	—
Solanky J. W. (Gm)	1973	15	25	5	452	71	22.60	—	3	2	—
†Solkar E. D. (Ind)	—	15	27	2	709	109	28.36	1	3	9	—
Spencer C. T. (Le)	1952	3	1	0	1	1	1.00	—	—	—	—
Spencer J. (Sx)	1973	18	26	5	243	37	11.57	—	—	9	—
Squires P. J. (Y)	—	13	21	3	329	67	18.27	—	2	6	—
†Stallibrass M.J.D. (OU)	—	11	16	6	119	24	11.90	—	—	4	—
†Stead B. (Nt/TNP)	1969	24	31	2	258	32*	8.89	—	—	6	—
Steele D. S. (No)	1965	21	36	3	1022	104	30.96	1	7	20	—
Steele J. F. (Le)	1971	24	41	5	953	116*	26.47	1	5	28	—
Stephenson G. R. (H)	1969	21	24	7	390	69*	22.94	—	2	61	1
Stevenson G. B. (Y)	—	4	4	0	25	18	6.25	—	—	4	—
Stevenson K. (D)	—	9	10	2	83	33	10.37	—	—	2	—
Storey S. J. (Sy)	1964	17	23	4	744	111	39.15	2	3	14	—
Stovold A. W. (Gs)	—	15	28	1	652	102	24.14	1	2	13	1
Stretton T. K. (Le)	—	2	4	2	13	6*	6.50	—	—	1	—
†Swarbrook F. W. (D)	—	20	32	11	490	65	23.33	—	2	18	—
Swart P. D. (DHR)	—	1	2	0	9	6	4.50	—	—	2	—
Swetman R. (Gs)	1972	6	8	4	63	14*	15.75	—	—	12	2
Swinburne J. W. (No)	—	3	3	1	5	4*	2.50	—	—	2	—
Swindell R. S. (D)	—	1	1	0	11	11*	—	—	—	—	—
†Tait A. (No)	—	16	26	0	545	99	20.96	—	4	3	—
Tavare C. J. (K)	—	9	11	1	152	31	15.20	—	—	2	—
Taylor D. J. S. (So)	1971	23	40	5	994	179	28.40	1	5	45	5
Taylor M. N. S. (H)	1973	21	24	2	479	68	21.77	—	3	12	—
Taylor R. W. (D/Res/DHR)	1962	22	33	4	488	54	16.82	—	1	52	3
Taylor W. (Nt)	—	14	13	5	51	14*	6.37	—	—	4	—
Thackeray P. R. (OU)	—	8	15	4	315	65*	28.63	—	2	3	—
Thomas R. J. (Gm)	—	1	1	1	8	8*	—	—	—	—	—
Thompson E. R. (Sc)	—	1	2	0	6	6	3.00	—	—	—	—
Thorn P. L. (Gs)	—	4	6	2	45	25	11.25	—	—	4	—
Tidy W. N. (Wa)	—	1	—	—	—	—	—	—	—	—	—
Titmus F. J. (M/DHR)	1953	22	26	6	366	81*	18.30	—	1	6	—
Todd P. A. (Nt)	—	10	18	1	232	37	13.64	—	—	6	—
Tolchard J. G. (Le)	—	19	26	3	419	64*	18.21	—	2	5	—
Tolchard R. W. (Le/MCC)	1966	24	34	9	743	103	29.72	1	3	46	7
Topley P. A. (K)	—	1	—	—	—	—	—	—	—	—	—
Torrens R. (Ire)	—	1	2	1	20	16	20.00	—	—	1	—
†Townsley R. A. J. (Y)	—	1	2	0	2	2	1.00	—	—	—	—
†Tunnicliffe C. J. (D)	—	4	6	0	18	14	3.00	—	—	—	—
Tunnicliffe H. T. (Nt)	—	11	19	5	357	87	25.50	—	2	2	—

	Cap	M	I	NO	Runs	HS	Avge	100	50	Ct	St
†Turner D. R. (H)	1970	21	29	2	977	152	36.18	3	5	7	—
Turner G. M. (Wo)	1968	20	31	9	1332	202*	60.54	3	5	13	—
Turner J. B. (MCo)	—	1	2	0	127	106	63.50	1	—	1	—
Turner S. (Ex/TNP)	1970	22	33	4	963	118*	33.20	1	6	12	—
Underwood D. L. (E/K/EXI/DHR)	1964	16	16	5	116	43	10.54	—	—	7	—
Venkataraghavan S. (Ind/D)	—	21	28	6	349	33*	15.86	—	—	16	—
Vernon M. J. (M)	—	10	12	4	99	27	12.37	—	—	1	—
Verrinder A.O.C. (Sy)	—	1	2	0	0	0	0.00	—	—	1	—
Virgin R. T. (No)	1974	23	39	5	1936	144*	56.94	7	10	25	—
Viswanath G. R. (Ind)	—	15	26	3	705	106	30.65	2	2	7	—
†Wadekar A. L. (Ind)	—	14	24	2	783	138	35.59	1	5	7	—
Waller C. E. (Sx)	—	20	29	4	182	25	7.28	—	—	11	—
Waller G. W. (OU)	—	11	21	1	176	29	8.80	—	—	8	—
Ward A. (D)	1969	18	16	6	92	32	9.20	—	—	8	—
Ward J. M. (D)	—	10	16	0	170	37	10.62	—	—	3	—
Warrington A. G. (MCo)	—	1	2	0	35	20	17.50	—	—	—	—
Wasim Bari (Pak)	—	14	14	3	104	30*	9.45	—	—	35	5
Wasim Raja (Pak)	—	11	15	4	486	139*	54.00	1	2	5	—
†Watts P. J. (No)	1962	21	33	7	1040	104*	40.00	1	7	13	—
†White R. A. (Nt)	1966	23	38	3	563	83	16.08	—	3	9	—
Wilcock H. G. (Wo)	—	14	19	3	302	44	18.87	—	—	40	1
†Wilkinson K.W. (Wo)	—	4	7	0	296	141	42.28	1	1	5	—
Wilkinson P. A. (Nt)	1974	15	21	8	148	28*	11.38	—	—	2	—
Wilkinson S. G. (So)	—	3	4	1	84	32*	28.00	—	—	—	—
Willey P. (No)	1971	23	37	3	790	100*	23.23	1	2	11	—
†Williams D. L. (Gm)	1971	20	22	11	84	18	7.63	—	—	2	—
Williams R. G. (No)	—	1	2	0	79	64	39.50	—	1	—	—
Willis R. G. D. (E/Wa/EXI)	1972	19	22	16	159	24	26.50	—	—	10	—
†Wilson D. (Y)	1960	8	12	4	64	22	8.00	—	—	1	—
Wisdom N. (Sx)	—	2	2	1	35	31*	35.00	—	—	—	—
Wood B. (La)	1968	22	35	1	893	101	26.26	1	4	10	—
Woolmer R. A. (K/DHR)	1970	23	34	4	840	112	28.00	3	1	14	—
†Yardley T. J. (Wo)	1972	22	31	8	656	66*	28.52	—	5	34	—
†Yeabsley D. I. (MCo)	—	1	2	1	1	1	1.00	—	—	—	—
†Younis Ahmed (Sy)	1969	19	33	4	907	116	31.27	1	4	17	—
Zaheer Abbas (Pak/Gs)	—	21	30	4	1182	240	45.46	5	2	12	—

BOWLING

	Type	Overs	Mdn	Runs	Wkt	Avge	Best	5wI	10wM
Abid Ali S. (Ind)	RM	324.4	64	965	32	30.15	6–23	2	—
Abrahams J. (La/MCo)	OB	6	2	24	0	—	—	—	—
Acfield D. L. (Ex/MCC)	OB	303.2	82	709	18	39.38	5–52	1	—
Aftab Baloch (Pak)	OB	21	2	106	2	53.00	2–91	—	—
Amiss D. L. (E/Wa/EXI/MCC/DHR)	LM/SLA	6	1	17	1	17.00	1–17	—	—
Anderson I.J. (Ire)	OB	19	7	21	5	4.20	5–21	1	—
Armstrong G.D. (Gm)	RF	20	2	101	2	50.50	2–101	—	—
Arnold G. G. (E/Sy/MCC)	RFM	487	139	1069	75	14.25	6–32	4	1
Asif Iqbal (Pak/K)	RM	79	20	205	10	20.50	4–46	—	—
Asif Masood (Pak)	RFM	260	64	603	29	20.79	5–35	1	—
Aworth C.J. (Sy/CU)	SLA	18	2	71	0	—	—	—	—
Baker R. P. (Sy)	RM	207.1	48	511	27	18.92	6–29	1	—
Balderstone J.C. (Le)	SLA	134.4	33	351	19	18.47	4–19	—	—
Barclay J.R.T. (Sx)	OB	96	22	272	8	34.00	3–41	—	—
Bedi B. S. (Ind/No/TNP)	SLA	1085.3	307	2760	112	24.64	7–75	8	1
Birch J. D. (Nt)	RM	45	5	169	5	33.80	3–45	—	—
Birkenshaw J. (Le/Res)	OB	514.2	135	1262	47	26.85	7–56	4	—
Blenkiron W. (Wa)	RFM	160.4	34	473	15	31.53	5–45	1	—
Booth P. (Le)	RFM	124.5	17	380	14	27.14	3–57	—	—
Bore M. K. (Y)	LM	44.1	17	129	0	—	—	—	—
Bose A. (Ind)	OB	15.4	1	42	4	10.50	4–23	—	—
Botham I. T. (So)	RM	309	76	779	30	25.96	5–59	1	—
Botton N. D. (OU)	LM	109	26	316	4	79.00	2–64	—	—
Bourne W. A. (Wa)	RFM	166	29	578	17	34.00	3–31	—	—
Boyce K. D. (Ex)	RFM	313.4	55	868	35	24.80	6–76	3	1
Bradley P. (MCo)	RM	41.3	8	137	2	68.50	2–39	—	—
Brain B. M. (Wo)	RFM	633.1	121	1752	84	20.85	6–58	2	—
Breakwell D. (So)	SLA	346.1	109	957	27	35.44	4–56	—	—
Brooker M.E.W. (CU)	RM	103	21	360	5	72.00	2–84	—	—
Brown A. S. (Gs)	RM	346.4	86	925	35	26.42	5–49	1	—
Brown D. J. (Wa)	RFM	495	134	1143	56	20.41	5–45	1	—
Burgess G. I. (So)	RM	437.1	114	1140	41	27.80	3–18	—	—
Buss A. (Sx)	RFM	93.2	30	219	5	43.80	2–27	—	—
Buss M. A. (Sx)	LM	350	122	797	32	24.90	6–74	2	—
Butcher A. R. (Sy)	LM	191	42	478	18	26.55	3–31	—	—
Carrick P. (Y)	SLA	405.4	167	840	47	17.87	6–43	2	1
Cartwright T. W. (So)	RM	273	130	493	22	22.40	4–45	—	—
Chandrasekhar B. S. (Ind)	RM/LBG	258.5	33	789	26	30.34	5–80	1	—
Cheatle R. G. L. (Sx)	SLA	14	3	53	0	—	—	—	—
Clapp R. J. (So)	RM	7	1	24	0	—	—	—	—
Clark J. (Sc)	RM	22	9	31	4	7.75	4–26	—	—
Clinton G. S. (K)	RM	1	0	1	0	—	—	—	—

168

	Type	Overs	Mdn	Runs	Wkt	Avge	Best	5wI	10 wM
Close D.B. (So/DHR)	RM/OB	164	31	287	14	20.50	5-70	—	—
Cook C. J. (Nt)	OB	35	7	105	1	105.00	1-50	—	—
Cooke R. M. O. (Ex)	LBG	20	1	90	1	90.00	1-37	—	—
Cooper H. P. (Y)	RM	21	8	54	2	27.00	1-23	—	—
Cope G. A. (Y)	OB	742.5	260	1681	77	21.83	7-101	5	1
Cordle A. E. (Gm)	RFM	289	39	914	30	30.46	5-101	1	—
Corlett S. C. (Ire)	RM/OB	12	2	38	0	—	—	—	—
Cottam R.M.H. (No)	RFM	454	113	1101	56	19.66	6-88	4	—
Coverdale S. P. (CU)	RM	1	1	0	1	0.00	1-0	—	—
Cowdrey M. C. (K)	LBG	15	0	54	2	27.00	1-14	—	—
Cowley N. G. (H)	OB	71	31	148	6	24.66	3-31	—	—
Cumbes J. (Wo)	RFM	243.5	49	595	21	28.33	4-25	—	—
Davey J. (Gs)	LFM	286	46	812	26	31.23	3-49	—	—
Davis R. C. (Gm)	OB	444.5	136	956	22	43.45	4-92	—	—
Davison B. F. (Le)	RM	47.3	14	113	4	28.25	2-39	—	—
Denning P. W. (So)	OB	4	1	4	1	4.00	1-4	—	—
Dixon J. H. (Gs)	RM	82.4	11	323	4	80.75	3-97	—	—
D'Oliveira B.L. (Wo)	RM/OB	345.3	105	697	40	17.42	5-49	1	—
Doshi D. R. (Nt)	SLA	130	39	327	10	32.70	2-49	—	—
Dudleston B. (Le)	SLA	23	3	72	2	36.00	1-9	—	—
Dye J. C. J. (No)	LFM	541.1	110	1512	69	21.91	5-54	2	—
East R.E. (Ex/Res)	SLA	571.1	151	1431	50	28.62	5-27	1	—
Edmeades B.E.A. (Ex)	RM	170.4	35	419	13	32.23	3-19	—	—
Edmonds P. H. (M/MCC)	SLA	815.5	266	1888	77	24.51	7-38	3	1
Elder J. W. G. (Ire)	RFM	10	3	21	1	21.00	1-13	—	—
Ellis G. P. (Gm)	RM	90	15	299	4	74.75	2-48	—	—
Elms R. B. (K)	LFM	290.4	68	870	23	37.82	5-76	1	—
Emburey J. E. (M)	OB	21	2	74	0	—	—	—	—
Faber M. J. J. (Sx)	RM	9.4	3	17	1	17.00	1-11	—	—
Featherstone N. G. (M/TNP)	OB	45.5	9	145	6	24.16	2-14	—	—
Field M. N. (Wa/CU)	RM	268.4	51	827	24	34.45	4-76	—	—
Fleming R. C. J. (CU)	OB	129	18	522	7	74.57	3-91	—	—
Fletcher K. W. R. (E/Ex/EXI/MCC)	LB	11.4	0	60	2	30.00	2-20	—	—
Fursdon E. D. (OU)	RM	330.3	79	870	33	26.36	6-60	1	—
Gardom B. K. (Wa)	LB	195.2	31	696	17	40.94	6-139	1	—
Gavaskar S. M. (Ind)	RM/LB	19	3	60	2	30.00	1-7	—	—
Gifford N. (Wo)	SLA	617	197	1333	69	19.31	7-15	3	—
Glover T. R. (OU)	OB	1	1	0	0	—	—	—	—
Goddard G. F. (Sc)	OB	15	5	37	3	12.33	3-28	—	—
Gomes L. A. (M)	RM	105	24	308	6	51.33	2-21	—	—
Gooch G. A. (Ex)	RM	56	11	153	3	51.00	1-17	—	—
Graham J. N. (K)	RM	465.3	107	1138	39	29.17	5-60	1	—
Graham-Brown J.M.H. (K)	RM	30	7	77	1	77.00	1-4	—	—
Graveney D. A. (Gs)	SLA	384.5	105	1014	47	21.57	8-85	3	1
Graves P. J. (Sx)	SLA	1	0	6	0	—	—	—	—
Greenidge G.A. (Sx)	LBG	7	0	45	0	—	—	—	—
Greig A. W. (E/Sx/EXI/MCC)	RFM	551.5	122	1677	55	30.49	6-50	1	—

	Type	Overs	Mdn	Runs	Wkt	Avge	Best	5wI	10 wM
Griffith M. G. (Sx)		1	0	8	0	—	—	—	—
Griffiths B. J. (No)	RM	110	23	385	10	38.50	3-54	—	—
Hacker P. J. (Nt)	LFM	7	1	31	0	—	—	—	—
Hampshire J. H. (Y)	LB	11	7	6	0	—	—	—	—
Hanley R. W. (DHR)	RFM	36	5	125	5	25.00	5-52	1	—
Hardie B. R. (Ex)	RM	2	0	19	0	—	—	—	—
Hardie K. M. (Sc)	SLA	17.3	8	37	3	12.33	2-36	—	—
Hare W. H. (Nt)		4	0	18	0	—	—	—	—
Harris M. J. (Nt)	LBG	4	0	24	0	—	—	—	—
Harrison S. C. (Gm)	RM	14	2	65	1	65.00	1-65	—	—
Harvey-Walker A. J. (D)	OB	30	7	108	1	108.00	1-16	—	—
Hassan B. (Nt)	RM	3	0	14	0	—	—	—	—
Hayes F. C. (La/Res/DHR)	RM	1	0	1	0	—	—	—	—
Hayes P. J. (CU)	RM	76	19	184	1	184.00	1-32	—	—
Hemmings E. E. (Wa)	RM/OB	738	213	1855	84	22.08	7-57	6	1
Hemsley E. J. O. (Wo)	RM	40.4	10	121	4	30.25	2-28	—	—
Hendrick M. (E/D/EXI/MCC)	RFM	531.1	127	1288	65	19.81	5-13	1	—
Herman R. S. (H)	RFM	657.4	202	1426	73	19.53	6-15	3	—
Higgs K. (Le)	RFM	421.1	107	996	39	25.53	5-53	2	—
Hills R. W. (K)	RM	10	1	30	1	30.00	1-30	—	—
Hobbs R. N. S. (Ex/DHR)	LBG	368.1	98	1061	34	31.20	5-73	1	—
Hodgson A. (No)	RFM	284.2	67	751	31	24.22	5-36	1	—
Holder V. A. (Wo)	RFM	659	146	1493	94	15.88	7-40	5	1
Howarth G. P. (Sy)	OB	37	7	132	0	—	—	—	—
Hughes D. P. (La)	SLA	591.3	196	1428	51	28.00	5-38	2	—
Hutton R.A. (Y/TNP)	RFM	259.2	70	620	24	25.83	6-85	1	—
Illingworth R. (Le)	OB	535.1	204	1014	57	17.78	7-18	4	—
Imran Khan (Pak/OU)	RFM	610.3	126	1808	60	30.13	5-44	4	1
Inchmore J. D. (Wo)	RFM	283.2	55	858	39	22.00	5-50	1	—
Intikhab Alam (Pak/Sy)	LBG	489	119	1459	58	25.15	5-60	4	—
Jackman R. D. (Sy/MCC)	RFM	664.1	146	1744	84	20.76	6-58	4	—
Jackson E.J.W. (CU)	LFM	250.2	49	849	19	44.68	4-48	—	—
Jameson J. A. (Wa/DHR)	RM/OB	205.5	42	641	12	53.41	4-47	—	—
Jarrett G. M. (MCo)	LBG	14	4	56	0	—	—	—	—
Jesty T. E. (H)	RM	321.1	96	749	26	28.80	4-47	—	—
Johnson A. A. (MCo)	RM	35	6	135	0	—	—	—	—
Johnson C. (Y)	OB	4	2	6	0	—	—	—	—
Johnson G. W. (K/MCC)	OB	468.2	140	1172	44	26.63	5-51	1	—
Johnson I. N. (Wo)	SLA	51	16	98	5	19.60	4-61	—	—
Jones A. A. (So)	RFM	565	122	1539	67	22.97	6-37	5	—
Jones K. V. (M)	RM	278.5	69	778	27	28.81	5-78	1	—
Joshi U. C. (Sx)	OB	182	54	431	13	33.15	4-79	—	—
Julien B. D. (K)	LMetc	93	21	266	12	22.16	5-91	1	—

170

	Type	Overs	Mdn	Runs	Wkt	Avge	Best	5wI	10 wM
Kallicharran A. I. (Wa)	LBG	34	4	119	2	59.50	2-87	—	—
Kanhai R. B. (Wa)	RM	3	0	9	0	—	—	—	—
Kerslake R. C. (MCo)	OB	9	3	22	1	22.00	1-22	—	—
Kahn M. J. (Pak/Gm)	RM/OB	2	0	10	0	—	—	—	—
Knight R. D. V. (Gs/Res/MCC)	RM	388.3	85	1127	34	33.14	6-44	1	—
Knott A. P. E. (E/K/EXI)	OB	0.2	0	4	0	—	—	—	—
Lamb T. M. (M/OU)	RM	395.5	87	997	36	27.69	5-57	2	—
Langford B. A. (So)	OB	412.1	153	937	42	22.30	5-51	3	—
Larkins W. (No)		7	2	27	0	—	—	—	—
Latchman H.C. (Nt)	LBG	351.3	66	1158	47	24.63	6-31	3	—
Lee P. (La)	RFM	341.2	85	902	29	31.10	5-62	1	—
Lee R. J. (OU)	RM	10	3	16	1	16.00	1-6	—	—
Lever J. K. (Ex/Res/DHR)	LFM	492.2	78	1355	31	43.70	3-38	—	—
Lever P. (La)	RFM	562.1	142	1401	57	24.57	4-20	—	—
Lewington P.J. (Wa)	OB	90	29	227	4	56.75	2-40	—	—
Lloyd B. J. (Gm)	OB	75.2	13	278	7	39.71	3-26	—	—
Lloyd C. H. (La)	RM	23	9	47	2	23.50	2-3	—	—
Lloyd D. (E/La/EXI)	SLA	70	19	206	7	29.42	4-36	—	—
Luckhurst B. W. (K)	SLA	23	9	60	2	30.00	2-23	—	—
McEwan K. S. (Ex/TNP)		0.2	0	0	1	0.00	1-0	—	—
McKenzie G. D. (Le)	RFM	531.3	131	1345	71	18.94	5-36	4	—
McVicker N. M. (Le)	RFM	511.1	113	1357	61	22.24	6-19	2	—
Madan Lal Sharma (Ind)	RM	412.4	89	1263	31	40.74	7-95	1	—
Maltby N. (No)	RM	10	1	42	0	—	—	—	—
Mankad A.V. (Ind)	OB/RM	15	1	58	1	58.00	1-43	—	—
Marriott D. A. (M)	LM	38	9	91	4	22.75	3-49	—	—
Marshall R.P.T. (Sx)	LFM	41	3	128	2	64.00	2-51	—	—
Maslin M. (MCo)	RM	2	0	16	0	—	—	—	—
Mazullah Khan (Pak)	RM/OB	68	16	183	1	183.00	1-32	—	—
Milburn C. (No)	RM	146	29	353	12	29.41	3-25	—	—
Miller G. (D)	OB	380	90	1020	42	24.28	5-88	1	—
Mohammad Nazir (Pak)	OB	118	33	366	4	91.50	2-83	—	—
Monteith J. D. (Ire)	SLA	28.4	14	33	7	4.71	5-29	1	—
Morley J. D. (Sx)		1	1	0	0	—	—	—	—
Mortimore J. B. (Gs/TNP)	OB	529.2	110	1481	33	44.87	4-26	—	—
Moseley H. R. (So)	RFM	661.5	198	1420	81	17.53	5-24	3	—
Moses G. H. (CU)	RFM	71	16	176	9	19.55	5-31	1	—
Murray D. L. (Wa)	LBG	7	3	23	0	—	—	—	—
Mushtaq Mohammad (Pak/No/DHR)	LBG	370.3	103	1106	53	20.86	7-59	3	—
Nanan N. (Nt)	LBG	5	0	10	1	10.00	1-7	—	—
Naseer Malik (Pak)	RM	127.1	14	538	20	26.90	5-61	2	—
Nash M. A. (Gm)	LM	539.5	124	1463	63	23.22	7-126	3	—
Nicholls R. B. (Gs)	OB	3	0	12	0	—	—	—	—

171

	Type	Overs	Mdn	Runs	Wkt	Avge	Best	5wI	10 wM
Nicholson A.G. (Y)	RM	471	152	1100	44	25.00	5-74	1	—
Old C.M. (E/Y/EXI)	RFM	526.3	132	1366	72	18.97	5-21	3	—
Oldham S. (Y)	RFM	20.5	5	69	4	17.25	3-7	—	—
Page J. T. (CU)	LM	28	2	95	1	95.00	1-14	—	—
Parker J. M. (Wo)	LBG	1	0	1	0	—	—	—	—
Parks J. M. (So)	LB	5.3	3	21	0	—	—	—	—
Parsons A.E.W. (Sx)	LB	0.2	0	4	0	—	—	—	—
Phillipson C. P. (Sx)	RM	189	50	439	16	27.43	5-30	1	—
Pilling H. (La/MCC)	OB	3	0	13	0	—	—	—	—
Pocock P. I. (Sy)	OB	628.5	192	1576	60	26.26	5-30	3	—
Pont K. R. (Ex)	RM	91	20	229	7	32.71	3-50	—	—
Prasanna E.A.S. (Ind)	OB	425.4	88	1261	28	45.03	4-59	—	—
Price J. S. E. (M)	RFM	153	33	451	21	21.47	6-54	1	—
Pridgeon A. P. (Wo)	RM	26	7	61	2	30.50	2-29	—	—
Procter M. J. (Gs)	RF	311.3	80	776	47	16.51	5-29	1	—
Randall D. W. (Nt/MCC)	RM	3	0	22	0	—	—	—	—
Ratcliffe R. M. (La)	RM	18	7	44	5	8.80	5-44	1	—
Reidy B. W. (La)	SLA	5	0	20	0	—	—	—	—
Rice C. E. B. (DHR)	RFM	34	7	117	2	58.50	1-45	—	—
Rice J. M. (H)	RM	5	3	9	0	—	—	—	—
Richards B. A. (H/DHR)	OB	37	13	96	2	48.00	1-8	—	—
Richards G. (Gm)	OB	8	1	33	0	—	—	—	—
Richards I. V. A. (So)	OB	95	31	273	6	45.50	2-53	—	—
Roberts A. M. E. (H)	RF	727.4	198	1621	119	13.62	8-47	6	—
Roberts C. P. (Wo)	RM	21	4	40	1	40.00	1-34	—	—
Robertson F. (Sc)	RM	31	11	68	4	17.00	2-31	—	—
Robinson A. L. (Y)	LFM	375.5	103	880	43	20.46	6-61	2	—
Robinson P. J. (So)	SLA	4	0	19	0	—	—	—	—
Roope G. R. J. (Sy)	RM	315.2	76	857	32	26.78	3-5	—	—
Rouse S. J. (Wa)	LM	164.5	34	489	27	18.11	4-26	—	—
Rowe C. J. C. (K)	OB	75.4	12	246	5	49.20	2-60	—	—
Rowe L. G. (D)	RM	27.4	7	84	1	84.00	1-22	—	—
Russell D. P. (CU)	RM	159	32	564	8	70.50	3-69	—	—
Russell P. E. (D)	RM/OB	554.3	154	1413	44	32.11	5-75	1	—
Sadiq Mohammad (Pak/Gs)	LBG	96.5	25	357	13	27.46	5-126	1	—
Sainsbury P. J. (H)	SLA	425.2	196	813	35	23.22	4-30	—	—
Sarfraz Nawaz (Pak/No)	RFM	559	153	1356	68	19.94	8-27	4	—
Schofield D. (Y)	RM	21.2	3	52	5	10.40	5-42	1	—
Selvey M. W. W. (M)	RFM	414.3	82	1246	35	35.60	6-109	2	—
Senghera R. (Wo/DHR)	OB	107	32	276	15	18.40	5-81	1	—
Shackleton J. H. (Gs)	RM	103	19	379	6	63.16	4-108	—	—
Shepherd D. R. (Gs)	RM	5.5	2	12	0	—	—	—	—
Shepherd J. N. (K/DHR)	RM	641	154	1691	55	30.74	6-42	2	—
Shuttleworth K. (La)	RFM	566.1	162	1418	53	26.75	7-61	2	—
Simmons J. (La)	OB	592.1	177	1467	58	25.29	5-79	2	—
Siviter K. (OU)	RM	20.3	1	79	4	19.75	3-24	—	—

	Type	Overs	Mdn	Runs	Wkt	Avge	Best	5wI	10wM
Smith A. C. (Wa)	RM	291.4	70	729	26	28.03	4-49	—	—
Smith M. J. (M/Res/MCC/DHR/TNP)	SLA	1	0	2	0	—	—	—	—
Smith M. J. K. (Wa)	RM	1	1	0	0	—	—	—	—
Snellgrove K. L. (La)		20	5	27	3	9.00	2-23	—	—
Snow J. A. (Sx/Res)	RF	569.1	122	1517	76	19.96	6-14	6	2
Snowden W. (CU)	RM	1.5	0	5	0	—	—	—	—
Sobers G. S. (Nt)	LFMetc	350.4	79	925	29	31.89	4-48	—	—
Solanky J. W. (Gm)	RM/OB	290	59	880	24	36.66	5-78	1	—
Solkar E. D. (Ind)	LM/SLA	250.2	62	680	14	48.57	3-73	—	—
Spencer C. T. (Le)	RM	36	5	112	0	—	—	—	—
Spencer J. (Sx)	RM	464.3	112	1243	47	26.44	6-19	3	—
Stallibrass M. J. D. (OU)	OB	197	56	600	9	66.66	2-2	—	—
Stead B. (Nt/TNP)	LFM	628	147	1713	62	27.62	6-65	1	1
Steele D. S. (No)	SLA	161	59	405	13	31.15	3-68	—	—
Steele J. F. (Le)	SLA	397.5	136	866	30	28.86	4-38	—	—
Stevenson G. B. (Y)	RM	29	9	88	2	44.00	2-43	—	—
Stevenson K. (D)	RM	171.2	16	654	18	36.33	4-127	—	—
Storey S. J. (Sy)	RM	180	48	401	16	25.06	3-2	—	—
Stretton T. K. (Le)	RM	54	16	136	3	45.33	2-71	—	—
Swarbrook F. W. (D)	SLA	427.4	138	1168	21	55.61	4-51	—	—
Swart P. D. (DHR)	RM	23	2	77	3	25.66	3-28	—	—
Swinburne J. W. (No)	OB	80	20	219	10	21.90	5-22	1	—
Swindell R. S. (D)	OB	14	1	58	2	29.00	2-40	—	—
Tavare C. J. (K)	RM	1	0	6	0	—	—	—	—
Taylor M. N. S. (H)	RM	541	147	1259	72	17.48	6-26	3	—
Taylor R. W. (D/Res/DHR)	RM	3	0	9	0	—	—	—	—
Taylor W. (Nt)	RFM	303.5	58	885	34	26.02	5-83	1	—
Thackeray P. R. (OU)	RM	0.3	0	1	0	—	—	—	—
Thomas R. J. (Gm)	RM	10.2	2	40	1	40.00	1-40	—	—
Thompson E. R. (Sc)	RFM	31.2	16	41	6	6.83	3-20	—	—
Thorn P. L. (Gs)	SLA	48	5	227	4	56.75	2-53	—	—
Titmus F.J. (M/DHR)	OB	941.2	312	1953	88	22.19	7-39	6	2
Torrens R. (Ire)	RFM	25.2	6	53	7	7.57	7-40	1	—
Tunnicliffe C. J. (D)	LFM	73	12	238	1	238.00	1-15	—	—
Tunnicliffe H. T. (Nt)	RM	72	11	255	7	36.42	3-55	—	—
Turner S. (Ex/TNP)	RFM	615.5	166	1317	73	18.04	6-87	4	—
Underwood D. L. (E/EXI/DHR)	LM	563	229	1181	65	18.16	8-51	7	3
Venkataraghavan S. (Ind/D)	OB	667.2	136	1923	49	39.24	7-102	2	—
Vernon M. J. (M)	RFM	155	19	586	20	29.30	6-58	2	1
Verrinder A.O.C. (Sy)	RFM	6	1	18	1	18.00	1-18	—	—
Virgin R. T. (No)	LB	1	1	0	0	—	—	—	—
Viswanath G. R. (Ind)	LB	3	0	26	0	—	—	—	—
Waller C. E. (Sx)	SLA	582.5	151	1580	47	33.61	5-69	2	—
Waller G. W. (OU)	RM/OB	1	0	4	0	—	—	—	—
Ward A. (D)	RF	400.4	82	1174	56	20.96	7-42	5	—

	Type	Overs	Mdn	Runs	Wkt	Avge	Best	5wI	10 wM
Wasim Raja (Pak)	LBG	123	23	400	9	44.44	3–92	—	—
Watts P. J. (No)	RM	65.1	25	119	1	119.00	1–18	—	—
White R. A. (Nt)	OB	704.4	197	1909	79	24.16	6–41	4	1
Wilkinson P. A. (Nt)	RM	377.1	98	953	28	34.03	4–46	—	—
Willey P. (No)	RM	238.1	69	595	15	39.66	3–94	—	—
Williams D. L. (Gm)	RFM	511	93	1586	55	28.83	5–67	2	—
Williams R. G. (No)	OB	22	5	76	2	38.00	1–36	—	—
Willis R. G. D. (E/Wa/EXI)	RF	471.2	92	1369	62	22.08	5–85	1	—
Wilson D. (Y)	SLA	157.4	39	469	17	27.58	5–36	1	—
Wisdom N. (Sx)	RM	13.5	3	33	2	16.50	1–0	—	—
Wood B. (La)	RM	405.4	136	892	43	20.74	6–33	3	—
Woolmer R. A. (K/DHR)	RM	467.4	138	1065	56	19.01	5–41	2	—
Yeabsley D. I. (MCo)	LM	44	11	105	5	21.00	3–45	—	—
Younis Ahmad (Sy)	LM/ SLA	6	2	11	0	—	—	—	—
Zaheer Abbas (Pak/Gs)			0	5	0	—	—	—	—

CAREER RECORDS
Compiled by Michael Fordham

The following career records are for all players appearing in first-class cricket in the 1974 season. A few cricketers who did not reappear for their counties this season, but who may do so next year, as well as others who appeared only in John Player League matches, are also included.

BATTING AND FIELDING

	M	I	NO	Runs	HS	Avge	100s	Ct	St
Abberley R. N.	192	327	19	7360	117*	23.89	2	131	—
Abid Ali S.	176	282	31	7214	173*	28.74	12	141	5
Abraham J.	16	27	4	355	78	15.43	—	13	—
Acfield D. L.	173	201	89	1030	42	9.19	—	58	—
Aftab Baloch	49	75	17	2869	428	49.46	6	41	—
Aftab Gul	89	155	7	5672	140	38.32	11	39	—
Amiss D. L.	328	553	71	19298	262*	40.03	38	225	—
Anderson I. J.	10	19	5	355	44	25.35	—	5	—
Armstrong G. D.	6	7	2	46	15*	9.20	—	3	—
Arnold G. G.	226	228	48	2445	73	13.58	—	83	—
Asif Iqbal	276	433	47	13808	175	35.77	22	212	—
Asif Masood	92	85	33	380	24*	7.30	—	34	—
Aworth C. J.	28	51	4	1146	97	24.38	—	12	—
Bailey D.	29	40	1	965	136	24.74	1	11	—
Bairstow D. L.	111	150	26	2194	79	17.69	—	257	36
Baker R. K.	20	34	3	505	59*	16.29	—	25	1
Baker R. P.	16	14	9	14	5	2.80	—	6	—
Balderstone J. C.	116	157	15	3941	140	27.75	2	52	—
Barclay J. R. T.	26	42	2	391	52	9.77	—	17	—
Barker P. D.	1	2	0	15	14	7.50	—	—	—
Barlow G. D.	18	31	2	651	70	22.44	—	4	—
Bedi B. S.	210	245	61	2103	61	11.42	—	107	—
Birch J. D.	7	12	1	102	26	9.27	—	7	—
Birkenshaw J.	368	517	86	9652	131	22.39	3	218	—
Blenkiron W.	118	139	30	1467	62	13.45	—	55	—
Bolus J. B.	449	795	77	24378	202*	33.95	37	193	—
Bond J. D.	362	548	80	12125	157	25.90	14	223	—
Booth P.	12	14	1	134	57	10.30	—	3	—
Bore M. K.	62	65	17	406	37*	8.45	—	20	—
Borrington A. J.	37	68	2	1341	75	20.31	—	22	—
Bose G.	55	92	5	2567	170	29.50	6	23	—
Botham I. T.	18	29	3	441	59	16.96	—	15	—
Botton N. D.	10	20	4	249	38*	15.56	—	8	—
Bourne W. A.	14	20	4	322	84	20.12	—	13	—
Boyce K. D.	227	345	20	7185	147*	22.10	3	179	—
Boycott G.	342	563	81	26686	261*	55.36	82	136	—
Bradley P.	2	3	2	11	9*	11.00	—	3	—
Brain B. M.	134	139	35	774	38	7.44	—	31	—
Brassington A. J.	4	6	2	17	8*	4.25	—	4	1
Breakwell D.	106	132	28	1905	97	18.31	—	42	—

	M	I	NO	Runs	HS	Avge	100s	Ct	St
Brearley J. M.	255	442	54	13477	312*	34.73	17	248	12
Briers N. E.	2	4	2	26	12*	13.00	—	—	—
Brooker M. E. W.	4	7	4	8	4*	2.66	—	1	—
Brown A. S.	455	742	88	11765	116	17.98	3	458	—
Brown D. B. S.	2	4	0	115	58	28.75	—	2	—
Brown D. J.	305	354	86	3209	79	11.97	—	110	—
Burgess G. I.	188	315	20	5580	129	18.91	2	81	—
Buss A.	310	412	76	4415	83	13.13	—	131	—
Buss M. A.	248	436	33	9689	159	24.04	10	182	—
Butcher A. R.	26	25	6	271	57	14.26	—	9	—
Butcher R. G.	5	8	1	150	53*	21.42	—	3	—
Carrick P.	33	37	4	514	46	15.57	—	21	—
Cartwright H.	23	40	5	612	63	17.48	—	13	—
Cartwright T. W.	468	722	91	13630	210	21.60	7	327	—
Cass G. R.	139	204	29	3573	104*	20.41	1	187	25
Chandrasekhar B. S.	152	151	77	413	25	5.58	—	73	—
Cheatle R. G. L.	1	1	0	0	0*	—	—	—	—
Clapp R. J.	4	3	0	4	3	1.33	—	—	—
Clark J.	5	6	2	11	4	2.75	—	5	—
Clinton G. S.	1	2	0	23	20	11.50	—	—	—
Close D. B.	715	1105	152	31633	198	33.19	50	751	1
Colhoun O. D.	23	33	18	66	9*	4.40	—	35	1
Collyer F. E.	4	7	1	50	31	8.33	—	9	1
Cook C. J.	1	1	0	1	1	1.00	—	1	—
Cook G.	77	130	12	2766	122*	23.44	1	76	—
Cooke R. M. O.	37	61	5	1331	139	23.76	2	19	—
Cooper H. P.	33	39	11	274	47	9.78	—	20	—
Cope G. A.	121	134	43	968	66	10.63	—	41	—
Cordle A. E.	211	305	41	3855	81	14.60	—	91	—
Corlett S. C.	19	31	6	319	40*	12.76	—	14	—
Cottam R. M. H.	263	245	88	1018	62*	6.48	—	136	—
Coverdale S. P.	11	19	0	250	52	13.15	—	7	1
Cowdrey M. C.	666	1085	127	41618	307	43.44	105	618	—
Cowley N. G.	11	13	1	242	43	20.16	—	1	—
Cumbes J.	61	43	22	145	25*	6.90	—	18	—
Davey J.	123	139	72	442	37*	6.59	—	22	—
Davis R. C.	185	313	25	5849	134	20.30	3	186	—
Davison B. F.	148	238	18	7513	142	34.15	11	124	—
Denness M. H.	361	605	46	18378	178	32.87	23	318	—
Denning P. W.	80	130	13	2363	85*	20.19	—	37	—
Dixon J. H.	6	7	2	13	7	2.60	—	1	—
Docwra E. D.	1	2	0	26	20	13.00	—	—	—
D'Oliveira B. L.	280	437	63	14575	227	38.97	36	180	—
Doshi D. R.	52	54	13	331	31*	8.07	—	19	—
Dudleston B.	177	297	31	8479	171*	31.87	20	145	1
Dudley-Jones R. D. L.	5	7	2	15	5	3.00	—	1	—
Dunstan M. S. T.	12	20	3	283	52	16.64	—	4	—
Dye J. C. J.	217	191	98	510	29*	5.48	—	46	—
Ealham A. G. E.	176	268	44	5834	105	26.04	3	114	—
East R. E.	218	277	73	3354	89*	16.44	—	148	—
Edmeades B. E. A.	302	494	64	10729	163	24.95	13	96	—
Edmonds P. H.	67	97	14	1345	76	16.20	—	61	—
Edrich J. H.	479	830	82	34342	310*	45.91	90	258	—

	M	I	NO	Runs	HS	Avge	100s	Ct	St
Edwards M. J.	256	452	26	11378	137	26.70	12	273	—
Elder J. W. G.	2	4	1	7	5	2.33	—	5	—
Ellis G. P.	37	66	8	1279	116	22.05	1	9	—
Ellis R.	10	13	3	133	35	13.30	—	6	—
Elms R. B.	44	43	14	229	28*	7.89	—	8	—
Emburey J. E.	6	3	3	5	4*	—	—	6	—
Engineer F. M.	287	433	43	11487	192	29.45	12	578	113
Faber M. J. J.	49	91	7	1655	112*	19.70	1	29	—
Featherstone N. G.	150	245	26	6222	125	28.41	3	138	—
Field M. N.	10	15	5	122	39*	12.20	—	1	—
Fisher P. B.	7	13	1	136	29	11.33	—	13	—
Fleming R. C. J.	9	15	7	60	13*	7.50	—	5	—
Fletcher K. W. R.	386	655	92	21269	228*	37.77	37	359	—
Foat J. C.	25	41	5	527	62*	14.63	—	15	—
Francis D. A.	16	28	6	306	52*	13.90	—	10	—
Fursdon E. D.	12	20	5	245	55	16.33	—	1	—
Gardom B. K.	17	25	2	427	79*	18.56	—	6	—
Gavaskar S. M.	102	181	19	7469	282	46.10	22	103	—
Gifford N.	406	490	145	4549	89	13.18	—	203	—
Gilliat R. M. C.	200	324	28	8446	223*	28.53	12	149	—
Glover T. R.	14	26	1	455	103*	18.20	1	7	—
Goddard G. F.	15	24	3	281	39	13.38	—	6	—
Gomes H. A.	38	57	7	1201	123	24.02	1	14	—
Gooch G. A.	16	26	3	655	114*	28.47	1	5	—
Good A. J.	1	1	0	6	6	6.00	—	—	—
Goodwin K.	124	153	43	636	23	5.78	—	229	27
Graham J. N.	169	159	64	372	23	3.91	—	33	—
Graham-Brown J. M. H.	7	7	3	99	29*	24.75	—	2	—
Graveney D. A.	45	62	15	587	50*	12.48	—	16	—
Graves P. J.	198	344	36	7915	145*	25.69	6	157	—
Greenidge C. G.	109	188	12	6215	273*	35.31	10	95	—
Greenidge G. A.	164	301	21	8535	205	30.48	16	80	—
Greig A. W.	259	431	35	11557	156	29.18	16	247	—
Griffith M. G.	276	455	90	8890	158	24.35	5	268	20
Griffiths B. J.	5	7	2	6	6	1.20	—	2	—
Groome J. J.	9	16	0	181	59	11.31	—	3	—
Hacker P. J.	1	2	0	0	0	0.00	—	1	—
Hampshire J. H.	364	581	65	16164	183*	31.32	22	278	—
Hanley R. W.	15	17	12	17	4*	3.40	—	10	—
Hardie B. R.	36	64	4	1809	133	30.15	2	23	—
Hardie K. M.	9	10	3	93	20	13.28	—	1	—
Hare W. H.	9	16	4	156	36	13.00	—	5	—
Harris M. J.	215	373	29	13092	201*	38.05	31	143	5
Harrison S. C.	5	10	0	139	65	13.90	—	3	—
Harrison S. C.	3	4	0	28	15	7.00	—	1	—
Harvey-Walker A. J.	47	85	4	2002	117	24.71	2	15	—
Hassan B.	164	271	26	6882	125*	28.08	7	134	1
Hayes F. C.	107	165	26	4817	187	34.65	8	88	—
Hayes P. J.	5	8	1	61	21*	8.71	—	—	—
Headley R. G. A.	423	758	61	21695	187	31.12	32	357	—
Hemmings E. E.	95	140	29	2572	80	23.17	—	44	—
Hemsley E. J. O	102	168	25	4224	138*	29.53	2	75	—
Hendrick M.	86	80	27	442	46	8.33	—	53	—

	M	I	NO	Runs	HS	Avge	100s	Ct	St
Herman R. S.	162	156	44	1076	56	9.60	—	65	—
Higgs K.	406	461	170	3209	63	11.02	—	227	—
Hignell A. J.	8	14	1	161	27	12.38	—	9	—
Hill A.	34	66	6	1417	140*	23.61	2	11	—
Hill L. W.	58	97	15	1993	96*	24.30	—	30	1
Hill M. J.	1	2	1	17	17*	17.00	—	—	—
Hills R. W.	4	4	1	72	36*	24.00	—	—	—
Hobbs R. N. S.	383	480	113	4374	100	11.91	1	255	—
Hodgson A.	42	46	5	362	41	8.82	—	13	—
Holder V. A.	190	208	49	1862	122	11.71	1	67	—
Hopkins J. A.	28	46	3	589	88	13.69	—	18	1
Howarth G. P.	51	85	7	2174	159	27.87	2	41	—
Howick N. K.	5	10	0	51	14	5.10	—	1	—
Hughes D. P.	167	196	41	2756	88*	17.78	—	93	—
Humpage G. W.	2	2	0	13	13	6.50	—	5	—
Humphries D. J.	3	6	1	74	60	14.80	—	3	1
Hutton R. A.	279	408	57	7547	189	21.50	5	216	—
Illingworth R.	667	942	181	21386	162	28.10	20	379	—
Imran Khan	62	97	10	2528	170	29.05	4	23	—
Inchmore J. D.	28	30	11	274	113	14.42	1	12	—
Intikhab Alam	328	481	47	10231	182	23.57	8	174	—
Jackman R. D.	205	225	81	2380	92*	16.52	—	80	—
Jackson E. J. W.	10	18	3	203	33	13.53	—	—	—
Jameson J. A.	318	532	42	16269	240*	33.20	25	220	1
Jarrett D. W.	7	13	0	138	51	10.61	—	7	—
Jarrett G. M.	3	4	2	32	24*	16.00	—	—	—
Jesty T. E.	137	198	34	3697	90	22.54	—	81	—
Johnson A. A.	27	37	4	289	45	8.75	—	24	—
Johnson C.	58	87	10	1585	107	20.58	1	31	—
Johnson G. W.	155	253	19	5607	158	23.96	6	125	—
Johnson P. D.	31	52	7	988	82	21.95	—	14	—
Johnson I. N.	29	38	9	578	55	19.93	—	11	—
Jones A.	431	783	50	23274	187*	31.75	33	230	—
Jones A. A.	121	125	44	485	27	5.98	—	25	—
Jones A. L.	5	9	0	110	54	12.22	—	—	—
Jones E. W.	221	336	76	5006	146*	19.25	2	484	51
Jones K. V.	117	155	37	2031	57*	17.21	—	48	—
Joshi U. C.	131	168	44	1552	64	12.51	—	56	—
Julien B. D.	99	130	16	2822	127	24.75	2	65	—
Kallicharran A. I.	115	180	15	6981	197	42.30	18	72	—
Kanhai R. B.	365	587	64	25964	256	49.64	77	270	7
Kennedy A.	24	39	5	919	81	27.02	—	13	—
Kerslake R. C.	84	130	13	1875	80	16.02	—	64	—
Khan M. J.	264	453	38	18251	241	43.97	51	292	—
Kirmani S. M. H.	54	76	17	1600	78	27.11	—	55	26
Kitchen M. J.	296	516	28	13100	189	26.84	14	117	—
Knew G. A.	4	6	1	59	25	11.80	—	—	—
Knight R. D. V.	163	295	16	8230	164*	29.49	10	127	—
Knott A. P. E.	304	444	81	10206	156	28.11	9	727	92
Laing J. G. B.	19	32	4	651	93	23.25	—	11	—
Laing J. R.	3	6	0	100	34	16.66	—	2	—
Lamb T. M.	21	22	10	134	40*	11.16	—	2	—
Lanchbury R. J.	13	22	3	357	50*	18.78	—	2	—

178

	M	I	NO	Runs	HS	Avge	100s	Ct	St
Langford B. A.	510	720	162	7588	68*	13.59	—	231	—
Larkins W.	25	37	5	312	109	9.75	1	10	—
Latchman H. C.	193	216	58	1984	96	12.55	—	93	—
Leadbeater B.	112	182	21	3936	99*	24.44	—	52	—
Lee P.	97	77	31	369	26	8.02	—	16	—
Lee R. J.	24	45	1	951	130	21.61	1	14	—
Lever J. K.	178	193	92	1144	91	11.32	—	85	—
Lever P.	260	281	60	3286	88*	14.86	—	86	—
Lewington P. J.	44	40	13	216	34	8.00	—	19	—
Lewis A. R.	409	708	76	20495	223	32.42	30	193	—
Lewis R. V.	85	153	13	2713	136	19.37	2	53	—
Linehan A. J.	2	4	0	29	16	7.15	—	2	—
Llewellyn M. J.	40	67	6	1151	112*	18.86	1	31	—
Lloyd B. J.	21	30	5	162	45*	6.48	—	12	—
Lloyd C. H.	220	346	46	14216	217*	47.38	35	135	—
Lloyd D.	212	345	46	9567	214*	31.99	17	175	—
Lloyd M. F. D.	5	9	0	65	36	7.22	—	2	—
Loney J. K.	2	2	0	4	2	2.00	—	—	—
Long A.	352	412	90	5064	92	15.72	—	701	101
Luckhurst B. W.	351	594	72	20465	215	39.20	44	352	—
Lumb R. G.	59	99	6	2562	123*	27.54	5	45	—
Lyon J.	19	19	4	187	48	12.46	—	33	1
Lyon S. K. J.	54	89	13	1513	92	19.90	—	26	—
McEwan K. S.	42	72	6	1821	126	27.59	2	47	2
McKenzie G. D.	365	452	97	5474	76	15.41	—	193	—
McVicker N. M.	130	158	38	2182	65*	18.19	—	37	—
Madan Lal Sharma	50	77	18	2288	119*	38.77	4	35	—
Maltby N.	9	14	4	185	59	18.50	—	2	—
Mankad A. V.	135	210	39	7311	171	42.75	12	69	—
Mansell A. W.	38	58	14	650	72*	14.77	—	68	7
Marriott D. A.	30	26	13	139	24*	10.69	—	5	—
Marshall R. P. T.	7	11	8	124	26	41.33	—	1	—
Maslin M.	5	10	1	274	66*	30.44	—	2	—
Mazullah Khan	29	45	4	721	130	17.58	1	16	—
Mendis G. D.	1	1	0	1	1	1.00	—	—	—
Milburn C.	255	435	34	13262	243	33.07	23	226	—
Miller G.	28	45	4	759	71	18.51	—	16	—
Milton C. A.	620	1078	125	32150	170	33.73	56	759	—
Mitchell S.	1	2	0	29	27	14.50	—	1	—
Mitra A.	4	8	0	104	30	13.00	—	2	—
Mohammad Nazir	69	89	21	1662	113*	24.44	2	33	—
Monteith J. D.	9	15	1	205	78	14.64	—	8	—
More H. K.	15	30	2	571	89	20.39	—	22	—
Morley J. D.	54	98	8	2085	127	23.16	2	22	1
Morris A.	3	6	1	113	37	22.60	—	1	—
Mortimore J. B.	638	986	122	15870	149	18.36	4	346	—
Moseley H. R.	84	93	38	748	67	13.60	—	36	—
Moses G. H.	3	4	2	37	24*	18.50	—	—	—
Mottram T. J.	21	18	9	55	15*	6.11	—	6	—
Murray D. L.	252	382	54	9332	166*	28.45	9	475	76
Murray J. T.	617	908	131	18307	142	23.56	16	1230	252
Murrills T. J.	20	36	3	516	53	15.63	—	11	—
Murtagh A. J.	7	12	2	142	47	14.20	—	3	—

	M	I	NO	Runs	HS	Avge	100s	Ct	St
Mushtaq Mohammad	392	651	80	23900	303*	41.85	53	268	—
Naik S. S.	62	99	11	3449	200*	39.19	7	35	—
Nanan N.	19	35	3	433	72	13.53	—	12	—
Naseer Malik	29	40	3	436	55	11.78	—	20	—
Nash M. A.	177	246	36	3539	89	16.85	—	87	—
Nicholls D.	169	291	14	5966	211	21.53	2	261	10
Nicholls R. B.	531	948	52	23474	217	26.19	18	283	1
Nicholson A. G.	277	261	123	1594	50	11.55	—	84	—
Norman M. E. J. C.	361	636	44	17423	221*	29.43	24	161	—
Northcote-Green S. R.	3	6	0	38	20	6.33	—	2	—
Old C. M.	152	185	33	2761	116	18.16	1	85	—
Oldham S.	2	1	1	5	5*	—	—	1	—
Ormrod A. J.	299	499	63	11948	204*	27.40	9	263	—
Owen-Thomas D. R.	96	162	17	4292	182*	29.60	7	41	—
Page J. T.	2	4	0	31	11	7.75	—	—	—
Page M. H.	236	417	46	10501	162	28.30	8	235	—
Parker J. M.	76	130	11	4138	195	34.77	8	59	3
Parks J. M.	735	1219	170	36483	205*	34.77	51	1086	93
Parsons A. E. W.	8	15	2	257	57	19.76	—	2	—
Patel B. P.	60	94	14	2594	168	32.42	7	24	—
Paver R. G. L.	16	26	2	290	34	12.08	—	33	5
Perryman S. P.	1	—	—	—	—	—	—	—	—
Phillipson C. P.	34	35	19	91	11*	5.68	—	8	—
Figot D. R.	10	20	0	366	88	18.30	—	7	—
Pilling H.	268	440	54	12367	144	32.03	20	63	—
Pocock P. I.	304	342	71	3249	75*	11.98	—	100	—
Pont K. R.	40	65	9	1228	113	21.92	1	24	—
Porteous T. W.	2	4	0	18	18	4.50	—	5	—
Prasanna E. A. S.	166	198	47	1875	81	12.41	—	94	—
Prentice C. N. R.	1	2	0	23	19	11.50	—	—	—
Price J. S. E.	275	220	91	1090	53*	8.44	—	104	—
Prideaux R. M.	444	805	75	25090	202*	34.36	41	301	—
Pridgeon A. P.	15	12	6	32	18*	5.33	—	6	—
Procter M. J.	230	381	37	13122	254	38.14	35	201	—
Pullan D. A.	95	106	36	613	34	8.75	—	206	28
Radley C. T.	256	411	64	11673	139	33.63	18	251	—
Randall D. W.	58	106	7	2367	107	23.90	2	32	—
Ratcliffe R. M.	10	9	2	50	12*	7.14	—	1	—
Reidy B. W.	5	6	2	164	60	41.00	—	7	—
Rhodes H. J.	321	399	143	2427	48	9.48	—	85	—
Rice C. E. B.	35	54	13	1021	81	24.90	—	14	—
Rice J. M.	21	24	4	214	29	10.70	—	15	—
Richards B. A.	238	399	37	20894	356	57.71	60	252	—
Richards G.	30	53	3	858	61	17.16	—	15	—
Richards I. V. A.	42	73	3	2146	107	30.65	2	26	—
Roberts A. M. E.	42	54	22	353	48*	11.03	—	5	—
Roberts C. P.	1	1	0	0	0*	—	—	—	—
Robertson F.	4	7	0	38	9	5.42	—	1	—
Robinson A. L.	31	22	12	116	28*	11.60	—	12	—
Robinson P. J.	183	285	54	4923	140	21.31	3	169	—
Roebuck P. M.	2	4	0	54	46	13.50	—	—	—
Roope G. R. J.	223	355	68	9900	171	34.49	12	306	1
Rose B. C.	37	60	4	943	125	16.83	1	16	—

	M	I	NO	Runs	HS	Avge	100s	Ct	St
Ross N. P. D.	7	12	1	137	30	12.45	—	1	—
Rouse S. J.	55	62	12	651	55	13.02	—	32	—
Rowe C. J. C.	14	16	8	237	58*	29.62	—	2	—
Rowe L. O.	72	119	7	4977	302	44.43	12	65	—
Russell D. P.	8	16	1	291	56*	19.40	—	2	—
Russell P. E.	108	134	30	1462	72	14.05	—	18	—
Sadiq Mohammad	144	243	16	8701	184*	38.33	17	117	—
Sainsbury P. J.	581	890	189	18826	163	26.85	6	593	—
Sarfraz Nawaz	88	99	27	1337	59	18.56	—	52	—
Saville G. J.	126	218	29	4474	126*	23.67	3	103	—
Schepens M.	2	3	0	19	11	6.33	—	1	—
Schofield D.	3	4	4	13	6*	—	—	—	—
Selvey M. W. W.	69	64	28	307	42	8.52	—	16	—
Senghera R.	3	—	—	—	—	—	—	—	—
Shackleton J. H.	9	12	6	74	18	12.33	—	4	—
Shafiq Ahmed	54	92	18	3380	155*	45.67	7	59	—
Sharp G.	85	113	25	1617	76*	18.37	—	152	34
Sharpe P. J.	453	742	78	20449	203*	30.87	25	570	—
Shepherd D. R.	199	346	25	7728	153	24.07	11	69	—
Shepherd J. N.	210	301	40	6190	170	23.71	4	166	—
Short J. F.	1	2	0	72	48	36.00	—	—	—
Shuttleworth K.	185	187	66	1901	71	15.71	—	82	—
Sidebottom A.	2	2	0	1	1	0.50	—	—	—
Simmons J.	140	155	50	2196	112	20.91	1	87	—
Siviter K.	2	4	1	31	26	10.33	—	—	—
Skinner L. E.	18	30	3	583	84	21.59	—	12	1
Smedley M. J.	261	447	54	12324	149	31.35	24	191	—
Smith A. C.	427	611	85	11012	145	20.93	3	715	61
Smith A. J. S.	20	33	7	782	87	30.07	—	71	1
Smith D. M.	4	1	1	8	8*	—	—	3	—
Smith K. D.	3	4	0	66	49	16.50	—	—	—
Smith M. J.	306	506	68	13958	181	31.86	26	182	—
Smith M. J. K.	624	1067	138	39129	204	42.11	68	587	—
Smith N.	42	62	14	729	77	15.18	—	70	15
Smyth R. I.	13	25	1	507	61	21.12	—	3	—
Snellgrove K. L.	106	172	16	3948	138	25.30	2	36	—
Snow J. A.	289	366	91	3409	73	12.39	—	101	—
Snowden W.	29	53	1	978	108*	18.80	2	9	—
Sobers G. S.	383	609	93	28315	365*	54.87	86	407	—
Solanky J. W.	50	81	12	1484	71	21.50	—	13	—
Solkar E. D.	133	196	26	4975	145*	29.26	5	138	—
Spencer C. T.	506	687	142	5871	90	10.77	—	380	—
Spencer J.	107	148	36	1029	55	9.18	—	41	—
Squires P. J.	28	47	6	677	67	16.51	—	12	—
Stallibrass M. J. D.	21	31	7	194	24	8.08	—	7	—
Stead B.	199	215	62	1806	58	11.80	—	55	—
Steele D. S.	275	450	56	12151	140*	30.84	16	314	—
Steele J. F.	124	197	21	5026	195	28.55	6	154	—
Stephenson G. R.	150	194	37	2656	82	16.91	—	357	45
Stevenson G. B.	5	6	0	33	18	5.50	—	5	—
Stevenson K.	9	10	2	83	33	10.37	—	2	—
Storey S. J.	316	469	59	10445	164	25.47	12	318	—
Stovold A. W.	22	40	2	915	102	24.07	1	20	4

	M	I	NO	Runs	HS	Avge	100s	Ct	St
Stretton T. K.	5	6	2	15	6*	3.75	—	2	—
Sullivan J.	153	239	32	4261	81*	20.58	—	84	—
Swarbrook F. W.	126	182	49	2426	90	18.24	—	81	—
Swart P. D.	51	73	7	1245	109	18.86	2	25	—
Swetman R.	286	411	73	6495	115	19.21	2	530	66
Swinburne J. W.	29	36	8	160	25	5.71	—	13	—
Swindell R. S.	20	27	10	229	38	13.47	—	10	—
Tait A.	45	74	0	1421	99	19.20	—	9	—
Tavaré C. J.	9	11	1	152	31	15.20	—	2	—
Taylor D. J. S.	133	179	40	2751	179	19.79	1	254	32
Taylor M. N. S.	273	371	85	5371	105	18.77	1	165	—
Taylor R. W.	375	536	106	6995	74*	16.26	—	856	102
Taylor W.	68	66	27	205	26*	5.25	—	14	—
Thackeray P. R.	8	15	4	315	65*	28.63	—	3	—
Thomas R. J.	1	1	1	8	8*	—	—	—	—
Thompson E. R.	16	20	7	135	29*	10.38	—	11	—
Thorn P. L.	4	6	2	45	25	11.25	—	4	—
Tidy W. N.	36	34	14	70	12*	3.50	—	17	—
Titmus F. J.	727	1053	188	20477	137*	23.67	5	451	—
Todd P. A.	18	32	2	453	66*	15.10	—	14	—
Tolchard J. G.	62	88	14	1408	66	19.02	—	17	—
Tolchard R. W.	259	353	101	7279	126*	28.88	6	498	68
Topley P. A.	12	12	3	110	22	12.22	—	8	—
Torrens R.	3	5	1	25	16	6.25	—	1	—
Townsley R. A. J.	1	2	0	2	2	1.00	—	—	—
Tunnicliffe C. J.	14	18	7	95	34*	8.63	—	4	—
Tunnicliffe H. T.	12	21	5	365	87	22.81	—	2	—
Turner D. R.	158	255	22	6386	181*	27.40	9	93	—
Turner G. M.	251	432	61	17313	259	46.66	46	228	—
Turner J. B.	1	2	0	127	106	63.50	1	1	—
Turner S.	149	220	40	3644	121	20.24	3	104	—
Underwood D. L.	344	368	95	2457	80	9.00	—	149	—
Venkataraghavan S.	201	293	53	4486	137	18.69	1	196	—
Vernon M. J.	10	12	4	99	27	12.37	—	1	—
Verinder A. O. C.	1	2	0	0	0	0.00	—	1	—
Virgin R. T.	371	653	32	18703	179*	30.11	31	356	—
Viswanath G. R.	111	183	21	6317	230	38.99	15	74	—
Wadekar A. L.	235	358	33	15377	323	47.31	36	270	—
Waller C. E.	60	60	17	355	47	8.25	—	24	—
Waller G. de W.	13	25	1	203	29	8.45	—	10	—
Ward A.	114	110	34	695	44	9.14	—	40	—
Ward J. M.	40	70	4	1425	85	21.59	—	19	—
Warrington A. G.	2	4	0	152	92	38.00	—	—	—
Wasim Bari	140	182	46	3042	101	22.36	1	322	68
Wasim Raja	67	107	15	3310	165	35.97	4	43	—
Watts P. J.	323	541	76	13569	145	29.18	10	252	—
White R. A.	329	529	84	10481	116*	23.55	5	150	—
Whitehouse J.	60	101	8	2724	173	29.29	2	28	—
Wilcock H. G.	57	73	16	877	44	15.38	—	113	10
Wilkinson K. W.	33	48	9	960	141	24.61	1	22	—
Wilkinson P. A.	42	55	19	289	28*	8.02	—	14	—
Wilkinson S. G.	18	27	5	452	69	20.54	—	11	—
Willey P.	158	251	41	4939	158*	23.51	5	72	—

	M	I	NO	Runs	HS	Avge	100s	Ct	St
Williams D. L.	140	136	68	369	37*	5.42	—	36	—
Williams R. G.	1	2	0	79	64	39.50	—	—	—
Willis R. G. D.	106	108	60	833	34	17.35	—	54	—
Wilson D.	422	533	91	6230	112	14.09	1	250	—
Wisdom N.	2	2	1	35	31*	35.00	—	—	—
Wood B.	209	347	39	9636	186	31.28	15	173	—
Woolmer R. A.	136	183	47	3376	112	24.82	3	89	—
Yardley T. J.	134	202	37	4239	135	25.69	3	110	2
Yeabsley D. I.	1	2	1	1	1	1.00	—	—	—
Younis Ahmed	225	379	54	11784	155*	36.25	19	121	—
Zaheer Abbas	143	230	31	10021	274	50.35	32	109	—

BOWLING

NB Players who have not bowled in first-class cricket are omitted from the following list.

	Runs	Wkts	Avge	BB	5w inns	10w match	100w season
Abberley R. N.	231	4	57.75	2–19	—	—	—
Abid Ali S.	8986	317	28.34	6–23	12	—	—
Abrahams J.	24	0	—	—	—	—	—
Acfield D. L.	10733	378	28.39	7–36	14	—	—
Aftab Baloch	2276	76	29.94	8–171	4	1	—
Aftab Gul	346	11	31.45	2–20	—	—	—
Amiss D. L.	603	15	40.20	3–21	—	—	—
Anderson I. J.	104	15	6.93	5–21	1	—	—
Armstrong G. D.	540	13	41.53	4–45	—	—	—
Arnold G. G.	15894	748	21.24	8–41	31	2	1
Asif Iqbal	7249	241	30.07	6–45	5	—	—
Asif Masood	6580	231	28.48	8–97	8	—	—
Aworth C. J.	71	0	—	—	—	—	—
Baker R. P.	844	37	22.81	6–29	1	—	—
Balderstone J. C.	2303	96	23.98	6–84	2	—	—
Barclay J. R. T.	853	24	35.54	5–28	1	—	—
Bedi B. S.	19470	910	21.39	7–19	61	8	2
Birch J. D.	261	5	52.20	3–45	—	—	—
Birkenshaw J.	23338	876	26.64	8–94	42	4	2
Blenkiron W.	8149	287	28.39	5–37	7	—	—
Bolus J. B.	886	24	36.91	4–40	—	—	—
Bond J. D.	69	0	—	—	—	—	—
Booth P.	520	23	22.60	4–18	—	—	—
Bore M. K.	3922	131	29.93	6–63	3	—	—
Borrington A. J.	15	0	—	—	—	—	—
Bose G.	1543	55	28.05	4–23	—	—	—
Botham I. T.	779	30	25.96	5–59	1	—	—
Botton N. D.	316	4	79.00	2–64	—	—	—
Bourne W. A.	732	20	36.60	3–31	—	—	—
Boyce K. D.	16824	668	25.18	9–61	27	5	—
Boycott G.	977	22	44.40	3–47	—	—	—

	Runs	Wkts	Avge	BB	5w inns	10w match	100w season
Bradley P.	249	9	27.66	4–57	—	—	—
Brain B. M.	10881	456	23.86	6–32	18	4	—
Breakwell D.	5434	188	28.90	8–39	6	1	—
Brearley J. M.	99	1	99.00	1–21	—	—	—
Brooker M. E. W.	360	5	72.00	2–84	—	—	—
Brown A. S.	29199	1144	25.52	8–80	52	8	2
Brown D. J.	22075	904	24.41	8–64	33	4	—
Burgess G. I.	9201	327	28.13	6–51	13	1	—
Buss A.	23989	958	25.04	8–23	44	3	3
Buss M. A.	12248	437	28.02	7–58	16	—	—
Butcher A. R.	996	39	25.53	6–48	1	—	—
Carrick P.	2214	91	24.32	8–33	6	1	—
Cartwright T. W.	28874	1517	19.03	8–39	94	18	8
Chandrasekhar B. S.	14764	689	21.42	9–72	53	15	—
Cheatle R. G. L.	53	0	—	—	—	—	—
Clapp R. J.	249	6	41.50	2–48	—	—	—
Clark J.	267	10	26.70	4–26	—	—	—
Clinton G. S.	1	0	—	—	—	—	—
Close D. B.	29134	1119	26.03	8–41	43	3	—
Cook C. J.	105	1	105.00	1–50	—	—	—
Cook G.	1	0	—	—	—	—	—
Cooke R. M. O.	108	1	108.00	1–37	—	—	—
Cooper H. P.	1964	78	25.17	4–37	—	—	—
Cope G. A.	7790	331	23.53	7–36	16	3	—
Cordle A. E.	11613	460	25.24	9–49	12	2	—
Corlett S. C.	1269	25	50.76	4–34	—	—	—
Cottam R. M. H.	19559	944	20.71	9–25	55	5	3
Coverdale S. P.	0	1	1.00	1–0	—	—	—
Cowdrey M. C.	3238	62	52.22	4–22	—	—	—
Cowley N. G.	148	6	24.66	3–31	—	—	—
Cumbes J.	4159	171	24.32	6–35	6	—	—
Davey J.	8126	290	28.02	6–95	3	—	—
Davis R. C.	6570	212	30.99	6–82	4	—	—
Davison B. F.	2319	78	29.73	5–52	1	—	—
Denness M. H.	47	1	47.00	1–36	—	—	—
Denning P. W.	33	1	33.00	1–4	—	—	—
Dixon J. H.	396	9	44.00	3–97	—	—	—
D'Oliveira B. L.	11836	449	26.36	6–29	14	2	—
Doshi D. R.	4305	219	19.65	7–29	13	1	—
Dudleston B.	717	22	32.59	4–6	—	—	—
Dudley-Jones R. D. L.	351	13	27.00	4–31	—	—	—
Dye J. C. J.	13838	588	23.53	7–45	20	1	—
Ealham A. G. E.	94	2	47.00	1–1	—	—	—
East R. E.	13441	525	25.60	8–63	24	4	—
Edmeades B. E. A.	9187	362	25.37	7–37	10	1	1
Edmonds P. H.	5740	217	26.45	7–38	9	3	—
Edrich J. H.	49	0	—	—	—	—	—
Edwards M. J.	179	2	89.50	2–53	—	—	—
Elder J. W. G.	47	1	47.00	1–13	—	—	—
Ellis G. P.	427	7	61.00	2–35	—	—	—
Ellis R.	379	6	63.16	1–3	—	—	—
Elms R. B.	2853	74	38.55	5–38	3	—	—

	Runs	Wkts	Avge	BB	5w inns	10w match	100w season
Emburey J. E.	473	8	59.12	3–50	—	—	—
Engineer F. M.	117	1	117.00	1–40	—	—	—
Faber M. J. J.	33	1	33.00	1–11	—	—	—
Featherstone N. G.	1155	39	29.61	3–32	—	—	—
Field M. N.	827	24	34.45	4–76	—	—	—
Fleming R. C. J.	522	7	74.57	3–91	—	—	—
Fletcher K. W. R.	1222	26	47.00	4–50	—	—	—
Foat J. C.	10	0	—	—	—	—	—
Fursdon E. D.	977	35	27.91	6–60	1	—	—
Gardom B. K.	700	17	41.17	6–139	1	—	—
Gavaskar S. M.	602	16	37.62	3–43	—	—	—
Gifford N.	25584	1264	20.24	8–28	65	11	3
Gilliat R. M. C.	106	2	53.00	1–3	—	—	—
Glover T. R.	0	0	—	—	—	—	—
Goddard G. F.	661	30	22.03	8–34	1	1	—
Gomes H. A.	532	12	44.33	4–22	—	—	—
Gooch G. A.	153	3	51.00	1–17	—	—	—
Good A. J.	63	1	63.00	1–63	—	—	—
Graham J. N.	12330	561	21.97	8–20	26	3	1
Graham-Brown J. M. H.	77	1	77.00	1–4	—	—	—
Graveney D. A.	2650	94	28.19	8–85	5	1	—
Graves P. J.	789	15	52.60	3–69	—	—	—
Greenidge C. G.	313	10	31.30	5–49	1	—	—
Greenidge G. A.	907	13	69.76	7–124	1	—	—
Greig A. W.	17989	643	27.97	8–25	25	7	—
Griffith M. G.	28	1	28.00	1–4	—	—	—
Griffiths B. J.	385	10	38.50	3–54	—	—	—
Hacker P. J.	31	0	—	—	—	—	—
Hampshire J. H.	1448	27	53.62	7–52	2	—	—
Hanley R. W.	1206	50	24.12	6–34	2	—	—
Hardie B. R.	19	0	—	—	—	—	—
Hardie K. M.	495	31	15.96	4–23	—	—	—
Hare W. H.	18	0	—	—	—	—	—
Harris M. J.	3165	74	42.77	4–16	—	—	—
Harrison S. C.	255	6	42.50	3–55	—	—	—
Harvey-Walker A. J.	262	9	29.11	2–8	—	—	—
Hassan B.	140	0	—	—	—	—	—
Hayes F. C.	15	0	—	—	—	—	—
Hayes P. J.	184	1	184.00	1–32	—	—	—
Headley R. G. A.	588	12	49.00	4–40	—	—	—
Hemmings E. E.	6280	207	30.33	7–57	8	1	—
Hemsley E. J. O.	1685	52	32.40	3–5	—	—	—
Hendrick M.	5411	234	23.12	8–45	7	2	—
Herman R. S.	11074	443	24.90	8–42	13	—	—
Higgs K.	30481	1293	23.57	7–19	41	5	5
Hill A.	34	0	—	—	—	—	—
Hill L. W.	36	0	—	—	—	—	—
Hills R. W.	173	5	34.60	4–24	—	—	—
Hobbs R. N. S.	25978	991	26.21	8–63	47	8	2
Hodgson A.	2194	86	25.51	5–36	1	—	—
Holder V. A.	13904	613	22.68	7–40	26	3	—
Howarth G. P.	853	32	26.65	5–32	1	—	—

185

	Runs	Wkts	Avge	BB	5w inns	10w match	100w season
Hughes D. P.	11411	381	29.95	7-24	15	2	—
Hutton R. A.	14866	625	23.78	8-50	21	3	—
Illingworth R.	37233	1882	19.78	9-42	98	11	10
Imran Khan	4842	171	28.31	6-54	7	1	—
Inchmore J. D.	1800	65	27.69	5-50	1	—	—
Intikhab Alam	30018	1146	26.19	8-54	69	12	1
Jackman R. D.	15875	679	23.37	8-40	31	3	—
Jackson E. J. W.	849	19	44.68	4-48	—	—	—
Jameson J. A.	3083	82	37.59	4-22	—	—	—
Jarrett G. M.	260	2	130.00	2-83	—	—	—
Jesty T. E.	6445	214	30.11	5-24	5	—	—
Johnson A. A.	1717	49	35.04	4-13	—	—	—
Johnson C.	260	4	65.00	2-22	—	—	—
Johnson G. W.	5703	176	32.40	6-35	3	1	—
Johnson I. N.	1175	27	43.51	4-61	—	—	—
Johnson P. D.	730	9	81.11	3-34	—	—	—
Jones A.	224	2	112.00	1-24	—	—	—
Jones A. A.	8244	297	27.75	9-51	15	3	—
Jones K. V.	6519	241	27.04	7-52	7	—	—
Joshi U. C.	11640	399	29.17	6-33	29	3	—
Julien B. D.	7175	256	28.02	7-63	7	—	—
Kallicharran A. I.	736	10	73.60	2-22	—	—	—
Kanhai R. B.	897	14	64.07	2-5	—	—	—
Kerslake R. C.	2491	109	22.85	6-77	4	—	—
Khan M. J.	6023	188	32.03	6-67	3	—	—
Kirmani S. M. H.	14	0	—	—	—	—	—
Kitchen M. J.	79	2	39.50	1-4	—	—	—
Knight R. D. V.	5856	169	34.65	6-44	2	—	—
Knott A. P. E.	77	1	77.00	1-40	—	—	—
Lamb T. M.	1639	63	26.01	5-57	2	—	—
Langford B. A.	34964	1410	24.79	9-26	83	16	5
Larkins W.	27	0	—	—	—	—	—
Latchman H. C.	12407	453	27.38	7-91	21	1	—
Leadbeater B.	5	1	5.00	1-1	—	—	—
Lee P.	7446	273	26.87	8-53	13	1	1
Lee R. J.	1081	29	37.27	4-56	—	—	—
Lever J. K.	11683	429	27.23	7-90	12	—	—
Lever P.	17209	669	25.72	7-70	24	2	—
Lewington P. J.	3086	103	29.96	6-37	2	—	—
Lewis A. R.	432	6	72.00	3-18	—	—	—
Lewis R. V.	104	1	104.00	1-59	—	—	—
Llewellyn M. J.	598	22	27.18	4-35	—	—	—
Lloyd B. J.	948	23	41.21	4-49	—	—	—
Lloyd C. H.	3824	106	36.07	4-48	—	—	—
Lloyd D.	3988	140	28.48	7-38	2	1	—
Luckhurst B. W.	2712	63	43.04	4-32	—	—	—
Lyon S. K. J.	205	1	205.00	1-36	—	—	—
McEwan K. S.	0	1	0.00	1-0	—	—	—
McKenzie G. D.	31649	1172	27.00	8-71	48	5	—
McVicker N. M.	9332	367	25.42	7-29	16	—	—
Madan Lal Sharma	3730	130	28.69	7-53	5	1	—
Maltby N.	97	2	48.50	2-43	—	—	—

	Runs	Wkts	Avge	BB	5w inns	10w match	100w season
Mankad A. V.	2125	46	46.19	5–21	2	—	—
Marriott D. A.	1990	67	29.70	5–71	1	—	—
Marshall R. P. T.	473	13	36.38	4–37	—	—	—
Maslin M.	44	0	—	—	—	—	—
Mazullah Khan	1844	79	23.34	8–97	3	1	—
Milburn C.	3171	99	32.03	6–59	1	—	—
Miller G.	1180	48	24.58	5–88	1	—	—
Milton C. A.	3630	79	45.94	5–64	1	—	—
Mohammad Nazir	4793	247	19.40	7–99	17	3	—
Monteith J. D.	542	33	16.42	7–38	3	1	—
Morley J. D.	2	0	—	—	—	—	—
Mortimore J. B.	41775	1802	23.18	8–59	75	8	3
Moseley H. R.	5021	209	24.02	5–24	5	—	—
Moses G. H.	176	9	19.55	5–31	1	—	—
Mottram T. J.	1659	77	21.54	6–63	3	—	—
Murray D. C.	235	4	58.75	2–50	—	—	—
Murray J. T.	243	6	40.50	2–10	—	—	—
Murrills T. J.	4	0	—	—	—	—	—
Murtagh A. J.	55	0	—	—	—	—	—
Mushtaq Mohammad	17397	755	23.04	7–18	31	2	—
Naik S. S.	151	4	37.75	2–75	—	—	—
Nanan N.	156	7	22.28	3–12	—	—	—
Naseer Malik	2284	83	27.51	8–160	6	—	—
Nash M. A.	12258	513	23.89	7–15	23	1	—
Nicholls D.	23	2	11.50	1–0	—	—	—
Nicholls R. B.	592	8	74.00	2–19	—	—	—
Nicholson A. G.	17118	866	19.76	9–62	39	3	2
Norman M. E. J. C.	164	2	82.00	2–0	—	—	—
Old C. M.	9221	419	22.00	7–20	13	1	—
Oldham S.	69	4	17.25	3–7	—	—	—
Ormrod A. J.	1015	25	40.60	5–27	1	—	—
Owen-Thomas D. R.	798	20	39.90	3–20	—	—	—
Page J. T.	95	1	95.00	1–14	—	—	—
Page M. H.	510	7	72.85	1–0	—	—	—
Parker J. M.	98	3	32.66	1–14	—	—	—
Parks J. M.	2230	51	43.72	3–23	—	—	—
Parsons A. E. W.	84	1	84.00	1–41	—	—	—
Patel B. P.	124	5	24.80	1–0	—	—	—
Phillipson C. P.	1914	57	33.57	6–56	2	—	—
Pilling H.	195	1	195.00	1–42	—	—	—
Pocock P. I.	23761	949	25.03	7–57	35	5	1
Pont K. R.	459	12	38.25	3–50	—	—	—
Prasanna E. A. S.	15756	688	22.90	8–50	44	6	—
Price J. S. E.	18989	807	23.53	8–48	26	4	—
Prideaux R. M.	176	3	58.66	2–13	—	—	—
Pridgeon A. P.	1006	19	52.94	3–50	—	—	—
Proxter M. J.	14561	802	18.15	9–71	32	7	1
Radley C. T.	24	2	12.00	1–7	—	—	—
Randall D. W.	36	0	—	—	—	—	—
Ratcliffe R. M.	467	9	51.88	5–44	1	—	—
Reidy B. W.	82	1	82.00	1–58	—	—	—
Rhodes H. J.	21113	1072	19.69	7–38	42	4	3

	Runs	Wkts	Avge	BB	5w inns	10w match	100w season
Rice C. E. B.	2333	103	22.65	5-65	1	—	—
Rice J. M.	1349	34	39.67	4-64	—	—	—
Richards B. A.	2179	59	36.93	7-63	1	—	—
Richards G.	33	0	—	—	—	—	—
Richards I. V. A.	750	19	39.47	3-49	—	—	—
Roberts A. M. E.	3257	181	17.99	8-47	7	—	—
Roberts C. P.	40	1	40.00	1-34	—	—	—
Robertson F.	233	17	13.70	6-58	1	—	—
Robinson A. L.	1775	73	24.31	6-61	3	—	—
Robinson P. J.	8031	293	27.40	7-10	10	1	—
Roope G. R. J.	5973	170	35.13	5-14	4	—	—
Rose B. C.	5	1	5.00	1-5	—	—	—
Rouse S. J.	3381	121	27.94	5-47	1	—	—
Rowe C. J. C.	246	5	49.20	2-60	—	—	—
Rowe L. G.	160	1	160.00	1-22	—	—	—
Russell D. P.	564	8	70.50	3-69	—	—	—
Russell P. E.	7178	240	29.90	6-61	4	—	—
Sadiq Mohammad	3552	135	26.31	5-29	5	—	—
Sainsbury P. J.	29355	1195	24.56	8-76	30	3	2
Sarfraz Nawaz	7436	285	26.09	8-27	11	2	—
Saville G. J.	76	3	25.33	2-30	—	—	—
Schepens M.	13	0	—	—	—	—	—
Schofield D.	112	5	22.40	5-42	1	—	—
Selvey M. W. W.	5183	174	29.78	6-43	8	—	—
Senghera R.	276	15	18.40	5-81	1	—	—
Shackleton J. H.	555	19	29.21	4-38	—	—	—
Shafiq Ahmed	1033	29	35.62	3-47	—	—	—
Sharpe P. J.	168	2	84.00	1-1	—	—	—
Shepherd D. R.	68	2	34.00	1-1	—	—	—
Shepherd J. N.	14777	567	26.06	8-40	33	1	—
Shuttleworth K.	11879	487	24.39	7-41	17	1	—
Sidebottom A.	140	5	28.00	3-61	—	—	—
Simmons J.	8684	306	28.37	7-64	9	2	—
Siviter K.	79	4	19.75	3-24	—	—	—
Smedley M. J.	4	0	—	—	—	—	—
Smith A. C.	3074	131	23.46	5-32	2	—	—
Smith D. M.	258	5	51.60	1-19	—	—	—
Smith M. J.	1820	57	31.92	4-13	—	—	—
Smith M. J. K.	305	5	61.00	1-0	—	—	—
Snellgrove K. L.	27	3	9.00	2-23	—	—	—
Snow J. A.	22263	1003	22.19	7-29	50	7	2
Snowden W.	13	0	—	—	—	—	—
Sobers G. S.	28941	1043	27.74	9-49	36	1	—
Solanky J. W.	2380	87	27.35	5-37	4	—	—
Solkar E. D.	6471	224	28.88	6-38	9	1	—
Spencer C. T.	36486	1367	26.69	9-63	47	6	1
Spencer J.	7258	275	26.39	6-19	10	1	—
Stallibrass M. J. D.	993	22	45.13	5-80	1	—	—
Stead B.	15129	551	27.45	8-44	19	2	—
Steele D. S.	4970	216	23.00	8-29	3	—	—
Steele J. F.	5131	191	26.86	7-29	4	—	—
Stephenson G. R.	10	0	—	—	—	—	—

	Runs	Wkts	Avge	BB	5w inns	10w match	100w seaso
Stevenson G. B.	138	5	27.60	2–23	—	—	—
Stevenson K.	654	18	36.33	4–127	—	—	—
Storey S. J.	12940	490	26.40	8–22	11	2	1
Stretton T. K.	293	4	73.25	2–71	—	—	—
Sullivan J.	2216	76	29.15	4–19	—	—	—
Swarbrook F. W.	8536	248	34.41	6–48	6	—	—
Swart P. D.	3480	134	25.97	6–85	2	1	—
Swetman R.	69	1	69.00	1–10	—	—	—
Swinburne J. W.	2281	83	27.48	6–57	4	1	—
Swindell R. S.	1466	43	34.09	6–97	3	—	—
Tavaré C. J.	6	0	—	—	—	—	—
Taylor D. J. S.	14	0	—	—	—	—	—
Taylor M. N. S.	17207	658	26.15	7–53	18	—	—
Taylor R. W.	25	0	—	—	—	—	—
Taylor W.	4712	175	26.92	6–42	5	1	—
Thackeray P. R.	1	0	—	—	—	—	—
Thomas R. J.	40	1	40.00	1–40	—	—	—
Thompson E. R.	1118	35	31.94	5–11	2	—	—
Thorn P. L.	227	4	56.75	2–53	—	—	—
Tidy W. N.	2775	81	34.25	5–24	3	—	—
Titmus F. J.	57876	2615	22.13	9–52	159	25	16
Todd P. A.	3	0	—	—	—	—	—
Tolchard J. G.	5	0	—	—	—	—	—
Tolchard R. W.	4	1	4.00	1–4	—	—	—
Topley P. A.	438	9	48.66	2–52	—	—	—
Torrens R.	166	13	12.76	7–40	1	—	—
Tunnicliffe C. J.	919	15	61.26	3–96	—	—	—
Tunnicliffe H. T.	274	7	39.14	3–55	—	—	—
Turner D. R.	68	1	68.00	1–4	—	—	—
Turner G. M.	188	5	37.60	3–18	—	—	—
Turner S.	7966	326	24.43	6–87	7	—	—
Underwood D. L.	25923	1333	19.44	9–28	90	29	7
Venkataraghavan S.	19753	834	23.68	9–93	48	15	—
Vernon M. J.	586	20	29.30	6–58	2	1	—
Verrinder A. O. C.	18	1	18.00	1–18	—	—	—
Virgin R. T.	321	4	80.25	1–6	—	—	—
Viswanath G. R.	323	6	53.83	2–45	—	—	—
Wadekar A. L.	908	21	43.23	2–0	—	—	—
Waller C. E.	3775	143	26.39	7–64	6	—	—
Waller G. de W.	4	0	—	—	—	—	—
Ward A.	7597	354	21.46	7–42	13	4	—
Wasim Bari	6	0	—	—	—	—	—
Wasim Raja	5640	210	26.85	8–65	16	3	—
Watts P. J.	8140	318	25.59	6–18	7	—	—
White R. A.	13863	490	28.29	7–41	19	3	—
Whitehouse J.	190	3	63.33	1–39	—	—	—
Wilkinson K. W.	1492	46	32.43	5–60	1	—	—
Wilkinson P. A.	2560	70	36.57	4–46	—	—	—
Wilkinson S. G.	9	0	—	—	—	—	—
Willey P.	4626	156	29.65	5–14	4	—	—
Williams D. L.	9150	341	26.83	7–60	12	1	—
Williams R. G.	76	2	38.00	1–36	—	—	—

	Runs	Wkts	Avge	BB	5w inns	10w match	100w season
Willis R. G. D.	7647	297	25.74	8–44	5	—	—
Wilson D.	24977	1189	21.00	8–36	50	8	5
Wisdom N.	33	2	16.50	1–0	—	—	—
Wood B.	5571	198	28.13	7–52	7	—	—
Woolmer R. A.	6061	254	23.86	7–47	11	1	—
Yardley T. J.	14	0	—	—	—	—	—
Yeabsley D. I.	105	5	21.00	3–45	—	—	—
Younis Ahmed	895	20	44.75	3–12	—	—	—
Zaheer Abbas	261	8	32.62	4–54	—	—	—

FIRST-CLASS CRICKET RECORDS

COMPLETE TO 30 SEPTEMBER 1974

Highest Innings Totals

1107	Victoria v New South Wales (Melbourne)	1926–27
1059	Victoria v Tasmania (Melbourne)	1922–23
951–7d	Sind v Baluchistan (Karachi)	1973–74
918	New South Wales v South Australia (Sydney)	1900–01
912–8d	Holkar v Mysore (Indore)	1945–46
910–6d	Railways v Dera Ismail Khan (Lahore)	1964–65
903–7d	England v Australia (Oval)	1938
887	Yorkshire v Warwickshire (Birmingham)	1896
849	England v West Indies (Kingston)	1929–30

NB   There are 22 instances of a side making 800 or more in an innings, the last occasion being 951–7 declared by Sind as above.

Lowest Innings Totals

12†	Oxford University v MCC and Ground (Oxford)	1877
12	Northamptonshire v Gloucestershire (Gloucester)	1907
13	Wellington v Nelson (Nelson)	1862–63
13	Auckland v Canterbury (Auckland)	1877–78
13	Nottinghamshire v Yorkshire (Nottingham)	1901
15	MCC v Surrey (Lord's)	1839
15†	Victoria v MCC (Melbourne)	1903–04
15†	Northamptonshire v Yorkshire (Northampton)	1908
15	Hampshire v Warwickshire (Birmingham)	1922
16	MCC and Ground v Surrey (Lord's)	1872
16	Derbyshire v Nottinghamshire (Nottingham)	1879
16	Surrey v Nottinghamshire (Oval)	1880
16	Warwickshire v Kent (Tonbridge)	1913
16	Trinidad v Barbados (Bridgetown)	1941–42
16	Border v Natal (East London)	1959–60

†Batted one man short.

NB   There are 26 instances of a side making less than 20 in an innings, the last occasion being 16 and 18 by Border v Natal at East London in 1959–60. The total of 34 is the lowest by one side in a match.

Highest Aggregates in a Match

2376	(38)	Bombay v Maharashtra (Poona)	1948–49
2078	(40)	Bombay v Holkar (Bombay)	1944–45
1981	(35)	England v South Africa (Durban)	1938–39
1929	(39)	New South Wales v South Australia (Sydney)	1925–26
1911	(34)	New South Wales v Victoria (Sydney)	1908–09
1905	(40)	Otago v Wellington (Dunedin)	1923–24

In England the highest are:

1723	(31)	England v Australia (Leeds) 5 day match	1948
1601	(29)	England v Australia (Lord's) 4 day match	1930
1502	(28)	MCC v New Zealanders (Lord's)	1927
1499	(31)	T. N. Pearce's XI v Australians (Scarborough)	1961

1496	(24)	England v Australia (Nottingham) 4 day match	1938
1494	(37)	England v Australia (Oval) 4 day match	1934
1492	(33)	Worcestershire v Oxford U (Worcester)	1904
1477	(32)	Hampshire v Oxford U (Southampton)	1913
1477	(33)	England v South Africa (Oval) 4 day match	1947
1475	(27)	Northamptonshire v Surrey (Northampton)	1920

Lowest Aggregates in a Match

105	(31)	MCC v Australians (Lord's)	1878
134	(30)	England v The B's (Lord's)	1831
147	(40)	Kent v Sussex (Sevenoaks)	1828
149	(30)	England v Kent (Lord's)	1858
151	(30)	Canterbury v Otago (Christchurch)	1866–67
153	(37)	MCC v Sussex (Lord's)	1843
153	(31)	Otago v Canterbury (Dunedin)	1896–97
156	(30)	Nelson v Wellington (Nelson)	1885–86
158	(22)	Surrey v Worcestershire (Oval)	1954

Wickets that fell given in parentheses.

Tie Matches

Due to the change of law made in 1948 for tie matches, a tie is now a rarity. The law states that only if the match is played out and the scores are equal is the result a tie.

The most recent tied matches are as follows:

Yorkshire (351-4d & 113) v Leicestershire (328 & 136) at
Huddersfield   1954
Sussex (172 & 120) v Hampshire (153 & 139) at Eastbourne   1955
Victoria (244 & 197) v New South Wales (281 & 160) at
Melbourne (St Kilda)   1956–57
(The first tie in Sheffield Shield cricket)
T. N. Pearce's XI (313-7d & 258) v New Zealanders (268 & 303-
8d) at Scarborough   1958
Essex (364-6d & 176-8d) v Gloucestershire (329 & 211) at Leyton   1959
Australia (505 & 232) v West Indies (453 & 284) at Brisbane   1960–61
(The first tie in Test cricket)
Bahawalpur (123 & 282) v Lahore B (127 & 278) at Bahawalpur   1961–62
Middlesex (327-5d & 123-9d) v Hampshire (277 & 173) at Portsmouth 1967
England XI (312-8d & 190-3d) v England Under-25 XI (320-9d &
182) at Scarborough   1968
Yorkshire (106-9d & 207) v Middlesex (102 & 211) at Bradford   1973

Highest Individual Scores

499	Hanif Mohammad, Karachi v Bahawalpur (Karachi)	1958–59
452*	D. G. Bradman, New South Wales v Queensland (Sydney)	1929–30
443*	B. B. Nimbalker, Maharashtra v Kathiawar (Poona)	1948–49
437	W. H. Ponsford, Victoria v Queensland (Melbourne)	1927–28
429	W. H. Ponsford, Victoria v Tasmania (Melbourne)	1922–23
428	Aftab Baloch, Sind v Baluchistan (Karachi)	1973–74
424	A. C. McLaren, Lancashire v Somerset (Taunton)	1895
385	B. Sutcliffe, Otago v Canterbury (Christchurch)	1952–53
383	C. W. Gregory, New South Wales v Queensland (Brisbane)	1906–07
369	D. G. Bradman, South Australia v Tasmania (Adelaide)	1935–36

365*	C. Hill, South Australia v New South Wales (Adelaide)	1900–01
365*	G. S. Sobers, West Indies v Pakistan (Kingston)	1957–58
364	L. Hutton, England v Australia (Oval)	1938
359*	V. M. Merchant, Bombay v Maharashtra (Bombay)	1943–44
359	R. B. Simpson, New South Wales v Queensland (Brisbane)	1963–64
357*	R. Abel, Surrey v Somerset (Oval)	1899
357	D. G. Bradman, South Australia v Victoria (Melbourne)	1935–36
356	B. A. Richards, South Australia v Western Australia (Perth)	1970–71
355	B. Sutcliffe, Otago v Auckland (Dunedin)	1949–50
352	W. H. Ponsford, Victoria v New South Wales (Melbourne)	1926–27

NB There are 88 instances of a batsman scoring 300 or more in an innings, the last occasion being 302 by L. G. Rowe for West Indies v England at Bridgetown in 1973–74.

Most Centuries in a Season

18	D. C. S. Compton	1947
16	J. B. Hobbs	1925
15	W. R. Hammond	1938
14	H. Sutcliffe	1932

Most Centuries in an Innings

6	for Holkar v Mysore (Indore)	1945–46
5	for New South Wales v South Australia (Sydney)	1900–01
5	for Australia v West Indies (Kingston)	1954–55

Most Centuries in Successive Innings

6	C. B. Fry	1901
6	D. G. Bradman	1938–39
6	M. J. Procter	1970–71
5	E. D. Weekes	1955–56

NB The feat of scoring 4 centuries in successive innings has been achieved on 27 occasions.

Most Centuries in Succession in Test Matches

5	E. D. Weekes, West Indies	1947–48 and 1948–49
4	J. H. Fingleton, Australia	1935–36 and 1936–37
4	A. Melville, South Africa	1938–39 and 1947

Two Double Centuries in a Match

A. E. Fagg, 244 and 202* for Kent v Essex (Colchester)	1938

A Double Century and a Century in a Match

C. B. Fry, 125 and 229, Sussex v Surrey (Hove)	1900
W. W. Armstrong, 157* and 245, Victoria v South Australia (Melbourne)	1920–21
H. T. W. Hardinge, 207 and 102* for Kent v Surrey (Blackheath)	1921
C. P. Mead, 113 and 224, Hampshire v Sussex (Horsham)	1921
K. S. Duleepsinhji, 115 and 246, Sussex v Kent (Hastings)	1929
D. G. Bradman, 124 and 225, Woodfull's XI v Ryder's XI (Sydney)	1929–30
B. Sutcliffe, 243 and 100*, New Zealanders v Essex (Southend)	1949
M. R. Hallam, 210* and 157, Leicestershire v Glamorgan (Leicester)	1959
M. R. Hallam, 203* and 143* Leicestershire v Sussex (Worthing)	1961

Hanumant Singh, 109 and 213*, Rajasthan v Bombay (Bombay)   1966–67
Salahuddin, 256 and 102*, Karachi v East Pakistan (Karachi)   1968–69
K. D. Walters, 242 and 103, Australia v West Indies (Sydney)   1968–69
S. M. Gavaskar, 124 and 220, India v West Indies (P. of Spain)   1970–71
L. G. Rowe, 214 and 100*, West Indies v New Zealand (Kingston)   1971–72
G. S. Chappell, 247* and 133, Australia v New Zealand
(Wellington)   1973–74
L. Baichan, 216* and 102, Berbice v Demerara (Georgetown)   1973–74

Two Centuries in a Match on Most Occasions
7 W. R. Hammond   6 J. B. Hobbs   5 C. B. Fry

NB 9 batsmen have achieved the feat on four occasions, 20 batsmen
on three occasions and 36 batsmen on two occasions.

Most Centuries
J. B. Hobbs, 197 (175 in England); E. Hendren 170 (151); W. R.
Hammond, 167 (134); C. P. Mead, 153 (145); H. Sutcliffe, 149 (135);
F. E. Woolley, 145 (135); L. Hutton, 129 (105); W. G. Grace, 124 (123);
D. C. S. Compton, 123 (92); T. W. Graveney, 122 (91); D. G. Bradman,
117 (41); A. Sandham, 107 (87); M. C. Cowdrey, 105 (79); T. Hayward,
104 (100); E. Tyldesley, 102 (94); L. E. G. Ames, 102 (89).

Highest Individual Batting Aggregates in a Season

Runs		Season	Inngs	NO	HS	Avge	100s
3,816	D. C. S. Compton	1947	50	8	246	90.85	18
3,539	W. J. Edrich	1947	52	8	267*	80.43	12

NB The feat of scoring 3,000 runs in a season has been achieved on
28 occasions, the last instance being by W. E. Alley (3,019 runs, av. 59.96)
in 1961.

Partnerships for First Wicket
555	H. Sutcliffe and P. Holmes, Yorkshire v Essex (Leyton)	1932
554	J. T. Brown and J. Tunnicliffe, Yorkshire v Derbyshire (Chesterfield)	1898
490	E. H. Bowley and John Langridge, Sussex v Middlesex (Hove)	1933
456	W. H. Ponsford and E. R. Mayne, Victoria v Queensland (Melbourne)	1923–24
428	J. B. Hobbs and A. Sandham, Surrey v Oxford U (Oval)	1926
424	J. F. W. Nicholson and I. J. Siedle, Natal v Orange Free State (Bloemfontein)	1926–27
413	V. Mankad and P. Roy, India v New Zealand (Madras)	1955–56
405	C. P. S. Chauhan and M. Gupte, Maharashtra v Vidarbha (Poona)	1972–73

Partnerships for Second Wicket
465*	J. A. Jameson and R. B. Kanhai, Warwickshire v Gloucestershire (Birmingham)	1974
455	K. V. Bhandarkar and B. B. Nimbalkar, Maharashtra v Kathiawar (Poona)	1948–49
451	D. G. Bradman and W. H. Ponsford, Australia v England (Oval)	1934
446	C. C. Hunte and G. S. Sobers, West Indies v Pakistan (Kingston)	1957–58

429* J. G. Dewes and G. H. G. Doggart, Cambridge U v Essex
(Cambridge)   1949
398 W. Gunn and A. Shrewsbury, Nottinghamshire v Sussex
(Nottingham)   1890

Partnerships for Third Wicket

445 P. E. Whitelaw and W. N. Carson, Auckland v Otago
(Dunedin)   1936–37
434 J. B. Stollmeyer and G. E. Gomez, Trinidad v British
Guiana (Port of Spain)   1946–47
424* W. J. Edrich and D. C. S. Compton, Middlesex v Somerset
(Lord's)   1948
410 R. S. Modi and L. Amarnath, India v Rest (Calcutta)   1946–47
399 R. T. Simpson and D. C. S. Compton, MCC v NE
Transvaal (Benoni)   1948–49

Partnerships for Fourth Wicket

577 Gul Mahomed and S. Hazare, Baroda v Holkar (Baroda) 1946–47
574* C. L. Walcott and F. M. Worrell, Barbados v Trinidad
(Port of Spain)   1945–46
502* F. M. Worrell and J. D. C. Goddard, Barbados v Trinidad
(Bridgetown)   1943–44
448 R. Abel and T. Hayward, Surrey v Yorkshire (Oval)   1899
424 I. S. Lee and S. O. Quin, Victoria v Tasmania (Melbourne) 1933–34
411 P. B. H. May and M. C. Cowdrey, England v West Indies
(Birmingham)   1957
410 G. Abraham and B. Pandit, Kerala v Andhra (Pulghat)   1959–60
402 W. Watson and T. W. Graveney, MCC v British Guiana
(Georgetown)   1953–54
402 R. B. Kanhai and K. Ibadulla, Warwickshire v
Nottinghamshire (Nottingham)   1968

Partnerships for Fifth Wicket

405 D. G. Bradman and S. G. Barnes, Australia v England
(Sydney)   1946–47
397 W. Bardsley and C. Kellaway, New South Wales v South
Australia (Sydney)   1920–21
393 E. G. Arnold and W. B. Burns, Worcestershire v
Warwickshire (Birmingham)   1909
360 V. M. Merchant and M. N. Raiji, Bombay v Hyderabad
(Bombay)   1947–48
347 D. Brookes and D. Barrick, Northamptonshire v Essex
(Northampton)   1952

Partnerships for Sixth Wicket

487* G. Headley and C. C. Passailaigue, Jamaica v Lord
Tennyson's XI (Kingston)   1931–32
428 W. W. Armstrong and M. A. Noble, Australians v Sussex
(Hove)   1902
411 R. M. Poore and E. G. Wynyard, Hampshire v Somerset
(Taunton)   1899
376 R. Subba Row and A. Lightfoot, Northamptonshire v
Surrey (Oval)   1958
371 V. M. Merchant and R. S. Modi, Bombay v Maharashtra
(Bombay)   1943–44

Partnerships for Seventh Wicket

347 D. Atkinson and C. Depeiza, West Indies v Australia
(Bridgetown)   1954–55
344 K. S. Ranjitsinhji and W. Newham, Sussex v Essex (Leyton) 1902
340 K. J. Key and H. Philipson, Oxford U v Middlesex
(Chiswick Park)   1887
336 F. C. W. Newman and C. R. Maxwell, Cahn's XI v
Leicestershire (Nottingham)   1935
335 C. W. Andrews and E. C. Bensted, Queensland v New
South Wales (Sydney)   1934–35

Partnerships for Eighth Wicket

433 V. T. Trumper and A. Sims, Australians v Canterbury
(Christchurch)   1913–14
292 R. Peel and Lord Hawke, Yorkshire v Warwickshire
(Birmingham)   1896
270 V. T. Trumper and E. P. Barbour, New South Wales v
Victoria (Sydney)   1912–13
263 D. R. Wilcox and R. M. Taylor, Essex v Warwickshire
(Southend)   1946
255 E. A. V. Williams and E. A. Martindale, Barbados v
Trinidad (Bridgetown)   1935–36

Partnerships for Ninth Wicket

283 A. R. Warren and J. Chapman, Derbyshire v Warwickshire
(Blackwell)   1910
251 J. W. H. T. Douglas and S. N. Hare, Essex v Derbyshire
(Leyton)   1921
245 V. S. Hazare and N. D. Nagarwalla, Maharashtra v Baroda
(Poona)   1939–40
239 H. B. Cave and I. B. Leggat, Central Districts v Otago
(Dunedin)   1952–53
232 C. Hill and E. Walkley, South Australia v New South Wales
(Adelaide)   1900–01

Partnerships for Tenth Wicket

307 A. F. Kippax and J. E. H. Hooker, New South Wales v
Victoria (Melbourne)   1928–29
249 C. T. Sarwate and S. N. Bannerjee, Indians v Surrey (Oval) 1946
235 F. E. Woolley and A. Fielder, Kent v Worcestershire
(Stourbridge)   1909
230 R. W. Nicholls and W. Roche, Middlesex v Kent (Lord's)   1899
218 F. H. Vigar and T. P. B. Smith, Essex v Derbyshire
(Chesterfield)   1947

Most Wickets in a Season

W		Season	O	M	R	Avge
304	A. P. Freeman	1928	1,976.1	423	5,489	18.05
298	A. P. Freeman	1933	2,039	651	4,549	15.26

NB The feat of taking 250 wickets in a season has been achieved on
12 occasions, the last instance being by A. P. Freeman in 1933 as above.
200 or more wickets in a season have been taken on 59 occasions, the last
instance being by G. A. R. Lock (212 wkts, av 12.02) in 1957.

All Ten Wickets in an Innings

The feat has been achieved on 69 occasions.

On three occasions: A. P. Freeman, 1929, 1930, and 1931.

On two occasions: J. C. Laker, 1956, H. Verity, 1931 and 1932, V. E. Walker 1859 and 1865.

Instances since the war:
W. E. Hollies, Warwickshire v Nottinghamshire (Birmingham) 1946; J. M. Sims of Middlesex playing for East v West (Kingston) 1948; J. K. Graveney, Gloucestershire v Derbyshire (Chesterfield) 1949; T. E. Bailey, Essex v Lancashire (Clacton) 1949; R. Berry, Lancashire v Worcestershire (Blackpool) 1953; S. P. Gupte, Bombay v Pakistan Services (Bombay), 1954-55; J. C. Laker, Surrey v Australians (Oval) 1956; J. C. Laker, England v Australia (Manchester) 1956; G. A. R. Lock, Surrey v Kent, (Blackheath) 1956; K. Smales, Nottinghamshire v Gloucestershire (Stroud) 1956; P. Chatterjee, Bengal v Assam (Jorhat) 1956-57; J. D. Bannister, Warwickshire v Combined Services (Birmingham) 1959; A. J. G. Pearson, Cambridge U v Leicestershire (Loughborough) 1961; N. I. Thomson, Sussex v Warwickshire (Worthing) 1964; P. Allan, Queensland v Victoria (Melbourne) 1965-66; I. Brayshaw, Western Australia v Victoria (Perth) 1967-68; Shahid Mahmood, Karachi Whites v Khairpur (Karachi) 1969-70.

Nineteen Wickets in a Match

J. C. Laker 19-90 (9-37 and 10-53), England v Australia (Manchester), 1956.

Eighteen Wickets in a Match

H. A. Arkwright 18-96 (9-43 and 9-53), MCC v Gentlemen of Kent (Canterbury) 1861, (twelve-a-side match).

Seventeen Wickets in a Match

The feat has been achieved on 18 occasions.

Instances between the two wars were: A. P. Freeman (for 67 runs), Kent v Sussex (Brighton) 1922; F. C. L. Matthews (89 runs), Nottinghamshire v Northamptonshire (Nottingham) 1923; C. W. L. Parker (56 runs) Gloucestershire v Essex (Gloucester) 1925; G. R. Cox (106 runs), Sussex v Warwickshire (Horsham) 1926; A. P. Freeman (92 runs), Kent v Warwickshire (Folkstone) 1932; H. Verity (91 runs), Yorkshire v Essex (Leyton) 1933; J. C. Clay (212 runs), Glamorgan v Worcestershire (Swansea) 1937; T. W. Goddard (106 runs), Gloucestershire v Kent (Bristol) 1939. There has been no instance since the last war.

Most hat-tricks in a Career

7 D. V. P. Wright.

6 T. W. Goddard, C. W. L. Parker.

5 S. Haigh, V. W. C. Jupp, A. E. G. Rhodes, F. A. Tarrant.

NB 8 bowlers have achieved the feat on four occasions and 24 bowlers on three occasions.

The 'Double' Event

3,000 runs and 100 wickets: J. H. Parks, 1937.

2,000 runs and 200 wickets: G. H. Hirst, 1906.

2,000 runs and 100 wickets: F. E. Woolley (4), J. W. Hearne (3), G. H. Hirst (2), W. Rhodes (2), T. E. Bailey, E. Davies, W. G. Grace, G. L. Jessop, V. W. C. Jupp, James Langridge, F. A. Tarrant, C. L. Townsend, L. F. Townsend.

1,000 runs and 200 wickets: M. W. Tate (3), A. E. Trott (2), A. S. Kennedy.

Most 'Doubles': W. Rhodes (16), G. H. Hirst (14), V. W. C. Jupp (10)

'Double' in first season: D. B. Close, 1949. At the age of 18, Close is the youngest player ever to perform this feat.

The feat of scoring 1,000 runs and taking 100 wickets has been achieved on 302 occasions, the last instance being by F. J. Titmus in 1967.

Fielding

Most catches in a season:	78 W. R. Hammond	1928
	77 M. J. Stewart	1957
Most catches in a match:	10 W. R. Hammond, Gloucestershire v Surrey (Cheltenham)	1928
Most catches in an innings:	7 M. J. Stewart, Surrey v Northamptonshire (Northampton)	1957
	7 A. S. Brown, Gloucestershire v Nottinghamshire (Nottingham)	1966

Wicket-keeping

Most Dismissals in a Season

127 (79 ct 48 st), L. E. G. Ames   1929

NB   The feat of making 100 dismissals in a season has been achieved on 12 occasions, the last instance being by R. Booth (100 dismissals— 91 ct 9 st) in 1964.

Most dismissals in a match:	12 E. Pooley (8 ct 4 st) Surrey v Sussex (Oval)	1868
	12 D. Tallon (9 ct 3 st), Queensland v New South Wales (Sydney)	1938–39
	12 H. B. Taber (9 ct 3 st), New South Wales v South Australia (Adelaide)	1968–69
Most catches in a match:	11 A. Long, Surrey v Sussex (Hove)	1964
	10 A. E. Wilson, Gloucestershire v Hampshire (Portsmouth)	1953
	10 L. A. Johnson, Northamptonshire v Sussex (Worthing)	1963
	10 R. W. Taylor, Derbyshire v Hampshire (Chesterfield)	1963
Most dismissals in an innings:	8 A. T. W. Grout (8 ct) Queensland v W. Australia (Brisbane)	1959–60

TEST CRICKET RECORDS

(To 31 October 1974)

Matches between England and Rest of the World 1970 and between
Australia and Rest of the World 1971–72 are excluded

HIGHEST INNINGS TOTALS

903—7d	England v Australia (Oval)	1938
849	England v West Indies (Kingston)	1929–30
790—3d	West Indies v Pakistan (Kingston)	1957–58
758—8d	Australia v West Indies (Kingston)	1954–55
729—6d	Australia v England (Lord's)	1930
701	Australia v England (Oval)	1934
695	Australia v England (Oval)	1930
681—8d	West Indies v England (Port of Spain)	1953–54
674	Australia v India (Adelaide)	1947–48
668	Australia v West Indies (Bridgetown)	1954–55
659—8d	Australia v England (Sydney)	1946–47
658—8d	England v Australia (Nottingham)	1938
657—8d	Pakistan v West Indies (Bridgetown)	1957–58
656—8d	Australia v England (Manchester)	1964
654—5	England v South Africa (Durban)	1938–39
652—8d	West Indies v England (Lord's)	1973
650—6d	Australia v West Indies (Bridgetown)	1964–65

The highest innings for the countries not mentioned above are:

622—9d	South Africa v Australia (Durban)	1969–70
551—9d	New Zealand v England (Lord's)	1973
539—9d	India v Pakistan (Madras)	1960–61

NB There are 39 instances of a side making 600 or more in an innings in a Test Match.

LOWEST INNINGS TOTALS

26	New Zealand v England (Auckland)	1954–55
30	South Africa v England (Port Elizabeth)	1895–96
30	South Africa v England (Birmingham)	1924
35	South Africa v England (Cape Town)	1898–99
36	Australia v England (Birmingham)	1902
36	South Africa v Australia (Melbourne)	1931–32
42	Australia v England (Sydney)	1887–88
42	New Zealand v Australia (Wellington)	1945–46
42†	India v England (Lord's)	1974
43	South Africa v England (Cape Town)	1888–89
44	Australia v England (Oval)	1896
45	England v Australia (Sydney)	1886–87
45	South Africa v Australia (Melbourne)	1931–32
47	South Africa v England (Cape Town)	1888–89
47	New Zealand v England (Lord's)	1958

†Batted one man short

The lowest innings for the countries not mentioned above are:

76	West Indies v Pakistan (Dacca)	1958–59
87	Pakistan v England (Lord's)	1954

HIGHEST INDIVIDUAL INNINGS

365* G. S. Sobers: West Indies v Pakistan (Kingston)   1957–58
364 L. Hutton: England v Australia (Oval)   1938
337 Hanif Mohammad: Pakistan v West Indies (Bridgetown)   1957–58
336* W. R. Hammond: England v New Zealand (Auckland)   1932–33
334 D. G. Bradman: Australia v England (Leeds)   1930
325 A. Sandham: England v West Indies (Kingston)   1929–30
311 R. B. Simpson: Australia v England (Manchester)   1964
310* J. H. Edrich: England v New Zealand (Leeds)   1965
307 R. M. Cowper: Australia v England (Melbourne)   1965–66
304 D. G. Bradman: Australia v England (Leeds)   1934
302 L. G. Rowe: West Indies v England (Bridgetown)   1973–74
299* D. G. Bradman: Australia v South Africa (Adelaide)   1931–32
287 R. E. Foster: England v Australia (Sydney)   1903–04
285* P. B. H. May: England v West Indies (Birmingham)   1957
278 D. C. S. Compton: England v Pakistan (Nottingham)   1954
274 R. G. Pollock: South Africa v Australia (Durban)   1969–70
274 Zaheer Abbas: Pakistan v England (Birmingham)   1971
270* G. A. Headley: West Indies v England (Kingston)   1934–35
270 D. G. Bradman: Australia v England (Melbourne)   1936–37
266 W. H. Ponsford: Australia v England (Oval)   1934
262* D. L. Amiss: England v West Indies (Kingston)   1973–74
261 F. M. Worrell: West Indies v England (Nottingham)   1950
260 C. C. Hunte: West Indies v Pakistan (Kingston)   1957–58
259 G. M. Turner: New Zealand v West Indies (Georgetown)   1971–72
258 T. W. Graveney: England v West Indies (Nottingham)   1957
258 S. M. Nurse: West Indies v New Zealand (Christchurch) 1968–69
256 R. B. Kanhai: West Indies v India (Calcutta)   1958–59
256 K. F. Barrington: England v Australia (Manchester)   1964
255* D. J. McGlew: South Africa v New Zealand (Wellington) 1952–53
254 D. G. Bradman: Australia v England (Lord's)   1930
251 W. R. Hammond: England v Australia (Sydney)   1928–29

The highest individual innings for India is:

231 V. Mankad: India v New Zealand (Madras)   1955–56

NB There are 104 instances of a double-century being scored in a Test Match.

HIGHEST RUN AGGREGATES IN A TEST RUBBER

R		Season	T	I	NO	HS	Avge	100s	50s
974	D. G. Bradman (A v E)	1930	5	7	0	334	139.14	4	—
905	W. R. Hammond (E v A)	1928–29	5	9	1	251	113.12	4	—
834	R. N. Harvey (A v SA)	1952–53	5	9	0	205	92.66	4	3
827	C. L. Walcott (WI v A)	1954–55	5	10	0	155	82.70	5	2
824	G. S. Sobers (WI v P)	1957–58	5	8	2	365*	137.33	3	3
810	D. G. Bradman (A v E)	1936–37	5	9	0	270	90.00	3	1
806	D. G. Bradman (A v SA)	1931–32	5	5	1	299*	201.50	4	—
779	E. D. Weekes (WI v I)	1948–49	5	7	0	194	111.28	4	2
774	S. M. Gavaskar (I v WI)	1970–71	4	8	3	220	154.80	4	3
758	D. G. Bradman (A v E)	1934	5	8	0	304	94.75	2	1
753	D.C.S. Compton (E v SA)	1947	5	8	0	208	94.12	4	2

RECORD WICKET PARTNERSHIPS—ALL TEST CRICKET

1st 413 V. Mankad & P. Roy: I v NZ (Madras)   1955–56
2nd 451 W. H. Ponsford & D. G. Bradman: A v E (Oval)   1934
3rd 370 W. J. Edrich & D. C. S. Compton: E v SA (Lord's)   1947

4th 411 P. B. H. May & M. C. Cowdrey: E v WI (Birm'ham) 1957
5th 405 S. G. Barnes & D. G. Bradman: A v E (Sydney) 1946–47
6th 346 J. H. Fingleton & D. G. Bradman: A v E (Melbourne) 1936–37
7th 347 D. Atkinson & C. C. Depeiza: WI v A (Bridgetown) 1954–55
8th 246 L. E. G. Ames & G. O. Allen: E v NZ (Lord's) 1931
9th 190 Asif Iqbal & Intikhab Alam: P v E (Oval) 1967
10th 151 B. F. Hastings & R. O. Collinge: NZ v P (Auckland) 1972–73

WICKET PARTNERSHIPS OF OVER 300
451 2nd W. H. Ponsford & D. G. Bradman: A v E (Oval) 1934
446 2nd C. C. Hunte & G. S. Sobers: WI v P (Kingston) 1957–58
413 1st V. Mankad & P. Roy: I v NZ (Madras) 1955–56
411 4th P. B. H. May & M. C. Cowdrey: E v WI (Birm'ham) 1957
405 5th S. G. Barnes & D. G. Bradman: A v E (Sydney) 1946–47
399 4th G. S. Sobers & F. M. Worrell: WI v E (Bridgetown) 1959–60
388 4th W. H. Ponsford & D. G. Bradman: A v E (Leeds) 1934
387 1st G. M. Turner & T. W. Jarvis: NZ v WI (Georgetown) 1971–72
382 2nd L. Hutton & M. Leyland: E v A (Oval) 1938
382 1st W. M. Lawry & R. B. Simpson: A v WI (Bridgetown) 1964–65
370 3rd W. J. Edrich & D. C. S. Compton: E v SA (Lord's) 1947
369 2nd J. H. Edrich & K. F. Barrington: E v NZ (Leeds) 1965
359 1st L. Hutton & C. Washbrook: E v SA (Johannesburg) 1948–49
350 4th Mushtaq Mohammad & Asif Iqbal: P v NZ (Dunedin) 1972–73
347 7th D. Atkinson & C. C. Depeiza: WI v A (Bridgetown) 1954–55
346 6th J. H. Fingleton & D. G. Bradman: A v E (Melbourne) 1936–37
341 3rd E. J. Barlow & R. G. Pollock: SA v A (Adelaide) 1963–64
338 3rd E. D. Weekes & F. M. Worrell: WI v E (Port of Spain) 1953–54
336 4th W. M. Lawry & K. D. Walters: A v WI (Sydney) 1968–69
323 1st J. B. Hobbs & W. Rhodes: E v A (Melbourne) 1911–12
319 3rd A. Melville & A. D. Nourse, Jun: SA v E (Nottingham) 1947
308 7th Waqar Hasan & Imtiaz Ahmed: P v NZ (Lahore) 1955–56
301 2nd A. R. Morris & D. G. Bradman: A v E (Leeds) 1948

HAT-TRICKS
F. R. Spofforth	Australia v England (Melbourne)	1878–79
W. Bates	England v Australia (Melbourne)	1882–83
J. Briggs	England v Australia (Sydney)	1891–92
G. A. Lohmann	England v South Africa (Port Elizabeth)	1895–96
J. T. Hearne	England v Australia (Leeds)	1899
H. Trumble	Australia v England (Melbourne)	1901–02
H. Trumble	Australia v England (Melbourne)	1903–04
T. J. Matthews (2)†	Australia v South Africa (Manchester)	1912
M. J. C. Allom‡	England v New Zealand (Christchurch)	1929–30
T. W. Goddard	England v South Africa (Johannesburg)	1938–39
P. J. Loader	England v West Indies (Leeds)	1957
L. F. Kline	Australia v South Africa (Cape Town)	1957–58
W. W. Hall	West Indies v Pakistan (Lahore)	1958–59
G. M. Griffin	South Africa v England (Lord's)	1960
L. R. Gibbs	West Indies v Australia (Adelaide)	1960–61

†Matthews achieved the hat-trick in each innings.
‡Allom took four wickets with five consecutive balls.

NINE OR TEN WICKETS IN AN INNINGS
10–53 J. C. Laker: England v Australia (Manchester) 1956
9–28 G. A. Lohmann: England v South Africa (Johannesb'g) 1895–96

9—37 J. C. Laker: England v Australia (Manchester)   1956
9—69 J. M. Patel: India v Australia (Kanpur)   1959–60
9—95 J. M. Noreiga: West Indies v India (Port of Spain)   1970–71
9—102 S. P. Gupte: India v West Indies (Kanpur)   1958–59
9—103 S. F. Barnes: England v South Africa (Johannesburg)   1913–14
9—113 H. J. Tayfield: South Africa v England (Johannesburg)   1956–57
9—121 A. A. Mailey: Australia v England (Melbourne)   1920–21

NB There are 32 instances of a bowler taking 8 wickets in an innings in a Test Match.

FIFTEEN OR MORE WICKETS IN A MATCH

19—90 J. C. Laker: England v Australia (Manchester)   1956
17—159 S. F. Barnes: England v South Africa (Johannesburg)   1913–14
16—137 R. A. L. Massie: Australia v England (Lord's)   1972
15—28 J. Briggs: England v South Africa (Cape Town)   1888–89
15—45 G. A. Lohmann: England v South Africa (Pt. Elizabeth)   1895–96
15—99 C. Blythe: England v South Africa (Leeds)   1907
15—104 H. Verity: England v Australia (Lord's)   1934
15—124 W. Rhodes: England v Australia (Melbourne)   1903–04

NB There are 6 instances of a bowler taking 14 wickets in a Test Match.

HIGHEST WICKET AGGREGATES IN A TEST RUBBER

W.		Season	Tests	Balls	Mdns	Runs	Avge	5 wI	10 wM
49	S. F. Barnes (E v SA)	1913–14	4	1356	56	536	10.93	7	3
46	J. C. Laker (E v A)	1956	5	1703	127	442	9.60	4	2
44	C. V. Grimmett (A v SA)	1935–36	5	2077	140	642	14.59	5	3
39	A. V. Bedser (E v A)	1953	5	1591	48	682	17.48	5	1
38	M. W. Tate (E v A)	1924–25	5	2528	62	881	23.18	5	1
37	W. J. Whitty (A v SA)	1910–11	5	1395	55	632	17.08	2	—
37	H. J. Tayfield (SA v E)	1956–57	5	2280	105	636	17.18	4	1
36	A. E. E. Vogler (E v SA)	1909–10	5	1349	33	783	21.75	4	1
36	A. A. Mailey (A v E)	1920–21	5	1463	27	946	26.27	4	2
35	G. A. Lohmann (E v SA)	1895–96	3	520	38	203	5.80	4	2
35	B. S. Chandrasekhar (I v E)	1972–73	5	1747	83	662	18.91	4	—

MOST WICKET-KEEPING DISMISSALS IN AN INNINGS

6 (6ct) A. T. W. Grout, Australia v South Africa (Johannesburg) 1957–58
6 (6ct) D. Lindsay, South Africa v Australia (Johannesburg)   1966–67
6 (6ct) J. T. Murray, England v India (Lord's)   1967

MOST WICKET-KEEPING DISMISSALS IN A MATCH

9 (8ct, 1st) G. R. A. Langley, Australia v England (Lord's)   1956

MOST WICKET-KEEPING DISMISSALS IN A SERIES

26 (23ct, 3st) J. H. B. Waite, South Africa v New Zealand   1961–62
24 (22ct, 2st) D. L. Murray, West Indies v England   1963
24 (24ct) D. Lindsay, South Africa v Australia   1966–67
24 (21ct, 3st) A. P. E. Knott, England v Australia   1970–71

HIGHEST WICKET-KEEPING DISMISSAL AGGREGATES

Total			Tests	Ct	St
219	T. G. Evans	(E)	91	173	46
187	A. T. W. Grout	(A)	51	163	24
185	A. P. E. Knott	(E)	61	170	15

141	J. H. B. Waite	(SA)	50	124	17		
130	W. A. Oldfield	(A)	54	78	52		
114	J. M. Parks	(E)	46	103	11		
100	R. W. Marsh	(A)	25	94	6		

NB Parks' figures include 2 catches as a fielder.

HIGHEST RUN AGGREGATES

Runs			Tests	Inns	NO	HS	Avge	100s	50s
8032	G. S. Sobers	(WI)	93	160	21	365*	57.78	26	30
7459	M. C. Cowdrey	(E)	109	179	15	182	45.48	22	38
7249	W. R. Hammond	(E)	85	140	16	336*	58.45	22	24
6996	D. G. Bradman	(A)	52	80	10	334	99.94	29	13
6971	L. Hutton	(E)	79	138	15	364	56.67	19	33
6806	K. F. Barrington	(E)	82	131	15	256	58.67	20	35
6227	R. B. Kanhai	(WI)	79	137	6	256	47.53	15	28
6149	R. N. Harvey	(A)	79	137	10	205	48.41	21	24
5807	D. C. S. Compton	(E)	78	131	15	278	50.06	17	28
5410	J. B. Hobbs	(E)	61	102	7	211	56.94	15	28
5234	W. M. Lawry	(A)	67	123	12	210	47.15	13	27
4882	T. W. Graveney	(E)	79	123	13	258	44.38	11	20
4579	G. Boycott	(E)	63	110	14	246*	47.69	12	26
4555	H. Sutcliffe	(E)	54	84	9	194	60.73	16	23
4537	P. B. H. May	(E)	66	106	9	285*	46.77	13	22
4502	E. R. Dexter	(E)	62	102	8	205	47.89	9	27
4455	E. D. Weekes	(WI)	48	81	5	207	58.61	15	19
4230	J. H. Edrich	(E)	65	106	7	310*	42.72	11	18
4131	R. B. Simpson	(A)	52	92	7	311	48.60	8	24
3922	I. M. Chappell	(A)	56	100	6	196	41.72	12	17
3915	Hanif Mohammad	(P)	55	97	8	337	43.98	12	15
3860	F. M. Worrell	(WI)	51	87	9	261	49.48	9	22
3798	C. L. Walcott	(WI)	44	74	7	220	56.68	15	14
3690	I. R. Redpath	(A)	54	97	10	171	42.41	4	26
3633	K. D. Walters	(A)	47	80	8	242	50.45	11	22
3631	P. R. Umrigar	(I)	59	94	8	223	42.22	12	14
3533	A. R. Morris	(A)	46	79	3	206	46.48	12	12
3525	E. H. Hendren	(E)	51	83	9	205*	47.63	7	21
3471	B. Mitchell	(SA)	42	80	9	189*	48.88	8	21
3431	J. R. Reid	(NZ)	58	108	5	142	33.31	6	22
3412	C. Hill	(A)	49	89	2	191	39.21	7	19
3283	F. E. Woolley	(E)	64	98	7	154	36.07	5	23
3245	C. C. Hunte	(WI)	44	78	6	260	45.06	8	13
3209	V. L. Manjrekar	(I)	55	92	10	189*	39.13	7	15
3164	V. T. Trumper	(A)	48	89	8	214*	39.06	8	13
3106	C. C. McDonald	(A)	47	83	4	170	39.31	5	17
3104	B. F. Butcher	(WI)	44	78	6	209*	43.11	7	16
3073	A. L. Hassett	(A)	43	69	3	198*	46.56	10	11
3061	C. G. Borde	(I)	55	97	11	177*	35.59	5	18

HIGHEST WICKET AGGREGATES

Wkts.			Tests	Balls	Mdns	Runs	Avge	5 wI	10 wM
307	F. S. Trueman	(E)	67	15178	522	6625	21.57	17	3
265	L. R. Gibbs	(WI)	66	22982	1114	7673	28.95	15	2

252	J. B. Statham	(E)	70	16056	595	6261	24.84	9	1
248	R. Benaud	(A)	63	19090	805	6704	27.03	16	1
246	G. D. McKenzie	(A)	60	17681	547	7328	29.78	16	3
236	A. V. Bedser	(E)	51	15923	572	5876	24.89	15	5
235	G. S. Sobers	(WI)	93	21599	995	7999	34.03	6	—
228	R. R. Lindwall	(A)	61	13666	418	5257	23.05	12	—
216	C. V. Grimmett	(A)	37	14513	735	5231	24.21	21	7
193	J. C. Laker	(E)	46	12009	673	4099	21.23	9	3
192	W. W. Hall	(WI)	48	10415	312	5066	26.38	9	1
189	S. F. Barnes	(E)	27	7873	356	3106	16.43	24	7
186	A. K. Davidson	(A)	44	11665	432	3838	20.58	14	2
176	J. A. Snow	(E)	42	10566	368	4609	26.18	8	1
174	G. A. R. Lock	(E)	49	13147	819	4451	25.58	9	3
172	D. L. Underwood	(E)	47	12210	733	4063	23.62	12	5
170	K. R. Miller	(A)	55	10474	338	3905	22.97	7	1
170	H. J. Tayfield	(SA)	37	13568	602	4405	25.91	14	2
162	V. Mankad	(I)	44	14686	777	5235	32.31	8	2
160	W. A. Johnston	(A)	40	11048	370	3825	23.90	7	—
158	S. Ramadhin	(WI)	43	13939	813	4579	28.98	10	1
155	M. W. Tate	(E)	39	12523	581	4055	26.16	7	1

MOST TEST APPEARANCES FOR EACH COUNTRY

NB   The abandoned match at Melbourne in 1970–71 is excluded from these figures.

England

M. C. Cowdrey	109
T. G. Evans	91
W. R. Hammond	85
K. F. Barrington	82
T. W. Graveney	79
L. Hutton	79

Australia

R. N. Harvey	79
W. M. Lawry	67
R. Benaud	63
R. R. Lindwall	61
G. D. McKenzie	60
S. E. Gregory	58

South Africa

J. H. B. Waite	50
A. D. Nourse, Senior	45
B. Mitchell	42
H. W. Taylor	42
T. L. Goddard	41
R. A. McLean	40

West Indies

G. S. Sobers	93
R. B. Kanhai	79
L. R. Gibbs	66
F. M. Worrell	51
W. W. Hall	48
E. D. Weekes	48

New Zealand

J. R. Reid	58
B. E. Congdon	48
B. Sutcliffe	42
G. T. Dowling	39
R. C. Motz	32
V. Pollard	32

India

P. R. Umrigar	59
C. G. Borde	55
V. L. Manjrekar	55
V. Mankad	44
P. Roy	43
Mansur Ali Khan	42

Pakistan

Hanif Mohammad	55
Imtiaz Ahmed	41
Intikhab Alam	41
Saeed Ahmed	41
Mushtaq Mohammad	36
Fazal Mahmood	34

Why must an umpire be sure of his shave?

Time was, before GII, when many a batsman died of fright through a certain umpire's habit of stroking his chin. Imagine it: you've padded up to one that was a bit too close, there's a yell from behind and up goes the umpire's hand...only to feel his whiskers! Finally, somebody bought him a GII—the razor with two blades. The first shaves you close, the second even closer. It's made a world of difference to everyone's nerves.

GII is easier on close shaves

TEST CAREER RECORDS

These do not include the recent series between Australia and England, New Zealand and England, India and West Indies, and Pakistan and West Indies.

ENGLAND

BATTING AND FIELDING

	M	I	NO	Runs	HS	Avge	100	50	Ct	St
D. L. Amiss	32	56	7	2488	262*	50.77	8	7	13	—
G. G. Arnold	27	37	8	393	59	13.55	—	1	8	—
J. Birkenshaw	5	7	0	148	64	21.14	—	1	3	—
G. Boycott	63	110	14	4579	246*	47.69	12	26	2	—
M. C. Cowdrey	109	179	15	7459	182	45.48	22	38	117	—
M. H. Denness	20	32	2	1098	118	36.60	2	6	21	—
J. H. Edrich	65	106	7	4230	310*	42.72	11	18	36	—
K. W. R. Fletcher	39	64	10	2260	178	41.85	5	13	30	—
A. W. Greig	30	47	3	1948	148	44.27	5	9	46	—
F. C. Hayes	7	13	1	219	106*	18.25	1	—	4	—
M. Hendrick	5	3	2	8	6	8.00	—	—	6	—
J. A. Jameson	4	8	0	214	82	26.75	—	1	—	—
A. P. E. Knott	61	92	10	2671	116	32.57	2	18	170	15
P. Lever	12	14	1	322	88*	24.76	—	2	7	—
D. Lloyd	5	7	2	356	214*	71.20	1	1	5	—
B. W. Luckhurst	19	37	5	1244	131	38.87	4	5	14	—
C. M. Old	18	25	4	341	65	16.23	—	1	8	—
P. I. Pocock	15	23	1	152	33	6.90	—	13	—	—
F. J. Titmus	49	68	11	1311	84*	23.00	—	9	35	—
D. L. Underwood	47	60	25	506	45*	14.45	—	—	27	—
R. G. D. Willis	11	16	9	102	24	14.57	—	—	9	—

BOWLING

	Balls	Runs	Wkts	Avge	Best	5 wI	10 wM
G. G. Arnold	5915	2455	94	26.11	6–45	5	—
J. Birkenshaw	1017	469	13	36.07	5–57	1	—
G. Boycott	792	346	7	49.42	3–47	—	—
M. C. Cowdrey	119	104	0	—	—	—	—
J. H. Edrich	30	23	0	—	—	—	—
K. W. R. Fletcher	249	173	1	173.00	1–48	—	—
A. W. Greig	5531	2428	80	30.35	8–86	4	1
M. Hendrick	918	410	20	20.50	4–28	—	—
J. A. Jameson	42	17	1	17.00	1–17	—	—
P. Lever	2476	979	27	36.25	5–70	1	—
D. Lloyd	24	17	0	—	—	—	—
B. W. Luckhurst	57	32	1	32.00	1–9	—	—
C. M. Old	3284	1731	60	28.85	5–21	2	—
P. I. Pocock	4116	1850	43	43.02	6–79	3	—
F. J. Titmus	14139	4571	146	31.30	7–79	7	—
D. L. Underwood	12210	4063	172	23.62	8–51	12	5
R. G. D. Willis	1938	997	30	33.23	4–64	—	—

AUSTRALIA

BATTING AND FIELDING

	M	I	NO	Runs	HS	Avge	100	50	Ct	St
G. S. Chappell	24	41	6	1823	247*	52.08	7	6	32	—
I. M. Chappell	56	100	6	3922	196	41.72	12	17	83	—
I. C. Davis	6	9	0	143	50	15.88	—	1	5	—
A. R. Dell	2	2	2	6	3*	—	—	—	—	—
G. Dymock	3	3	1	13	13	6.50	—	—	—	—
R. Edwards	11	17	1	657	170*	41.06	1	5	7	—
G. J. Gilmour	3	4	0	60	52	15.00	—	1	2	—
A. G. Hurst	1	1	0	16	16	16.00	—	—	—	—
T. J. Jenner	6	10	3	102	30	14.57	—	—	2	—
D. K. Lillee	11	14	5	44	14	4.88	—	—	3	—
A. A. Mallett	20	28	6	243	43*	11.04	—	—	7	—
R. W. Marsh	25	39	4	1285	132	36.71	2	7	94	6
K. J. O'Keeffe	15	20	3	426	85	25.05	—	1	9	—
I. R. Redpath	54	97	10	3690	171	42.41	4	26	64	—
A. P. Sheahan	31	53	6	1594	127	33.91	2	7	17	—
K. R. Stackpole	43	80	5	2807	207	37.42	7	14	47	—
J. R. Thomson	1	1	0	19	19*	—	—	—	—	—
M. H. N. Walker	11	13	5	110	23*	13.75	—	—	2	—
K. D. Walters	47	80	8	3633	242	50.45	11	22	15	—
A. J. Woodcock	1	1	0	27	27	27.00	—	—	1	—

BOWLING

	Balls	Runs	Wkts	Avge	Best	5 wI	10 wM
G. S. Chappell	2724	1022	24	42.58	5–61	1	—
I. M. Chappell	2421	1097	16	68.56	2–21	—	—
A. R. Dell	559	160	6	26.66	3–65	—	—
G. Dymock	1040	322	13	24.76	5–58	1	—
G. J. Gilmour	768	347	15	23.13	5–64	1	—
A. G. Hurst	232	73	1	73.00	1–56	—	—
T. J. Jenner	1353	523	19	27.52	5–90	1	—
D. K. Lillee	2959	1232	51	24.15	6–66	4	1
A. A. Mallett	6091	2263	88	25.71	8–59	6	1
K. J. O'Keeffe	3140	1103	30	36.76	4–57	—	—
I. R. Redpath	64	41	0			—	—
K. R. Stackpole	2321	1001	15	66.73	2–33	—	—
J. R. Thomson	152	110	0			—	—
M. H. N. Walker	3305	1108	54	20.51	6–15	4	—
K. D. Walters	2519	1102	38	29.00	5–66	1	—

WEST INDIES

BATTING AND FIELDING

	M	I	NO	Runs	HS	Avge	100	50	Ct	St
A. G. Barrett	4	5	0	33	19	6.60	—	—	—	—
K. D. Boyce	12	16	1	322	72	21.46	—	1	2	—
M. L. C. Foster	12	20	5	548	125	36.53	1	1	2	—
R. C. Fredericks	32	59	3	2283	163	40.76	2	15	39	—
L. R. Gibbs	66	90	30	407	25	6.78	—	—	46	—
G. A. Greenidge	5	9	2	209	50	29.85	—	1	3	—
V. A. Holder	16	22	3	290	42	15.26	—	—	8	—
Inshan Ali	10	14	2	132	25	11.00	—	—	4	—
B. D. Julien	8	10	1	392	121	43.55	1	3	3	—
A. I. Kallicharran	15	24	2	1122	158	51.00	4	6	13	—
R. B. Kanhai	79	137	6	6227	256	47.53	15	28	50	—
C. H. Lloyd	36	64	5	2282	178	38.67	5	12	19	—
D. L. Murray	22	34	5	568	90	19.58	—	2	62	4
A. M. E. Roberts	1	1	1	9	9*	—	—	—	—	—
L. G. Rowe	12	17	1	1131	302	70.68	5	2	8	—
G. S. Sobers	93	160	21	8032	365*	57.78	26	30	110	—
E. T. Willett	3	5	2	19	12	6.33	—	—	—	—

BOWLING

	Balls	Runs	Wkts	Avge	Best	wI	10 wM
A. G. Barrett	1228	454	11	41.27	3–43	—	—
K. D. Boyce	2101	1017	41	24.80	6–77	2	1
M. L. C. Foster	1332	435	5	87.00	1–3	—	—
R. C. Fredericks	408	182	1	182.00	1–12	—	—
L. R. Gibbs	22982	7673	265	28.95	8–38	15	2
G. A. Greenidge	156	75	0		—	—	—
V. A. Holder	3811	1366	40	34.15	4–41	—	—
Inshan Ali	3190	1338	28	47.78	5–59	1	—
B. D. Julien	1704	644	23	28.00	5–57	1	—
A. I. Kallicharran	66	34	0		—	+	—
R. B. Kanhai	183	85	0		—	—	—
C. H. Lloyd	1472	523	10	52.30	2–13	—	—
A. M. E. Roberts	300	124	3	41.33	2–49	—	—
L. G. Rowe	48	34	0		—	—	—
G. S. Sobers	21599	7999	235	34.03	6–73	6	—
E. T. Willett	870	327	7	46.71	3–33	—	—

NEW ZEALAND

BATTING AND FIELDING

	M	I	NO	Runs	HS	Avge	100	50	Ct	St
B. Andrews	2	3	2	22	17	22.00	—	—	1	—
M. G. Burgess	27	49	4	1465	119*	32.55	4	8	16	—
B. L. Cairns	1	2	1	4	4*	4.00	—	—	—	—
R. O. Collinge	23	30	7	364	68*	15.82	—	2	9	—
J. V. Coney	4	7	0	123	45	17.57	—	—	6	—
B. E. Congdon	48	91	6	2853	176	33.56	6	15	35	—
D. R. Hadlee	19	31	3	390	56	13.92	—	1	6	—
R. J. Hadlee	7	12	1	155	46	14.09	—	—	5	—
B. F. Hastings	28	51	6	1488	117*	33.06	4	7	23	—
H. J. Howarth	24	32	16	188	29*	11.75	—	—	30	—
J. F. M. Morrison	6	11	0	336	117	30.54	1	1	4	—
D. R. O'Sullivan	4	8	1	29	8	4.14	—	—	—	—
J. M. Parker	10	16	0	313	108	19.56	1	—	12	—
M. J. F. Shrimpton	10	19	0	265	46	13.94	—	—	2	—
G. M. Turner	27	49	6	2196	259	51.06	5	11	27	—
K. J. Wadsworth	28	44	4	789	80	19.72	—	3	79	4
M. G. Webb	3	2	0	12	12	6.00	—	—	—	—

BOWLING

	Balls	Runs	Wkts	Avge	Best	5 wI	10 wM
B. Andrews	256	154	2	77.00	2–40	—	—
M. G. Burgess	450	190	5	38.00	3–23	—	—
B. L. Cairns	168	73	2	36.50	2–73	—	—
R. O. Collinge	5157	2224	83	26.79	5–74	2	—
J. V. Coney	16	13	0	—	—	—	—
B. E. Congdon	3854	1597	49	32.59	4–46	—	—
D. R. Hadlee	3526	1737	56	31.01	4–30	—	—
R. J. Hadlee	1410	735	20	36.75	4–33	—	—
B. F. Hastings	22	9	0	—	—	—	—
H. J. Howarth	7599	2683	77	34.84	5–34	2	—
D. R. O'Sullivan	605	309	5	61.80	5–148	1	—
M. J. F. Shrimpton	257	158	5	31.60	3–35	—	—
G. M. Turner	12	5	0	—	—	—	—
M. G. Webb	732	471	4	117.75	2–114	—	—

PAKISTAN

BATTING AND FIELDING

	M	I	NO	Runs	HS	Avge	100	50	Ct	St
Asif Iqbal	32	53	2	1737	175	34.05	4	7	22	—
Asif Masood	13	14	6	58	17*	7.25	—	—	4	—
Imran Khan	4	7	1	97	31	16.16	—	—	3	—
Intikhab Alam	41	68	10	1389	138	23.94	1	8	19	—
Majid Khan	24	39	1	1433	158	37.71	2	7	27	—
Mushtaq Mohammad	36	63	5	2452	201	42.27	6	15	22	—
Sadiq Mohammad	18	32	0	1359	166	42.46	3	6	13	—
Sarfraz Nawaz	11	14	4	138	53	13.80	—	1	11	—
Shafiq Ahmad	1	2	0	25	18	12.50	—	—	—	—
Wasim Bari	24	34	6	467	72	16.67	—	2	52	8
Wasim Raja	6	11	3	273	53	34.12	—	1	1	—
Zaheer Abbas	15	26	1	978	274	39.12	2	2	8	—

BOWLING

	Balls	Runs	Wkts	Avge	Best	5 wI	10 wM
Asif Iqbal	3240	1241	47	26.40	5–48	2	—
Asif Masood	2519	1280	33	38.78	5–111	1	—
Imran Khan	840	313	5	62.60	2–48	—	—
Intikhab Alam	8879	3865	102	37.89	7–52	5	2
Majid Khan	2228	951	19	50.05	2–32	—	—
Mushtaq Mohammad	2535	1108	40	27.70	5–49	1	—
Sadiq Mohammad	154	74	0	—	—	—	—
Sarfraz Nawaz	2555	1076	27	39.85	4–53	—	—
Wasim Raja	486	240	6	40.00	3–32	—	—
Zaheer Abbas	12	2	0	—	—	—	—

INDIA

BATTING AND FIELDING

	M	I	NO	Runs	HS	Avge	100	50	Ct	St
S. Abid Ali	27	49	3	956	81	20.78	—	6	31	—
B. S. Bedi	35	55	16	292	22	7.48	—	—	16	—
B. S. Chandrasekhar	26	36	20	87	22	5.43	—	—	11	—
F. M. Engineer	41	78	3	2389	121	31.85	2	14	58	15
S. M. Gavaskar	15	30	4	1359	220	52.26	5	8	9	—
S. Madan Lal	2	4	0	11	7	2.75	—	—	1	—
A. V. Mankad	14	28	2	701	97	26.96	—	5	7	—
Mansur Ali Khan	42	76	3	2698	203*	36.95	6	16	25	—
S. S. Naik	1	2	0	81	77	40.50	—	1	—	—
B. P. Patel	2	4	0	10	5	2.50	—	—	—	—
E. A. S. Prasanna	30	51	9	477	37	11.35	—	—	9	—
E. D. Solkar	21	37	6	866	75	27.93	—	6	41	—
S. Venkataraghavan	26	40	8	462	51	14.43	—	1	23	—
G. R. Viswanath	18	35	3	1162	137	36.31	2	7	6	—
A. L. Wadekar	37	71	3	2113	143	31.07	1	14	46	—

BOWLING

	Balls	Runs	Wkts	Avge	Best	5 wI	10 wM
S. Abid Ali	3960	1820	46	39.56	6–55	1	—
B. S. Bedi	11584	3934	131	30.03	7–98	6	—
B. S. Chandrasekhar	7624	3109	112	27.75	8–79	7	1
S. M. Gavaskar	126	63	0	—	—	—	—
S. Madan Lal	438	188	2	94.00	2–56	—	—
A. V. Mankad	41	43	0	—	—	—	—
Mansur Ali Khan	132	88	1	88.00	1–10	—	—
E. A. S. Prasanna	9535	3933	137	28.70	6–74	8	1
E. D. Solkar	1911	866	16	54.12	3–28	—	—
S. Venkataraghavan	6837	2531	83	30.49	8–72	3	1
G. R. Viswanath	24	18	0	—	—	—	—
A. L. Wadekar	61	55	0	—	—	—	—

PRINCIPAL FIXTURES 1975

Will continue on Sunday if necessary

Friday 18 April
Edgbaston: Warwicks v Middx
(one-day friendly)

Saturday 19 April
Cambridge: Cambridge U v Leics

Monday 21 April
Taunton: Somerset v Worcs
(one-day friendly)
The Oval: Surrey v Middx
(two one-day friendlies)

Tuesday 22 April
Taunton: Somerset v Hants
(two-day friendly)

Wednesday 23 April
Leicester: Leics v Notts
(non-Championship)
Lord's: MCC v Worcs
Oxford: Oxford U v Glos
Cambridge: Cambridge U v Surrey

Thursday 24 April
Cardiff: Glam v Warwicks
(one-day friendly)

Saturday 26 April
Oxford: Oxford U v Sussex
Benson & Hedges Cup
Derby: Derbys v M Counties (N)
*Southampton: Hants v Surrey
Canterbury: Kent v M Counties (S)
Old Trafford: Lancs v Yorks
Leicester: Leics v Northants
Lord's: Middx v Essex
Taunton: Somerset v Glam
Worcester: Worcs v Warwicks

Wednesday 30 April
Derby: Derbys v Worcs
Bristol: Glos v Leics
Bournemouth: Hants v Essex

Lord's: Middx v Kent
Trent Bridge: Notts v Glam
Taunton: Somerset v Sussex
Edgbaston: Warwicks v Lancs
Headingley: Yorks v Surrey

Saturday 3 May
Benson & Hedges Cup
Chelmsford: Essex v Kent
Bristol: Glos v Hants
Cambridge: Oxford U & Cambridge
U v Worcs
The Oval: Surrey v Somerset
Edgbaston: Warwicks v Leics

Sunday 4 May
John Player League
Chelmsford: Essex v Somerset
Moreton-in-Marsh: Glos v
Warwicks
Old Trafford: Lancs v Derbys
Leicester: Leics v Kent
Lord's: Middx v Northants
Trent Bridge: Notts v Glam
Hove: Sussex v Surrey
Worcester: Worcs v Hants

Monday 5 May
Benson & Hedges Cup
Trent Bridge: Notts v Lancs
Hove: Sussex v Middx
Bradford: Yorks v Derbys

Wednesday 7 May
Chelmsford: Essex v Leics
Cardiff: Glam v Glos
Dartford: Kent v Yorks
Northampton: Northants v Somerset
The Oval: Surrey v Lancs
Worcester: Worcs v Notts
Oxford: Oxford U v Derbys
Cambridge: Cambridge U v
Warwicks

Saturday 10 May

Benson & Hedges Cup
Chesterfield: Derbys v Notts
Cardiff: Glam v Surrey
Canterbury: Kent v Sussex
Leicester: Leics v Oxford U & Cambridge U
Scunthorpe (Appleby & Frodingham): M Counties (N) v Yorks
Bedford (Goldington Bury): M Counties (S) v Essex
Northampton: Northants v Warwicks
Street: Somerset v Glos

Sunday 11 May

John Player League
Swansea: Glam v Surrey
Folkestone: Kent v Middx
Northampton: Northants v Sussex
Bristol (Imperial Grnd): Somerset v Glos
Edgbaston: Warwicks v Lancs
Huddersfield: Yorks v Derbys

Wednesday 14 May

Swansea: Glam v Hants
Leicester: Leics v Sussex
Lord's: Middx v Somerset
Northampton: Northants v Warwicks
The Oval: Surrey v Derbys
Worcester: Worcs v Yorks
Oxford: Oxford U v Kent
Cambridge: Cambridge U v Notts

Saturday 17 May

Benson & Hedges Cup
Bristol: Glos v Glam
Bournemouth: Hants v Somerset
Old Trafford: Lancs v Derbys
Lord's: Middx v Kent
Northampton: Northants v Worcs
Newark: Notts v M Counties (N)
Hove: Sussex v M Counties (S)
Coventry (Courtaulds): Warwicks v Oxford U & Cambridge U

Sunday 18 May

John Player League
Derby: Derbys v Middx

Southampton: Hants v Sussex
Canterbury: Kent v Yorks
Trent Bridge: Notts v Essex
Yeovil: Somerset v Leics
The Oval: Surrey v Worcs

Wednesday 21 May

Edgbaston: Warwicks v Scotland
Benson & Hedges Cup
Chelmsford: Essex v Sussex
Swansea: Glam v Hants
Stoke-on-Trent (Longton): M Counties (N) v Lancs
Amersham: M Counties (S) v Middx
Oxford: Oxford U & Cambridge U v Northants
The Oval: Surrey v Glos
Worcester: Worcs v Leics
Barnsley: Yorks v Notts

Saturday 24 May

Bristol: Glos v Somerset
Southampton: Hants v Kent
Old Trafford: Lancs v Yorks
Leicester: Leics v Northants
Trent Bridge: Notts v Derbys
The Oval: Surrey v Warwicks
Hove: Sussex v Middx
Worcester: Worcs v Essex
Oxford: Oxford U v Free Foresters

Sunday 25 May

John Player League
Ebbw Vale: Glam v Essex
Bristol: Glos v Northants
Old Trafford: Lancs v Notts
Leicester: Leics v Worcs
Lord's: Middx v Hants
Edgbaston: Warwicks v Yorks

Wednesday 28 May

Chesterfield: Derbys v Kent
Bristol: Glos v Glam
Lord's: Middx v Leics
Northampton: Northants v Lancs
Hove: Sussex v Hants
Edgbaston: Warwicks v Notts
Oxford: Oxford U v Somerset

Saturday 31 May

Buxton: Derbys v Lancs
Colchester: Essex v Kent
Bournemouth: Hants v Notts
Lord's: Middx v Surrey
Northampton: Northants v Glam
Hastings: Sussex v Warwicks
Worcester: Worcs v Glos
Bradford: Yorks v Leics
Oxford: Oxford U v MCC

Sunday 1 June

John Player League
Buxton: Derbys v Glam
Colchester: Essex v Lancs
Southampton: Hants v Notts
Tring: Northants v Kent
Guildford: Surrey v Somerset
Hastings: Sussex v Warwicks
Worcester: Worcs v Glos
Hull: Yorks v Leics

Wednesday 4 June

(Venues to be decided): Benson &
Hedges Cup (quarter-finals)
Oxford: Oxford U v Comb Services

Saturday 7 June

Ilford: Essex v Lancs
Swansea: Glam v Warwicks
Southampton: Hants v Middx
Leicester: Leics v Worcs
Bath: Somerset v Derbys
Oxford: Oxford U v Northants
Prudential Cup
Headingley: Australia v Pakistan
Lord's: England v India
Edgbaston: New Zealand v East
Africa
Old Trafford: West Indies v Sri
Lanka

Sunday 8 June

John Player League
Swansea: Glam v Warwicks
Bristol: Glos v Middx
Bournemouth: Hants v Kent
Trent Bridge: Notts v Sussex
Bath: Somerset v Derbys
The Oval: Surrey v Northants
Worcester: Worcs v Yorks

Wednesday 11 June

Ilford: Essex v Notts
Bristol: Glos v Yorks
Maidstone: Kent v Worcs
Bath: Somerset v Hants
Oxford: Oxford U v Warwicks
Prudential Cup
The Oval: Australia v Sri Lanka
Trent Bridge: England v New Zealand
Headingley: India v East African
Edgbaston: Pakistan v West Indies

Saturday 14 June

Cardiff: Glam v Surrey
Bristol: Glos v Hants
Maidstone: Kent v Sussex
Northampton: Northants v Derbys
Scarborough: Yorks v Middx
Cambridge: Cambridge U v MCC
Prudential Cup
The Oval: Australia v West Indies
Edgbaston: England v East Africa
Old Trafford: India v New Zealand
Trent Bridge: Pakistan v Sri Lanka

Sunday 15 June

John Player League
Ilford: Essex v Derbys
Cardiff: Glam v Hants
Gloucester: Glos v Lancs
Canterbury: Kent v Worcs
Leicester: Leics v Warwicks
Bath: Somerset v Notts

Wednesday 18 June

Headingley & The Oval: Prudential
Cup (semi-finals)
Swansea: Glam v Kent
Old Trafford: Lancs v Middx
Leicester: Leics v Somerset
Trent Bridge: Notts v Sussex
Edgbaston: Warwicks v Yorks
Worcester: Worcs v Northants

Saturday 21 June

Lord's: Prudential Cup (final)
Old Trafford: Lancs v Derbys
Leicester: Leics v Hants
Worksop: Notts v Northants
Hove: Sussex v Surrey

214

Edgbaston: Warwicks v Somerset
Cambridge: Cambridge U v Essex
Eastbourne: D. H. Robins' XI v
  Oxford U

Sunday 22 June

John Player League
Old Trafford: Lancs v Hants
Northampton: Northants v Leics
Trent Bridge: Notts v Glos
The Oval: Surrey v Middx
Hove: Sussex v Glam
Edgbaston: Warwicks v Essex
Bradford: Yorks v Somerset

Wednesday 25 June

Burton-on-Trent: Derbys v
  Warwicks
Westcliff: Essex v Glos
Canterbury: Kent v Australians
Worcester: Worcs v Oxford U
Sheffield: Yorks v Hants
Eastbourne: D. H. Robins' XI v
  Cambridge U
Edinburgh: Scotland v MCC
Gillette Cup (1st round)
March: Cambs v Northants
Lord's: Middx v Bucks
Trent Bridge: Notts v Sussex
Oxford (Morris Motors): Oxon v
  Cornwall
Stoke-on-Trent (Longton): Staffs v
  Leics
The Oval: Surrey v Somerset

Saturday 28 June

Derby: Derbys v Oxford U
Westcliff: Essex v Sussex
Bristol: Glos v Northants
Southampton: Hants v Australians
Tunbridge Wells: Kent v Lancs
Leicester: Leics v Glam
Lord's: Middx v Worcs
Trent Bridge: Notts v Surrey
Harrogate: Yorks v Somerset
Portsmouth: Comb Services v
  Cambridge U

Sunday 29 June

John Player League
Chesterfield: Derbys v Glos

Westcliff: Essex v Sussex
Maidstone: Kent v Lancs
Leicester: Leics v Glam
Lord's: Middx v Worcs
Edgbaston: Warwicks v Northants
Scarborough: Yorks v Surrey

Wednesday 2 July

(Venues to be decided): Benson &
  Hedges Cup (semi-finals)
Aldershot: Army v Oxford U
†Lord's: MCC v Australians
Harrogate: Yorks v D. H. Robins'
  XI

Saturday 5 July

Derby: Derbys v Essex
Swansea: Glam v Australians
Bournemouth: Hants v Glos
Old Trafford: Lancs v Somerset
Northampton: Northants v Kent
Trent Bridge: Notts v Middx
The Oval: Surrey v Leics
Hove: Sussex v Yorks
Worcester: Worcs v Warwicks
Lord's: Oxford U v Cambridge U

Sunday 6 July

John Player League
Long Eaton (Trent College): Derbys
  v Kent
Southampton: Hants v Surrey
Old Trafford: Lancs v Somerset
Lord's: Middx v Leics
Luton: Northants v Essex
Hove: Sussex v Yorks
Worcester: Worcs v Notts

Wednesday 9 July

Basingstoke: Hants v Glam
Southport: Lancs v Worcs
Lord's: Middx v Glos

Thursday 10 July

**EDGBASTON: ENGLAND v
  AUSTRALIA (First Test)**

†*Alternative venue if Middx drawn
  at home in B & H Cup*

215

Saturday 12 July

Chesterfield: Derbys v Yorks
Dover: Kent v Notts
Leicester: Leics v Essex
Taunton: Somerset v Northants
The Oval: Surrey v Middx

Sunday 13 July

John Player League
Chelmsford: Essex v Middx
Lydney: Glos v Glam
Basingstoke: Hants v Warwicks
Dover: Kent v Notts
Leicester: Leics v Surrey
Torquay: Somerset v Northants
Headingley: Yorks v Lancs

Wednesday 16 July

Trent Bridge or Hove: Notts or
Sussex v Australians (loser of
1st round G Cup match)
Gillette Cup (2nd round)
Bristol: Glos v Oxon or Cornwall
Southampton: Hants v Glam
Old Trafford: Lancs v Cambs or
Northants
Trent Bridge or Hove: Notts or
Sussex v Kent
The Oval or Taunton: Surrey or
Somerset v Derbys
Edgbaston: Warwicks v Middx or
Bucks
Worcester: Worcs v Essex
Headingley: Yorks v Staffs or Leics

Saturday 19 July

Lord's: Benson & Hedges Cup (final)
Chesterfield: Derbys or Glos or
Worcs. v Australians

Sunday 20 July

John Player League
Burton-on-Trent: Derbys v Leics
Chelmsford: Essex v Worcs
Bournemouth: Hants v Glos
Northampton: Northants v Yorks
Trent Bridge: Notts v Middx
The Oval: Surrey v Lancs
Hove: Sussex v Somerset
Edgbaston: Warwicks v Kent

Wednesday 23 July

Cardiff: Glam v Derbys
Old Trafford: Lancs v Australians
Northampton: Northants v Sussex
Weston-super-Mare: Somerset v
Worcs
The Oval: Surrey v Essex
Coventry (Courtaulds): Warwicks v
Leics
Sheffield: Yorks v Notts

Saturday 26 July

Ilkeston: Derbys v Notts
Swansea: Glam v Lancs
Cheltenham: Glos v Kent
Leicester: Leics v Australians
Northampton: Northants v Middx
Weston-super-Mare: Somerset v
Hants
The Oval: Surrey v Yorks
Edgbaston: Warwicks v Essex
Worcester: Worcs v Sussex

Sunday 27 July

John Player League
Ilkeston: Derbys v Notts
Swansea: Glam v Lancs
Cheltenham: Glos v Kent
Leicester: Leics v Sussex
Lord's: Middx v Yorks
Weston-super-Mare: Somerset v
Hants
Dudley: Worcs v Northants

Wednesday 30 July

Cheltenham: Glos v Warwicks
Canterbury: Kent v Hants
Blackpool: Lancs v Leics
Hove: Sussex v Glam

Thursday 31 July

**LORD'S: ENGLAND v
AUSTRALIA (Second Test)**

Saturday 2 August

Cheltenham: Glos v Worcs
Canterbury: Kent v Middx
Old Trafford: Lancs v Warwicks
Leicester: Leics v Derbys
Northampton: Northants v Essex

Sunday 3 August

John Player League
Cardiff: Glam v Yorks
Cheltenham: Glos v Essex
Canterbury: Kent v Sussex
Old Trafford: Lancs v Leics
The Oval: Surrey v Notts
Edgbaston: Warwicks v Somerset
Worcester: Worcs v Derbys

Wednesday 6 August

(Venues to be decided): **Gillette Cup** (quarter-finals)
Taunton: Somerset (or Surrey if Somerset still in Gillette Cup) v Australians

Saturday 9 August

Leyton: Essex v Somerset
Liverpool: Lancs v Hants
Leicester: Leics v Notts
Lord's: Middx v Glam
Northampton: Northants v Australians
Eastbourne: Sussex v Glos
Edgbaston: Warwicks v Kent
Worcester: Worcs v Surrey
Scarborough: Yorks v Derbys

Sunday 10 August

John Player League
Chesterfield: Derbys v Surrey
Old Trafford: Lancs v Worcs
Leicester: Leics v Essex
Lord's: Middx v Somerset
Wellingborough: Northants v Glam
Trent Bridge: Notts v Warwicks
Eastbourne: Sussex v Glos
Bradford: Yorks v Hants

Wednesday 13 August

Leyton: Essex v Glam
Bournemouth: Hants v Surrey
Lord's: Middx v Yorks
Hove: Sussex v Derbys

Thursday 14 August

HEADINGLEY: ENGLAND v AUSTRALIA (Third Test)

Saturday 16 August

Cardiff: Glam v Yorks
Bournemouth: Hants v Northants
Trent Bridge: Notts v Lancs
Taunton: Somerset v Glos
The Oval: Surrey v Sussex
Edgbaston: Warwicks v Worcs

Sunday 17 August

John Player League
Cardiff: Glam v Kent
Southampton: Hants v Northants
Old Trafford: Lancs v Middx
Trent Bridge: Notts v Leics
Byfleet: Surrey v Essex
Arundel: Sussex v Derbys
Edgbaston: Warwicks v Worcs

Wednesday 20 August

(Venues to be decided): **Gillette Cup** (semi-finals)

Saturday 23 August

Derby: Derbys v Glos
Chelmsford: Essex v Australians
Swansea: Glam v Worcs
Folkestone: Kent v Surrey
Lord's: Middx v Sussex
Northampton: Northants v Leics
Taunton: Somerset v Notts
Edgbaston: Warwicks v Hants
Headingley: Yorks v Lancs

Sunday 24 August

John Player League
Chelmsford: Essex v Hants
Maidstone: Kent v Surrey
Lord's: Middx v Warwicks
Northampton: Northants v Derbys
Taunton: Somerset v Glam
Worcester: Worcs v Sussex
Scarborough: Yorks v Glos

Wednesday 27 August

Chelmsford: Essex v Northants
Folkestone: Kent v Somerset
Lord's: Middx v Warwicks
Trent Bridge: Notts v Leics
Edgbaston: Warwick Pool U-25 County Cricket Comp

217

Thursday 28 August

THE OVAL: ENGLAND v
  AUSTRALIA (Fourth Test)

Saturday 30 August

Chesterfield: Derbys v Middx
Chelmsford: Essex v Worcs
Cardiff: Glam v Somerset
Bristol: Glos v Surrey
Southampton: Hants v Sussex
Tunbridge Wells: Kent v Leics
Old Trafford: Lancs v Notts
Bradford: Yorks v Northants

Sunday 31 August

John Player League
Chelmsford: Essex v Kent
Bristol: Glos v Surrey
Bournemouth: Hants v Leics
Old Trafford: Lancs v Northants
Lord's: Middx v Sussex
Trent Bridge: Notts v Yorks
Edgbaston: Warwicks v Derbys

Wednesday 3 September

Leicester: Leics v Middx
Trent Bridge: Notts v Warwicks
Taunton: Somerset v Essex
Guildford: Surrey v Northants
Worcester: Worcs v Glam
Scarborough: Fenner Trophy
  Knock-Out Comp (3 days)

Saturday 6 September

Lord's: Gillette Cup (final)
Scarborough: T. N. Pearce's XI v
  D. H. Robins' Overseas XI

Sunday 7 September

Scarborough: T. N. Pearce's XI v
  D. H. Robins' Overseas XI
John Player League
Darley Dale: Derbys v Hants
Canterbury: Kent v Somerset
Leicester: Leics v Glos
Brackley: Northants v Notts
The Oval: Surrey v Warwicks
Hove: Sussex v Lancs
Worcester: Worcs v Glam

Wednesday 10 September

Southampton: Hants v Derbys
Old Trafford: Lancs v Glos
Hove: Sussex v Kent

Saturday 13 September

Chesterfield: Derbys v Leics
Trent Bridge: Notts v Glos
Taunton: Somerset v Glam
The Oval: Surrey v Kent
Hove: Sussex v Lancs
Edgbaston: Warwicks v Northants
Worcester: Worcs v Hants
Middlesbrough: Yorks v Essex

Sunday 14 September

John Player League
Cardiff: Glam v Middx
Taunton: Somerset v Worcs
Bradford: Yorks v Essex

MINOR COUNTIES FIXTURES

Indicates that second day's play is on a Sunday

MAY

11 Penrith: Cumberland v Lincs
13 Jesmond: Northumberland v Lincs
25 Sleaford: Lincs v Suffolk
   Jesmond: Northumberland v Durham
28 Old Trafford: Lancs II v Cheshire

JUNE

1 Northwich: Cheshire v Somerset II
   Kendal: Cumberland v Northumberland
3 Wroxeter: Salop v Somerset II
4 March: Cambs v Beds
5 Southport: Lancs II v Somerset II
9 Southport: Lancs II v Northumberland
11 Papworth: Cambs v Norfolk
   Cleethorpes: Lincs v Northumberland
   Walsall: Staffs v Salop
15 Chester (Boughton Hall): Cheshire v Staffs
18 Wisbech: Cambs v Lincs
22 Grimsby (Ross Group): Lincs v Norfolk
29 Jesmond: Northumberland v Cumberland
   Stone: Staffs v Cheshire

JULY

2 Radlett: Herts v Cambs
   St Georges: Salop v Staffs
5 *Buckingham: Bucks v Beds
6 Falmouth: Cornwall v Somerset II
   Durham City: Durham v Cumberland
9 (Venue undecided): Herts v Norfolk
11 Truro: Cornwall v Devon
12 Luton (Vauxhall Motors): Beds v Cambs
   *Reading U: Berks v Bucks

13 Stamford (Burghley Park): Lincs v Cumberland
14 Alderley Edge: Cheshire v Northumberland
   Camborne: Cornwall v Wilts
   Hartlepool: Durham v Salop
16 (Venue undecided): Somerset II v Wilts
   Wolverhampton: Staffs v Northumberland
19 Southill Park: Beds v Herts
20 Macclesfield: Cheshire v Durham
21 Dunstable: Beds v Salop
   Penzance: Cornwall v Berks
   Old Trafford: Lancs II v Cumberland
   Norwich (Lakenham): Norfolk v Cambs
22 Oxford (Morris Motors): Oxon v Wilts
23 Plymouth: Devon v Berks
   Stevenage: Herts v Suffolk
   Taunton: Somerset II v Lancs II
24 Banbury Town: Oxon v Dorset
25 Trowbridge (County Ground): Wilts v Berks
26 Bedford (Goldington Bury): Beds v Bucks
27 Lincoln: Lincs v Staffs
28 Wimborne: Dorset v Wilts
   Hertford: Herts v Bucks
   Norwich (Lakenham): Norfolk v Suffolk
   Jesmond: Northumberland v Lancs II
   Shrewsbury (London Rd): Salop v Durham
29 Shipton-under-Wychwood: Oxon v Devon
30 Norwich (Lakenham): Norfolk v Bucks
31 Reading (CC Ground): Berks v Devon

AUGUST

1 Ipswich (Ransomes): Suffolk v Bucks
2 *Sherborne School: Dorset v Devon
  *Oxford (St Edward's School): Oxon v Berks
3 Wellington: Salop v Beds
4 Oxton (Birkenhead): Cheshire v Lancs II
  South Shields: Durham v Staffs
  Norwich (Lakenham): Norfolk v Herts
5 Wadebridge: Cornwall v Dorset
  Swindon (County Ground): Wilts v Oxon
6 Cambridge (Fenners): Cambs v Herts
  Norwich (Lakenham): Norfolk v Lincs
  Jesmond: Northumberland v Staffs
7 Sidmouth: Devon v Dorset
  Beaconsfield: Bucks v Oxon
  Ipswich (Ransomes): Suffolk v Herts
9 *Reading (Courage's): Berks v Wilts
  Glastonbury (Morland's): Somerset II v Salop
10 Chesham: Bucks v Suffolk
  Whitehaven: Cumberland v Durham
  Spalding: Lincs v Cambs
11 Exeter (County Ground): Devon v Salop
  Devizes: Wilts v Dorset
12 Luton (Wardown Park): Beds v Suffolk
  Maidenhead (Boyne Hill): Berks v Cornwall
  Witney Mills: Oxon v Bucks
13 Blandford: Dorset v Salop
  Stoke-on-Trent (Longton): Staffs v Lincs
14 Abingdon (CC Ground): Berks v Oxon
  Salisbury (Bemerton): Wilts v Cornwall
16 *Wing (Ascott Park): Bucks v Berks
  Ludlow: Salop v Dorset
17 Jesmond: Northumberland v Cheshire
  (Venue undecided): Somerset II v Cornwall
  Felixstowe: Suffolk v Beds
18 High Wycombe: Bucks v Herts
19 Paignton: Devon v Oxon
  Poole Park: Dorset v Cornwall
  Blackhill: Durham v Cheshire
20 Hitchin: Herts v Beds
  Felixstowe: Suffolk v Norfolk
21 Torquay: Devon v Somerset II
  Weymouth: Dorset v Oxon
24 Amersham: Bucks v Norfolk
  Millom: Cumberland v Lancs II
  Chester-le-Street: Durham v Northumberland
  Bury St Edmunds: Suffolk v Lincs
26 Exmouth: Devon v Cornwall
  Chippenham: Wilts v Somerset II
27 Burton-on-Trent (Bass Worthington Ground): Staffs v Durham
28 Bath: Somerset II v Devon
30 *Market Drayton: Salop v Devon
31 (Venue undecided): Somerset II v Cheshire

SECOND XI FIXTURES

APRIL

28/29   Glos v Warwicks   (Bristol)
30/1 May   Lancs v Worcs   (Old Trafford)

MAY

5/6   Notts v Northants   (Colston Bassett)
      Glam v Somerset   (Chepstow)
      Warwicks v Leics   (Rugby)

7/8   Glam v Lancs   (Barry)
      Leics v Yorks

7/8/9   Middx v Kent   (Teddington)
      Hants v Sussex   (Southampton

8/9   Glos v Worcs   (Bristol)

12/13   Lancs v Northants   (Old Trafford)
      Worcs v Warwicks   (Kidderminster)
      Sussex v Essex   (Haywards Heath)
      Hants v Somerset   (Andover)

14/15/16   Hants v Middx   (Southampton)
      Notts v Warwicks   (Newark)

19/20   Glam v Warwicks   (BP Llandarcy)
      Leics v Notts   (Leicester)
      Surrey v Northants   (Beddington)
      Worcs v Yorks   (Dudley)

19/20/21   Kent v Hants   (Dover)
21/22/23   Notts v Yorks   (Shireoaks, Worksop)
22/23   Northants v Lancs   (Bletchley)
      Glos v Glam   (Bristol)

26/27   Yorks v Lancs   (Harrogate)
28/29   Somerset v Warwicks   (Taunton)
28/29/30   Kent v Surrey
      Middx v Sussex   (Harefield)

JUNE

2/3   Leics v Warwicks   (Lutterworth)
      Lancs v Notts   (Old Trafford)

4/5   Worcs v Leics   (Old Hill)
5/6   Northants v Glos   (Wellingborough)
      Glam v Notts   (Abergavenny)

9/10   Surrey v Essex   (NW Bank, Norbury)
      Worcs v Glos   (Worcester)

11/12   Worcs v Lancs   (Stourbridge)
      Northants v Notts   (Finedone [Dolben])

11/12/13   Hants v Glam   (Bournemouth)
      Sussex v Kent   (Hastings)

16/17   Middx v Warwicks   (Harrow)
      Leics v Northants   (Blaby)
      Yorks v Glam   (Harrogate)

18/19   Leics v Glam   (Lutterworth)
      Middx v Essex   (Crouch End) (N. Middlesex)

18/19/20   Surrey v Hants   (Guildford)
      Warwicks v Lancs   (M & B, Birmingham)

23/24   Warwicks v Glam   (Knowle & Dorridge, Birmingham)
      Notts v Leics   (Mansfield Colliery)

24/25   Glos v Hants   (Bristol)

25/26	Glam v Worcs (Cardiff)
26/27	Warwicks v Northants (Bedworth)
30/1/2 July	Lancs v Warwicks (Blackpool)

JULY

2/3/4	Surrey v Sussex (Guildford)
3/4	Glam v Northants (Cardiff [Sophia Gdns])
	Somerset v Worcs
	Warwicks v Glos (Stratford-upon-Avon)
7/8	Essex v Warwicks (Chelmsford)
	Yorks v Leics (Marske by Sea)
9/10	Somerset v Hants (Paulton)
	Northants v Worcs (Corby)
	Lancs v Leics (East Lancs Blackburn)
9/10/11	Surrey v Kent (NW Bank, Norbury)
	Sussex v Middx (Hove)
	Yorks v Notts (Bradford)
14/15	Essex v Kent (Thames Board Mills)
	Middx v Glam (North Ealing)
	Worcs v Northants (Redditch)
	Glos v Lancs (Bristol)
17/18	Northants v Yorks (Horton)
	Glam v Glos (Neath)
21/22	Essex v Sussex (Dagenham Cables)
	Northants v Warwicks (Northampton)
	Glam v Yorks (Swansea)
23/24	Worcs v Somerset (Worcester)
	Somerset v Lancs (Taunton)
	Worcs v Notts (Colwall)
23/24/25	Warwicks v Yorks (Edgbaston)
	Middx v Hants (Uxbridge)
28/29	Hants v Surrey (Southampton)
30/31	Yorks v Northants (Scarborough)
	Leics v Lancs (Leicester)
	Sussex v Somerset (Chichester)
	Notts v Glam (Nottm HS Grd)
30/31/1	Hants v Kent (Bournemouth)
	Surrey v Middx (Oval)
31/1 August	Warwicks v Essex (Nuneaton [Griff & Coton])

AUGUST

4/5	Worcs v Glam (Worcester)
	Warwicks v Somerset (Moseley)
6/7/8	Warwicks v Notts (Coventry & N. Warwick)
7/8	Essex v Middx (Chingford)
	Surrey v Glam (Sunbury)
11/12	Glam v Leics (Swansea)
13/14	Northants v Leics (Northampton)
	Notts v Lancs (Wollaton)
	Somerset v Glam (Taunton)
14/15	Hants v Glos (Southampton)
13/14/15	Warwicks v Worcs (M & B, Birmingham)
	Kent v Middx

18/19	Kent v Essex (E. Greenwich)
	Glos v Northants (Staverton)
	Lancs v Glam (Blackpool)
	Yorks v Worcs (Bradford)
	Warwicks v Middx (Blossomfield)
20/21	Notts v Worcs (Collingham)
20/21/22	Sussex v Surrey (Hove)
	Yorks v Warwicks (Barnsley)
21/22	Northants v Glam (Northampton)
25/26	Middx v Surrey (Roehampton)
	Leics v Worcs
27/28/29	Sussex v Hants (Hove)
	Lancs v Yorks (Old Trafford)

SEPTEMBER

3/4/5	Kent v Sussex (Canterbury)
4/5	Essex v Surrey (Chelmsford)

Future Cricket Tours

TO ENGLAND	MCC TOURS OVERSEAS
1976 West Indies	1975–76 No tour
1977 Australia	1976–77 South Africa
1978 Pakistan and New Zealand	1977–78 India and Pakistan
1979 India	1978–79 Australia and N. Zealand
1980 West Indies and S. Africa	1979–80 No tour
1981 Australia	1980–81 West Indies

OTHER TOURS

1975–76	Australia to Pakistan
	India to West Indies
1976–77	India to Australia
	New Zealand to Pakistan
	Pakistan to New Zealand and West Indies
1977–78	West Indies to Australia
1978–79	India to West Indies
1979–80	Australia to West Indies
1981–82	New Zealand to West Indies
1982–83	Pakistan to West Indies

Young Cricketer of the Year

At the end of each season the members of the Cricket Writers' Club select by ballot the player they consider the best young cricketer of that season.
P. H. Edmunds of Middlesex was elected last year.

The selections to date are:

1950 R. Tattersall (Lancashire)	1963 G. Boycott (Yorkshire)
1951 P. B. H. May (Surrey)	1964 J. M. Brearley (Middlesex)
1952 F. S. Trueman (Yorkshire)	1965 A. P. E. Knott (Kent)
1953 M. C. Cowdrey (Kent)	1966 D. L. Underwood (Kent)
1954 P. J. Loader (Surrey)	1967 A. W. Greig (Sussex)
1955 K. F. Barrington (Surrey)	1968 R. M. H. Cottam
1956 B. Taylor (Essex)	(Hampshire)
1957 M. J. Stewart (Surrey)	1969 A. Ward (Derbyshire)
1958 A. C. D. Ingleby-	1970 C. M. Old (Yorkshire)
Mackenzie (Hampshire)	1971 J.Whitehouse(Warwickshire)
1959 G. Pullar (Lancashire)	1972 D.R. Owen-Thomas (Surrey)
1960 D.A. Allen (Gloucestershire)	1973 M. Hendrick (Derbyshire)
1961 P. H. Parfitt (Middlesex)	1974 P. H. Edmunds (Middlesex)
1962 P. J. Sharpe (Yorkshire)	

ISBN 0362 00226 6

© Queen Anne Press Limited,
12 Vandy Street, London EC2A 2EN.
Printed by John Gardner (Printers) Limited, Liverpool.